JOHN J. DUFF, a native New Yorker, has practiced law in New York since 1927; he has been an avid Lincoln scholar since childhood. A. LINCOLN: *Prairie Lawyer*, his first book, combines all his professional skill with his avocation. He is a member of the Illinois State Historical Society, the Lincoln Fellowship of Wisconsin, the New York Civil War Round Table and the New York County Lawyers' Association.

A. Lincoln
PRAIRIE LAWYER

A. Lincoln

PRAIRIE LAWYER

By John J. Duff

HOLT, RINEHART AND WINSTON
NEW YORK

Grateful acknowledgment is hereby made for permission to quote from "The Lawyers Know Too Much" in SMOKE AND STEEL by Carl Sandburg, Copyright 1920, by Harcourt Brace and Company, Inc.; Copyright 1948, by Carl Sandburg.

Published, February, 1960
Second Printing, May, 1960

In Canada, Holt, Rinehart and
Winston of Canada, Limited

ACKNOWLEDGMENTS

Tʜɪs is a book about an unpretentious Midwestern lawyer, whose career at the bar, though freighted with significance, rests in comparative obscurity. In undertaking the task of re-creating a vision of that career, the writer's problems have been eased beyond acknowledgment by his many benefactors in the field of Lincoln scholarship, without whose perceptive criticisms and unstinting service this book could not have been written.

Though its exact genesis is uncertain, the work derives from a long-felt craving for details of Lincoln's law career, and the belief that an account of his work at the bar, written in a manner that any literate non-lawyer might understand, has been a crying need in Lincoln literature. Among those sharing this belief was Harry E. Pratt, late Illinois State Historian, whose untimely passing on February 12, 1956, deprived the nation of one of its outstanding contemporary students of Abraham Lincoln. The evolution of this book was influenced, in its early stages, by his constant reiteration of the thought that it would be a terrible mistake to permit what we now know of Lincoln's work in the courts to go unrecorded, and by his helpful advice on the necessary works and source materials to be consulted. He was an unfailing friend and counselor.

A primary obligation is to Margaret A. Flint, Assistant Illinois State Historian and reference librarian at the Illinois State Historical Library. She has been patient and kind, always ready and eager to help with research and suggestions. It is devastating to think of the errors which might have been committed, were it not for the assistance which she so cheerfully and expertly rendered. Whenever the writer was uncertain where to turn for documentation, her uncanny gift for placing her finger unerringly on the source invariably saved the day.

In the quest for new materials to illuminate the story of Lincoln as a lawyer, a most indefatigable guide to public archives in the Lincoln country has been James T. Hickey, of Elkhart, Illinois, and the staff of the Illinois State Historical Library, to whom the writer is enormously indebted. But his influence extends far beyond the purely investigatory realm, for his belief in this book has been a sustaining factor from the time of its inception to the moment of completion. In the throes of doubt which the intricacy and magnitude of the task often inflicted upon the writer, his approval and encouragement went far to reassure and strengthen him.

A particular word of thanks is due to Clyde C. Walton, present Illinois State Historian, for his generosity in giving access to the priceless contents of that great institution, the Illinois State Historical Library, which he so genially administers, for permitting the writer to "set up shop" there for weeks on end, as well as for permission to reproduce documents and photographs that appear in this volume.

Among those who contributed pertinent items were Howard F. Rissler and S. Ambrose Wetherbee, both of the staff of the Illinois State Historical Library. The writer has been fortunate in being enabled to lean on their efforts and make use of their inventories of facts in the matters, respectively, of Illinois courthouses and Lincoln's pardon petitions. James N. Adams has rendered gracious assistance in making available the Historical Library's vast collection of mid-nineteenth-century Illinois newspaper files, which present, perhaps, the finest picture of Lincoln on the circuit.

Marion D. Pratt, assistant editor of *The Collected Works of Abraham Lincoln*, has been most kind in passing on to the writer important nuggets of information come upon by her in the Archives Department of the Illinois State Library and elsewhere.

A special tribute is due the memory of that most modest of men, Benjamin P. Thomas, whose book *Abraham Lincoln* was acclaimed by scholars in 1952 as the outstanding one-volume biography of the Civil War President. His numerous articles in the Bulletin and Quarterly of the Abraham Lincoln Association, his short history of New Salem and his *Portrait for Posterity* have contributed greatly to this work, as have our discussions, in the course of which he evinced his informed interest in the subject of Lincoln as a lawyer. It is sad to reflect that no more writings will come from his gifted pen.

Arnold Gates, literary editor of the *Lincoln Herald*, has read the whole manuscript and given helpful comments. This long-time Lincoln student is living disproof of the maxim that a historical critic must always carry a knotty club and be endowed with a chronically perverse disposition. While no easy man to please where Lincoln writing is concerned, he has nevertheless helped give the writer the strength to swim the turbulent waters until he could make port.

Others who have found ways to be helpful are King V. Hostick, of Springfield, a loyal friend, whose holdings in the field of historical Americana have proved so indispensable; Ivan Huber Light, attorney and gentleman farmer of Shirley, Illinois, whose knowledge of McLean County history and the early members of the Bloomington bar is nothing short of encyclopedic; Wayne C. Temple, Director of the Department of Lincolniana and professor of history at Lincoln Memorial University, in Harrogate, Tennessee; his predecessor, R. Gerald McMurtry, now Director of the Lincoln National Life Foundation of Fort Wayne, Indiana; Louis Warren, retired Director of the Lincoln National Life Foundation; Charles H. Coleman and Lavern M. Hamand, professors at Eastern Illinois University, Charleston, Illinois; Justin G. Turner, of Los Angeles, and Alfred W. Stern, of Chicago, distinguished Lincoln collectors;

Marguerite J. Pease, of the University of Illinois; Helen Newman, Librarian of the United States Supreme Court; David A. Jonah and John R. Turner Ettlinger, of the Brown University Library, and C. C. Tisler, of the Ottawa [Illinois] *Daily Republican-Times*.

David C. Mearns and C. Percy Powell have the writer's gratitude for assistance during weeks of research in the Manuscript Division of the Library of Congress. The members of the staffs of the New York Public Library, the Columbia University Library, the Brown University Library and the Library of The Lincoln National Life Foundation of Fort Wayne, Indiana, have effectively helped in this book's preparation.

J.J.D.

CONTENTS

A. Lincoln
PRAIRIE LAWYER

I L L I N O I S

Chicago •

WOODFORD
Metamora
20
30
Pekin
20
McLEAN
TAZEWELL
55
Tremont
50
Bloomington
35
LOGAN
DEWITT
CHAMPAIGN
VERMILION
Mt.
Pulaski
Clinton
Urbana
Danville
20
20
30
MACON
20
Monticello
35
Decatur
PIATT
Springfield
25
MOULTRIE
EDGAR
SANGAMON
20
Sullivan
30
15
Paris
Taylorville
55
CHRISTIAN
Shelbyville
SHELBY

The
EIGHTH JUDICIAL
CIRCUIT
as traveled by
LINCOLN
in 1850

Miles
0   10   20   30   40   50

CHAPTER I

Early Contacts

O N A March day in 1837 there fatefully stood before the Clerk of the Illinois Supreme Court a tall, melancholy man of twenty-eight who, with right hand upraised, swore to "in all things faithfully execute the duties of Attorney and Counsellor at Law." The place was Vandalia, but recently rendered expendable as capital of the prairie commonwealth of Illinois, due largely to the political capers of a group of irreconcilables known to history as "The Long Nine." Statewise, the strident issue of the day was the Internal Improvement Act, calling for a huge program of public works—the "grand system," as it was derisively called; on the national level, it was still Jacksonism. Generally speaking, the subject of slavery, as a great moral and national issue, was a relatively new topic, though on December 29, 1836, Governor Duncan had submitted to the Legislature resolutions and memorials from six states, warning of the dangers inherent in abolition agitation. On January 12, 1837, the Joint Select Committee of that body affirmed the "sacred" right of property in slaves, at the same time deploring the activities of abolition societies.

In this setting there "came to the bar," on that significant first day of March, one who, through his wit, wisdom and understanding of humankind, rather than through any extensive knowledge of abstract legal principles, was to rise to a position of primacy at the Illinois bar. Though his years of practice were to end with his accession to the Presidency, he would remain indelibly the lawyer down to the last conscious moment, in Ford's

Theatre, on Tenth Street, Washington, D.C., at about twenty minutes past ten on the tragic evening of Good Friday, April 14, 1865. His name, as entered on the roll of attorneys of the Central Grand Division, was, it is hardly necessary to point out, Abraham Lincoln.

1.

The event of March 1, 1837, had a tortuous pedigree, for Lincoln had traveled a long road since his first contact with the law. During his years in the Midwest he had tested his powers, in a ragtag sort of way and with but indifferent success, in various activities: farm laborer, flatboat pilot, grocery clerk, unsoldierly soldier, country storekeeper, village postmaster, surveyor and self-taught student of law.

Working backward in time, one learns that in 1827 he had a foretaste of his future calling when hailed before Squire Samuel Pate, farmer and justice of the peace near Lewisport, Kentucky —charged, on the complaint of two licensed ferrymen, John and Lin Dill, with operating a ferryboat without a license, in violation of the Ohio River ferry ordinance. Unaware of any statutory restriction, Lincoln, having built a small flatboat, was transporting travelers, for hire, from the Indiana shore of the Ohio River to steamers in midstream. The complainants, owners of the duly licensed ferryboat operating from the Kentucky shore, after luring the unsuspecting Lincoln to their bank of the river, induced him to accompany them to the home of Squire Pate, where John Dill sued out a warrant.

Lincoln's defense was ignorance of the law, which, as every layman now knows, is no defense at all. Squire Pate, doubtless impressed with the forthrightness of the youthful defendant, proceeded to consult the statute book and, after reading the pertinent section, came up with the legally sound observation that the statute was directed against transportation *across* the river, and not to steamers located in midstream. The proceeding was dismissed, whereupon Lincoln expressed his gratitude to the Squire, who invited him to attend his "court" whenever in the neighborhood, an invitation which one may be sure Lincoln was not slow in taking advantage of.

It is said that in his Indiana days Lincoln read his first law book, *The Revised Statutes of Indiana*. How he came by this rather forbidding tome is not certain. Dennis Hanks, married to Elizabeth Johnston Lincoln, the eldest of Lincoln's two step-sisters, claimed to have brought the book to Lincoln's attention.[1] One is constrained to take Hanks's account with a grain of skeptical salt, for it has been suspected that this lovable character, devoted to strong drink and possessed of an untrammeled imagination, was not above manufacturing anecdotes pretty freely. One correspondent, who evaluated his recollections as being something less than on a par with the tablets from Sinai, was moved to refer to him as "that cheerful and multifarious liar, Dennis Hanks."[2] When in quest of material for his *Life of Lincoln*, William H. Herndon, Lincoln's biographer and law partner from 1844 to 1861, pumped Hanks at length, yet even Herndon, with his penchant for fictional elaboration, refused to be taken in by his more exaggerated claims. In a memorandum made shortly after an interview with Hanks in 1865, Herndon noted that, when his informant became "gloriously tight," his facts bore little or no resemblance to the truth.[3]

Another unverified legend has it that Lincoln's friend and employer, David Turnham, the constable at Gentryville, possessed a copy as a necessary adjunct to the performance of his official duties, and in this way Lincoln, a frequent visitor at his home, came under its dubious spell.[4] This version, first launched by Herndon, was credited by him to Turnham. Jesse W. Weik, Herndon's close collaborator, who did the actual writing of that challenging volume, *Herndon's Lincoln*, cites as Herndon's authority Lincoln's stepmother.[5] Lincoln's own writings, including his correspondence with Turnham, fail to mention the book.

The Hanks claim and the Herndon hearsay, each given wide

currency, suffer from the infirmity of being founded on recollections had many years after the event they were supposed to record, to say nothing of their inherent improbability. That Lincoln's interest in the law should have been aroused by anything so painfully dull as a compendium of statutes is distinctly on the improbable side, the statement by Albert J. Beveridge that Lincoln "read it repeatedly" notwithstanding.[6] When Herndon states, supposedly on the authority of Turnham, that Lincoln "fairly devoured the book in his eager efforts to abstract the store of knowledge that lay between the lids,"[7] one is inevitably reminded that his biography of his former law partner is chock-full of inaccuracies and what Huck Finn would have called "stretchers." Refutation of the statement was furnished by Herndon, himself, when he wrote, in a letter to Weik, in 1887: "Lincoln never read much law, and never did I see him read a law book through, and no one else ever did."[8]

It probably more nearly approximates the truth that Lincoln came across the book at some time during the Indiana period, that he studied the Declaration of Independence, the Constitutions of the United States and Indiana, as well as the Ordinance of 1787, all included as a sort of prefix, but quailed at the thought of wading through the rest of the volume. The story of the Indiana statute book is but one of a multitude of examples of the temptation that Lincoln's life affords to mingle fact with fiction.

Partly for want of something better to do, partly, perhaps, because his destiny was calling, Lincoln, acting as a sort of legal "buff," spent much of his time during his later years in Indiana lounging around the courthouses (if they could be given such a pretentious title) of the towns of Rockport and Boonville, to which he went afoot from Gentryville to hear the trials. The earliest courthouses of the Middle West were constructed of logs, and in appearance differed but little from the early log churches. These primitive structures were later replaced, around the middle 'twenties, by frame buildings of severely simple architectural design. Governor Ford, in his *History of Illinois,* pointed out that in early times in that state judges very frequently held court "in the bar-rooms of taverns, fitted up with a temporary bench for the judge and chairs or benches for the lawyers and jurors."[9]

It was at the circuit court in Boonville, seat of justice of Warwick County, that Lincoln caught his first glimpse of circuit practice, that distinctive institution long vanished from the American scene. It was a colorful way of life which—in spite of the monotony of travel across the broad expanse of open prairie, with only here and there an occasional house or inn, and all the attendant rigors and inconveniences—was to afford Lincoln his most pleasurable years. Thus enabled to get glimpses of the actual processes of the law, he doubtless found a slew of pettifogging squabbles that must have struck him as beneath the dignity of the court even to consider. Many of the cases were of the type which, during the first years of Midwestern history, were litigated at church sessions, at times taxing the Solomonic wisdom of the elders. As for the judges, the aura of judicial omnipotence doubtless proved somewhat of an illusion. Though the scales began to fall from Lincoln's eyes as he heard the cross-examination of the witnesses and the arguments of counsel, something may have stirred within him—the realization that here was a calling in which he might find himself quite capable of holding his own.

The researcher in quest of details of Lincoln's years in Indiana, relevant to this study for whatever light they might throw upon his early interest in the law, is restricted for the most part to recollections, often hazy and sometimes contradictory, gathered by Herndon in 1865 and 1866 from neighbors who knew Lincoln a generation and more before. Lincoln himself divulged comparatively little about his late adolescence and early manhood. When John Locke Scripps of the Chicago *Press and Tribune* interviewed him for the purpose of securing data for the Scripps campaign biography of 1860, his difficulty, he later wrote, "was to induce him to communicate the homely facts . . . of his early life."[10] All in all, the evidence upon which one must rely in tracing the various stages in the evolution of Lincoln, the lawyer, gives, at best, an unclear picture of the pre-New Salem years.

2.

Though the impressionable Indiana years may have seen his first tentative leaning toward the law, they played no part in the systematic, even though informal preparation for it as a calling. Which brings one, in logical order, to New Salem, the little hamlet perched on a ridge overlooking the Sangamon River, where Lincoln made his home from 1831 to 1837, after a rather aimless year spent in Decatur, Macon County, Illinois. He came to New Salem a rustic, uneducated youth without any sense of direction —"a piece of floating driftwood," as he later described himself. He left it a lawyer, with definite political ambitions, and with a knowledge of people that shaped his point of view for the rest of his life.

Here in New Salem, the quaint little prairie town where his peculiar kind of greatness began to take shape, he would form an invaluable friendship with the profoundly wise Mentor Graham, attend frequently at the court of Bowling Green, justice of the peace, and come to know the carefree, philosophic dreamer, Jack Kelso, who brought him the revelation of Burns and Shakespeare; here, while learning surveying and at the same time improving his grammar and knowledge of mathematics, he was to make his first effort at public speaking; and from here he would be elected to the state legislature, there to learn at first hand how laws are made and, for good measure, something of the shenanigans of politicians. Here, in a society where books were relatively few and hard to come by, he would study *Blackstone's Commentaries* and works borrowed from John Todd Stuart's law library in nearby Springfield. Taken all in all, it was invaluable preparation, a course of study which not even the most respected traditional institution could have offered.

There is an interesting side light on all this. Though he

viewed with skepticism the Ann Rutledge tale, as embroidered by Herndon, William E. Barton, Lincoln biographer of the post-World War I period, wrote that Ann sought to have Lincoln attend Illinois College, in Jacksonville, while she pursued her studies at the Female Academy, in the same town.[11] It is intriguing to consider the effect a college education might have had on Lincoln's future and the course of history. Although it is idle to venture into the realm of what might have been, one cannot but reflect that exposure to formalized teaching may have proved a poor substitute for the liberal education of a different sort which Lincoln acquired in New Salem from 1831 to 1837, as well as in the state legislature following his election to that body in 1834. As his horizons were widened by reading, by association with all manner of people, and by service in the legislature, Lincoln took on stature which no purely formal educational contacts could have conferred.[12]

In those preceptorial days, when an apprentice attached himself to a lawyer, studying law in the Midwest was, for the most part, a matter of reading the standard law commentaries, usually under the more or less random supervision of some practicing attorney, and observing the courts in action, as Lincoln had ample opportunity to do. While Midwestern standards of legal learning may not have been too lofty, that incredibly prodigal period in the history of Illinois (roughly, 1835 to 1860) produced some of the most eminent lawyers in the Union, men who, taken by and large, bear favorable comparison to the bar of any other place and period in American jurisprudence. Few generalizations are more annoying than sweeping glorifications of the past, yet it is a fact, evidence for which literally abounds, that there were titans at the Illinois bar in those days.

Attendance at schools of higher learning was not common in the eighteen thirties. Of Lincoln's early contemporaries who had the benefit of a formal education there were only Henry E. Dummer, who studied at Bowdoin College, and later at Harvard Law School; John T. Stuart, who attended Centre College, at

Danville, Kentucky, followed by a period of apprenticeship in
the law office of a distant relative at Richmond, Kentucky; Dan
Stone, a graduate of Middlebury College, in his native Vermont;
Ninian W. Edwards and John J. Hardin, both of Transylvania
College Law School, at Lexington, Kentucky; Edward Jones,
who studied at Virginia Law School, in Winchester; and Herndon, who attended the preparatory department at Illinois College,
in Jacksonville.

3.

It can be said that for the most part Lincoln was self-taught.
When in need of guidance, however, in his almost obsessive
desire to learn, he was not wanting for advisers, each of whom, in
his own fashion, contributed something to Lincoln's preparation
for the law. Salient among them was Mentor Graham, the New
Salem schoolmaster who pointed the way to the study of grammar and mathematics. It was Graham who, having the perception
to early sense something of the dimensions of this raw youth with
less than a year of conventional schooling, introduced him to the
Columbian Orator, to Webster's *Speller* and Kirkham's *Grammar*, to which Lincoln applied himself with almost fanatical
single-mindedness, and through the patient study of which he
was to acquire something of his singular felicity in the use of language. It was not knowledge alone which Lincoln craved at this
stage; he sought, with equal ardor, the ability to express himself
with precision and with beauty—to make words, simple words,
and not too many of them, do his bidding. He became, in time,
their master, for he could make each one count: a fact evidenced
in widely varying ways ranging from the aridities of legal
phraseology to the exquisitely worded letter of condolence to
Lydia Bixby on the death of her sons in the Civil War. Even in
his early days, the rambling discursion so common to his time
was foreign to Lincoln.

It was Graham who helped him acquire in six weeks a good

working knowledge of surveying, tying it in with the study of mathematical calculation, a knowledge later to stand Lincoln in good stead in connection with his numerous chancery cases in the courts. R. B. Rutledge, Ann's brother, writing of him, said: "I know of my own knowledge that Graham did more than all others to educate Lincoln."[13] Lincoln always spoke with the highest respect of "my old teacher," whose proudest moment must have been when, as Lincoln's guest, he sat on the platform while his one-time pupil was inaugurated President of the United States.

Indifferent to the charms of work, and filled with visionary thoughts about the poetic nature of life, John A. Kelso, when not fishing or hunting, was given to quoting extensively from Shakespeare and Burns. For a while Lincoln boarded with Kelso and his wife, and doubtless was an avid listener while Jack, himself with the soul of a poet, read or recited from memory portions of their works. Throughout his life Lincoln preserved a devotion to Shakespeare. In a note to James H. Hackett, Shakespearean actor whom Lincoln had seen portray the role of Falstaff, he was to refer to his own keen appreciation of certain of the Bard's plays, notably *King Lear, Richard III, Henry VIII, Hamlet,* "and especially *Macbeth,*" all of which he acknowledged having "gone over perhaps as frequently as any unprofessional reader."[14]

In addition to contributing to his cultural development, Lincoln's familiarity with the plays of the great poet unquestionably had a distinct utilitarian value in connection with his work in the courts. As any trial lawyer will attest, the closing peroration or summation affords infinite opportunity for apt excursion into Shakespeare, who seemingly anticipated every situation and emotion appurtenant to the concerns of life. There is proof, as we shall see, that Lincoln was fully alive to the possibility of dramatizing the issue with appropriate allusion to the symbolic dramas of him who seemed to know everything about the vagrant souls of human beings.[15]

Kelso must be counted among the liberal-minded eggheads

of his day, for his reading extended to works then considered radical and not for consumption by the better class of people. Together, Lincoln and he read Tom Paine's *Age of Reason*, Volney's *Ruins of Empire* and parts of Voltaire.[16]

Another of the vivid figures who impinged so forcefully upon the consciousness of young Lincoln was the local Democratic leader, justice of the peace and former member of the legislature, the genial, potbellied Bowling Green. The picture of him that has come down to us is that of a leader in civic affairs, though one with all the trappings of the bustling politician, even down to the traditional aldermanic midriff. A perpetual office-holder, his political activities began soon after filing on his homestead land. In 1817 he was appointed constable for Sugar Creek Township. Thereafter he served, in turn, as deputy sheriff and sheriff of Washington County. Green was hardly a stranger to the mechanics of court procedure before taking over the office of justice of the peace. He was foreman of the jury which tried Nathaniel Van Noy for the murder of his wife, a prosecution which resulted in the first hanging in Sangamon County. On several occasions Green was himself hauled into court on the charge of being drunk and disorderly. On October 5, 1824, appearing before the Sangamon Circuit Court to answer an indictment for assault and battery, he was acquitted by a jury.[17]

Green's influence on Lincoln's career was of considerable significance, for, though we must assume that the latter formed no very high opinion of the "court" where his friend held forth, he nevertheless assiduously attended at same, and even, on occasions, was permitted by courtesy of the Squire to try cases before him. It would be pleasant to contemplate Lincoln, at such times, calling upon a knowledge of the laws of Illinois supposedly acquired at some time during the "Winter of the Deep Snow" (1830–1831),[18] while Lincoln was confined with frozen feet to the home of William Warnick, Sheriff of Macon County, who must have possessed (so the reasoning goes) a compilation of

Illinois statutes. As that meticulous Lincoln scholar, Harry E. Pratt, late Illinois State Historian, observes, dryly and with puckish realism, "the story grew that Lincoln spent many hours absorbed in the dull pages of a law book despite the distraction offered by the presence of the sheriff's pretty daughter."[19]

One of the earliest-known legal documents in Lincoln's autograph, except for the printed portion and the signature of Bowling Green as Justice of the Peace, is a Summons dated May 23, 1833, in an action brought by Nelson Alley, New Salem tavern keeper, against Dr. Jason Duncan for $21.57. It is reproduced here for the first time, so far as the writer has been able to learn. The top six lines of the endorsement on the back of the summons are also in Lincoln's hand. The question naturally presents itself whether Lincoln, in this firsthand contact with legal process, was acting on behalf of the plaintiff, or simply helping out Bowling Green. Several weeks prior to the issuance of the process, upon his appointment as postmaster on May 7, 1833, Lincoln was required to furnish bond in the sum of five hundred dollars. Alley acted as one of his bondsmen,[20] and so it may well have been that Lincoln was repaying the favor. In either case it would appear that he was, even then, not only rich in the confidence and esteem of the community, but looked upon as a sort of counselor without portfolio.

STATE OF ILLINOIS, } SANGAMON COUNTY.

THE PEOPLE OF THE STATE OF ILLINOIS, TO ANY CONSTABLE OF SAID COUNTY, GREETING:

YOU are hereby commanded to summon Jason Duncan to appear before me, at my office in N. Salem, on the 30th day of this Inst. at 10 o'clock A.M., to answer the complaint of Nelson Alley. for a failure to pay him a certain demand not exceeding one hundred dollars: And hereof make due return as the law directs.

Given under my hand and seal, this 23rd day of May, 1833.

Bowling Green   Justice Peace

[Reverse side]

N. Alley

vs.

Jason Duncan

Demand on Due Bill

$21-57

cost   −31   ?

executed the within according to law

Serving 25

2 miles 10

J. Clary.   C.S.C.[21]

Few justices of the peace were lawyers, yet the list of actionable wrongs under their jurisdiction was wide. For his part, Green took no overly modest view concerning the extent of his powers, and resolved all such questions by sustaining his own jurisdiction. This fact was humorously revealed in an episode related on the floor of the United States Senate by Edward D. Baker, Senator from Oregon, who, prior to moving west, served in the Illinois House with Lincoln. Green had inquired of Baker if he (Green) had jurisdiction to entertain a case of slander. When informed that under the law he had no such authority, Green declared: "Now, sir, I know I can; for, by Heaven, I have done it."[22]

There was, perhaps, some justification for Green's refusal to conform to statutory limitations. Despite their superior jurisdiction, some of the Illinois circuit courts functioned in a manner decidedly on the informal side, with, like as not, counsel, jurors, witnesses, spectators and even the presiding judge chewing away at plug tobacco and regularly relieving themselves. A visitor unfamiliar with statutory differentiations would have been justified in rating some of these same circuit courts as inferior in many respects to that of Squire Green. We are fortunate in having descriptions of several of the former, of which the following is an apt example:

Judge Reynolds, afterward the governor of the state, presided. The clerk of the court made his home with one of the farmers in the

vicinity of the present city of Hillsboro, in a house consisting of two
rooms. In one of these rooms the first court was held. The judge sat
upon the side of the bed and impannelled the first grand jury, which,
being duly sworn in, retired to the adjacent woods, where the jurors
sat upon a log and made their investigation of the lawlessness of the
county. After mature deliberation they presented to the court that
they had no indictments to return, and they were discharged from
further labors, "with the thanks of the court for the efficient and
fearless manner in which they had discharged their duties."[23]

Though the foregoing account refers to the Circuit Court
of Montgomery County at a time shortly after its organization
in 1821, the general atmosphere differed but little from that of
the Circuit Court of Sangamon County in 1835. "Upon the
bench," wrote a visitor to Springfield, "was seated the judge, with
his chair tilted back and his heels as high as his head, and in his
mouth a veritable corn cob pipe; his hair standing nine ways for
Sunday, while his clothing was more like that worn by a wood-
chopper than anybody else. There was a railing that divided the
audience; outside of which smoking and chewing and spitting of
tobacco seemed to be the principal employment."[24]

Bowling Green frequently entertained Lincoln at his home,
where the embryo lawyer would look over the former's modest
law library, borrowing from it until he had exhausted its meager
contents. Green, for whom Lincoln had conceived a vast admiration, died in February, 1842. It was altogether fitting that his
protégé, who by then had become established in Springfield,
should be the one called upon by Mrs. Green to make a few remarks at the grave.[25]

4.

It was on *Blackstone's Commentaries on the Common Law*,
published in 1765 and 1769, that early American lawyers were
bred for a century or more. Few more enduring clichés have
won their way into the currency of Lincolniana than the notion
that Lincoln came upon a copy of this work at the bottom of a

barrel of junk which he had purchased for fifty cents from a traveler heading west in a covered wagon.[26] Like the Ann Rutledge legend, the Blackstone barrel tale died hard, for it was for a long time firmly established in the public mind, a fact difficult to understand, as Lincoln's own memory clashed so sharply with the pleasant anecdote. In the summer of 1860, after Lincoln's nomination for the Presidency, William Dean Howells prepared a ninety-four-page biography for use in the campaign. Lincoln, at the request of Samuel C. Parks, of Lincoln, Illinois, read the work through and, with considerable care, made a total of nineteen marginal corrections in pencil in the Parks copy.[27] While a few minor errors escaped his notice, in the main Lincoln's editing is minute. At page 31 there appears the following printed matter, unmarked by any penciled revision: "He bought an old copy of Blackstone, one day, at auction, in Springfield, and on his return to New Salem, attacked the work with characteristic energy."

In a letter written in 1858 Lincoln suggests a course of reading for the prospective lawyer. "Let Mr. Widner read Blackstone's Commentaries, Chitty's Pleadings—Greenleaf's Evidence, Story's Equity, and Story's Equity Pleading's [sic], get a license, and go to the practice, and still keep reading."[28] In 1860 Lincoln took time out from the presidential campaign to advise a young school teacher of Pleasant Plains, Illinois, on "the best mode of obtaining a thorough knowledge of the law." He wrote: "The mode is very simple, though laborious and tedious. It is only to get books and read and study them carefully. Begin with Blackstone's 'Commentaries,' and after reading it carefully through, say twice, take up Chitty's 'Pleadings,' Greenleaf's 'Evidence,' and Story's 'Equity,' etc., in succession. Work, work, work, is the main thing."[29]

It is from the latter communication that the belief has grown that Lincoln had the stamina to read through the *Commentaries* —not once, but twice. The clarity, grace, and elegance of style of *Blackstone*, and its attentive regard to the needs of students, as shown by the frequent explanation of technical expressions—

these are qualities which must have rendered the work especially attractive to Lincoln, and may account for his preference for it, even to the extent of recommending, as part of the intellectual fodder of law students, a careful reading, "say twice."

On the subject of advice to others, one is moved to comment that Lincoln, like most of us, was sometimes better able to tell what should be done than to follow his own prescription. In his "Notes for a Law Lecture," prepared in 1850, Lincoln stressed the necessity for prompt attention to correspondence, and leaving nothing for tomorrow which could be done today. This from a lawyer who carried his letters around in a battered stovepipe hat until, becoming lost, they answered themselves! The same absence of method or system, in connection with important letters and state documents, was later to cause his wartime secretaries to view the President's headgear with never-ending despair. Perhaps the crowning embarrassment caused by this careless habit was the occasion when Lincoln had to confess to a correspondent that, upon receipt of his letter, "I put it in my old hat, and buying a new one the next day, the old one was set aside, and so, the letter lost sight of for a time."[30] The ever-present top hat, with its high and capacious crown, if not especially ornamental, was certainly, to Lincoln's way of thinking, extremely useful.[31]

Students of Lincoln's law career would do well to ponder the fact that, though his reading of *Blackstone* may have given him a working grasp of the basic principles of the English common law, and brought him into contact with their deeper significance, the greatest single factor in his qualification to practice his chosen calling was something which no amount of law book learning could have imparted—Lincoln's knowledge that the sources of law were human beings of all sorts. With the sagacity which propelled him to the forefront of the Illinois bar, Lincoln could represent and contend with all kinds of men—clients, opposing counsel, judges and juries—because he knew them so well and accepted them as partners in the struggle with fate.

5.

A group brought together by Dr. John Allen, a leading force in the cultural activity of New Salem, formed, in 1831, the New Salem Debating Society. As one might gather, their tastes were intellectual, in contrast to those of Lincoln's somewhat raffish followers, the Clary's Grove Boys. Shortly after its founding, Lincoln was welcomed to membership in New Salem's most learned body, and it was here, at one of its regular weekly meetings, before an audience composed of the village's budding intellectuals, that he made his initial attempt at public speaking. After the meeting the president of the society remarked to his wife that "there was more than wit and fun in Abe's head; that he was already a fine speaker; . . ."[32] Seemingly born to the hustings, Lincoln had early showed an aptitude for expressing himself effectively as a speaker, which was to be one of his most valuable acquisitions. In Indiana he had been wont to declaim extemporaneously, in his high, thin voice, using the stumps of trees as his imaginary audience. Consciously or not, Lincoln was storing up proficiency in the technique of thinking on his feet, against the days when he would be engaged in the cut and thrust of debate on the floor of the state legislature, and, later, trying cases on the inspiration of the moment on the Eighth Judicial Circuit.

Despite the uplifting influence of Dr. Allen, it must be recorded that New Salem, in its heyday, was a lusty place in more ways than one. Herndon tells us that "At this time in its brief history [during the period of Lincoln's residence] New Salem was what in the parlance of large cities would be called a fast place; and it was difficult for a young man of ordinary moral courage to resist the temptations that beset him on every hand."[33] Even though there were those among his associates who may have enjoyed something of a local reputation for drinking and wenching, Herndon states that "Lincoln was able to retain his popularity with the hosts of young men of his own age, and still not join them in their drinking bouts and carousals."[34] Though no plaster saint or self-righteous bluenose, Lincoln managed to steer clear of most of the less admirable peccadillos then in vogue, his only deviation being a fondness for cockfighting. There was about him a certain fastidiousness of character that earned for him the respect and admiration of all—from the reputable gentry down to the village roustabouts. Not one to make showy virtue of his lack of vices, he liked to tell the story on himself of the occasion when a fellow traveler offered him a cigar on a stage journey during one of his grueling campaigns of the Illinois years. Lincoln declined, stating jocularly that he "had no vices." The man looked him over, went on smoking in silence, and after a while snorted contemptuously: "It's my experience that men with no vices have plaguey few virtues!"[35]

Lincoln's proficiency as a draftman of legal documents is well known. His skill in this direction was developed during the New Salem period, when he was called upon to draw up miscellaneous papers of a legal and quasi-legal nature, including a deed, mortgage, bill of sale, will, several bonds and various petitions to the county commissioners, as well as certificates of survey. The will of Joshua Short, written entirely in Lincoln's hand, and dated August 22, 1836,[36] by which date the embryo lawyer was cropping out, is a sample of the economy of verbiage which Lincoln practiced even at that early date, a model for those lawyers who would cover pages of legal cap saying the same thing. It is probably true that Lincoln had access to a form book, yet a scrutiny of the document shows rather clearly that he could not *wholly* have depended on any such work.

In April, 1832, Governor Reynolds issued a call for volunteers to help drive Black Hawk and his warriors from northern Illinois, an incident which has been described as "a detail of Indian swindling which history obscures behind the respectable name of the Black Hawk War."[37] Lincoln, who at the time was clerking in the store of Denton Offutt, enrolled for thirty days' service, at the end of which period he re-enlisted for another twenty days, and again, on June sixteenth, for a further thirty days. Lincoln's service in the Black Hawk War is important to this study principally because of the contacts it enabled him to make. In addition to John Todd Stuart, a young attorney from Springfield, who was to play a part in influencing Lincoln in his decision seriously to study law, there were Joseph Gillespie, John J. Hardin, Orville Hickman Browning, Edward D. Baker and John A. McClernand—all of them significant figures in Illinois history with whom Lincoln would later be associated in close professional contact.

CHAPTER II

The Shape of Things to Come

1.

THE YEARS 1832 to 1834 were among the most critical in the life of this man for whom history had so much in store. In the third-person autobiographical sketch prepared by him in 1860 for the guidance of Scripps, Lincoln states, referring to the period immediately following his return to New Salem from the Black Hawk War: "He studied what he should do—thought of learning the blacksmith trade—thought of trying to study law —rather thought he could not succeed at that without a better education."[1] The local smithy, the only one for miles around, was Josh Miller, who toiled at his anvil from early morning until late at night. His need for a helper, coupled with Lincoln's desire to remain in New Salem, would suggest that Lincoln, if in fact he ever *seriously* thought of becoming a blacksmith, may have explored the possibility of going to work for Miller.

The Scripps "autobiography," however, presents a question which has never been fully explored, much less answered. Why, one may justifiably ask, should Lincoln in 1832 have been so conscious of his educational limitations when considering the law as a calling? On the basis of what he had witnessed in the courts of Lewisport and Rockport, or in the court of Bowling Green, or even the circuit court in Boonville, there was no valid reason for putting aside, for want of "a better education," the pursuit of that for which he had shown a certain inclination. For the most part, those practicing at the time had enjoyed about as much formal education as had Lincoln—a fact of which he was unquestionably aware.

Lincoln was as well equipped for the study of law in 1832 as he was in 1834, the year of his momentous decision to go at it "in good earnest." As Pratt has pointed out: "Only two years separated Lincoln's two decisions. In that period his only advance, educationally, was his mastery of trigonometry."[2] Moreover, Lincoln was ordinarily not one to be deterred by self-doubt; for all his essential humility, his realization of himself as a fallible human being, he was not without his share of self-confidence. Herndon comments in this connection: "Lincoln thought that he could do anything that other men could or would try to do; he had unbounded confidence in himself, in his capacity and powers; . . ."[3]

Lincoln was never known to have made a calculated misstatement, and so, though it makes little sense, we must accept as true that he believed, in 1860, that in 1832 he entertained misgivings, based on a feeling of inadequacy. Somewhere along the way, just prior to, or at or about the time of his return from the Black Hawk War, had his thinking really changed? Though every available scrap of material about him has been impounded and subjected to critical analysis by the field's outstanding academicians—men like James G. Randall, Paul M. Angle, Harry E. Pratt and Benjamin P. Thomas—the answer to this question remains a difficult one. Lincoln was a man of paradox, an exasperatingly complex individual, as well as a person of intense reserve, seldom vouchsafing more than a glimpse of his inner feelings and impulses. He was a man, in all matters private, the most reticent and contained; his was not the confessional temperament.

The writer has searched in vain among the writings and available papers of Lincoln's close friends for some clue revelatory of the motivating factor which might have prompted him in arriving at the decision of 1832. An examination of the recently disimpounded papers of the *Robert Todd Lincoln Collection*[4] has proved no more revealing. The answer is probably as many-sided as the man himself, but certainly includes a feeling that his decision was tentative in the extreme, and that the deprecatory self-estimate which led to his inner doubts was but a fluctuating phase, stemming from some emotional confusion.

2.

There is a strong tradition that Stuart was chiefly instrumental in bringing about Lincoln's eventual decision to enter the field of the law. During the legislative campaign of 1834, Lincoln was much in the company of Stuart, who was then a fellow candidate for the lower house. In Howells' *Life of Lincoln* there appears the following: "During the Legislative canvass of 1834, John T. Stuart advised Lincoln to study law, and after the election he borrowed some of Stuart's books and began to read."[5] This is the basis for the theory, grown to become accepted fact, that it was in response to Stuart's "urging," as some biographers put it, that Lincoln embraced the law as a calling. It is more than possible that there has been an overemphasis upon the Stuart influence. To a certain extent it may have furnished the spark which rekindled Lincoln's always smoldering interest in the law and resolved his crucial dilemma; but *only* to a certain extent. Granted that Lincoln entertained the suggestion hospitably, the feeling persists that he also had his own sufficient reasons for going at it "in good earnest." Lincoln was hardly the man to be talked or stampeded into doing anything which he had not already thought through for himself; he had a mind of his own that was not easily made up except on its reasoned conclusions. He listened with courteous patience to the suggestions of others, but in the end his own independent judgment resolved the decision.

Speaking at memorial services for Stuart, on the occasion of the annual meeting of the Illinois State Bar Association January 13, 1886, Judge David Davis, under whom Lincoln and Stuart traveled the circuit, gave Stuart sole credit for Lincoln's decision to study law: "When the subject was introduced [by Stuart] it appeared that Lincoln had never entertained the idea of becoming a lawyer, and stated difficulties which he deemed insurmountable. These Stuart overcame, and Lincoln agreed to give the matter thoughtful consideration. The result was that he yielded to Stuart's solicitation and read law. . . ."[6]

It is a rash thing to look for authentic biographical data in memorial perorations; the results are sometimes quite startling. Davis's indiscriminate eulogy of his friend Stuart is a case in point, for there is no factual basis whatever for this extreme statement. That the law as a possible means of livelihood had never occurred to Lincoln prior to his conversation with Stuart, seems too considerable an exaggeration to require extended comment. John Pitcher, the Rockport lawyer, who remembered Lincoln from the latter's Indiana days, recalls that even in those early years Lincoln "wanted to become a lawyer."[7] Before he had lived six months in New Salem, he drew a bond for a deed, by which James Estep agreed to convey a tract of land in St. Clair County to Solomon Teter. And in January, 1833, he drew another bond for a deed, involving part of a lot "South of Main Street" in New Salem. On the basis of what evidence there is to go on, it seems clear that the thought of becoming a lawyer had been incubating in Lincoln's mind for some time.

Pratt has marshaled evidence to show that a latent factor in Lincoln's arrival at the decision of 1834 may be discerned in the records of the Sangamon Circuit Court in Springfield.[8] These reveal that on April 16, 1833, Abraham Lincoln appeared as a witness in the case of *Simmons* v. *Bale*, tried by Judge Samuel D. Lockwood, sitting without a jury. While in court, waiting to testify, Lincoln was pressed into service as a juror in three other cases, the practice apparently having been to select the veniremen from among those present in the courthouse.

The following week found Lincoln in the Circuit Court once again, having been called as a witness in the case of *Close* v. *Ritter*. We may be sure that he was favorably impressed by the new two-story brick courthouse in the center of the public square, the finest structure in town, and that he observed closely everything which went on inside of it during the weeks he was in attendance. Of the eleven members of the Sangamon County bar who were present at the term—and whom Lincoln had occasion to observe in the trial of cases, which involved for the most part small amounts and were relatively uncomplicated— only four had attended college or law school. Observing closely their methods, Lincoln must have realized, if anything more pointedly than before, that a formal education was no passport to success at the bar—that acumen, intelligence and the ability to express one's self clearly and convincingly were the prime requisites of a jury lawyer.

3.

To these girders of circumstantial evidence in support of the thesis that Lincoln's determination to follow the law owed its inception to something more than the prompting of Stuart, one ventures to add another prop. It is the writer's conviction that the turning-point decision is indissolubly linked to the fact that Lincoln had by then come to the definite conclusion that politics and public life, to which the law was the one sure approach, were to be his real domain, to which all things else would be auxiliary. Political ambition was already in his blood. Despite his defeat at the polls in 1832, he had come back to offer himself as a candidate for the Legislature at the next election. Lincoln doubtless sensed that his chances of success were something better than fair; as it turned out, he was elected with the second highest vote cast for any of the candidates.

Today "politician" is (very often not without cause) a term in bad repute, calling for a defensive posture on the part of one so characterized. It was not always so. "Politicking" and office-seeking seem to have become something akin to a mania in Lincoln's day, the be-all and end-all of national life. At least 75 per cent of the text of newspapers was devoted to politics. It was an age when everyone who was anyone (and many who weren't) coveted public office. The term "politician," far from being an opprobrious epithet, was a term of distinction, marking the designee as a person of importance. Lawyers, doctors and even ministers were attracted to the young republic's most fascinating game, like moths to the flame. As one contemporary writer stated: "Office seeking seems to have been a mania of the period, and became a mad passion with all professional men—lawyers, doctors and even ministers became attracted with the maelstrom of politics."[9]

The case of Lincoln's friend, Dr. Anson G. Henry, furnishes an apt example of the political activity of some members of the medical profession. From 1839 to 1844 Henry was continually busy with Whig politics, neglecting his practice to such an extent that he went bankrupt. It is perhaps significant that in 1849 he found it necessary to assure his patients that in the future he would pay more attention to his practice, as witness the following announcement appearing in the *Illinois Journal* of August 18, 1849:

> Dr. A. G. Henry, office with Dr. Cabaniss—residence on Jefferson, between 5th and 6th Streets. Dr. Henry will devote the remainder of his life exclusively to his profession.

Was this fetish of the times a factor in the evolution of the uncertain, inquiring youth into the man who was to gain statewide celebrity as a lawyer? In the absence of documentation, let us here put a witness on the stand who, though not always unimpeachable, is on the whole reliable where he speaks of Lincoln's political activities. David Donald, Herndon's biographer, who is not unaware of his subject's defects, cites "seven major counts on which *Herndon's Lincoln* has drawn sharp criticism, . . ." Herndon's treatment of Lincoln's political career does not figure among them.[10] If Herndon is to be believed, and there is reason to feel that in this regard he should be, "Lincoln's restless ambition found its gratification only in the field of politics. He used the law merely as a stepping-stone to what he considered a more attractive condition in the political world."[11] Again we find Herndon stating: "Mr. Lincoln was an extremely ambitious man and that ambition found its gratification only in the political field. Politics were his life and newspapers his food, merely using the law as a stepping stone to a political life and it was in this field that he seemed to be happy."[12]

So, to Stuart's encouragement and Lincoln's attendance at court in the spring of 1833, as furnishing clues to the mental processes by which he had come at last to the momentous decision of 1834, after the strange interlude of two years, the writer would add Lincoln's choice of politics as his life's calling, and his (Lincoln's) belief that admission to the bar was in the nature of a *sine qua non*. While it would be inexact to say that Lincoln's interest in the law was negligible, everything seems to point to the fact (though one not always acknowledged by lawyers) that he had a consuming love for politics which transcended his attachment to the law. As one who served as a law student in the office of Lincoln & Herndon aptly observed: "He took up the law as a means of livelihood, but his heart was in politics. . . . He delighted, he reveled in it, as a fish does in water, as a bird disports itself on the sustaining air."[13]

Legal pietists may be disturbed by the thought that Lincoln, than whom few men knew more about the highways and byways of Illinois politics, was first and foremost a politician. They shouldn't be. Lincoln knew that to demonstrate his capacity as a statesman, or even just a holder of public office, he must first be a politician, and a practical, vote catching one at that. His greatness derives from this awareness. Let there be no quibbling about it: Were he the most accomplished lawyer of his time, possessed of the same love of the Union, the same wisdom, faith in the people and appreciation of the essential equality of all men, those traits which formed the wellspring of his greatness, without the opportunity which politics afforded he would have been bypassed by history. However it may be argued that the law prepared Lincoln for the many legal and constitutional problems created by the grave national crisis ahead, it was his affinity for and his ability to cope with the processes of politics, and not the law, which brought about his emergence from the prairie and comparative obscurity to national prominence. The political Lincoln, who rose in the hurly-burly of Illinois politics, where the devil took the hindmost, is a part of his immortality.

4.

Possibly the single most important factor in Lincoln's preparation for the law was the experience gained as a member of the general assembly, for which he ran a losing race in 1832, and to which he was elected for successive terms in 1834, 1836, 1838 and 1840. Lincoln was a legislator before he was a lawyer. The bills and resolutions he offered show him to have been a born draftsman. Returning to New Salem in July of 1832, after being mustered out as a soldier, following his brief period of service in the Black Hawk War, the budding young politician resumed his campaign for the legislature, having previously announced his candidacy on March ninth. In a field of thirteen candidates for the four posts of representative in the lower house to which Sangamon County was entitled, Lincoln ran eighth.

In 1834, having rebuilt his political fences, he again ran for the legislature, and was elected, together with John Dawson, who received 1390 votes, William Carpenter, 1170, and John T. Stuart, 1164. Lincoln received 1376. Arriving in Vandalia, the wilderness capital of the state, and seat of justice of Fayette County, in late November, wearing a tailor-made sixty dollar suit, Lincoln proceeded to look about him before entering upon his legislative duties.

He found a teeming community of some 800 inhabitants, 200 dwellings and, as noted by the *Illinois Advocate and State Register*, Vandalia's Democratic newspaper, "fifteen wholesale and retail establishments, all doing a fair business, besides many curious manufacturers."[14] Like most Illinois towns, with their center squares inherited from the village greens of the East (though the Midwesterner may deny it), Vandalia was built around a public square, across the street from which was the two-story brick building known as the State House, a structure rather down-at-the-heels in appearance despite its comparative newness, having been completed only ten years before. Its appointments were severely functional. "The furniture . . . was as plain and primitive as the structure. No cushioned chairs, but long, hard benches were the seats of the members."[15]

The taverns dispensed imported vintages, and living, generally, was on a high scale, as befitted the political and social capital of the state. At session times the normal population was augmented by the presence of folks of various categories, not all good—lawyers, lawmakers, lobbyists, office seekers, wirepullers, drummers, itinerant hucksters, pretty ladies of every gradation of virtue, sundry hangers-on, and a rogue or two. It was a colorful and exciting, if motley assemblage which greeted the freshman Whig from Sangamon County.

The House convened on December 1, 1834, and recessed February 13, 1835. Lincoln's absorption in his legislative duties is evidenced by the fact that his presence was recorded on every day that a roll call was taken, though it must be noted that on occasions he was wont to steal away from the ennui-provoking monotony of legislative humdrum to attend sessions of the Federal Court for the District of Illinois and the State Supreme Court. Here he listened to the trial of cases and made important contacts with lawyers from different parts of the state.

His evenings were spent in the company of fellow members of the legislature, many of them actively identified with the legal profession, listening to the usual chitchat of legislative and legal shoptalk. Among those who attended the nightly talkfests, Lincoln doubtless met Alexander Pope Field, a brilliant speaker and raconteur, who enjoyed a considerable reputation as the leading criminal lawyer in the state. He also had a lucrative negligence practice. Juries, rising to great heights of adequacy under his tutelage, brought in very substantial verdicts on behalf of plaintiffs represented by Field. He was later to figure as a princi-

pal in one of Lincoln's important "political cases." A member of
the House for three terms before becoming Secretary of State in
1828, the convivial Field never lost touch with the members of the
legislature. Lincoln, one may be sure, paid rapt attention to the
exciting stories of his courtroom experiences.

The significance of this session, in its relation to the present
study, resides in the educative value of participating in the process of enacting legislation, including the preparation, in proper,
foolproof form, of proposed laws; of attendance at the Federal
Court and the State Supreme Court; and the daily association and
nightly discussions with prominent lawyers of the state.

By his successful advancement, as one of the Sangamon delegation of nine, of the interests of Springfield as seat of the state
government, Lincoln has taken his place as one of the wisest
and cagiest political practitioners ever to come down the Illinois
pike. In this matter of the relocation of the state capital, it is
noteworthy that Alton, Jacksonville, Peoria and Iliopolis were
rival aspirants, all of them ably represented. Vandalia's representatives, led by John Dement, who had entered the House to
protect Vandalia's interests as capital of the state, resisted the
move to the bitter end. Stephen A. Douglas, who presented
Jacksonville's bid, was no less energetic. Acting as a unit under
Lincoln, the Long Nine (so dubbed because they averaged six
feet in height) outmaneuvered the opposition at every stage
of the contest. His fellow legislators soon found that he could
take care of himself when the going got rough. For all his
sensitiveness and inner dignity, there was a hard, tough, unyielding core in Lincoln—an invaluable asset in those early brass-
knuckle days of Illinois politics. And yet, for all that Lincoln was
stoutly partisan, alike in his espousal of the Whig and Springfield
causes, he was tremendously popular with his fellow lawmakers
of both parties. His remarks almost invariably had the saving
grace of humor, coupled with the frank admission of his own
fallibility.

His equipment for the law enriched by service in the two regular sessions and the special one of 1835–1836, Lincoln, on March 7, 1837, returned to New Salem, to remain but a few weeks before moving on to Springfield. All in all, the importance of Vandalia, in connection with the legal education of Lincoln, was such that one is moved to wonder if it didn't surpass that of New Salem.

5.

Between sessions of the legislature Lincon had applied himself assiduously to the study of law. "When the Legislature met, the law-books were dropped, but were taken up again at the end of the session."[16] He had the run of Stuart's law library in Springfield, where the firm of Stuart & Dummer had maintained an office since May 24, 1833. Dummer told Herndon in 1865: "Lincoln used to come to our office—Stuart's and mine—in Springfield from New Salem and borrow law books. Sometimes he walked but generally rode. He was the most uncouth looking young man I ever saw. He seemed to have but little to say; seemed to feel timid, with a tinge of sadness visible in the countenance, but when he did talk all this disappeared for the time and he demonstrated that he was both strong and acute. He surprised us more and more at every visit."[17]

Even though Stuart possessed what passed in those days for an ample law library, the probability is that Lincoln's reading took in only a part of its contents. In preparation for the law, as in other fields of inquiry which stirred his questing mind, Lincoln verified the maxim that it is better to know, thoroughly, a few good books than to read many. His reading was highly selective, never desultory, and because so thorough, never wide. What he read he knew. In addition to *Blackstone*, there were *Greenleaf On Evidence*, *Chitty's Pleadings*, *Story's Equity* and *Story's Equity Pleadings*.

6.

It remains to speak of one significant influence which gave direction to his life toward the career in which his talents found full flowering. With his appointment by President Jackson as postmaster of New Salem on May 7, 1833, an office he held until May 30, 1836, when the post office was discontinued, he became an omnivorous reader of newspapers. The publications delivered at the post office and read by him before being called for by addressees came, many of them, from scattered towns in Illinois, others from distant points. Life on the Illinois frontier was marked by an excess of litigation; folks were wont to "go to law" over the slightest provocation. As a consequence, considerable space was devoted in the press to the doings of the different courts. (Apart from occasional references in diaries and memoirs, the only sources of information concerning many of the cases referred to in this work, as to which official court records are unavailable or disappointingly meager, are the contemporary press, the small-town newspapers from which this book largely draws its ingredients.)

And so not only was Lincoln's general knowledge enriched by reading newspapers, but, even allowing for a certain amount of journalistic inaccuracy in the coverage of trials, and the flamboyance which was then the fashion in American newspaper writing, his familiarity with court procedure and trial tactics was undoubtedly enhanced by reading the accounts of the more prominent cases.

The self-teaching between sessions of the legislature, frequent attendance at the circuit court in Springfield, as well as occasional visits to the Federal Court and Supreme Court, where he had ample opportunity to watch the leading members of the Illinois bar in action, coupled with his service in the lower house, combined to form one of the most gratifying experiences of his life. Long years later, when his eldest son, Robert, came home to the White House, following his graduation from Harvard, Lincoln inquired as to his intentions and when Robert informed him that he wished to return to Harvard, to study law,[18] the father commented: "If you do, you should learn more than I ever did, but you will never have so good a time."[19]

7.

It is not recorded that the event of March 1, 1837, was signalized by the customary celebration, which "took every form from dinner to drinks all around."[20] Cristopher C. Brown, son-in-law of John T. Stuart, in describing the occasion of his own admission to the bar twenty years later, told how, in accordance with established custom, his two examiners, Lincoln and Herndon, accompanied him to Chatterton's Restaurant, on the west side of Hoffman's Square, in Springfield, "and partook of oysters and fried pickled pigs feet at my expense."[21]

Difficult though it be to learn the thoughts of a man who liked to keep his own counsel, one is perhaps justified in thinking that Lincoln was in no mood for celebrating—that this climactic event was followed by a characteristic pessimistic reaction. The temperament of the newly inducted member of the legal profession inclined him to look beyond the elation of any success to the difficulties ahead.

Six weeks after his admission to practice, Lincoln bade farewell to his friends and neighbors in the little village of New Salem, where he had spent his young manhood and developed his interest in law and politics, and set out for Springfield, where he was to live and practice for almost a quarter of a century, before moving on to history and legend. Near the entrance to New Salem State Park, one of this nation's great historic shrines, there stands a majestic nine-foot statue, depicting Lincoln as he is about to leave for his new career in Springfield. The only Lincoln statue in the restored village, it symbolizes the story of New Salem in its relation to Lincoln's evolution as a lawyer; in his left hand is the frontiersman's axe which he is laying aside, in his right a large book intended to represent a copy of *Blackstone's*

Commentaries. Viewing this work of heroic proportions, cast in bronze, one pictures Lincoln coming to the little frontier outpost in 1831, a gangling, rawboned youth, altogether at loose ends, and leaving it on that historic fifteenth day of April, 1837, when he stood at the crossroads of his career, the most remarkable in American history. New Salem, to which Lincoln owed so much in the formation of his interests and attitudes during the years when he was struggling to find himself, will always hold a luminous place in the story of Lincoln's genesis as a lawyer.

CHAPTER III

Stuart & Lincoln

1.

LINCOLN'S was not a case of a briefless country lawyer embarking upon the difficult task of establishing himself in a city of strangers. Thanks to a fortunate concatenation of circumstances he was enabled, virtually upon admission to the bar, to step into an established practice, as the partner of John Todd Stuart. No one who has not experienced the heartaches of the novitiate in the struggle to get a start in the law, can fully appreciate Lincoln's good fortune. Henry E. Dummer, who had been Stuart's law partner for almost four years, had decided, about that time, to move on to Beardstown, where he was to build up a large and, for those times, lucrative practice. On April 15, 1837, the *Sangamo Journal*[1] carried the announcement: "The partnership heretofore existing between the undersigned, has been dissolved by mutual consent. The business will be found in the hands of John T. Stuart. April 12, 1837. John T. Stuart. Henry E. Dummer." Congenial though the personal relations of the partners had been, Dummer was dissatisfied, perhaps for the same reason which later moved Lincoln to sever the Stuart connection—the latter's increasing preoccupation with politics. As with so many of his contemporaries, politics came close to being the central fact of Stuart's existence.

Considering the close relationship which had existed between them since the days of the Black Hawk War, when Stuart first met and instantly took to the young captain of militia, and the high estimate which Stuart had come to place on Lincoln's ability, to say nothing of the latter's enhanced reputation and popularity as prime mover in effecting transfer of the state capital to Springfield, it is not surprising that, with the withdrawal of Dummer, Stuart should have offered Lincoln a junior partnership in what was then the busiest law firm in Sangamon County.

For Lincoln it was an ideal arrangement. It is a fair guess that there was not a lawyer in Springfield but would have jumped at the opportunity to form an association with Stuart, and the fact that the latter chose Lincoln strongly suggests that he saw something of the inner qualities of the man. Educated beyond the standards of his day, Stuart was a cultivated individual, a man of fine sensibilities—which gives one pause for skeptical thought at the suggestion that Lincoln was, at the time, the loutish fellow he has been pictured by some writers. Stuart had taken the full measure of his man, and sensed with salient intuition that, though countrified and rugged in appearance and informal in manner, he was a sensitive and intelligent individual, capable of reaching intellectual heights. However one may view the matter of Stuart's responsibility for Lincoln's decision to enter the law, one comes back inevitably to the fact that his contribution to the Lincoln story is incalculable, if only for the reason that he early perceived in him something of his considerable potential as a lawyer.

On April 15, 1837, in the same issue noting the withdrawal of Dummer, the *Sangamo Journal* recorded the forming of the new partnership of Stuart & Lincoln:

> John T. Stuart and A. Lincoln, Attorneys and Counsellors at Law, will practice, conjointly, in the Courts of this Judicial Circuit. — Office No. 4 Hoffman's Row, up stairs. Springfield, April 12, 1837.[2]

On that same day Lincoln packed his few belongings in his saddlebags, rode into Springfield on a borrowed horse and, after securing lodging with a local merchant, Joshua F. Speed, proceeded to fling himself energetically into the usual miscellany of civil and criminal cases that come a lawyer's way. However subordinate to the lure of politics may have been his early attraction to the law, there is no gainsaying the fact that Lincoln was extremely industrious at his calling. Even in its purely physical aspects, his achievement as a lawyer is amazing. It would be tedious to pass in review all the vast number of cases, important and trivial, in which he participated as counsel during the years 1837–1860; a representative sampling (not, it is to be hoped, a mere skimming over), as presented in this work, will give but a small notion of how really busy a practitioner he came to be. Though the law was not his sole and exclusive mistress, he devoted himself to her with unflagging zeal. From the outset of his association with Stuart, Lincoln was called upon to handle the bulk of the firm's work; the working arrangement constituted a strenuous apprenticeship of inestimable benefit to one whose training in the law had been less than complete. In the legal profession there is no substitute for the crucible of experience.

A fine figure of a man, six feet tall, of pleasing presence, urbane and dignified, Stuart, a Kentuckian by birth, was the soul of Southern courtliness, the "compleat gentleman." It was said of him that he always had "as fine and gallant a bow for his laundress as for a duchess." Graduating from college in 1826, he went to Richmond, Kentucky, where, after studying law in the office of a distant relative, he received his license to practice in 1827. In October of the following year he packed some clothing and a few books in his saddlebags, and set out for Illinois. After riding for ten days, he arrived, on October 25, 1828, in the young town of Springfield, a community of some three hundred inhabitants, among them five lawyers. Almost from the date of his arrival, Stuart became an integral part of the cultural and business life of the town. His growth in the confidence and attachment of the people of Sangamon and the adjoining counties was such that soon there was a pressing demand for his services.

In the same year that Lincoln joined forces with him, Stuart married Mary V. Nash, and sired a brood of three sons and three daughters. Shortly before his marriage, he purchased the property on which the historic Stuart mansion, at 529 South Fourth Street, was erected the same year. Lincoln was a frequent visitor there, as were Logan and other members of the Sangamon bar. (The home was razed in 1956, and a motel erected on the site.) That Stuart was able to raise a large family and live in a manner befitting one who moved in the best social circles, is the more remarkable in view of his timidity when it came to asking fees. Christopher C. Brown, who married Stuart's daughter, Bette, and joined the Stuart & Edwards law firm in 1860, writing of his father-in-law's inability to demand compensation commensurate with the value of the services rendered, said of him: "Accustomed in his early life to very low fees,—when he devoted more time to politics than the law,—he naturally placed a low estimate on legal services. When a suit was terminated and the time reached for fixing fees, if there was any possible chance to escape, he would leave the office."[3]

Lawyers will wince at the incredibly moderate (if that is the word) fee which he once fixed for drawing a will disposing of an estate the value of which, for those days, was somewhat staggering. Called on, in the early 'sixties, to draw a will for a client who was ill, he was obliged to travel by foot to the client's home several miles outside of Springfield, the roads being impassable at the time. After spending the day going over with the testator provisions disposing of an estate in excess of one hundred thousand dollars, drawing the will by hand and attending to its execution, he returned home after dark. The following morning he prepared a bill for legal services rendered, in the amount of five dollars. One of his partners, possessed of a vastly different notion of the value of a lawyer's services, prevailed upon him to make it fifty dollars. In a few days the client sent him one hundred dollars and a note stating that he hoped to be able to see him soon about the balance.[4] Clients, too, were different in those days.

2.

Lincoln came to Springfield at a time when it was settling down to a semblance of normalcy, after having been in a state of excitement over the event in the consummation of which he had played such a conspicuous role. It was an auspicious time, for the transfer of the seat of government meant enlarged opportunity for the lawyer. As county seat of Sangamon County, Springfield already boasted a circuit court, and, as befitted the capital city, it was only a question of time until the higher courts—the Supreme Court and the United States Courts—would remove there. With its rapidly expanding population, it was, from every point of view, an ideal springboard from which to launch a career at the bar. Even without the inducement of a law partnership with Stuart, the move to Springfield would have been an inevitable sequence to the favorable impression Lincoln had made in bringing about relocation of the state capital.

In attempting to dig out the source material on the frontier community of Springfield in 1837, with especial reference to the physical surroundings of Lincoln's start in the law, one soon finds that the "reminiscers" were considerably muddled in their recollections. On one thing, however, all accounts seem agreed—the town whose streets, said Vachel Lindsay in his famous poem, Lincoln walks at midnight, was then a rather unbeautiful place. John Hay irreverently speaks of "the dreary wastes of Springfield—a city combining the meanness of the North with the barbarism of the South." Other contemporary accounts describe it as a pretty soggy place—streets, especially, were quagmires and worse.

With prescient optimism, businessmen of the town had begun, in late 1835 or early 1836, the construction of a row of six two-story buildings on the west side of North Fifth Street. Though Hoffman's Row was somewhat effusively described as "a striking and handsome improvement upon the other buildings" of Springfield, there was nothing especially distinguished about the jumble of façades facing the east side of the street. Even to

Lincoln, fresh from the log-cabin community of New Salem, Springfield's main stem, with its unlighted streets deep in mud, could not have seemed much more prepossessing than was the town itself.

Elsewhere in town, one's ears were everywhere assailed by the sound of the hammer as dwellings and business buildings, the latter mostly two-story brick affairs, were going up in all directions; new shops were being opened, new doctors and lawyers were coming to live and practice. Soon the brick courthouse, built in 1831, would be razed, and in its place would be erected the new statehouse. A fresh and vigorous spirit was plainly astir. According to the Springfield census of 1836, there were eighteen doctors and eleven lawyers, and a population of twelve to thirteen hundred potential patients and clients to draw from.

No discussion of Springfield would be adequate that did not put large emphasis upon the "hog nuisance." The porkers roamed at large and lived on terms of intimacy with the community. Hog holes, filled with filth and mud, greeted one at every turn. The smell, so positive and unequivocal, and the orchestration of the nonstop grunting, were a constant source of irritation. The condition, however, was not indigenous to Springfield. There is an anecdote concerning Lincoln, involving an amusing incident which supposedly occurred in Taylorville, county seat of Christian County. The courthouse was raised several feet above the ground, resting on stone pilings; the space between afforded an ideal meeting place for the town's hogs. On one occasion, Lincoln was arguing a case, having difficulty making himself heard above the porcine chorus. Finally, he suspended the argument and, in mock earnestness, begged the judge to issue a writ of quietus, directed to the Sheriff, to abate the nuisance.[5]

Even in the frontier community of Springfield, the stratification of society was somewhat rigid. Lincoln's sensitiveness about his poverty and lack of practice in the social graces contributed to the feeling of not belonging, which is revealed in a letter to Mary Owens, written three weeks after his arrival. "There is a great deal of flourishing about in carriages here. . . . I am quite as lonesome here as [I] ever was anywhere in my life."[6] Within a few months, however, he began to feel more at home. No doubt Stuart, a member of one of Kentucky's "first families," with entrée, of right, to upper-crust Springfield society, had invited him to some of the social affairs—parties, dances, picnics and house-warmings—which marked the lighter side of life among the town's aristocracy. It is amusing to learn that Lincoln's political opponents—partly because of his partnership with the socially prominent Stuart, and partly because of his marriage into a Kentucky family of aristocratic background—should, in time, have come to refer to him as the candidate of wealth and social position.[7]

3.

The creaky office in the front room on the second floor in Hoffman's Row, at 109 North Fifth Street, in which Stuart and Lincoln conducted their partnership (the site now designated by a bronze marker), was anything but pretentious. The few items of furniture, consisting of a small couch, a chair, a wooden bench, "a feeble attempt at a book-case," and a table which answered the purpose of a desk, bore little resemblance to each other. The physical appearance of "Office No. 4" was not untypical of the law offices of that year of grace. To the lawyer of today, accustomed to all the conveniences of the modern law factory, with its sleek, almost treadmill efficiency, it is hard to conceive of a time when the typewriter and all the other time- and labor-saving devices were unknown. The paper work of lawyers was onerous in those days, since it had to be done laboriously by pen. (In the *Herndon-Weik Collection*, in the Library of Congress, there are a few printed legal forms used by the firm of Lincoln & Herndon, which in those days were evidently a novelty.)

Lincoln was from the outset an uncommonly good draftsman; starting with the year of his admission to practice, we find document after document written in his neat and pleasing hand, corrected only now and then, and subscribed either in the firm name or his own. (There would appear to have been no uniform practice in the matter of subscription.) In contrast to the pleadings of most of his contemporaries, marked as they are by corrections in profusion, those of Lincoln show relatively few, indicating that when he set about drawing up a declaration (statement of the plaintiff's cause of action) or other pleading, even the Lincoln of the late 'thirties knew pretty much what he was about and how he wanted to say it. He did not become flustered or panicky; he was calm; one can see it in his pleadings.

In an age when the art of orthography was not taken as seriously as it is today, Lincoln's occasional spelling lapses do not appear to have been very grievous. True, he wrote "colateral" and "colatteral" for collateral, "prossecution" and "prossecutor," "docketted," "guarranty," "afforesaid" and "aforsaid," "alledge" and "alledged," "consedation" and "considderation."[8] Yet, compared with those of most of his contemporaries, some of whom had had the benefit of a formal education, his legal papers would appear, on the whole, to be substantially free of eccentric spelling. As one who has made a careful study of the subject puts it: ". . . we are not justified in calling Abraham Lincoln a poor speller, although at times he was a careless one."[9]

When one has waded through the ocean of legal documents and memoranda prepared by Lincoln—some of them engrossing, some of them dull, a number of them (those not taken from *Chitty On Pleadings*) marked by his distinct, tight prose—it is not so much for his undoubted skill as a legal draftsman that one remembers him as for his prodigious gifts in the domain of perspicuity. The absence of extensive alteration and the conciseness of his way of putting down his thoughts on paper are significant of the clarity of Lincoln's thinking. The simplest words in the simplest order, and not too many of them, was his rule—this despite the copiousness of language in nineteenth-century legal documents. It was a lawyerly age, which delighted in many words for saying comparatively little. Which conjures up Lincoln's remarks on a paper drawn by a fellow lawyer best known for his uncontrollable verbosity: "It's like the lazy preacher that used to write long sermons, and the explanation was, he got to writin' and was too lazy to stop."

Defeated in 1836 by William L. May in his bid for election to Congress, Stuart was preparing for the Congressional contest of 1838 against the redoubtable Stephen A. Douglas. In consequence, he was away from the office the major part of the time, and the burden of preparing papers for court, drawing up business documents, and attending to the firm's correspondence—the purely utilitarian and relatively unspectacular aspects of practice —fell upon Lincoln. Despite long, toilsome hours of penmanship and composition, Lincoln performed this work conscientiously and well—never scrawling, writing always in a hand severely graceful. His industry was prodigious. Considering the amazing number of pleadings and miscellaneous legal documents in his handwriting to be found in the *Herndon-Weik Collection*, as well as those dispersed among various other repositories of primary source materials, the wonder is how he found time for anything else. Herndon, with whom accuracy was not always a fetish, couldn't have been wider of the mark than when he stated that Lincoln did less office work than any other lawyer in Illinois.[10]

The consistent, sustained quality of industry which Lincoln displayed in this phase of the practice was conspicuously absent when it came to attending to clerical work, at which he was woefully inefficient and which he always found exceedingly irksome. Lincoln was, as John Hay, one of his presidential secretaries, rightly noted, "extremely unmethodical."[11] A page of the fee book of Stuart & Lincoln, in Lincoln's handwriting, shows long time gaps between items apparently haphazardly entered. Instead of making entries in the book provided for that purpose, Lincoln was just as apt to jot down a casual memorandum, of which the following is typical, on any slip of paper conveniently at hand:

"I have received five dollars from Deed of Macon, five from Lewis Keeling, five from Andrew Finley, one-half of which belongs to Stuart and has not been entered on the books."

The page from the fee book[12] shown below appears to be especially interesting for the light it throws on the size of the average fee taken in. In one instance a coat purchased by Stuart for fifteen dollars is credited against a charge of fifty dollars, the largest fee shown on the page. Much of the litigation was of a petty nature, and the fees were accordingly small. Though the internal improvement fiasco had yet to run its course, financial panic struck the country with suddenness early in 1837. In April the State Bank at Springfield suspended specie payments. The financial crash created a situation whereby many folks were unable to meet their obligations, and in consequence there was an increase in collection business, of which work the firm of Stuart & Lincoln received their fair proportion. Unhappily for the legal profession, however, the economic plight of the nation communicated itself to lawyers, for, while there was enough business for all, cash fees were not to be had, except in small amounts. A number of the entries on the firm books indicate the acceptance of

Mather, Lamb & Co.
To Stuart & Lincoln Dr.
1837 — April — To attendance at trial of right of J. F. Davis'
property before Moffett $ 5.00

William Herndon
To Stuart & Lincoln Dr.
1837 — Oct. To Attachment case against Smith $ 5.00

Wiley & Wood
To defense of Chancery case of Ely $50.00
Credit by coat to Stuart   15.00
                                                          ‾‾‾‾‾‾
                                                          $35.00

Peyton L. Harrison
To Stuart & Lincoln Dr.
1838 — March — To case with Dickinson $10.00

Allen & Stowe
        To Stuart & Lincoln Dr.
1838 — Oct. To case with Centro $ 2.50

promissory notes in lieu of cash.

Not only were the cases, generally speaking, trivial in nature, but the rules of practice and procedure were relatively simple. American jurisprudence, like the republic itself, was still in its infancy, with no staggering mass of conflicting precedents to wrestle with, no mountain of authorities to be consulted in order to determine whether statutes or cases were still good law or whether subsequent decisions or supplementary legislation had impaired their value as controlling authorities. Issues were usually resolved in accordance with basic principles of abstract justice— "first principles," as they were sometimes called. While it is true that several of the Eastern states, principally New York and Massachusetts, had by then built up a fairly impressive body of legal precedent, founded on the English common law, quoting authorities from other jurisdictions, in the presence of a jury, was apt to prove, if anything, injurious to one's cause. Witness the experience of one prominent Illinois lawyer who cited from the New York reports, in support of his client's position: His adversary not only maintained that the authority referred to was without application, but launched a blistering attack on counsel for presuming to introduce into the case citations from a source so polluted. The jury was apparently in complete accord with this dim view of New York standards, for they found against the side which would contaminate justice in the sovereign State of Illinois by introducing foreign precedents.[13]

It is unhappily true that the whole changing trend of law has brought with it not only a steady piling up of precedents at an awesome rate, but the gradual decline in importance of the "all-round" lawyer, of which Lincoln was perhaps the prime example. This is not to say, however, that Lincoln was by any definition a village lawyer, as generally thought. Though Springfield was an important county seat and the capital of a flourishing state that boasted many outstanding lawyers, the impression somehow prevails that Lincoln practiced mainly before local magistrates, while spending most of his time spinning yarns for the amusement of witless rustics. The New York *Daily News* of October 30, 1860, likened him to "any other clever, awkward, jolly, common place, hum-drum lawyer and politician of a small country city." The fact of the matter is that he tried important matters and was not limited in his cases to those of purely regional concern.

4.

At the July, 1837, term of the Sangamon Circuit Court the firm had sixty cases, compared to forty-five for Logan & Baker, their closest competitors. Their cases ranged virtually the gamut of litigation, from simple assault to homicide, from small collection claims to actions in chancery involving the title to real estate. Out of this heterogeny of lawsuits there emerges one which attracted considerable attention by reason of its political overtones. Not alone did it focus attention on the new member of the Sangamon bar, but it provided him with an opportunity to give rein to his considerable epistolary talent.

To Springfield, in May of 1837, came Mary and Richard Anderson, the widow and son of Joseph Anderson, it being their intention, as his heirs, to take possession of and sell ten acres of land owned, at the time of his death (or so they believed), by the decedent, who resided in Fulton County. The property was in a section lying north of Springfield, situated where Oak Ridge Cemetery, Lincoln's final resting place, was subsequently located. To their consternation, they found the land to be occupied by General James Adams, a former attorney for Anderson. Adams predicated his claim to title upon a deed of record from the deceased. Upon the assertion of his claim, coupled with refusal to surrender possession, the Andersons consulted Lincoln, whose first move was to call in Logan. This done, Lincoln proceeded to draw up a contract for a contingent fee, whereby the firm of Stuart & Lincoln, and Logan would receive one half of the tract, conditioned upon their recovery of the same for the widow and her son.

> Whereas the heirs of Joseph Anderson deceased are about to commence an action in chancery in the Sangamon Circuit Court, for the recovery of a certain piece of ground [describing the land in controversy]; and whereas, Stephen T. Logan, John T. Stuart and A. Lincoln have engaged to prosecute the suit as attorneys for the said heirs, we, the subscribers, being the widow and one of the sons of the said Anderson deceased, agree to give to said Logan, Stuart and Lincoln one-half of the said piece of ground for their services, provided they recover the same; but are not bound to pay anything unless the piece of ground be recovered.[14]

An examination of the papers in the office of the Recorder[15] convinced Lincoln that the conveyance from Anderson to Adams was spurious. Accordingly, action was instituted to set it aside. Neither side being anxious to press the suit to a determination, it dragged on until November 29, 1843, when, by reason of the death of the defendant, an order of discontinuance was entered.[16] During the pendency of the action and after completion of his term as probate justice of the peace, Adams had moved on to Nauvoo, where he became active in Mormon affairs. He was run and elected as Mormon candidate for the office of probate justice of the peace, and died shortly after election.[17]

The suit having abated, the tract of land was inventoried in the estate of James Adams, and was sold by the executor to one Lewis, and by mesne conveyances title eventually became vested in the city of Springfield as part of Oak Ridge Cemetery. The Adams estate received the money from the sale of the land, and not a penny ever went to the widow and heirs of Anderson— from which one can safely conclude that Lincoln, Stuart and Logan received no compensation for their services.

There was a good deal behind the case which was not disclosed by the bare pleadings. Adams was at the time running for

probate justice of the peace of Sangamon County; he was opposed by Lincoln's friend and fellow Whig, Dr. Anson G.
Henry. Two days before the election there appeared on the
streets of Springfield a handbill, admittedly written by Lincoln
and turned out by the *Sangamo Journal*, charging that Adams
had acquired the Anderson property by fraud. Prior to that, someone, writing under the *nom de plume* of "Sampson's Ghost," had
conducted against Adams a campaign of denunciation in the
Journal, in the form of six letters spaced a week apart. The public
was quick to suspect that the "spectral" author of these letters
was none other than Abraham Lincoln. Though it has never been
established, with certainty, that they were, in fact, written either
by Lincoln or by Lincoln in collaboration with his colleagues,
Logan and Stuart, it is clear that only they could have been in
possession of the evidence upon which the charges were predicated.

The letters' strictures ranged beyond the issues of the case
to indulge in personalities, as well. Adams did not take the accusations lying down, but defended himself vigorously in the
columns of the *Republican*. The two newspapers devoted considerable space to the pre-trial skirmishing—the "news," in each
case, reflecting the editor's sympathies. Devoted, as all newspapers of the period were, to virulent personal journalism, the
case furnished grist to the mill. Viewing the picture objectively,
it is difficult to resist the feeling that Lincoln overreached himself.
The reaction to his preference for trying the case in the *Journal*
was distinctly unfavorable, and on August 7, 1837, Adams was
elected by a sizable majority, receiving 1025 votes to 792 for his
opponent.[18] Dr. Henry's defeat for the office was the first Whig
loss in Sangamon County in three years.

Lincoln's singularly maladroit use of the lawsuit as a weapon
to defeat Adams in his campaign for the judgeship stamps him at
the time as a harder fighter than he is sometimes made to appear.
Politics stir most men to acrimony. However, much water was
to flow under the bridge; even though, when the case required,

Lincoln could, without a blush, voice the sort of party claptrap calculated to stir the voters' blood, never again do we find him indulging in the squalid political campaigning which marked his effort on behalf of Dr. Henry.

5.

In the fall of 1837 Lincoln remained in Springfield while Stuart set out to cover the courts in the northern counties of the First Judicial Circuit. Entries in the partnership record indicate that this particular stint of circuit riding proved something less than a pronounced financial success, the net result being two cases in which fees of fifty dollars each were received, and one of forty dollars—hardly enough to keep the firm solvent for very long. It is likely that Stuart's energies were directed more toward strengthening his political contacts with the Whig leaders of Tazewell, McLean and Macon counties than digging up new cases.

During February of 1838 Lincoln may have been called upon to render advice to clients of Josephus Hewett's during the latter's absence from Springfield. The following item, appearing in the *Sangamo Journal*, is not untypical of the miscellaneous notices inserted by lawyers in those days:

A Card.

Being unexpectedly called from home on pressing business, likely to detain me until a week previous to our next Court, I take this method of informing those who have confided their business to the care of Walker & Hewett, that whenever *not* adversely employed, either Messrs. Logan & Baker, or Messrs. Stuart & Lincoln will give any advice or assistance needed during my absence.

Springfield, January 17, 1838. J. Hewett.

What some might consider an undignified means of developing new clients was practiced by Illinois lawyers throughout the nineteenth century, through insertion of "cards" in the local newspapers. Witness the following notice, inserted by Herndon in the *Illinois Journal:*

Law Business

By

Wm. H. Herndon

I have taken up my old profession, the prompt and vigorous practice of the law in this city, and will prepare and write out all needed contracts, leases, bonds, mortgages, deeds, last wills and testaments, obtain patents for all inventions, attend to the division of lands among heirs, dower, homestead cases, investigate titles to real estate, bring suits therefor or defend the same; will attend to all probate business, all collections of whatever nature, and any other matters left with me to arrange shall be promptly attend[ed] to. I will, speedily and cheaply, do all law business given over or entrusted to me. No person shall complain of my want of care to his business interests, nor to the fees, nor to the value of the labor. Strict and close attention to all business matters given to my charge, and cheapness of fees shall be my invariable rule.

Office on North Fifth Street, a few doors north of the old stand of the First National Bank.

Wm. H. Herndon.

Springfield, Ill., May 20, 1885.

CHAPTER IV

The Truett Murder Case

IF LINCOLN got off on the wrong foot in the Anderson case, he was not long in redeeming himself. It was this same resiliency, this power of recrudescence which he displayed throughout his life—the boundless capacity for bouncing back after defeats which would have permanently halted a lesser man—that gave Lincoln dimension. His first important criminal trial, one of the most celebrated in early Illinois legal history, came in October 1838. In it the tall young lawyer-politician not only made a notable comeback, but came close to stealing the show.

A proper picture of Lincoln's law career has been much obscured by myths and half-truths. Pre-eminent among these is the claim that Lincoln shunned the practice of criminal law. Joseph B. Oakleaf, the noted Lincoln collector, at a banquet of the Illinois State's Attorneys Association, held in Chicago December 7, 1912, spoke on the subject, "Lincoln as a Criminal Lawyer." Something of his distaste for the topic may be gathered from his apologetic opening remarks: "The subject assigned me was not of my own selection. I was invited to deliver an address on Lincoln, and I was pleased that the honor was accorded me, and, had the subject been left to me, I would have preferred to have addressed you on some other phase of Lincoln's life, inasmuch as there is so little to say concerning Lincoln from the standpoint of a criminal lawyer, for the reason that he abhorred criminal practice." It is significant that Oakleaf made no attempt to substantiate this broad statement, either by quotation or analysis.

Characteristic of the nonsense which has been written on

this subject is the statement of one writer that Lincoln would have no part of criminal practice because he didn't have the requisite "intellectual unscrupulousness."[1] James G. Randall, the late dean of the Lincoln scholars, has pointed out that the ratio of criminal cases to the total number of cases on a typical court docket on the Eighth Circuit exceeded the proportion which Lincoln had.[2] True enough, but the fact remains that he handled hundreds of such cases—involving crimes ranging all the way from gambling to rape and murder. Manifestly, any treatment of Lincoln's work in the courts, without somewhat extended consideration of his appearances in criminal cases, would be seriously incomplete.

Few judgments can be more grossly inaccurate than the one which would have us believe that Lincoln, with his sympathy for people in trouble, could ever have been guilty of the priggish thinking involved in a disinclination to handle criminal matters. What is more, Lincoln practiced in an era when there was no prejudice against lawyers representing people accused of crime; in the then current climate of social thought, the press and the "better elements" were not given to disapproving so loquaciously of lawyers for showing that under the law their socially unacceptable clients had to be "sprung."

It might also be noted that, in taking any and all cases, lawyers were animated by sound practical considerations. The lawyer who traveled the circuit could not afford to be choosy in selecting his clients or worry about courting social ostracism. From the time that Illinois was admitted into the Union, the practice of criminal law was most assiduously cultivated, and there was hardly one of the old pioneer lawyers, or even of Lincoln's contemporaries, but what had considerable to do with the trial of cases in the criminal courts. In the East, such lawyers as Webster and Choate were frequently engaged before the criminal bar. Choate, one of the most articulate advocates of the Anglo-Saxon tradition that a man is innocent until he is proved guilty, had almost a monopoly in that field in his own Essex County, where he was recognized as "the great criminal lawyer."

Spottswood's Rural Hotel, later to be known as the Globe Tavern, was the scene of one of Springfield's most dramatic episodes, an event which became a local *cause célèbre*. Like most small-town hotels of the time and section, it had a large public "parlor," with an open fireplace. On the evening of March 7, 1838, Jacob M. Early, a physician and Methodist preacher, who lived about five miles outside Springfield and who sometimes put up at the hotel overnight, was relaxing after dinner, seated before the fireplace, reading the *Sangamo Journal*. After first extracting his pistol from a pocket of his overcoat hanging on a rack in the hall, Henry Truett, ex-Register of the Galena land office, entered the room and seated himself nearby. Suddenly jumping to his feet, Truett demanded of Early if it was not a fact that he had authored certain resolutions adopted at a recent Democratic convention in Peoria, disapproving of Truett's appointment as Register and calling for his removal. Early remained silent, whereupon Truett drew his pistol. Early attempted to protect himself by holding a chair in front of him. Maneuvering his victim into a position where he could take an unobstructed shot at him, Truett pulled the trigger and Early fell, mortally wounded. He died three days later.[3] Truett fled from the scene, but was apprehended shortly thereafter. On March fourteenth he was indicted on a charge of murder. On the insistence of Douglas, acting prosecuting attorney, the accused was denied bail.

The killing was the outgrowth of a bitter political feud. Truett's father-in-law was William L. May, congressman from the Springfield district. Through the latter's influence, Truett had managed, early in 1837, to have himself appointed Register of the United States Land Office in Galena. His tenure of office was to be short-lived, for, at the district convention held at Peoria the following November, Stephen A. Douglas was nominated in his place. May had incurred the displeasure of the party workers by reason of his opposition to certain of Van Buren's fiscal measures.

If matters had rested there, probably Truett would have taken his medicine and charged it all up to the fortunes of politics. However, the convention, not content with denying him the nomination, proceeded to adopt the following resolution: "The recent appointment of H. B. Truett to the office of Register of the land office at Galena, was not in accordance with the wishes and feelings of the Democratic party, in this district, and . . . his standing is such as to require of us a recommendation to the President for his immediate removal." Truett believed that the author of the resolution was Early, a member of the resolutions committee and a leader of the Douglas faction in the Democratic Party.

In a letter to the *Sangamo Journal*, written in January of 1838, Lincoln was rather uncomplimentary in referring to his future client, whom he described as "a certain gentleman who resides in Sangamon County, and who has followed a variety of occupations both here and elsewhere, for a living and failed in all." Lincoln went on to speculate as to "when he should be called upon to close up his loafing operations."[4] One is led to think that Truett was of that breed of adventurers and scoundrels who stalk constantly through political life. Knockabout characters of his stamp generally have a tough hide, but apparently the rebuff was too much for him to take without resort to homicidal retaliation.

The defendant retained Lincoln, Stuart, Logan, Baker and Cyrus Walker, all of them Whigs. The last named, an experienced hand at the business, was considered a good man to have on one's side in a criminal case. With that yearning for new fields to conquer which brought so many restless Southerners to the Illinois country, he left Kentucky, where he had gained prominence as a criminal lawyer, and settled, in 1833, in Macomb.[5] It was not uncommon, in Illinois, for the different state's attorneys to engage outside counsel, and, though he held no public office, many was the prosecution in which Walker was so retained. It was frequently a race between the defense and the prosecution to enlist his services. In 1835 he formed a partnership with Josephus Hewett, a preacher noted for his eloquence, who switched callings after having "read law" in the office of Logan.[6] When the Mormon prophet, Joseph Smith, was arrested in 1843 in Lee County in connection with an extradition proceeding seeking his removal for trial to the State of Missouri, he sent for Walker, then a candidate for Congress, to represent him. A somewhat unusual retainer agreement was entered into between them, Smith promising Walker his vote in return for the latter's services.[7]

In view of his contemplated appearance as a witness for the state, the prosecuting attorney, John D. Urquhart, stepped aside, and Judge Jesse B. Thomas, Jr. appointed Douglas, Urquhart's law partner, to represent the People. A curious feature of the case is the fact that Urquhart, though a public official, was obliged to post one thousand dollars bail as a material witness.[8]

Upon the defendant's arraignment, his attorneys requested and were granted a continuance to the July term, because of the allegedly inflamed state of public opinion. Had Lincoln been senior counsel, instead of Logan, he almost certainly would have moved for a change of venue, for in virtually every criminal case which he handled, either on his own or as chief counsel, this was an automatic first move. In July a further adjournment was obtained until the October term, on the ground that certain material witnesses whom the defense planned calling were unavailable.[9] If Lincoln was not already, he soon became, as we shall presently see, a master of the art of delaying tactics. It is sometimes said that justice delayed is justice denied, but for Lincoln, who disliked seeing people condemned in haste, justice rushed was apt to be justice gone amiss. He realized that nothing is better calculated to dissipate passion and prejudice than a cooling-off period, during which inflamed public opinion has an opportunity to settle down and view the facts fairly and with some degree of objectivity. Thus, dilatory maneuvers by lawyers frequently have their valid purpose, even though contributing to the "law's delay," which Shakespeare, putting the complaint in the mouth of his favorite character, cited as one of "the whips and scorns of time."[10]

On October 8, 1838, the trial commenced in the little store which housed the Sangamon Circuit Court on Hoffman's Row, on the street level directly beneath the Stuart & Lincoln office. There was a trap door leading from the law office (later rented by an architectural firm) to the courtroom; on one occasion Lincoln was listening to Baker addressing a turbulent political meeting below, and when the speaker was rushed by several of the opposition, Lincoln dropped through the trap door and held off the attackers. The firm was enabled to defray part of its operating expenses by renting out the office to the County of Sangamon for use of grand and petit juries, at a rental of twelve dollars per term of court.

The county of Sangamon.

To Stuart & Lincoln   Dr.

To furnishing room for Grand an[d] Petit Juries at July & October terms of 1837—and March term of 1838—

$36–00[11]

At the prosecution table sat David M. Woodson, newly appointed state's attorney for the First Judicial District, and Douglas, who remained in the case as his associate. As the trial headed into the third day, selection of the jury was completed, after examination of 215 veniremen. The direct evidence pointed unmistakably to the guilt of the defendant, and amply warranted a conviction. A dying declaration, made by the deceased to Urquhart, and naming the defendant as the aggressor in an unprovoked attack, was admitted in evidence over the objection of the defense.[12] The State contended that the act of the defendant in arming himself prior to going to Spottswood's Hotel, and the picking of a quarrel with the deceased, coupled with the showing of a sufficient motive, plus the undisputed fact of the shooting and the defendant's flight, excluded, to a moral certainty, every hypothesis but that of guilt.

The creation of a reasonable doubt as to the defendant's guilt must have taken some doing, for it was clearly evident that the defendant's goose was now cooked to a turn. To counter the airtight case presented against their client, Logan, Lincoln *et al.*, advanced the disingenuous defense that Early, possessed of a deadly weapon, to wit, a chair, was intent on killing Truett (or so the latter had a right to believe), and that in shooting his assailant Truett was simply acting in self-defense. One need not be versed in the complex profundities of the law to recognize the contention for the unmitigated sham it really was. In fact, two eyewitnesses to the shooting testified for the People that the deceased had made no effort to strike the defendant with the chair, but merely held it before him as a shield. The case looked exceedingly grave against Truett; a hanging may reasonably have been anticipated.

When all the evidence was in, and both sides had rested, there arrived the great moment when Lincoln would address the jury. Most lawyers would have quailed before the task which confronted him. It was, indeed, a tribute to his ability to express himself convincingly that, in a capital case, he should have been entrusted with the closing argument by four such veteran campaigners as Logan, Baker, Stuart and Walker. Though only a year in practice, the rising young lawyer was already in fast company; it would not be long before he moved in their midst as an equal. Here was the climax of the trial, the opportunity to rescue a cause that until then might well have seemed lost, for the case for the prosecution seemed ironclad, and no amount of legal rationalization that the defense could devise could disguise the fact that the defendant had killed the deceased deliberately and with premeditation, and without provocation in law. Lincoln had his work cut out for him. If, as he gathered his thoughts, with the careful determination to make the best of a bad case, Lincoln realized, as he very probably did, the staggering weight of his responsibility, and his heart pounded with the fear that he might not measure up to the task, it could hardly have been wondered at.

The skill and economy with which the tyro discharged his assignment is attested by Logan's characterization of the plea as "a short but strong and sensible speech." Logan, with the caution of a seasoned veteran, was loath to bestow compliments haphazardly, and folks valued his approbation the more for the Scotch thrift he showed in giving it. That Lincoln's unannounced talent should so emphatically assert itself on first appearance was cause enough for Logan to depart from his usual taciturnity. That Lincoln abjured the temptation to expatiate is the more remarkable in view of the fact that, in that blustering age of Illinois law, there was no time limit placed on the closing argument of counsel, and the practice among lawyers was to hold forth, in summation, at great length and with flamboyant rhetoric.

Lincoln's showing in the Truett trial, as in numerous other of his cases, where the facts were overwhelmingly against his client, should dispose, with devastating finality, of the patent poppycock advanced by certain of his biographers—even by some of his contemporaries—that Lincoln could only put forth his best efforts when convinced of the justice of the cause which he advocated.[13] Certainly no lawyer will swallow such buncombe. Though possessed of a rare gift for objective detachment, he could, on occasions, be as technical and hairsplitting as all get-out, and when urging fine points, it sometimes mattered not whether justice and common sense were on his side. To the Lincoln canonizers this may sound like a harsh thing to say, but it is the exact truth. For one horrible example of pettifogging, there was the time when the clerk of court in Tazewell entered judgment for $939.41 in an action where the plaintiff had brought suit on two items of indebtedness totaling that amount. Judge Davis rendered judgment in the full amount against the defendants, Lincoln's clients. Because the clerk, in following the Court's finding, added the two items together, entering one judgment instead of two, Lincoln argued upon the appeal that there was "a fatal variance" between the amounts sued for and the judgment. Stuart & Edwards, in opposition, contended that the defendants should not be permitted, on a technicality, "to defeat a judgment in other respects righteous and just." The court was unimpressed with Lincoln's hairsplitting, and in affirming the judgment lumped the two items together.[14]

There was the time in Tazewell, on a change of venue from Peoria County, when the Shaffer brothers (a pair of larcenous scalawags who, for low-down knavery, stand high on the list of Lincoln's antisocial clients) were under indictment for cheating and fraud. As appears from the following excerpt, in Lincoln's hand, taken from the motion to quash the indictment, filed October 4, 1853, Lincoln moved on the captious ground that

> The principal charge; to wit, the charge that the defendants obtained the money &c. by false pretenses, is not presented by the Grand Jury 'in the name, and by the authority of the People of the State of Illinois—'[15]

Again, Lincoln's technical objection left the Court unmoved.

Whatever the merits of his closing remarks in the Truett case, it was generally acknowledged among his contemporaries of the next two decades that Lincoln, when he emerged from the woods, surpassed them all in summation. (It is uncertain whether, at that early stage, he had yet acquired the superb knack of cross-examination which marked his later trial work.) It was his extraordinary power of persuasion in the final summing up to the jury, his aptitude for illustration in the vernacular and homely similes folks could understand, which, probably as much as any other feature of his trial work, so often tipped the balance in his client's favor and earned for him a reputation as a first-rate jury lawyer. Intuitively adept at the art of establishing contact with men in groups of twelve, he would proceed to project himself and his client's cause across to them, better than almost anyone practicing in those parts. Possessed of an analytical mind and the ability to

express what was in it—qualities not often found in combination
—he had a way of "getting into the jury box." Even the conspicuously able Logan was later to concede Lincoln's superiority over
him in the matter of summation. Grant Goodrich, a leading
Chicago trial lawyer of Lincoln's day, writing to Herndon in
1866, said: "Mr. Lincoln was my associate first in the trial of three
cases *vs.* Grace Lawson in 1845 for fraud and misrepresentations,
in the sale of land. The cases were severely contested. Messrs.
Butterfield and Collins and Edw. Baker, Esqs., being counsel for
defendant. Mr. Lincoln in closing the case made the best jury
argument I ever heard him make. Judge Pope said it was one of
the best he ever heard."[16]

Despite his ungainliness and rather homely face, Lincoln
had what is known in the trade as "courtroom presence." Withal,
his demeanor was on the conservative side—this in an age of
Illinois law when restraint was not the dominant note, when lawyers were wont to pull out all the organ stops of courtroom dra-
matics. The technique of that day, with the old-time emphasis on
histrionics and spread-eagle oratory, called for lawyers to thun-
der, bellow and whisper. They leaned chummily on the jury rail;
they declaimed from across the room. And, into the bargain, they
very frequently resorted to logic.

On the fifth day Judge Thomas charged the jurors, who
thereupon repaired to the Stuart & Lincoln office upstairs, to
deliberate. In about three hours they returned to the courtroom.
The verdict? Not Guilty! Without detracting from the force of
Lincoln's plea and whatever other legal prestidigitation defense
counsel may have practiced upon the twelve good men and true,
it must be noted that juries were, as a rule, loath to convict in
murder cases. They would hang a man for stealing a horse, but
acquit him of shooting another man. However that may be, Lincoln was no longer a neophyte; he had won his spurs. His success
in this, his first important criminal case, undoubtedly contributed
to the confidence and self-reliance which he displayed in his trial
practice thereafter.

On March twenty-first, a week after the indictment, May gave two notes of $250 each to Lincoln and Stuart, secured by a deed intended to operate as a mortgage on land in the northern part of Sangamon, now Logan County. Under date of August 22, 1838, there appears a notation on the margin of the Deed Record of Logan County, showing that the same had that day been satisfied. Logan, Baker, and Walker received, among them, one thousand dollars.

Truett was dogged by the killing for the rest of his days, the Whig press, in particular, never failing to remind the public that he was an "acquitted murderer."[17] Several years after his acquittal, this unabashed rogue attended a Democratic Senatorial Convention in Dixon. His appearance as delegate evoked bitter remarks in the press. One Whig journal put it his way: "We wonder if all the delegates were as *pure* as this Mr. Truett? . . . Is there a democratic paper in the state, that has not again and again charged this man with a murder of the most atrocious character? We always knew the mantle of democracy was a broad one, but we cannot yet persuade ourselves that it can cover the heinous sin of murder. For the character of our State, we wish our opponents would pay a little more attention to character."[18]

CHAPTER V

Early Law Years

1.

ON AUGUST 6, 1838, Lincoln was elected to the legislature for the third time; as in 1836, he led a field of seventeen candidates. During that spring and summer, Stuart was engaged in a torrid campaign for Congress against Douglas, and in consequence devoted even less time than usual to the partnership affairs. While Stuart was making speeches and shaking hands on the campaign trail throughout the thirty-four northern counties, Lincoln not only took sole charge of the firm's business, handling cases in court and attending to the office phase of the practice, but campaigned for his partner as well. Stuart squeezed through by the narrow margin of thirty-six votes.

In his first two years of practice, during which Sangamon County was part of the First Judicial Circuit, extending north to Tazewell County and south to Calhoun County, Lincoln attended the courts to the north. It was not until 1839, when the Eighth Judicial Circuit was formed, that he became identified with the regular seasonal hegira, in which the various members of the peripatetic bar took off on the grueling trek each spring and fall. In the preceding two years, he got just a taste of what it was to be like traveling long distances over rugged roads, often with a driving rain or early winter snowstorm in his face, while he bucked the ruthless wind. Despite the many trying vicissitudes of travel and climate, he was to enjoy the experience, and everything about it, especially the courage and grim humor of the prairie settlers, the same grim humor which caused the Illinois landlord to assure Ralph Waldo Emerson, in a week when the temperature varied from ten to twenty below zero, that they had no cold weather in Illinois—"only now and then Indian summer and cool nights."

In April, 1839, Lincoln attended the Hancock County Circuit Court at Carthage, where he unsuccessfully represented William Fraim on a charge of murder. While there, Lincoln probably stayed at Artois Hamilton's, a boarding inn which catered to lawyers whose business in court necessitated their stopping over.

His associate in the Fraim trial was yet another Kentuckian who had felt the pull of Illinois—T. Lyle Dickey, of Ottawa. Originally a schoolteacher, Dickey switched to law at the urging of Cyrus H. Walker, and built up a good practice, in addition to editing a Whig newspaper. In common with many others, Dickey succumbed to the speculative urge and became deeply involved in real-estate deals. Scarred and bruised by the disastrous panic of 1837, in which he lost practically everything, he was obliged to start anew just about the time when he and Lincoln became associated in the Fraim murder trial. Leonard Swett, the most famous criminal lawyer of Lincoln's day, speaking of Dickey as a trial lawyer, said: "Here he was gentlemanly, overflowing with good nature, quick, sharp, and incisive as a Damascus blade. Playing with him under such circumstances was like playing with broken glass."[1] With Lincoln he joined the newly formed Republican Party, but soon quit it as being "too closely allied to the Abolitionists," whom he abominated. When Lincoln learned of Dickey's action, he told Henry C. Whitney that he "did not know of any of his friends he felt so badly about losing as Dickey." In later years Dickey was elected to the Illinois Supreme Court, on which he sat from 1876 to 1885. During the war he served on Grant's staff as chief of cavalry in the Western theater.

If Lincoln left Springfield on Saturday, as he very probably did, in order to be in Carthage for the convening of court on Monday, April twenty-second, he covered a distance of 115 miles in two days. On Tuesday the case was tried before Judge James H. Ralston and a jury. Fraim, a laborer on the steamboat

Hero, which plied the Illinois River, had killed a fellow worker in the course of a drunken brawl. The case originated in Schuyler County, but was tranferred to Hancock on the defendant's application for a change of venue. (On June 27, 1844, Joseph Smith, the Mormon Prophet, and his brother, Hyrum, were slain by an anti-Mormon mob in the same jail, in Carthage, where Fraim was held awaiting trial.)

Upon conviction of murder as charged, the prisoner was sentenced to be hanged. There remained to the defense one final recourse—the post-conviction remedy of a motion in arrest of judgment, the papers being drawn partly by Lincoln. This last-ditch effort failed, and on May eighteenth the sentence of the court was carried out in a field on the outskirts of the town, in the presence of a large crowd, the levity and callousness of which was characteristic of such turnouts. Among the less lovely aspects of life on the frontier was the festive mood in which the populace turned out to gape at these brutalizing and degrading public hangings. In the early Middle West, "rope parties" took on the character of national holidays.

Excruciatingly, almost pathologically sensitive as Lincoln was to the plight of others, and with his lively imagination, which put him in the other fellow's place and made him suffer with him, he doubtless endured many an agonizing moment thinking of omissions and mistakes which he may have made in the course of the trial. It is not easy to live with the thought that one might have saved a human life, but proved inadequate for the task.

The Fraim case furnishes an interesting example of the looting of official court documents in Lincoln's hand which became almost, one might say, a major industry after his death. Court clerks and others having access to official records, among them Herndon, developed taking ways, and many a court paper, even complete files of cases in which Lincoln participated, received the "basement door treatment." An example of solid, otherwise law-abiding citizenry not above a bit of filching where Lincoln documents are concerned, is the case of the West Coast banker. Among the yellowed papers on file in the Circuit Court of Hancock County, at Carthage, is the motion in arrest of judgment, partly in Lincoln's hand, in *People* v. *William Fraim*. Shortly after the turn of the century a dignified gentleman visited the courthouse in Carthage and, expressing deep interest in Lincoln, was shown the valued paper. Not long thereafter, it appeared on display, neatly framed, in a bank window in a West Coast city. An acquaintance of Circuit Court Reaugh's saw it by chance, and, knowing something of the document's history, communicated the fact to Reaugh, back in Carthage. The latter replied that it had unaccountably disappeared from the files, and asked his informant to do some discreet checking on how the legal paper had reached there. Upon being confronted, the light-fingered financier admitted appropriating it to his own use; a week later the paper reached Carthage by registered mail.[2]

2.

In June, 1839, Lincoln and Douglas opposed each other in the trial of a case in Decatur, seat of Macon County. David Adkins had been accused by one Robert Hines of stealing the latter's pigs, whereupon Adkins brought an action for slander against his accuser, the complaint praying damages in the sum of two thousand dollars. Associated with Lincoln, for the defendant, were Stuart and Charles Emerson, the first resident lawyer of Macon County. For Adkins there were Douglas and Kirby Benedict, who later became Chief Justice of the New Mexico Territory. The defendant's answer, drawn up by Lincoln and signed by Hines, alleged the truth of the statements attributed to him, the same being a complete defense in law. After a trial before Judge Samuel H. Treat, in which the plaintiff called seven witnesses and the defendant thirteen, the jury (of which Joseph Hanks, a cousin of Lincoln, was a member) found for the defendant. Thereupon Douglas prepared, in his own hand, and submitted an affidavit for a new trial, on the ground of newly discovered evidence. The case was not reopened.

In July, 1839, the Supreme Court met in Springfield for the first time. Though Lincoln had no matters in that court until June of 1840, it is likely that he attended as a spectator. Many distinguished visitors graced the gay capital for the occasion. Until completion of the new State House, the court held its sessions in the Episcopal Church, on Adams Street between Third and Fourth.

On October 31, 1839, while in attendance in Decatur, Lincoln was appointed by Judge Jesse B. Thomas to defend the aforementioned David Adkins on a charge of larceny. Lincoln never attended at the old courthouse in Decatur without adverting to the fact that it was there, in 1830, on the courthouse green, that the Lincoln caravan made its first stop in Illinois, on its way from Indiana.[3] The jury found the defendant not guilty.

It was common practice for the different judges to assign lawyers to represent indigent persons charged with the commission of crimes. Though there was no organization in existence in any way comparable to our present-day legal-aid societies, no person accused of a crime—in Illinois, at least—went unrepresented upon a showing of financial inability to engage counsel. In thus implementing the right to counsel, and so alleviating the natural disadvantages of indigents in criminal cases, Illinois was in the forefront among the states.

Not infrequently such an assignment entailed a trial lasting days, during which period counsel was obliged to pass up the bread and butter cases. During lean times, as in 1837 and 1838, it often meant real hardship for one to find, after journeying to some outlying court, enduring no end of discomfort to get there, that the better part of one's time and efforts were to be taken up in handling a "free case," so that justice might be had by all. Even so, there was in Lincoln's day, as there is now, and probably always will be, an aversion to that most maligned of all secular professions, a group which maintains itself upon the disputes and imperfections of other men—which conjures up Carl Sandburg's lines:

> Why is there always a secret singing
> When a lawyer cashes in?
> Why does a hearse horse snicker
> Hauling a lawyer away?

3.

Like every lawyer who is active in politics, Lincoln was obliged to handle a number of "political cases," in which services are rendered without any hope of remuneration. Political office holders, whenever they find themselves in legal difficulty, almost invariably look to the party's lawyers for free advice and assistance. The custom obtains even when the individual involved is himself a lawyer; as a class, lawyers are the first to recognize that the adage of the defendant who is his own lawyer having a fool for a client has not been perpetuated without some reason. *John A. McClernand, Secretary of State* v. *Robert Irwin & Co.*, in the Sangamon Circuit Court, an offshoot of the Supreme Court case of *Field* v. *The People*, presented such a situation. Alexander Pope Field, a Whig wheel horse, was, as has been noted, at one time considered among the forefront of the state's criminal lawyers. He also is said to have obtained some of the largest slander, seduction, breach of promise and negligence verdicts in the state. In 1828 he was appointed Secretary of State. When Governor Carlin, a Democrat, came into office in 1838 he proceeded to replace the incumbent with a member of his own party—that ineffable Illinois politician, John A. McClernand. Field, however, refused to surrender possession of the office, whereupon McClernand brought a proceeding in the Fayette County Court in the nature of *quo warranto* (a demand calling upon an individual to show by what authority he exercises certain rights). The proceeding was decided in McClernand's favor; Field appealed to the Supreme Court.

Before the appeal came up, Field, who must have possessed some of the toughness of his illustrious uncle, Judge Nathaniel Pope, removed his files, as well as the seal of the state, from Vandalia to Springfield, the new state capital, where they were placed for safekeeping with John Irwin & Co., a store which served as general headquarters for the Whig Party in Springfield. Lincoln was later to have a charge account there. Douglas, representing McClernand, sued out a writ of replevin (a possessory action for the recovery of the possession of goods or chattels wrongfully taken or detained) in the Sangamon Circuit Court. On July 5, 1839, Lincoln and Mason Brayman, appearing on behalf of Field, filed a motion to quash the writ, which motion was granted by Judge Treat. The same day, the Supreme Court upheld Field's right to the office of Secretary of State. By then, however, Field, a contentious individual, especially when in his cups (which was frequently), had proved such a headache to the Whigs, as well as to the Democrats, that enough of them voted with the latter to succeed in ousting him from office in November, 1840, by approving the appointment of Douglas.

On November 2, 1839, Stuart left to take his seat in Congress. The occasion was marked by an entry made by Lincoln in the firm's fee book, "Commencement of Lincoln's Administration."

4.

Writing of his childhood, Joseph Jefferson, famous actor of the succeeding generation, who won enduring fame in the role of Rip Van Winkle, told how his father, with a traveling company of actors which set out from Albany, New York, in open wagons, reached Springfield in the early winter of 1839, after brief stands en route in various towns like Galena, Burlington, Quincy, Peoria and Pekin. Springfield being the capital of the state, it was determined to devote an entire season to entertaining the members of the legislature. Having made some money prior to their arrival, the management rented a lot and proceeded to erect a small wooden theater about ninety feet deep and forty feet wide.[4]

Unfortunately for the venture, it coincided with a religious revival movement; not only did the ministers of the different faiths launch forth against the group in their sermons, but indignant church members saw to it that the little playhouse was taxed out of existence by means of a prohibitive license fee upon the contemplated "unholy" performance.[5] Jefferson's experience was typical of the tribulations of the nineteenth-century theater and trouping in the United States, when playgoing was frowned upon by the clergy and actors were a generally raffish lot.

As told by Jefferson, the story goes that, in the midst of their difficulties, a young lawyer, Abraham Lincoln by name, called upon the management and, stating that he had heard of their trouble, volunteered to make an application to have the tax rescinded. So strongly did he feel about the injustice of it all that he offered to represent the group, which operated under the name of the Illinois Theatrical Company, without fee. When the matter came on for a hearing before the local burgesses, Lincoln made a persuasive argument covering the history of acting from earliest times. So earnestly and effectively did he present the case for the actors, that the exorbitant tax was rescinded.[6]

Anecdotes, many of them apocryphal, have sprung up about so much of Lincoln's work as a lawyer that one is not surprised to learn that the minutes of the Springfield town council, of which body he was a member at the time the episode occurred, fail to disclose that Lincoln was present when the matter was considered[7]—which, of course, does not necessarily rule out the possibility of his having appeared on behalf of the players. Appearances may not have been noted so scrupulously in those days. If the charming legend was not exactly true, it could and should have been; only the spoil-sport will quibble about it. Lincoln was always fond of the play; what is more, he disliked seeing people pushed around. If the episode, as related by Jefferson, Jr., has any basis in fact, we may be sure that Lincoln considered the satisfaction of accomplishment in seeing to it that the little theater was permitted to remain, well worth the effort involved.

5.

Spring of 1840 found Lincoln on the circuit, covering McLean, Livingston, DeWitt, Macon, Christian, Menard and Sangamon counties. The Eighth Circuit had been reorganized on February 1, 1840, to include the foregoing counties, plus those of Tazewell and Logan. On May twenty-third, at Clinton, county seat of DeWitt County, Lincoln, together with Douglas and Kirby Benedict, represented Spencer Turner on a charge of murder. The principal interest of the case lies in the fact that it was the only murder trial in which Lincoln and Douglas appeared as co-counsel.[8]

The finding of the coroner's jury recited that the deceased, Matthew K. Martin, "came to his death by a severe blow upon his head with a club struck by Spencer Turner . . . together with his [decedent's] own imprudence in keeping himself in a state of intoxication and exposure in rain and inclemency of the weather on the night previous to his death"[9]—a finding that provided Lincoln with an argument he could get his teeth into. Lincoln had an extraordinary capacity for seizing upon the vulnerable spot in an adversary's case—what Justice Oliver Wendell Holmes called "the instinct for the jugular."

Upon the trial the prosecution subpoenaed fourteen witnesses, the defense nine. It is to be doubted, however, that all were called, inasmuch as the trial commenced on May twenty-third, and was concluded the same day. Lincoln summed up for the defense, and (not necessarily a case of cause and effect) the defendant was acquitted.

We the Jury find the Defendant Not
Clinton May 23rd, 1840   Guilty
Henry Willray
foreman
[Memorandum of jury's verdict, in hand of foreman][10]

While no transcript of the summation exists, for the reason that none was made, it is safe to assume that Lincoln, striking at the obvious flaw in the case for the prosecution, riddled the latter with well-aimed shafts based upon the finding of the coroner's inquest, *i.e.:* that the deceased was in an intoxicated condition at the time of the altercation resulting in his death. The advantage to be derived from this circumstance was, from the defendant's point of view, twofold, affording as it did plausible grounds for the contention, first, that the death of the deceased had been brought about, not as a result of the blow struck by the defendant, but, rather, by the decedent's "imprudence in keeping himself in a condition of intoxication and exposure," and second, that the deceased was the aggressor, any blow struck by the defendant having been delivered in self-defense.

The prosecution was conducted by David B. Campbell, a Democrat who, in 1839, had been elected by the legislature to the office of state's attorney for the Eighth Judicial District over his Whig opponent, David Davis. Campbell, a "noted fiddler," carried his violin with him while on circuit; it was a fine instrument which he frequently played when the other lawyers were not talking or playing cards into the small hours. John M. Palmer, in his *Bench and Bar of Illinois*, says of Campbell that he "would never prosecute one charged with crime unless thoroughly convinced of his guilt"[11] (rather an excessive claim, one feels). If true, it speaks well for Lincoln's ability, at that early stage of his career, to free his more antisocial clients.

The tale, which went the rounds for a while after Lincoln's death, that he received as compensation a horse which soon went blind, has been consigned to its proper place among those pleasant but decidedly suspect anecdotes in which the story of Lincoln's life abounds. For his services Lincoln received a ninety-day note for two hundred dollars. A year and a half later later, having received neither payment nor anything on account, he commenced action on the note. The defendant pleaded that he was under age when the note was executed, a defense which in the end availed him nothing, for, after prolonged litigation, judgment was awarded Lincoln for $213.50 and costs, which he did not succeed in collecting until April, 1846. Douglas, on the other hand, is said to have demanded and received his fee of two hundred dollars either before the commencement of the trial or immediately upon its conclusion.

6.

A called session of the lower house of the state legislature convened on November 23, 1840. The *Journal* of the House of Representatives of the Twelfth General Assembly reveals an intriguing item under date of November twenty-sixth. A prosecutor firmly opposed to capital punishment is uncommon enough in any day to warrant special mention. Such a man was Wickford Kitchell. On that date the Speaker laid before the House, for its consideration, a message of Attorney General Kitchell, recommending certain changes designed to introduce some relaxation in the criminal code, among them one calling for abolition of the death penalty.

It is rare to find a prosecuting official speaking out with such sincerity on the controversial subject of the efficacy of hanging (or other forms of capital punishment) as did Kitchell, who has been rightly described as a man "in advance of his time": [12] "While life remains, the most wicked may repent, the most abandoned may be brought to a sense of moral duty to God and his fellow men; his brutal and malignant passions may be brought under subjection to reason, his physical powers be made productive of benefit to community by a life of confinement at hard labor." [13] The futile method of society in dealing with the subject has found more eloquent and perhaps more scientific critics since; but Kitchell's voice in the wilderness was a pioneer argument of its sort in the State of Illinois, if not in the nation.

Of the four bills introduced at that session relative to revision of the criminal code, none pertained to capital punishment, and so Lincoln did not get to vote on the question. How the future war president, who issued so many pardons that he was criticized for demoralizing the army, would have voted, had the proposition been submitted to the House, seems an easy question to answer.

7.

By the end of 1840 the absence of Stuart in Washington and Lincoln's own preoccupation with politics were having a decidedly unhealthy effect on the partnership. Even when not in Washington, the former practiced law on an intermittent basis, and though the experience which Lincoln gained in the course of the life of the partnership was invaluable, both parties recognized that the situation could not continue indefinitely. Although the time had come for a change, especially in view of the fact that Stuart expected to be re-elected to Congress, from Lincoln's standpoint the association had been fruitful of knowledge and experience beyond measure. It had been a brief, though valuable apprenticeship, during which Lincoln compressed into a few years experiences which would have ordinarily occupied a decade or more. In those four years—years that were jammed with significance to the future of his law career—he had acquired a solid background of insight, which formed the basis for his later advancement to the forefront of the Illinois bar. It was precisely the kind of practical knowledge which he needed most in order to fill the gaps left by his course of self-study in preparation for the law.

This work does not pretend to completeness. Even if it were being written for the exclusive edification of lawyers, its reasonable limits would preclude discussion of the numerous cases, of almost every conceivable type, which Lincoln personally handled during those early, formative years while Stuart was away from the office, giving close attention to his political fences, campaigning or serving in Congress. Appearing before justices of the peace, traveling the circuit and trying such cases as could be picked up en route, practicing before the Illinois Supreme Court and the United States District Courts, Lincoln was thrown upon his own resources in deciding how best to cope with the multitudinous problems arising in connection with a practice so widely diverse. If the prodigality of his pleadings is staggering, the range and variety of his cases is scarcely less so.

During the four years of the Stuart partnership the Sangamon Circuit Court, with terms of two weeks each in the spring and fall and one in the summer, saw much of Lincoln, who had between twenty-five and thirty cases each term. Though the court itself possessed some of the attributes of a small-claims court, it was here, during this same period, that he met many distinguished members of the Illinois bar. No study of Lincoln as a lawyer would be complete without at least passing reference to the careers of some of his contemporaries of that early period of his practice. It would be particularly remiss not to mention, among those who appeared at the March term, 1840, of the Sangamon Circuit Court, in addition to Logan, Baker, Dummer and Douglas, that most remarkable man, Albert Taylor Bledsoe. After graduating from West Point, he taught mathematics in that institution; thereafter he studied for the ministry, becoming ordained in the Episcopal Church before turning to the law. From the time of his admission to the bar in 1839, he practiced law in Springfield until 1847, during which years he was a friend and associate of Lincoln. He resided at the Globe Tavern when Lincoln went to live there after his marriage. They were in daily contact, and at one time occupied adjoining offices. One who has made a close study of his life wrote: "Bledsoe had more to do with moulding Lincoln's intellect than any man who ever touched it."[14] Stuart rated him the strongest man at the Sangamon bar, for pure logic.

In the late 'forties Bledsoe went South, abandoning the law for the more congenial academic life. He became a member of the University of Virginia faculty, from which he resigned to take his commission as a colonel in the Confederate Army, later serving as Assistant Secretary of War in the Confederacy. At his own expense he published a book, *Is Davis a Traitor?*, justifying the right of secession on constitutional grounds. Thaddeus Stevens is said to have confessed, after reading it: "It is unanswerable." Stanton supposedly expressed the same opinion.[15] (The quotation could be apocryphal, when one considers the unyielding natures of Stevens, the grim old warrior, bitter and vituperative enemy of the South, and "the terrible Stanton.") Though, with the outbreak of war, Bledsoe's feelings toward Lincoln became extremely bitter, it is interesting to note that one of the President's last official acts was to issue a pass to Mrs. Bledsoe to go through the lines to see her children, and they both entered Richmond the day it fell.

There was David B. Campbell, who migrated to Springfield from New Jersey, his native state and, as noted, was elected prosecuting attorney in 1839. John C. Doremus was another who, finding the Sucker State a more suitable climate for his talents, emigrated from New Jersey. Still another who budded in the east and flowered in the Middle West was Schuyler Strong, who came to Springfield from New York; an inability to stay on the wagon for any length of time was all that prevented him from rising to a position at the top of the Illinois bar. One of the most conspicuous ornaments of the Sangamon bar, which included a high proportion of the best lawyers in the state, was James C. Conkling, a Princeton graduate, who came to Springfield from New York in 1838 and was admitted to practice the following year. As a lawyer he ranked among the ablest in the state.

There was Ninian Wirt Edwards, who was married to Mary Todd's sister, Elizabeth. Born in Kentucky the same year as Lincoln, he came to Illinois after graduating from the law department of Transylvania University in 1833. He made his office in Springfield, where he was an active practitioner, though not as active as his brother, the handsome, though vain, Benjamin S. Edwards. After graduating from Yale College and law school, the latter came to Springfield in 1838 and completed his legal

education in the office of Stephen T. Logan. In 1843 he formed
a partnership with Stuart, an association which was not to end
until Stuart's death. Though the bulk of their practice was in the
State Supreme Court and in the federal courts, they did a considerable amount of circuit work until the middle 'fifties, when
most attorneys had enough business at home to keep them active.

8.

Lincoln and Stuart severed relations on April 14, 1841; their
friendship remained undiminished, even though, upon the formation of the Republican Party in 1856, they parted political
company, Stuart going over to the Democrats. As a member of
Congress, he opposed Lincoln on the Emancipation Proclamation.
Herndon, unlike Lincoln, never could forgive Stuart for his
apostasy in wandering off the reservation. Just as the cause of
abolitionism was, with Herndon, an article of faith, in like manner
was he ferociously articulate in defending the political movement
that began in antislavery idealism, accompanied alike by Know-
Nothingism and a highly pragmatic attachment to the high tariff.
Always a good hater, intolerant, perverse and dogmatic, the man
was a militant crusader.

There is nothing strange about the fact that, in politics,
Herndon should appear as a narrow partisan. He belonged to a
generation and a group in which Republicanism (like Whiggism
before it) was something sacred.[16] (Nor is the judicial view of
politics very common among those today who have to participate
actively in party warfare.) Even so, there is no excuse for Herndon writing to his collaborator, Weik, on December 10, 1885:
"Between Lincoln and Stuart from 1843 to 1865 there was no
good feeling of an earnest friendship. Lincoln hated some of the
ways of Stuart. Lincoln felt no jealousy toward Stuart. Stuart did
toward Lincoln. Stuart in his heart hated Lincoln."[17] There is
no slight shred of evidence to support this arresting claim. One
generous explanation of Herndon's remarks is the suggestion that

the by then crotchety, broken and defeated old man may have hoisted a few too many before writing these lines to Weik. His dislike of Stuart was doubtless partly explicable by the fact that Stuart was of the social elite, in whose circle Herndon was never accepted, while Lincoln, who married into the Todd-Edwards clique, was. It rankled and ate into his soul.

With all that he failed to devote himself systematically to his practice while up to his neck in politics, Stuart never lost contact with the law. While as an appeals lawyer he does not appear to have been as successful as Lincoln was (he lost fifteen of the twenty-one cases in which they were opposed in the Illinois Supreme Court), contemporary accounts confirm that he was a trial lawyer of high rank, considered by some to be the best in the state. We shall meet him from time to time, sharing with Lincoln and the others the inconveniences of country taverns and the good fellowship that characterized circuit practice.

CHAPTER VI

Logan & Lincoln

1.

ON MAY 14, 1841, the *Sangamo Journal* carried the first "card" of the firm of Logan & Lincoln, though their association is said to have commenced on April fourteenth, the date of dissolution of the Stuart and Lincoln partnership. During the two-week term of the Sangamon Circuit Court, commencing on March twenty-third, Lincoln appeared with Logan in twelve cases, an indication that they had, even then, arrived at an understanding of some sort, if not formally entered into a partnership arrangement. The only authority for the April fourteenth date, as marking the termination of Lincoln's association with Stuart and the simultaneous launching of the Logan and Lincoln partnership, is Herndon's statement to that effect.[1] According to the newspaper announcement, their office was on Fifth Street, opposite Hoffman's Row (directly across the street from the office occupied by Stuart and Lincoln). It was later moved to the third floor of the Tinsley Building, a new structure at the corner of Sixth and Adams streets, which is still standing. The *Sangamo Journal* of January 4, 1844—and weekly thereafter until termination of the partnership in December of that year—carried the firm's "professional card," showing the new address, on the first page. It read:

Logan & Lincoln

Attorneys and Counsellors at Law, Springfield—
over the post office—third story.

Stephen T. Logan, soon to attain to a leading position in the state (the *Sangamo Journal* of April 13, 1843, opined that he was "perhaps the best lawyer in the state"), was already the acknowledged leader of the Sangamon bar. Nine years Lincoln's senior, he had come to Springfield in 1833, at the age of thirty-two, after having established himself as a successful lawyer in his native Kentucky. In January, 1835, he was commissioned by the Legislature circuit judge of the First Judicial Circuit; he resigned in March, 1837. The office had become irksome to him, his energetic nature and great talent requiring a less circumscribed field of activity. A likely contributing factor was the fact that the post paid a salary of but six hundred dollars a year.[2] To a lawyer of Logan's commanding talents and acquisitive ways, this meant a very real financial sacrifice.

He opened his first court in Sangamon County on March 9, 1835, the same day that Douglas began his career as State's Attorney. It was said of him that while on the Bench, Logan "had a mania for whittling and Court never moved smoothly until the sheriff had placed a number of white pine shingles beside the wool-sack, when the evolution of law and pine shavings proceeded with equal dignity and composure."[3]

There was about this pioneer lawyer a kind of Roman severity; himself a stickler for painstaking precision (every paper, it was said, underwent his close scrutiny), Logan would tolerate no slipshod methods on the part of one associated with him. With no one to check on him during the period of the Stuart partnership, Lincoln had been given, at times, to a somewhat haphazard reliance on his natural talents, in particular his ready wit, rather than on thorough preparation. Logan, exacting but not unkind, showed him the value of preparedness, as opposed to mere glibness. It was Herndon's contention, however, that "his [Lincoln's] old habits eventually overcame him." ". . . he trusted to his general knowledge of the law and the inspiration of the surroundings to overcome the judge or the jury."[4] Herndon notwithstanding, Lincoln benefited greatly by the example of Logan, and became, in time, a pretty thorough lawyer—more methodical and systematic than Herndon, who devoted little time to the preparation of his cases.

Small, spare, almost gnomelike in appearance, this stern-faced, craggy man looked out on the world from behind a countenance of startling homeliness. That the senior member was not much to look at may be inferred from the remarks of Stuart, made at a gathering of the Springfield bar, called to give expression to their sorrow on the occasion of Logan's passing: "In person he was of small stature. He discarded the ornamentations of dress. Nature had not given in his appearance any indication of his talent."[5] The dour little man was possessed, however, of a legal mind of the finest temper and vision, and a persistence in cross-examination which could be terrifying.

Handicapped by the fact that he had an unattractive voice, he was no orator, though this defect was amply compensated for by the logic of his arguments. Logan considered mere rhetoric the enemy of wisdom. The only real shortcoming of this courtroom genius was a tendency to provocative argument with the Bench, a proneness for advancing legal and procedural points with sometimes irritating pertinacity. As Herndon put it, he was "as technical as technicality itself."[6] Even so, as a trial lawyer he ranked with the best of his time, and his attainments as such were everywhere recognized.

Not without reason did Logan, who knew men, have confidence in Lincoln's promise as a lawyer. As a contemporary at the Sangamon bar, he was in an excellent position to evaluate the Lincoln of the late 'thirties and early 'forties in terms of his potentialities as an all-round practitioner. They had been associated in the Truett trial, in which Lincoln's summation, the subject of favorable comment by Logan, contributed mightily to the result. Lincoln's fluency of expression, his native horse sense, his dignified bearing and straightforward character—all these were qualities which recommended him to Logan.

2.

On April 15, 1841, the Circuit Court of Tazewell County opened at Tremont. The following day Lincoln appeared for the plaintiff in *Kellogg* v. *Crain*, an action in debt, which was tried before the Court without a jury. His client was awarded judgment in the sum of $16,000, plus $58.02 costs. This was by far the largest judgment secured by Lincoln up to then. En route to Tremont, Lincoln probably stopped at the Delavan House, built by the Delavan Colony, at Delavan, about 1836. It was one of the leading hostelries on the stagecoach line between Springfield and Peoria.

Returning from the Menard Circuit Court, at Petersburg, on June sixteenth, Lincoln found Springfield in a state of excitement over the disappearance on June second of Archibald Fisher. William Trailor and Archibald Fisher made their home together in Warren County; Archibald Trailor, a brother of the former, lived in Springfield, and Henry Trailor, another brother, in Clary's Grove. While the three brothers were visiting together in Springfield, Fisher vanished shortly after having been seen in their company. After his disappearance had been advertised in the newspapers, and a systematic search instituted, to no avail, the community bubbled with rumors of foul play. It was believed that Fisher, a somewhat eccentric old character, had on his person at the time of his disappearance a large number of gold coins, having gone to Springfield to enter land, the land office being located there.[7]

Suspicion fastened upon the impecunious Trailor brothers as perpetrators of the legendary "perfect crime"—the murder of a man and disposition of the remains so they could not be found. Considered strictly as drama, the story of this celebrated case is compelling. Referring to it in later years, Judge James H. Matheny said: "Probably the most remarkable trial that ever took place in Springfield, and beyond a doubt one of the most dramatic trials that ever took place in the whole country, was what is known among the old settlers as 'the Trailor case.' For fifty years it has served to impress upon the public mind of Sangamon county the fact that circumstantial evidence, no matter how strong it may appear, is never infallible."[8]

Henry, the first to be taken into custody, was held incommunicado and interrogated at length by the police, the mayor and Josiah Lamborn, one of the most picturesque characters at the early Illinois bar, then serving as Attorney General. After intensive questioning for the better part of three days, Henry finally confessed, the gist of his confession being that his brothers Archibald and William had killed the old man, "and made a temporary concealment of the body," later disposing of it "in a safe place." As so frequently is the case with confessing prisoners, Henry, once launched on his narrative, proceeded to expand, explaining how his brothers, on the day following the murder, enlisted his aid in making a permanent disposition of the body in the Hickox millpond, after first getting it from a dense brush thicket and carrying it to a buggy in which he had remained. He supplied the most precise details, complete with measurements and hours of the day and night.

It was charged that the confession had been extracted from him under circumstances demonstrating that it was coerced, mainly through the efforts of Lamborn.[9] There seems little doubt that the prisoner was subjected to prolonged interrogation while held incommunicado. Lincoln, writing of the case several years later, said concerning this feature of it: "The Mayor and Attorney Gen'l took charge of him [Henry], and set their wits to work to elicit a discovery from him. He denied, and denied, and persisted in denying. They still plied him in every conceivable way, till Wednesday, when . . . he stated that his brothers, William and Archibald had murdered Fisher; . . ."[10]

Two days after Henry confessed, William and Archibald were taken into custody and charged with the murder. Logan, Baker and Lincoln were retained to defend them. In Edward D. Baker the defense had a man who, like Logan and Lincoln, excelled in trial work. Lincoln and he opposed each other in many cases and were associated in others. Public opinion in this instance was decidedly against the defendants, the more rancorous among the populace even suggesting a lynching. With the empaneling of the jury on June 18, 1841, an atmosphere of intense excitement pervaded the old Christian Church, where the trial was held.

The prosecution's star witness was, of course, Henry, who furnished damning testimony against his brothers. By way of corroboration, Lamborn showed that since Fisher's disappearance the defendants had passed a number of gold pieces. There were witnesses who testified to signs of a struggle in the thicket and a trail leading to buggy tracks, which in turn led to the millpond, into which the body had supposedly been thrown. There was virtually an avalanche of circumstantial evidence against the defendants.

When Lamborn, with a triumphant air, rested the People's case, the all-but-convicted defendants gave every appearance of being likely candidates for the noose. The defense, however, had been holding back a hidden card. Amidst breathless silence, Lincoln rose and called, as their sole witness, Dr. Robert Gilmore, from Warren County, who swore that Fisher was, at that moment, in his (Gilmore's) home, very much alive, though in too enfeebled a condition to give an account of where he had been during his absence. The doctor further testified that he had known Fisher for several years and knew, for a fact, that the latter suffered from temporary mental blackouts, owing to a head injury which he had sustained early in life. As a result of the bizarre twist which the case took, the defendants were discharged. The following week Fisher was brought to Springfield; he could throw no light on the case, and many baffling circumstances were never explained.

There was the devil to pay about the prosecution's handling of the affair. Providing a striking illustration of the ebb and flow of public opinion, the populace, which, prior to Gilmore's testimony, had been clamoring for blood, now turned in their indignation upon Lamborn, who narrowly escaped being lynched on the spot, one spectator being heard to say that it was "too damned bad to have so much trouble and no hanging after all." The outcome of the trial certainly reflected no credit on the prosecution, especially as it was shown that the true facts had been known to the Attorney General in advance of the trial, and by him suppressed.

Lamborn's reputation was not savory. We have a contemporary judgment of him from the pen of Usher F. Linder, who, after first paying tribute to his capabilities as a lawyer, describes him as an altogether unattractive character: "He was wholly destitute of principle, and shamelessly took bribes from criminals prosecuted under his administration."[11] (Lamborn was among the very few who earned less than favorable comment in Linder's *Reminiscences*.) There was a duality in his make-up that made him at once both cold and considerate. This fact is summed up ably by the observation of Judge Matheny: "His character was remarkable for its many contradictions. He was almost criminally avaricious, yet suffering humanity never appealed to him in vain. . . . He was a strange mortal, uncertain and mysterious, with few personal friends, living seemingly in a world of his own, and yet when aroused from his dreams and called to the discharge of his duties as the prosecutor of criminals his soul kindled with a strange and vengeful fire. Nothing moved him from his purpose. With the instincts of a blood hound he tracked the skulking wretch to his lair and with pitiless heart crushed the hopeless victim."[12]

Lamborn was prominent in state politics—at times a Democrat and at other times a Whig. He was somewhat convivial in his habits and, together with some of his brethren at the bar who felt the need to keep their drinking within proper limits, formed a lawyers' temperance society. Lamborn invariably reported, at its monthly meetings, his inability to remain abstemious.[13]

Lincoln neglected to secure, in advance of the trial, his fee of one hundred dollars. After his acquittal William Trailor refused to pay; once again Lincoln was obliged to sue for services rendered. Upon Trailor's death, Logan & Lincoln brought suit against the estate in the Sangamon Circuit Court, the executor setting up the defense that the claim had been outlawed by the statute of limitations. The plaintiffs secured judgment, but were unable to collect. It has been said—so often that it has become a sort of bromide among lawyers—that in criminal cases the attorney either secures his fee in advance or not at all.

The time sometimes involved in collecting the small recompense of lawyers in those days is aptly illustrated by the case of *Dorman* v. *Lane*, an action involving the sale of real estate to satisfy the debts of an estate. After working on the case for a year and a half, Lincoln finally, in January, 1844, secured a judgment on behalf of the plaintiff, and did not succeed in collecting his fee of one hundred dollars until 1853—eleven years after being retained.[14] Herndon claimed that "Lincoln never believed in suing for a fee. If a client did not pay on request he never sought to enforce collection."[15] The records show, however, six instances in which he sued to collect for legal services rendered.

While Lincoln made no fetish of money, he was not exactly (all legends to the contrary) what one might call indifferent to it. Something of his mounting annoyance over the failure of clients to pay, once the matter at hand was concluded, is reflected in a letter which he wrote to James S. Irwin, of Springfield, on November 2, 1843: "As to fees, it is impossible to establish a rule that will apply in all, or even a great many cases. We believe we are never accused of being unreasonable in this particular; and we would always be easily satisfied, provided we could see the money—but whatever fees we earn at a distance, if not paid before, we have noticed, we never hear of after the work is done. We, therefore, are growing a little sensitive on that point."[16]

3.

The summer term of the Illinois Supreme Court, which commenced on July 5, 1841, and closed on the twenty-fourth, saw much of Lawyer Lincoln. Though he came to be one of the foremost practitioners in that court in the 1840s and 1850s, he did not practice there at all in the late 'thirties, probably because so much of his time was taken up by his routine official duties in the Legislature.

One of the memorable cases which commanded Lincoln's attention during the court's summer term of 1841 was that of *Bailey* v. *Cromwell*, argued July twenty-third, and involving his first encounter with the legal aspects of slavery. Early in 1839 an action was brought by the administrators of Nathan Cromwell against David Bailey in the Circuit Court of Tazewell County, then held at Tremont, upon a promissory note made by Bailey and given to Cromwell in payment for a Negro girl named Nance. The seller, who represented that the subject of the sale was indentured to him and still had about seven years to serve, agreed to furnish the purchaser with proof that the girl was in fact a slave and bound to servitude.[17] This Cromwell failed to do and, the girl having left Bailey's service in the meantime, when the note matured the latter refused to pay.

Upon the trial, the defendant showed by the testimony of the girl and one Benjamin Kellogg that Nance had repeatedly stated that she would not work without pay, and had received from Cromwell, who operated a store, both goods and money in return for services rendered.[18]

Judgment was rendered by Judge William Thomas in favor of the plaintiff for $431.97. An appeal was taken to the Supreme Court, where Lincoln, representing the defendant, argued that the note was without consideration and hence void, inasmuch as it was given, in a free state, as the purchase price of a human being who was not legally the subject of sale. He maintained that the girl was free by virtue of both the Ordinance of 1787 and the constitution of the state prohibiting slavery. The Court, in an opinion by Judge Breese, reversed the lower court. The case, in which Lincoln was opposed by Logan, established the broad principle that "the presumption of the law in Illinois is that every person is free without regard to color," and "the sale of a free person is illegal."

There has long been some question whether Lincoln or Stuart tried the case, in the first instance, in the Tazewell Circuit Court. In 1957 there came to light the bill of exceptions filed in the lower court on September 28, 1839. While most of the bill was written by Stuart, the document reveals that Lincoln added the caption at the beginning, filled in the line "and that she was at that time above the age of twenty-one years," in the middle of the document, and at the end added the words "Whereupon the court gave judgment for the plaintiffs; to which opinion of the court, the defendant excepts, and prays this his bill of exceptions may be signed sealed and made part of the record in the cause—" Lincoln also wrote the caption appearing on the outside of the document. It would seem a fair assumption, from the somewhat unusual circumstance that the bill of exceptions (now in the Illinois State Historical Library) represents the joint efforts of the partners and reflects the intimate knowledge of each, that *both* Lincoln and Stuart participated in the trial.

On November 4, 1842, Lincoln and Mary Todd were married at the home of Ninian W. Edwards by the Reverend Charles Dresser, pastor of St. Paul's Episcopalian Church; they boarded at the Globe Tavern, where they occupied a one-room apartment, paying the weekly sum of four dollars.

4.

An interesting case, one which projected the popular young Springfield lawyer into statewide prominence, was the removal trial of Thomas C. Browne, Justice of the Supreme Court, before the Illinois House of Representatives in January, 1843, in which he appeared for the Judge. Though, at the time, the case attracted widespread interest, little is mentioned by Lincoln biographers concerning it.[19]

Browne's period of service on the Supreme Court covered

the entire thirty years (1818–1848) that the first Constitution
of the state was in force. Like Lincoln and so many others of his
contemporaries, he came on the scene by way of Kentucky,
where he was admitted to practice in 1812. Arrived in Illinois, he
settled in Shawneetown. For a brief spell prior to his election to
the Supreme Court, he served as State's Attorney for the Shawneetown district, and in 1822 was an unsuccessful candidate for governor, running on a pro-slavery platform.

On December 24, 1842, four upstate lawyers from Galena
introduced in the House a petition praying for Browne's removal for want of ability and qualification to discharge the duties
of his office. The House voted to investigate the charges, and the
Speaker thereupon appointed Stephen T. Logan of Sangamon,
Gustavus Koerner of St. Clair and Isaac N. Arnold of Cook to
conduct the investigation. The petitioners were represented by
Attorney General Lamborn and Giles A. Spring of Chicago.

The shifting intellectual climate, as new life and new culture
surged into the young state, may have suggested to some younger
members of the bar the desirability of eliminating from the Court
one who had come to it at a time when the standards were those
of the early frontier days. Time, in its usual role, had changed
somewhat the concept of fitness. And yet, though the petition for
his removal may have been symbolic of a new day, it is difficult to
escape the feeling that, whatever Browne's qualifications, the
move to oust him sprang, at least in part, from political motives.
Under the reorganization of the Supreme Court effected in 1841,
the judges of that court were required to cover the circuit courts,
in addition to performing their usual duties in the higher court.
It was felt by those seeking to replace him with a younger man
(preferably a Democrat) that his assignment to the Sixth Circuit
in the extreme northwestern part of the state would have the desired effect. In seeking to pressure Browne into resigning, they
reckoned without his stiff determination to see it through, for he
accepted the additional assignment without complaint. It was then
that the Galena group of lawyers hit upon the expedient of the
removal proceeding.

From the specifications submitted by the petitioners, it was clear that Browne's removal was sought on the most frivolous grounds. Dealing altogether in generalities, they charged that he suffered from a poverty of intellect, that he was deficient in legal and literary learning, "that by nature, education and habit, he is wholly and absolutely unfit for a station upon the bench of the Supreme Court of the State of Illinois."

On January third the House resolved itself into a committee of the whole and proceeded, with Orlando B. Ficklin of Coles in the chair, to try the charges. A reporter covering the trial wrote: "The feeling here, among all parties and classes, is strongly in his [Browne's] favor. The ladies, God bless them, are all for him; it was with great difficulty that I obtained a seat in the gallery, by the side of one of the fairest of Springfield's belles."[20]

After the parties were assigned to seats in front of the Speaker's desk, the charges were read, whereupon Lincoln commented that they were too vague and indefinite to be consistent with fairness to the accused. Though he stated his willingness to meet them "at this time," he reserved the right to later object. Lamborn, for the prosecution, contended that inasmuch as the defendant was not charged with the commission of a crime, the rules obtaining in criminal trials did not apply, and specific charges were not necessary. To the laity, the objection which Lincoln raised may seem technical in a derogatory sense of the term, but his position was well taken. There were in Lincoln's time, as there have always been, those who would prefer expediency and freedom from hampering rules of evidence, to the detriment of the safeguards and rights of a citizen on trial.

Throughout the proceedings, Lincoln kept thinking up such devilment to practice on the opposition as to make a shambles of the case for the petitioners. At the end of the third day, the charges were dismissed. One gathers from contemporary newspaper accounts that the verdict met with widespread approval. The *Sangamo Journal* had this to say editorially about the outcome: "The decision of the House meets with the unanimous approval of our citizens, . . . and Judge Browne now has a deeper hold on their affections and confidence than before this iniquitous prosecution commenced."[21]

Lincoln gained in professional recognition by his skillful defense of the Judge, in a contest which was closely followed throughout the state. With the dismissal of the charges, important doors opened to him, important people sought him out.

5.

Slander actions were rife in Lincoln's day, a fact of which lawyers were not heard to complain. At the November term, 1843, of the Menard Circuit Court, Lincoln tried, on behalf of the plaintiff, an action seeking five thousand dollars damages, brought by Eliza S. Cabot, a young schoolteacher recently of New England, against Francis Regnier, a physician, based on statements allegedly made by the latter imputing moral laxity to the plaintiff. The jury returned a verdict in her favor for twelve dollars, a sum hardly calculated to adequately assuage the plaintiff's injured feelings. Not surprisingly, Lincoln moved to set the verdict aside as being inadequate, and on the further ground that one of the jurors was heard to state, during the pendency of the case, that "he did not believe Miss Cabot ought to recover much if anything off of Dr. Regnier."[22] The motion was granted by Judge Treat, and on Lincoln's further application for a change of venue, the cause was ordered removed to Morgan County, where, on a retrial before Judge Lockwood and a jury in March, 1844, the plaintiff recovered a judgment of sixteen hundred dollars.

We the Jury find for the plaintiff—damages $1600
A. V. Putnam   Foreman[23]

The defendant, in due course, moved in arrest of judgment on the ground that the "jury separated contrary to law," in that one of the twelve absented himself from the deliberations of his colleagues, and while so absented was approached by the other

side. In opposing the motion, Lincoln submitted the affidavit of
John Bowen, the juror in question, who swore that he "went out
to find a place for his horse, and while going and returning and
during his absence he spoke to no one."[24] The motion was denied,
and the judgment stood.

From the defendant's bill of exceptions we learn that he
sought to prove through one Martha Cogdill that she saw the
plaintiff and Elijah Taylor in the defendant's bedroom "at a late
hour in the night, she sitting in the window in her night clothes,
no other person being in the room." The testimony was excluded on Lincoln's technical objection.

One who gave damaging evidence against Lincoln's client
was her landlady, Maria Bennett, whose deposition, taken March
12, 1844, appears in the file. It was in the hotel operated by Mrs.
Bennett, in Petersburg, that the acts which formed the basis for
the defendant's accusations were supposedly committed. (The
building is still standing.) The following were some of the
questions put and the answers made:

Q. Do you not think that the conduct which came under your view
between Mr. Elijah B. Taylor and Miss Eliza S. Cabott was highly
improvident for a virtuous female?
A. I certainly did.
Q. Do you believe Miss E. S. Cabot to be a Lady of veracity?
A. I did not.
Q. Did not her conduct appear while living with you to substantiate
the charge which Francis Regnier has against her as regards Mr.
E. Taylor?
A. I never approved, from the first, of her conduct with Mr. Taylor,
but the latter part of the time fully convinced me of the im-
propriety of it, and left not a shadow of doubt on my mind of the
charge advanced against her by Francis Regnier.
Q. Did you not some time previously to her leaving your house re-
quest her to do so?
A. I did so.

In the course of the second trial, held in Jacksonville on
March 14 and 15, 1844, the defendant sought to introduce evi-

dence of a specific act of fornication on the part of the plaintiff. Lincoln succeeded in having it excluded, on the ground that under the plea of General Denial which the defendant had interposed he should not be permitted to show specific facts which would tend to cast suspicion of guilt upon the plaintiff. A defendant in an action of slander who interposes a general denial, Lincoln contended, only declares that he did not speak the words charged in the plaintiff's declaration to have been spoken by him, and cannot, under the plea entered, prove affirmatively that the words spoken were true. This early declaration of a rule, now taken for granted, that the truth of the statements charged may only be shown when justification by way of truth is set up as an affirmative defense, was fully sustained on appeal, in an opinion written by Judge Norman H. Purple.[25]

This was the case of which Samuel C. Parks wrote: ". . . and his [Lincoln's] denunciation of a defendant (before a jury in Petersburg) who had slandered a small, friendless schoolmistress, was probably as bitter a Phillippic as was ever uttered."[26]

Old "Doc" Regnier, who knew Lincoln back in New Salem, was a somewhat eccentric individual.[27] In New Salem, to which he had emigrated from Ohio, he had his office and living quarters in a single room[28] where, in his treatment of his patients, he "purged, bled, blistered, puked, and salivated."[29]

For all his oddity, one wonders, going through the file of the case, if there wasn't more than a modicum of truth to what Regnier said concerning Lincoln's client, who wasn't, one suspects, quite the innocent young maiden her lawyer made her out to be. The thought gives rise to further doubts concerning the oft-made claim that Lincoln was not at his best as a lawyer when the facts were against his client. For years after his death, his biographers, with few exceptions, refused to bring themselves to believe or admit that Lincoln was other than a demigod. Going over his cases, the writer is sometimes struck by the shockingly irreverent thought that Lincoln would appear to have been a most dangerous adversary even when, to put it politely, the justice of his client's cause was not readily apparent.

6.

On March 5, 1844, Lincoln filed an affidavit for a continuance in Peoria, in connection with the little known "Jackass Suit" of *Jacob B. Backenstos* v. *Baldwin S. Samuel*, in which he represented the defendant. The case, a recent discovery, involved, among other things, a sale by the defendant to the plaintiff of a pair of jackasses, both of which turned out to be something less than sound—suffering, each, an untimely demise shortly after the sale. It was, for Lincoln's client, a case for the old admonition: *Caveat emptor*. In a letter from the plaintiff to Jacob Gale, Clerk of the Peoria Circuit Court, written on September 26, 1848, and requesting the issuance of an execution against the defendant,[30] Backenstos has something to say about the "viliny [sic]" of Lincoln's client. It would appear from the papers in the file that the litigation was commenced in 1842; one wonders if Lincoln was not principally responsible for the fact that it took six years for the case to wend its tortuous way to the execution stage.

Although Peoria was outside the Eighth Circuit, the place is rich in Lincoln associations. Lincoln made a number of appearances in its brick courthouse, construction of which was begun in 1834 and completed in 1836 at a cost of approximately fifteen thousand dollars. The building remained in use until May, 1876. An interesting thing about the capacious courthouse was the occupancy of several of the rooms on the ground floor as law offices.[31] The writer is of the opinion that this practice did not obtain in many Illinois courthouses, since most were too limited in size to have permitted it.

As will be seen from time to time, Peoria was not the only county outside the Eighth Circuit in which Lincoln appeared to try special cases. Discovery of such cases is, however, more or less a matter of chance, since it would be extremely difficult, if not downright impossible to make a special search in the archives of every county where he may have appeared.

7.

Sometime in the month of December, 1844, the partnership with Logan terminated. As in the case of Stuart, the dissolution was effected amicably. Logan told Herndon: "Our partnership continued perhaps three years. I then told him [Lincoln] that I wished to take my son David with me who had meanwhile grown up, and Lincoln was perhaps by that time willing to begin on his own account. So we talked the matter over and dissolved the partnership amicably and in friendship." Logan continued to stray in and out of the story of Lincoln's law career, with many interesting connotations.

The intellectual self-discipline acquired through association with the Spartanlike Logan was to stand Lincoln in good stead through many a trying period in the years ahead. All the rest of his life he was to draw heavily upon the bountiful storehouse of practical knowledge and experience acquired during the period of their partnership. It is fair to say that no man contributed more toward bringing Lincoln's natural gifts as a lawyer to their fullest fruition.

Writing with his customary disparagement, Herndon, one of the cattiest of men, says of Logan: "Here was a cold, avaricious, and little mean man for you as the people saw him."[32] There is nothing to substantiate this harsh estimate. Some writers, to be sure, have pictured the wizened little man as something of a curmudgeon, but Logan was an amiable host, urbane and hospitable. His home in Springfield, where his four sons and four daughters set a lively tempo, was a center of entertainment, and strangers were always welcome. That he was thrifty and not indifferent to making money seems undisputed, for he accumulated a comfortable fortune, but since when is that synonymous with "avaricious-ness" and "meanness"?

Of Lincoln's close associates, no one has had less to say about him than Logan, a fact which lends interest to the latter's description of Lincoln's approach to a case, given in an interview with Herndon in 1875: "So far as his reading knowledge of law went he had a quite unusual grasp of the principles involved. When he was with me, I have seen him get a case and seem to be bewildered at first, but he would go at it and after a while he would master it. He was very tenacious in his grasp of a thing that he once got hold of."[33]

Down through the crowded remaining years of Lincoln's practice, he and his old associate and mentor were to meet frequently, both as associate counsel and on opposite sides. In the Supreme Court, where they faced each other in thirty-two appeals, there was, from the standpoint of results achieved, little to choose between them, Lincoln prevailing in seventeen of them. A tally of those cases, in all courts, in which they were known to have been opposed, shows that Lincoln more than held his own, although it must always be borne in mind that a lawyer's percentage of victories is no sure criterion in determining his standing at the bar.

Nothing is more strikingly illustrative of this fact than the case of *James McCall, et al.* v. *Jacob Lesher, et al.*,[34] in which Lincoln took on a tough assignment and attempted the impossible. The action was upon a bill in chancery seeking specific performance of an agreement to convey four hundred acres of land lying at the Grand Rapids, in Wabash County. After the taking of testimony, though before rendition of judgment, two of the defendants died. On motion of the plaintiff, their heirs-at-law were thereupon made parties defendant to the suit, in place and stead of the deceased defendants, and a decree entered requiring the defendants (including those newly added) to convey the premises in question to the plaintiff.

Upon the appeal, which was heard at the December term, 1845, of the Supreme Court, Lincoln, who had not appeared upon the trial below, argued on behalf of the appellees. His argument was one for the books. Logan, attorney for the heirs-at-law, contended that his clients were necessary parties to the litigation, and as such should have been served with process, a contention which Lincoln dismissed with the astonishing irrelevancy that the heirs-at-law had not appeared in the action to assert their position. He followed this up with the equally curious, indeed tortured reasoning that their voluntary appearance should therefore be inferred as a matter of law. Judge Treat, in his opinion, summarily rejected Lincoln's contention, an argument which added nothing to the latter's stature as a lawyer.

CHAPTER VII

Lincoln & Herndon

1.

LIKE MANY another great personality, Lincoln was an exceedingly complex individual, almost defying delineation. Without any thought of dabbling in the psychoanalytical approach
with which so many biographers attempt to drag history's great
men retroactively to the couch, there are times when one is
moved to feel that without maladjustment there would be no
greatness; the well-adjusted individual would be content simply
to live. It is a queer reflection that Lincoln, an intense individualist, one of the most self-sufficient of men, was never without
a partner, either in the twenty-three years of his practice at the
bar or during the life of his unsuccessful business venture. While
his motives for entering into the Stuart and Logan associations,
from which valuable apprenticeships he gained so much in the
way of knowledge and practical experience, are understandable,
his reason for joining forces with Herndon defies analysis.

The garrulous, windy, opinionated, prodigiously indiscreet[1]
Herndon, oracularly sure of himself and forever spouting dicta,
was certainly not the happiest choice Lincoln could have made.
At the time, Lincoln was on his way to becoming one of the
ablest lawyers at the Sangamon bar; having already made something of a name for himself, he could have formed an alliance with
virtually any of the competent lawyers then practicing in Springfield. Instead, he chose to take in, *as a full partner*, one who was
altogether without experience, except for that picked up as a
clerk in the Logan & Lincoln office.

How Lincoln came to choose such an offbeat character as

was Herndon is a subject which has long had a peculiar fascination for Lincoln scholars; after nearly a century of exploration, it
would appear that the question must remain ever undetermined.
Herndon, himself, was frank to say that he was "surprised" when
Lincoln invited him to become his partner,[2] and never sought to
advance any reason for the selection. When queried as to "what
the motives were that actuated Lincoln in taking me into partnership," Herndon replied: "I don't know and no one else does."[3]
Speculation evoked in the minds of those gathered at the Library
of Congress on the memorable occasion of the opening for public
use of the locked papers of the *Lincoln Collection* doubtless included this matter. Not only was the mystery not dispelled, but
the papers yielded up not so much as a clue.

The *Illinois State Journal* credits Herndon with having
stated: "I, according to the best of my recollection, was at that
time, in 1844, the monied man of the firm."[4] There has been a
disposition in some quarters to conclude, from this remark, that
Herndon, born of parents fairly prosperous by the standards of
the time, was brought in for whatever financial assistance he
might be in a position to render. The soundness of this finding is
impugned by the fact that, though far from affluent, Lincoln
was getting along reasonably well at the time; morover, the practice of law requires no capital investment. Of the fees latterly
taken in by Logan & Lincoln, the portion which constituted
Lincoln's share represented a fair-to-middling income, based
upon a rather satisfactory volume of business, for approximately
a quarter of the some 243 cases in which Lincoln appeared in the
Supreme Court were handled during the period of the Logan
partnership. Even if there was a less than overpowering demand
for his services, Lincoln's annual income at the time was probably
in the neighborhood of fifteen hundred dollars, on which one
could buy ample food for the cupboard a hundred and sixteen
years ago, when the purchasing power of a dollar was several
times what it is today.

Others have said that Herndon's Whig affiliation may have

counted heavily with Lincoln. If political considerations were a motivating factor, then it is pertinent to observe that there was no shortage of *experienced* Whig lawyers from whom the latter could have made his selection.

In a letter to Judge David Davis, administrator of the Lincoln estate, dated March 4, 1867, Mrs. Lincoln, referring to Herndon as "this miserable man," wrote: "Out of pity he [Lincoln] took him into his office, when he was almost a hopeless inebriate. . . ."[5] Such was palpably not the case. In a lecture delivered in Springfield about four months before the writing of the letter, Herndon, whom Mary had mistrusted virtually from the moment when she first laid eyes on him, launched the Ann Rutledge legend. Speaking at the courthouse before a large audience, Herndon, with his flair for the dramatic, spoke on the topic with the (for Herndon) characteristically grandiose title "A. Lincoln—Miss Ann Rutledge, New Salem—Pioneering, and the poem called Immortality—or, 'Oh! Why should the Spirit of Mortal be Proud.' " The gist of his remarks was that "Abraham Lincoln loved Miss Ann Rutledge with all his soul, mind and strength." "They seemed made in heaven for each other. . . ."[6]

Up to this point, no great harm had been done by the engagingly idyllic tale of how Lincoln wooed this village maiden, this "beautiful, amiable, and lovely girl of nineteen." Never one to do things by halves, Herndon, a man of strong animosities, who left no stone unturned (and few unflung) when it came to making life miserable for those whom he fancied his enemies, went on to publicly state that Lincoln had never really loved his spouse, "never ended his letters with 'yours affectionately.' "

The indignation of this most harried of First Ladies was unsuppressed; and never was resentment more justified. Small wonder, then, that she should have lashed back, flaying her cruel tormentor in scathing language, with judgments for some of which there is no contemporary evidence. It is worth remembering that, while Herndon's drinking proclivity became more marked as time went on, it was not until 1865, or thereabouts, that he became a more or less habitual drunkard—with periodic swearing off, followed by varying periods of abstinence. Prior to then, his susceptibility to the bottle, though fairly pronounced, did not compare with that of some of his contemporaries—Richard Yates, Usher F. Linder and Stephen A. Douglas, in particular. In 1844, Herndon, though a tippler in an age neither averse to nor unacquainted with heavy drinking,[7] was very far from being "a hopeless inebriate." In so characterizing him and, as a correlate, declaring that his selection as partner was dictated by a feeling of pity on Lincoln's part, Mrs. Lincoln was being less than fair—which, under the circumstances, is not to be wondered at.

Benjamin P. Thomas, in his one-volume life of Lincoln, a work that must be considered as one of the great American biographies, advances the cogent thesis that cardinal in Lincoln's thoughts may have been the notion that he "could train him [Herndon] according to his own methods, and would no longer be dominated by an older man."[8] Henry C. Whitney, a colleague of Lincoln's later circuit days (1854–1860), wrote, in this connection, that Lincoln told him "that he took Herndon in partnership on the supposition that he was not much of an advocate, but that he would prove to be a systematic office lawyer."[9]

It also may well have been that Lincoln had had his fill of office-seeking partners, having, as he remarked, "learned that a law office could not be run when all the members wanted to be Congressmen." Though he later served a term as Mayor of Springfield and was at one time State Bank Examiner, Herndon was relatively without political ambitions. Nevertheless, one is prone to remark that—as of that time, certainly—weighing the few possible advantages against the many distinct disadvantages involved in entering into a partnership with Herndon, it is not clear on any rational ground why Lincoln, in the secret soul of him, should have made the choice he did. When all is said, one can only repeat that searching for motives among the labyrinths of a mind as complicated and elusive of analysis as was Lincoln's is apt to prove an unrewarding task.

2.

As divergent in temperament as the poles, this ill-assorted pair could hardly have differed more radically as to their personalities. Both were distinct individualists, and there any resemblance ends. Lincoln, though a man of granite traits of will and character, possessed the tact which Herndon so conspicuously lacked. Unlike the latter, with all his grandiloquent pedantry, when Lincoln spoke, it was with no pretended intellectuality—only with that unaffected clarity of mind which enabled him to state his views in the language of everyday conversation. Lincoln, devoid of pomposity, wrote forthright prose, modestly and without pretentiousness of any sort; Herndon wrote with the turgid effusiveness and unblushing self-importance of the intellectually vain. Lincoln was in everything the quintessence of moderation—a moderation shot through with large particles of sense and wit and understanding; with his volatile partner there was no half-way ground, no gray, indefinite, in-between shade between truth and error. Lincoln was by nature conservative; Herndon, a rambunctious radical who kicked over conventional traces with uninhibited gusto. In later years the former, though he had come to hate slavery, was frequently called upon to hose down the fires of abolitionism which his considerably left-of-center junior partner was forever fanning. The influence which Lincoln exercised in this regard was at best moderating, never restraining.

Lincoln was, for all his moments of withdrawal, essentially a friendly man, possessed of an unusual gift for getting along with people, which was later to prove so helpful in dealing with certain of his recalcitrant Cabinet members; Herndon, on the other hand, was an ornery critter, endowed with an impulse to opposition and provocation which was fundamental in his make-up. Though Lincoln's humor was at times, one suspects, of the Rabelaisian tinge, he was endowed with a broad and humane wit, much of it self-directed, by which he saw all in scale, as it were. During the war years, his sense of humor enabled him to abide follies which would have broken a humorless man. In this respect, as in so many others, Lincoln was the antithesis of Herndon, who was so completely lacking in a sense of humor that when Lincoln, speaking of Niagara Falls, facetiously remarked to him: "The thing that struck me . . . was where in the world did all that water come from?" Herndon failed to see it as a joke, but, rather, proof that Lincoln "had no eye for the magnificence and grandeur of the scene, . . ."[10] Lincoln was uncertain about many, if not most things in life; Herndon was positive about just about everything. While the senior member was never averse to conceding his fallibilities, mistrust of his own judgment was not one of Herndon's besetting weaknesses. Probably his most estranging fault was his excessive philosophizing, his predilection for indulging in metaphysical elaboration, which Lincoln must have found rather tedious.

On the credit side, which is by no means negligible, it must be noted that, whatever Herndon's faults—and they were many and glaring—he possessed certain compensating virtues. He enjoyed, in some quarters, a reputation as "a distinguished lawyer," and even though he considered himself a better lawyer than Lincoln, he constantly submerged his own ambitions to advance the reputation of his partner, his unswerving loyalty to whom was his most endearing trait. There is evidence that Lincoln recognized this quality in him. Some years later, upon suffering defeat in the legislature on the balloting for United States Senator, he stated: "I expect everybody to desert me now—except Bill Herndon." Another item on the credit side of the ledger, one which is amply evident from the documents extant, was Herndon's readiness to bear (however imperfectly at times) the brunt of the drudgery of office detail.

In Herndon's further defense, it should be noted that, for his part, he was obliged to put up with sundry annoyances; for it is, indeed, true that Lincoln, who was no more an altogether ideal law partner than he was an ideal husband, had his share of idiosyncracies. When not on the circuit, Sunday mornings usually found him at the office—frequently accompanied by Tad and Willie. The mischievous little devils, their growth unimpeded by paternal discipline ("They litterally [sic] ran over him"),[11] were a constant source of irritation to Herndon. To quote his words, they "were absolutely unrestrained in their amusement. If they pulled down all the books from the shelves, bent the points of all the pens, overturned inkstands, scattered law-papers over the floor, or threw the pencils into the spittoon, it never disturbed the serenity of their father's good-nature."[12] In fact, it is rather to be suspected that Lincoln not only enjoyed the antics and horseplay of the unruly little demons, but egged them on. While Herndon "felt many and many a time," when the exuberance of the boys got out of hand, that he "wanted to wring their little necks," he endured their vexations and, "out of respect for Lincoln,"[13] "kept his mouth shut" (not an easy thing for Herndon to do, one feels).

Among Lincoln's irritating mannerisms, his stories, some of them repeated over and over, *ad nauseam* ("I have heard him relate the same story three times within as many hours. . . ."),[14] must have proved as annoying to Herndon as was the senior partner's incorrigible habit of reading newspapers aloud.[15] Working in close daily contact (except for those months when the senior member was on the circuit) with a person of Lincoln's fluctuating moods, a man now all boyish exuberance, now self-contained and withdrawn, all melancholy and self-doubt, must have proved extremely trying at times. Herndon's partnership life, one is forced to conclude, was hardly a bed of roses.

3.

One of the tantalizing questions for anyone who tries to understand this combination without compare is how two men so dissimilar could have pulled together so long, for, though they seemed like incompatible bedfellows, the fact remains that the association lasted sixteen years, and nominally until Lincoln's death. When Lincoln left his law office for the last time, he told Herndon to allow the wooden sign at the entrance to the office bearing the inscription, Lincoln & Herndon, to remain swinging. "Give our clients to understand," he said, "that the election of a President makes no change in the firm of Lincoln & Herndon." (The sign was still swinging when the President's lifeless body was brought home to Springfield. The great funeral procession marched past it, but Herndon was not among the honored bearers of the President's remains. He was relegated to the Sixth Division. Lincoln would not have had it so.) Despite the tensions that must exist inevitably in a partnership, each respected the other, and they were always on speaking terms. They came, in time, to endure each other's vagaries.

Even though the relationship of the two was very much that of a senior and junior partner, Herndon always addressing his associate as "Mr. Lincoln" and the senior partner addressing the junior as "Billy," it would be a mistake to see Herndon as simply an appendage to Lincoln—his "Good Man Friday," as some were wont to refer to him. Anyone cherishing this delusion has but to cull the vast number of pleadings in Herndon's hand, and the records of his numerous court appearances, representing his own independent work as a lawyer, to realize that he was no part of a flunky.

Though, for the first several years, he had few cases of his own and seldom made a court appearance without Lincoln, the printed reports of the Illinois Supreme Court, from the date of Herndon's first appearance through the January 1861 term, list his appearance in thirty-six cases in which he was not associated with Lincoln. In addition to his practice in the state courts, Herndon was much occupied, before the United States Commissioner in Springfield, in defense of fugitive slaves in danger of being carried off into bondage. In nearby Menard County, which formed part of a different circuit, the court sessions of which conflicted with those of the Eighth Circuit, which Lincoln regularly covered, Herndon was an especially active practitioner, numbering among his clients Menard County and the county seat town of Petersburg. Such was the impression he made in Petersburg that an enthusiastic admirer there wrote Lincoln, proposing Billy for Congress: "I would like to suggest," he wrote, "that if they start the name of Wm. H. Herndon Menard will do something very handsome—there are many Democrats here anxious to vote for 'Bill'—& there is no other name half so potent here. . . . We are all for Bill."[16]

Of course, all these circumstances must be considered in the light of the fact that Lincoln's practice was suspended, from 1847 to 1849, by a term in Congress, and interrupted frequently from 1854 to 1860, by his efforts in opposition to the repeal of the Missouri Compromise. Neglecting his law practice for weeks at a time, in order to make speeches in the interest of his party (while paying most of his traveling expenses out of his own pocket), Lincoln necessarily delegated to Herndon much of the work which he would otherwise have attended to personally.

It is a mistake to undervalue Herndon's ability to bring in his share of the firm's business, for there is documentary proof that the junior partner had his own particular clients, quite a few in number, who apparently preferred him to Lincoln. A number of the original pleadings drawn by Herndon, covering the period of his partnership with Lincoln, and now in the Illinois State Historical Library, are signed "W. H. Herndon for [name of client]," and not "Lincoln & Herndon." Herndon had his own loyal clientele, who dealt with him, and him alone. Almost without exception, the pleadings involving a case of a particular client are all in the handwriting of the same partner. Also, where a client had repeat business, the same partner took care of his affairs each time.

Though at first his efforts consisted of the performance of routine tasks—he " 'toated books' & 'hunted up authorities' " for the senior partner[17]—in time Herndon came to bear his share of the work of the partnership. Whatever he may have lacked in sustained brilliance, he made up in industry and drive. His capacity for work, which was awe-inspiring, is the more remarkable in view of his strong distaste for the law. "A law office is a dry place for incident of a pleasing kind," Herndon once observed, adding, somewhat primly: "If you love the stories of murder—rape—fraud &c. a law office is a good place. . . ." With contempt for the "heated foaming discussion" of judges, he wrote: "*I hate the Law* [Herndon, like Lincoln, made a practice of underscoring certain words for emphasis]: it cramps me: it seems to me priestly barbaric. I am here above the suspicion of not knowing somewhat of the History—Spirit & Principles of the Law, and my flings do not come from Disappointment. I say I hate the Law."[18]

4.

Opinions about the character and attainments of this tremendously vital man have varied unceasingly with the passage of a century. About no other Illinois lawyer of that period have so many conflicting judgments been expressed. Putting to one side the opinions of others, and viewing the man solely on the basis of his course of conduct over the years, one can only say that of all Lincoln's contemporaries at the Illinois bar, Herndon is perhaps the most difficult to evaluate. There was a protean quality about him that gives an uncertainty to his true stature as a lawyer.

Acting invariably a role which he conceived to be that of one who knew all the answers—jurisprudential, moral, philosophical, metaphysical, psychoanalytical, political, or what have you—Herndon comported himself with an air of profundity. A windbag, a performer with a touch of the ham, Herndon was the least reticent of men; he had none of the customary inhibitions. To give him his due, it is only just to say that he was, in truth, something of a scholar (a fact he was not inclined to allow the world to forget), but at his birth some mischievous pixie had endowed him with a gift for humbug, so that the pundit and the quack in him were ever at odds with each other. And yet, for all that he may have been "a faddist to whom the latest book read gave the full answer,"[19] the man was a born crusader, a subversive at heart, holding militantly and resolutely to the things he truly believed in. Possibly the most distinctive thing about this most rugged of individualists was the intensity of his nature; he gave himself prodigally to every cause which enlisted his sympathy.

A man of multiple facets, which carried over into his legal work, Herndon, a chain talker who looked upon the law as a loquacious trade (as, indeed, it was), could talk the hind legs off a mule; with a natural fondness for disputation and knockdown tactics, he could be on occasions as overly technical and contentious and *gauche* as the most pettifogging frontier shyster, and at other times a well-informed student of the law—a far better one than his detractors have allowed. While he showed to advantage in the hurly-burly and rough infighting of a police-court hearing, it remains true that in the higher courts there were moments which exposed the true qualities of a lawyer, even though in between his work was mediocre. And while it is also true that the sum of his appearances before the higher courts would hardly be the record of a leader of the Illinois bar, yet to call him merely an inferior court lawyer would be to demean his intellectual quality.

More susceptible to emotion than reason, impulsive and intuitive as a woman, and possessed, at times, of sheer quixotism, the free-swinging Herndon was wont to act precipitately, plunging headlong into legal situations without having first made a careful examination of either the facts or the law.[20] Herndon's impetuosity and Lincoln's calm deliberateness amounted to a temperamental difference that accounted for their inability to see certain things alike. In his law work, as in other things, Herndon, a man without restraint or balance, was not always careful to sift the evidence and was altogether too prone to jump to conclusions. Charles S. Zane, the Springfield attorney, felt that "Mr. Herndon as a rule considered questions in the abstract, while Mr. Lincoln considered them more in the concrete."[21] Herndon, continued Zane, "did not spend much time in the preparation of his cases. . . . Mr. Lincoln was more methodical and systematic."

On the other hand, there was in the Oliver R. Barrett Collection (now dispersed) a large notebook, in Herndon's handwriting, filled with citations of authorities for cases handled by the firm from 1849 to 1860. They reflect his careful study, among others, of the Illinois, New York, Missouri, Kentucky and Arkansas reports, as well as the standard law commentaries and digests. In the *Herndon-Weik Collection* (opened to the public in 1942) there is a smaller book, containing a number of similar references. Though in his declining years, when he practiced intermittently and with inconspicuous success, and was more often off the wagon than on, Herndon was regarded as being "not strong as a lawyer,"[22] in his prime his intellectual resources appeared equal to any demands that the practice of law made of them.

5.

A strange man was Billy Herndon, almost as strange and paradoxical a personality as was Lincoln. It has been rightly observed that "It is safer for a biographer to exhibit his subject than attempt to explain him." Certainly that is the proper formula for a subject as rampageously individual as Herndon, in whose character the most contradictory traits and influences dwelt side by side. The son of a pro-slavery father, he early became passionately enamored of the cause of abolitionism; a solid rock of Whiggism, his political views were anathema to the Democratic elder Herndon. A capable lawyer, he had an aversion to the law. An intellectual of sorts, an omnivorous reader and genuine bibliophile, possessed of one of the finest libraries in the whole Middle West, in which were included the works of Montaigne, Kant, Hegel and Francis Bacon, he nevertheless numbered among his intimates Springfield's hooligan element. A leader in the temperance movement, his greatest failing was his addiction to alcohol.

Regarding the living Lincoln with an almost worshipful reverence, his subsequent judgments (as, for example, his at times condescending references to Lincoln as a lawyer) have brought down upon him deserved condemnation as an ingrate and fluent liar.

It is all very well to attempt to write off some of the bibulous Herndon's uncomplimentary references to Lincoln as the effusions of one who admitted to taking "a toddy *as exciter*," yet there is no slight justification for many of his cheaply belittling remarks. Herndon's repeated misrepresentations of Lincoln's motives sometimes make it very difficult for the reader to think other than ill of him. The probity of his approach to an assessment of Lincoln's character has never been more seriously impugned than in the astonishing observation that Lincoln was a "remorseless trimmer with men. They were his tools, and when they were used up he threw them aside as old iron and took up new tools."[23]

Of the law partner-biographer's numerous perversions of the truth, perhaps the most preposterous is the claim that Lincoln "was not always—to all persons & at all times *absolutely* Honest."[24] Herndon's piddling references to his deceased law partner; his unblushingly exalted opinion of his own legal ability, coupled with his shrugging off of that of Lincoln; indeed, his frequent excursions into wanton denigration, are altogether too many and seemingly calculated to be dismissed as the promptings of the "exciter." It is not without reason that a certain repugnance has attended many of the judgments to be found in Herndon's *Life* of his friend and partner. Emanuel Hertz's gushingly effusive characterization of the man as "Lincoln's Boswell par excellence"[25] finds little support among men of reputation in the field of Lincoln scholarship.

6.

In the spring of 1821, Archer G. Herndon brought his family from Green County, Kentucky and settled outside the young village of Springfield. With its selection as county seat, he moved into town, where he put up the "Indian Queen," Springfield's first tavern-hotel. The elder Herndon was a man of some consequence, having served eight years in the State Legislature, from 1834 to 1842, and having been one of the famous Long Nine. He was receiver of the land office from 1842 to 1849. Modestly successful in business, Herndon, Sr. sent his favorite son, William Henry, to a private academy. In 1836 he entered him in the preparatory department of Illinois College, in the nearby town of Jacksonville, the president of which institution was Edward Beecher, brother of Harriet Beecher Stowe, author of the great social document, *Uncle Tom's Cabin.*

The fanciful story goes that the youth's college career was terminated when, in November, 1837, he joined the faculty and the other students in antislavery demonstrations occasioned by the murder of Elijah P. Lovejoy, the abolitionist preacher-editor. The elder Herndon, a Democratic bigwig, supposedly took the incalculable *enfant terrible* out of college, saying that he would have no part in the education of "a damned Abolitionist pup." David Donald, who labored unremittingly in running down the facts of Herndon's life, has scotched the myth that he was ever at Jacksonville in November, 1837, by showing that the minutes of the Illinois College faculty for September fourteenth of that year disclose that Herndon was unable to meet the college entrance requirements, having failed in arithmetic.[26] As Donald goes on to point out, the 1837–38 college catalogue contains no mention of his enrollment.[27] Herndon himself said merely that his father felt "the college was too strongly permeated with the virus of Abolitionism." In any event, at the age of nineteen (he was nine years Lincoln's junior), Herndon went back to clerking in the store of Joshua Speed, taking up quarters in the spacious room above the store, along with Speed, Lincoln and Charles Hurst.

In 1842 he quit his job with Speed and entered the office of Logan & Lincoln. At the same time, following Lincoln's suggestion, he took up the study of law, reading law at night and in his spare moments during the day. As Herndon later recalled, he was "studious—too much so for . . . [his] own health—studied from 12 to 14 hours a day."[28] In the fall of 1843 and spring of 1844, Herndon served as a juror in the Sangamon Circuit Court; even though this entailed his being away from the office, Lincoln doubtless considered it fully justified by the practical benefits to be reaped from the experience.

On November 27, 1844, Herndon was, by order of the Circuit Court, granted a certificate of "good moral character" (written out by Lincoln) and, several weeks later, on December ninth, he "came to the bar." Although it is impossible to ascertain the exact date when, for better or for worse, the firm of Lincoln & Herndon was launched, it probably was soon after Herndon's admission to practice. Herndon gives the date of dissolution of Lincoln's partnership with Logan and the commencement of the firm of Lincoln & Herndon as December, 1843; this is obviously an error, inasmuch as Herndon was not admitted to practice until a year later. What is more, the docket of the Sangamon Circuit Court for the year 1844 shows the frequent appearances of Logan & Lincoln. The first case in that court in which Lincoln and Herndon appeared as partners was *Hope* v. *Beebe*, tried in March, 1845.

The firm located in the office previously occupied by Logan & Lincoln, on the third floor front of the Tinsley Building, the first three-story building on the south side of the square and the finest brick business building in central Illinois. On the second floor was located the United States Courtroom, in which Lincoln practiced. Here they remained until the late 'forties; after brief periods in several locations, they moved to the second floor of the brick building at 105 South Fifth Street (the site now commemorated by a bronze marker), where they supposedly remained until Lincoln bid Springfield "an affectionate farewell." Logan Hay, however, maintained that sometime during the period when Herndon was Mayor of Springfield (1854–1856), the partners moved their office to a location nearer the mayor's office and, at the expiration of his term, moved back to 105 South Fifth Street. After Lincoln's death Herndon continued to occupy the Fifth Street office for the remainder of his life, first in partnership with Charles Zane, who later became judge of the United States District Court for the Southern District of Illinois, and later as partner of Alfred Orendorff.

The original office, from all accounts an incredibly dingy place even for a pioneer law office, consisted of a single room, which overlooked Hoffman's Row; in the center of the room stood a long table, 10' x 3', with a smaller one at the end. In a corner stood a desk containing the firm's law papers; a bookcase against the wall (now on display in the Illinois State Historical Library) held some lawbooks and miscellaneous other volumes. The couch and a tall, unblackened stove were the only other articles of any consequence in this room which, from the standpoint of appointments, was destitute of legitimate claim to be called an office.

Over everything in the gloomy, dismal law office, where Lincoln ate meager lunches of cheese and crackers, lay a film of dust—and thereby hangs a tale. John H. Littlefield, who came with the firm as a student in 1859, describing the condition of another office which they then occupied, stated that seeds which had fallen to the floor, from a desk, actually sprouted in one corner of the room. This story may sound a mite too fanciful to swallow, yet Gibson W. Harris, who served as a clerk in the office occupied in 1845, described the place as drab and thoroughly unkempt, the floor unscoured, and with only an occasional sweeping of the "accumulated dirt" by the law clerk currently employed.[29] Probably each of the offices which they occupied at different times was alike in the matter of cleanliness, or, rather, its lack. It must be said for Herndon, however, that he displayed more interest in the acquisition of new office equipment and a library than did the senior member. A year after the partnership was formed, he purchased a desk for twenty dollars and books in the amount of $54.65.[30] (A bookcase against the wall of the Fifth Street office contained about two hundred law books and other volumes.)

The antiquated couch was an indispensable item of equipment so far as the senior partner was concerned. Upon arrival at the office in the morning, it was his custom to throw himself down upon it and, because his six feet four inches overhung, he would spread his legs "on two or three chairs or up against the wall,"[31] and proceed to read the newspaper aloud, greatly to the distraction of Herndon. "I have had to quit the office frequently," wrote Herndon, "because of this reading aloud."[32]

7.

The physical appearance of untidiness was only matched by the antique methods which the partners pursued in keeping records. Like Lincoln, Herndon was lacking in all the qualities of a businessman. For several years (1845–47) Herndon, one of whose duties it was to keep the books of the partnership, maintained a combination day book and fee book in rather desultory fashion. It listed the cases (or, to be more exact, some of the cases) which the partners handled in Springfield and in the adjoining counties of Logan, Menard and Christian, and the fees charged. This book, entirely in Herndon's fairly good handwriting, contains 125 numbered cases (1, 2, 3, etc.) of the two-year period before Lincoln went to Congress, with some others in the back of the book, entered after his return; it is among the possessions of the Illinois State Historical Library. There was an occasional fifty-dollar fee charged, and in one instance, in 1845, a hundred-dollar fee, but for the most part remuneration for work in the circuit courts ranged from ten dollars to twenty-five dollars per case (often enough not forthcoming). The prevailing low fees emphasized the need for volume and prevented lawyers from specializing. Most of them, like Lincoln, handled whatever cases they could get.

There is an entry of three dollars (the smallest fee known to have been charged) for drawing a power of attorney; the one-hundred-dollar fee was for a case in the Supreme Court. The list of cases is known to be incomplete, including, presumably, only those in which the fee was not paid in full at the outset. Even as to the cases listed, it would seem that the entries are completely perfunctory. Apparently it was Herndon's practice, when the fee charged was collected, to go back and write in across the case entry the word "Paid," though without noting the date of payment. The partners were sometimes obliged to accept promissory notes (not all of which were paid) in lieu of cash. For example, Item No. 17, showing a charge of fifty dollars in "Peo. v. Dormer (for Deft To attending to case in Circuit in Menard," bears the word "Note" written across it; there is no subsequent notation or record of the same having been paid.

With the passing years, the partners came to rely increasingly less on even such haphazard records as Herndon kept in the early stages of the partnership. Cash fees were usually split on the spot, so to speak. "Sometimes I went on the circuit," wrote Herndon, "and, if I were with Lincoln around in the counties, all the money collected by us was instantly divided. If I were not on the circuit, was at the office attending to our affairs at home, Lincoln would collect monies due us and our fees on the circuit and divide it, putting his half in his pocketbook and using it as he wanted to; he would wrap my half up in a roll, putting my name on a slip of paper and then wrapping it, the slip, around the roll of money and then putting it in his pocketbook and when he came home he would come to the office and hand me my money; . . ."[33] This practice of wrapping up Herndon's share in a piece of paper and writing his name on it, is probably traceable to Lincoln's obsession with death; if he should die away from home, Herndon would have no trouble in collecting. (Which recalls to mind the fact that Lincoln left no will—another of the unanswerable riddles in the life of this complicated man.)

The first bank in Springfield was not organized until 1851, when the Springfield Marine and Fire Insurance Company came into being. (Since the failure of the State Bank in 1837, banking institutions had been viewed with disfavor in the State of Illinois.) For several years the firm maintained a partnership account at the Marine and Fire, though very few transactions were recorded in it. It would appear to have been used simply for the collection of drafts. Though it originally functioned as an insurance company, the institution shortly branched out into the banking business, and, under the name of the Springfield Marine Bank, is still in business on the same site, the oldest bank in Illinois. Before 1851 the practice was for the more opulent Springfield residents (as well as some, like Lincoln, not quite so affluent) to leave their cash for safekeeping with the general store of Irwin & Company, which possessed one of the few iron safes in Springfield. Presumably, though, the money was put to work by Irwin & Company, for interest on these deposits was paid at the annual rate of twelve per cent.[34]

In November, 1954, that idefatigable Lincoln rummager, James T. Hickey, set out to explore the musty contents of a storage room above the Marine Bank. The prize was worth the hunt, for there, slumbering among the old records of the Springfield Marine and Fire Insurance Company, he came upon one of the most significant Lincoln finds in years—three journals and a store ledger of John Irwin & Company and Robert Irwin & Company, covering the years 1842 to 1853. Robert Irwin left the store about the latter year, to become cashier of the Springfield Marine and Fire Insurance Company, which explains the presence of the old books among the bank's records. Now in the possession of the Illinois State Historical Library, they throw fresh and valuable light on Lincoln's financial affairs during the period covered.

Most important, for the purpose of the present study, they have helped to set the record straight on the matter of the division of fees in the Logan & Lincoln partnership. One writer has concluded: "The terms of Lincoln's partnership with Judge Logan are not known, but it may reasonably be inferred that the junior member of the firm received only a small percentage of the fees, for the business was almost entirely Logan's, and he was not by nature over-generous."[35] Insofar as the statement refers to division of fees, it seems a considerable exaggeration. The common belief held, until Hickey's discovery, that Lincoln received a third of all fees taken in during the period of his association with Logan. Journal jottings in Lincoln's account for March 6, August 12 and September 11, 1844, show clearly, however, that the amounts indicated by those entries represent one half, rather than one third of the total fee received. In connection with one of the three items, papers filed upon the settlement of the estate of William G. Drennan disclose a fee of one hundred dollars paid Logan & Lincoln. The Irwin account shows the following entry, under date of August twelfth: "A Lincoln for ½ of fee from Drennan [Estate] 50.00."[36] It could very well have been, and likely was, that the percentage was increased during the final year of the partnership.[37]

The books of Irwin & Company show the last banking transaction to have been on November 23, 1848, when thirty dollars paid by one Ben Giger was credited to Lincoln's account. When Robert Irwin went with the bank, Lincoln followed him, opening an account there on March 1, 1853, with a deposit of $310,[38] which was continuously maintained until the time of his death.

The Library of Congress has recently acquired, as a gift from Lincoln's great-grandson, Lincoln Isham, of Dorset, Vermont, twenty-eight checks made out by Lincoln during the years 1859 and 1860, and drawn on his account with the Springfield Marine and Fire Insurance Company. The checks, which range in amount from $1.25 to $100, are rich in human interest, adding bits of knowledge about Lincoln's everyday life. The $100 check, for instance, was made out to a tailor only three weeks before he went to New York to deliver his historic Cooper Union address. It suggests the prairie lawyer was careful to dress suitably for his appearance in important Eastern political circles.

Case files of the firm were nonexistent; pleadings, correspondence and papers generally were in a perpetual state of chaos. Of system in filing there was none. Lincoln's capacious "stovepipe" hat, with its wide sweat band, very often served the purpose of a filing cabinet. Herndon says of it: "This hat of Lincoln's—a silk plug—was an extraordinary receptacle. It was his desk and his memorandum-book."[39] Writing to Weik in 1885, Herndon referred to the Lincoln top-piece "where he carried quite all his plunder, checkbook for the bank account, letters answered and unanswered, handkerchief, etc."[40] At other times, when he had finished with legal papers Lincoln would put them away in places known only to himself. After his death, Herndon discovered a bundle of papers, with the notation in Lincoln's hand: "When you can't find it anywhere else, look in this."

Something of the confusion which usually reigned in the untidy office, in the latter years of their association, may be gathered from several letters written by Herndon to Theodore Parker, the left-wing Congregationalist minister, in the early part of 1858. Writing from Springfield on January eighth, he said: "What I write to you is always written in my office amid bluster, confusion and 'malicious queries'; and you must therefore look over imperfections and mistakes. You know a country law office, and if you do not, just step into ours some day and see for yourself."[41] And again, on February twenty-fourth: "Just as I was writing my letter to you my office got full of people inquiring about three cent law suits."[42]

Herndon, whom Lincoln may have thought would furnish a needed corrective to his own woeful lack of method, proved no more organized or methodical than was Lincoln. And yet, if order never did emerge from confusion, the fact does not appear to have had any appreciably adverse effect on the functioning of the partnership and its ability to meet the stiff competition furnished by the rest of the Sangamon bar.

CHAPTER VIII

Law and Politics on the Prairie

1.

SPRING OF 1845 found Lincoln on the circuit, covering Tazewell, Woodford, McLean, DeWitt, Champaign and Christian Counties, while Herndon looked after things in Springfield. Though there is, for that term of court, no extant evidence of his activity in Piatt, Edgar, Moultrie and Macon Counties, all then included in the Eighth Circuit, it is likely that Lincoln accompanied the other members of the traveling bar to the county seat towns of Monticello, Paris, Sullivan and Decatur. He was still somewhat removed from being the most-sought-after lawyer on the circuit, and it is conceivable that his visits to these towns were not productive of business. Either that, or the records of his cases have become lost or destroyed.

At the May term, 1845, of the Champaign Circuit Court, held in Urbana, Lincoln and Asahel Gridley, lawyer, banker and Bloomington's first millionaire, were appointed by the Court to defend William Weaver, a no-account drunkard who, for no apparent reason, shot and killed a man with a rifle.[1] The docket shows that an order sentencing the defendant to be hanged was entered by the Court on May 10, 1845, and the date of execution set for June 27, 1845, "between the hours of two and four o'clock in the afternoon."[2] Before the date of execution Weaver escaped.

Returning from the circuit on June third, Lincoln was busy for a few days in Springfield. On the seventh, appearing in the United States Circuit Court, he obtained a judgment of $2,904.68 for the plaintiffs in *Hite, et al.* v. *Kerney*.[3] On Monday, the ninth, he attended at the Menard Circuit Court, in Petersburg, on behalf of James Dorman, held for manslaughter. It was charged that on February 25, 1845, the defendant attempted forcibly to enter the dwelling house of Ellen Cox by breaking in. She was inside, pregnant, and, as a result of her efforts to stop him, became ill and died. Appearing for the prosecution was James A. McDougall, Attorney General, whom Palmer regarded as "one of the most brilliant men ever connected with the Chicago bar."[4] When the gold craze broke out, he went to California, where he fell on evil days, "closing his career groveling with sots and borne down with the demon drink."[5]

In Springfield, where the case originated, Lincoln had previously appeared and invoked what was, for him, in a fair way of becoming the inevitable application for change of venue. One must not lose sight of the fact that, in the workaday task of helping his clients out of their difficulties, Lincoln, by resorting to this remedial measure, was serving their best interests—which, when one comes to think of it, was what he was being paid to do. The remedy finds its rationale in the sound reasoning that where there is a strong probability that bias exists throughout the community, the accused should not be compelled to take the risk of coming before a jury whose members, or some of whom, are influenced by adverse sentiments which preclude a detached consideration, and which may be undiscovered in the course of examination, or which, indeed, may not be fully appreciated by the jurors themselves.

One may justly believe that Lincoln was not one of those who believed that innocence is sufficient. His remarks on the Trailor murder case, contained in the narrative of the case published in the Quincy *Whig* on April 15, 1846,[6] leave no doubt of the fact that he realized that the machinery of the law is by no means infallible. Commenting on Lincoln's account of the case, the editor stated: "There is no doubt of the truth of every fact stated; and the whole affair is of so extraordinary a character as to entitle it to publication, and commend it to the attention of

those at present engaged in discussing reforms in criminal jurisprudence, and the abolition of capital punishment. Ed. *Whig*."

Though it is not, perhaps, germane to the main theme of
this work, for the reason that Lincoln's services were not involved,
the writer feels warranted in citing a case tried in 1848 in Mc-
Henry County, Illinois. The defendant, Henry Brydenbecker,
was charged with a particularly dastardly crime—the brutal killing of the girl he was soon to marry. Public feeling ran high.
Years later, Lincoln's friend Isaac N. Arnold, who undertook the
defense, writing in his *Recollections of Early Chicago and the
Illinois Bar*, said: "The trial lasted ten days, during which a Sunday intervened, when the jury were taken to a nearby camp-
meeting to attend religious services, consisting of prayer that the
guilty might not escape through any device or sham defense of
counsel, and that the jury might have the firmness to do their duty.
In addition, a sermon was preached to them in which they were
admonished not to be misled by prisoner's counsel." The jury
disagreed, and on a new trial a change of venue was secured to
Cook County, where the defendant was found not guilty because
insane. He died a few months later, in a mental institution, and
upon post-mortem examination was found to have an ulceration
of the brain.

Dorman's affidavit in support of the application, drawn in
Lincoln's hand, the original of which is in the Illinois State Historical Library, reads in pertinent part:

> James Dorman, the defendant in an Indictment for manslaughter,
> pending in the circuit court of the county aforesaid, being first duly
> sworn, states on oath that he fears he will not receive a fair and im-
> partial trial in the court aforesaid upon the Indictment aforesaid on
> account that the minds of the inhabitants of the county aforesaid, are
> prejudiced against him, and that affiant verily believes the minds of
> said inhabitants are so prejudiced against him—

The motion was granted, and the case removed to Menard
County. On June eleventh Lincoln & Herndon, in their first case

in Menard,[7] succeeded in obtaining an acquittal for their client.

Petersburg, the county seat where the case was tried, is two miles north of New Salem; it had become the home of many of Lincoln's old acquaintances when New Salem went into a decline. In 1839 the northwestern part of Sangamon was set off as Menard. The Menard Circuit Court met for the first time for a two-day session, June 17-18, 1839, in the home of John Taylor; Lincoln attended the first day. Thereafter, he was to be found in fairly regular attendance during the spring and fall terms, until Menard was removed from the Eighth Circuit in 1847.

One would naturally think that Lincoln's practice was more extensive in Menard than in any other county but Sangamon. There, at New Salem, he had lived for six years, and when the town gave way to Petersburg, many of his old friends moved to the new town. Oddly enough, his practice there, even before Menard's detachment from the Eighth Circuit, did not begin to compare with that of David Rutledge (Ann's brother, and the first practicing attorney in Menard County), who enjoyed the bulk of the county's business during the first few years of its existence, or Thomas L. Harris, who succeeded Rutledge in outranking all others. Even Springfield lawyers, among them Stuart, frequently had more cases in Menard than did Lincoln.[8]

The courthouse in which Lincoln appeared in connection with the Dorman case was in use from 1843 to approximately 1897, a longer time than most courthouses of the second half of the nineteenth century. It is fairly representative of those in which Lincoln practiced—old-fashioned wood or brick structures, architecturally undistinguished both inside and out, usually capped by cupola or tower, or both. The interiors were finished in a stiff, severe style, with white walls, unpainted woodwork, pine floors and wooden benches. They were usually heated by large Franklin stoves, "with yards of stovepipe running wildly through the air, searching for an exit, and threatening momentarily to unjoint and tumble in sections."[9]

2.

Lincoln, between court appearances, was actively engaged, in the spring and summer of 1846, in seeking the Whig nomination for Congress from the one dependable Whig congressional district in Illinois. Having twice failed to obtain it, when first John J. Hardin and then Edward D. Baker (after whom Lincoln named his second son) became the party choice and then congressman, he was determined to let no grass grow under his feet in an effort to win the 1846 nomination. It is an interesting fact that all three (Lincoln, Hardin and Baker) were lawyers who utilized the law as a vantage point for furtherance of their political careers.

When Baker returned from Washington in the summer of 1845, Lincoln inquired if he would abide by the rule of rotation and stand aside, in favor of him. Baker replied that he would gladly do so, were it not for the fact that he feared that Hardin would run again, defeat Lincoln, and deprive them both of the nomination. Lincoln then sought to get a commitment from Hardin, but the Morgan County leader indicated unmistakably that he had no thought of yielding. Whereupon Lincoln set about in earnest to insure his candidacy, overlooking no opportunity to strengthen his position with the Whig politicos in those county seat towns along the route of the Eighth Circuit which were comprised within the Seventh Congressional District, the while he attended to his circuit practice. It was customary for the nomadic practitioners to correlate their court practice and the establishment of political contacts while on seasonal exodus to the outlying precincts.

Before returning to Congress in November, 1845, Baker gave Lincoln assurance of his decision not to seek re-election, but Hardin hung on until, seeing his chances reduced to the vanishing point, he formally withdrew from the race on February 16, 1846. The following May first Lincoln was nominated by acclamation at the district convention at Petersburg. American politics has a way of treating the front-runner unkindly; Lincoln, however, not only got out in front early in the race for the nomination, but stayed there, eventually killing off the opposition by virtue of lining up the Whig leaders through personal appeals. His instinctive tact in personal relations made him a superb politician, for he was greatly liked by those who knew him and appears to have been disliked by practically none.

In court, Lincoln's treatment of his adversaries was uniformly exemplary, and so it was that his fellow lawyer-politicians, within the limits imposed by party discipline, felt, on the whole, kindly disposed toward his political aspirations. To a much greater degree than is usual in a profession where jealousy is not uncommon, Lincoln, with his never-failing courtesy to associate and opposing counsel alike, enjoyed, throughout his career at the Illinois bar, the esteem of his brother lawyers. "Mr. Lincoln's courtesy to young practitioners was little less than proverbial," wrote Gibson W. Harris, "and it was never more gracious than when he was the opposing counsel. He had a happy knack of setting them at ease and encouraging them to put forth their best efforts. In consequence they all liked him."[10]

What Whitney says about Lincoln's interest in young lawyers, a fact frequently referred to by other men who knew Lincoln, bears repeating: "I well recollect how kindly and cordially he aided and advised me about my business at court, it being my first appearance at the bar. I did not feel the slightest delicacy in approaching him for assistance; it seemed as if he wooed me to close intimacy and familiarity at once; and this from no selfish motive at all—but pure disinterested philanthrophy and goodness of heart toward a young lawyer just commencing his career."[11] Another contemporary, Adlai E. Stevenson, refers to the "words of encouragement" Lincoln spoke to young lawyers. "He was ever the generous, kindly gentleman," said Stevenson.[12] It is not an exaggeration to say that no other lawyer of his time and place so stimulated the respect and admiration of his colleagues, neophytes and oldsters alike, as did Lincoln.

Legend has it that during the campaign which followed, in which Lincoln was opposed by the sixty-one-year-old Bible-thumping, devil-wrasslin' Methodist circuit rider, Peter Cartwright, then presiding elder of the Bloomington, Illinois District of the Methodist Episcopal Church, the former attended one of his Democratic opponent's meetings. Mixing politics and "the old time religion," this redoubtable warrior for the Lord, who thundered against evil and the practitioners thereof, called upon all sinners to come forward and be saved. Lincoln got up to leave the hall. "Where are you going, Mr. Lincoln?" Cartwright called out. Lincoln had a ready answer; in a flash, he retorted: "To Congress, Mr. Cartwright." Which is where he went, for on August 3, 1846, the Seventh Congressional District, a rock-ribbed Whig bastion comprising eleven counties in the central part of the state, gave him an unprecedented majority of 1,511 votes. Lincoln thus became the sole Whig representative from Illinois.

3.

At the spring term, 1847, of the Tazewell Circuit Court, Lincoln appeared for the plaintiff in the case of *Case v. Snow Brothers*, the tale of which constitutes an interesting episode in the story of Lincoln's work in the courts. The defendants had purchased of the plaintiff a team of oxen and a plow and, being without funds, gave their promissory note in payment. The brothers were under age at the time, of which fact the seller was aware. When the note matured, the Snows resisted the plaintiff's efforts to collect, upon the ground that they were not of age when the note was given. Case engaged Lincoln as his attorney, and in due course action was instituted on the instrument.

Present throughout the trial was George W. Minier, who was detained in Tremont as a witness in a case which had been deferred. (Minier, an early settler in Tazewell and the person for whom the town of Minier was named, was a preacher of the

Christian Church and was once elected to the lower house of the legislature on the Prohibition ticket.) He has left an intriguing account of the skillful manner in which Lincoln got around the legal impediment to recovery on his client's just claim.[13]

The case went to the jury on what amounted to an agreed state of facts. In his summation Lincoln argued that the Snow brothers had received full value for the note, and that in pleading "the baby act" they had been poorly advised. Realizing, as he must have, that he had his work cut out for him in getting past the defense of infancy, Lincoln, after first conceding its validity in a proper case, where there was overreaching on the part of the seller, argued that it should not be permitted to become an instrument to facilitate cheating. At this point, as Minier remembered it, Lincoln changed the whole tenor of his plea—from one on behalf of his client to an appeal in the interest of the boys. His final words bear quoting: "Gentlemen of the Jury, are you willing to allow these boys to begin life with this shame and disgrace attached to their character? If you are, *I* am not. The best judge of human character that ever wrote has left these immortal words for all of us to ponder:

> 'Good name in man and woman, dear my lord,
> Is the immediate jewel of their souls:
> Who steals my purse steals trash; 'tis something, nothing;
> 'Twas mine, 'tis his, and has been slave to thousands;
> But he that filches from me my good name
> Robs me of that which not enriches him
> And makes me poor indeed.' "[14]

Without leaving their seats, the jury returned a verdict for the plaintiff in the amount of his claim.

It must be noted that, when it suited his client's purpose, Lincoln, like any other lawyer, was not above pleading the defense of infancy, as well as other technical defenses not exactly on the merits. This fact is amply revealed by an examination of the files of a number of his cases. In so doing, Lincoln was acting in the best interests of his client; to have done otherwise would have exposed him to deserved censure. In *Dorman* v. *Lane* we find him, representing the plaintiff, ready to plead the statute of limitations as a bar to the defendant's counterclaim.[15] In *Pearl* v. *Wellmans, et al.*, Lincoln, appearing for the defendant, sought unsuccessfully to defeat the plaintiff's claim by pleading that the plaintiff, in sleeping on his rights, had been guilty of *laches*.[16] In *Maus* v. *Worthing*, Lincoln succeeded in dismissing the appeal taken by his adversary on the technical ground that the appeal bond was not executed in the precise manner provided by statute.[17] In a sharp dissent from the ruling of his two colleagues, Judge Breese deplored adherence to a rule "so arbitrary, so technical, so wholly inappropriate to our condition, and so little calculated to promote justice."

For all his high-mindedness, Lincoln was a very clearheaded lawyer, realistic and practical in the safeguarding of his clients' legal rights. The records of the courts in which he practiced do not bear out the Herndon conclusion that he was strikingly deficient in the technical rules of the law. Possessed as he was of many admirable qualities as a lawyer, Lincoln was nevertheless not less human than other reputable members of his profession who did not fail to avail themselves of legal technicalities or legal devices to further the best interests of their clients. Despite the assertions of Nicolay and Hay, Herndon, Lamon, Whitney and other biographers, the court records prove conclusively that he resorted to every legitimate device and utilized every technical advantage to win his cause. To represent Lincoln as a lawyer either disinclined or without the know-how to take advantage of any technical defense is plainly a distortion of fact. In the law, as in everything else, Lincoln was endowed with a stern sense of down-to-earth realism.

4.

On May fourth, appearing in Petersburg, Lincoln represented the defendants in a larceny case, *People* v. *Lane, et al.*, in which the jury convicted. The defendants were sentenced to three months in the county jail and fined thirty dollars each. The case originated in Sangamon County, from which it was removed to Menard when Lincoln applied for a change of venue. Though one of the more prosaic of his cases, it is of interest because of the requests for instructions to the jury, four in number, which appear in Lincoln's handwriting,[18] all of which were charged by the Court, as requested. They show a sound grasp, on Lincoln's part, of the law of the case.

GIVEN
1. That unless they are satisfied, beyond a reasonable doubt, of the guilt of the defendants, they are to find them not guilty.

GIVEN
2nd. That they are at liberty to find some of the defendants guilty, and others not guilty; and that they are not to find one guilty, unless they are satisfied, beyond a reasonable doubt, that such one, was *Present* when the trees were stolen, or *encouraged* and *advised* their being stolen.

GIVEN
3rd. That if they believe some of the defendants are guilty and some not, they are not to find any guilty, unless they are satisfied beyond a reasonable doubt, which *one* or *two* is, or are, guilty.

GIVEN
4. That the mere *receipt* of the trees as they were stolen, is not sufficient to convict any one of the defendants, on this indictment.

5.

On July 1, 1847, Lincoln set out for Chicago, there to attend the River and Harbor Convention, called to protest against the veto, by the Democratic President Polk, of an appropriation for river and harbor development, passed by the Twenty-ninth Congress, which would have committed the Federal Government to internal improvement on a large scale. It was, for Lincoln, an event of considerable importance, the first time he had ever addressed a large representative gathering that was almost national in its scope. Representing Sangamon County, Lincoln was in attendance during the three-day session. The Chicago *Journal,* noting the attendance of "the only Whig representative from this State," welcomed him to the "commercial emporium of the State."[19] It was probably his first visit to the great urban community, then a place of 16,000 inhabitants, which was growing rapidly in population and importance. As the phenomenon of Chicago revealed itself to the unpretentious prairie lawyer, he may have recalled that the charter incorporating it as a city had been approved by the General Assembly in March of 1837, the month of his admission to practice. They had both, since then, come a long way.

Present were many notable figures from all sections of the country. Representing the New York *Tribune* was Horace Greeley, while Thurlow Weed, leader of the Whig Party in New York State, covered the proceedings for the Albany *Evening Journal.* Among the speakers and those who addressed the Convention by letter were Daniel Webster, Thomas Hart Benton, Edward Bates (later to become Lincoln's Attorney General), who presided as chairman of the Convention, Thomas Corwin and other figures of national repute. It was Lincoln's first opportunity to measure himself with men of national reputation, and he fully exploited it. Called upon to reply to David Dudley Field, spokesman for the administration and one of the leading lawyers in the country, who had criticized a resolution passed by the Convention as being too radical, his remarks elicited favorable comment from Greeley.

Between sessions, Lincoln and that hard-bitten Jacksonian from Missouri, most powerful spokesman of the new West, "Old Bullion" Benton, very likely had interesting things to say to each other, exchanging experiences on their respective judicial circuits. Benton had practiced for years in the "small fee circuit courts" of frontier Missouri. Like Lincoln, he knew what it was to endure the inconveniences of country taverns, irregular hours of sleep and irregularity of meals, which characterized circuit practice. Like Lincoln, his skill as a lawyer was developed in the stern crucible of that rough-and-tumble training ground.

Lincoln's attendance at the Rivers and Harbors Convention, and the impression which he made upon Norman B. Judd, another of the delegates, indirectly led to his being retained in the Rock Island Bridge Case, one of the most celebrated cases of his entire career. In 1857, after the owners of the *Effie Afton* steamboat had brought suit for damages against the Rock Island Bridge Company, Judd, Henry Farnam and Joseph Knox of Rock Island were seated in the lobby of the Tremont Hotel, in Chicago, discussing the case over their after-dinner cigars. Knox remarked that it would take "a strong, popular man to handle the case," to which Judd responded: "Well, gentlemen, there is only one man in this country who can take this case and win it, and that is Abraham Lincoln." "And who is Abraham Lincoln," queried Farnam. "A young lawyer from Sangamon County," replied Judd, "one of the best men to state a case forcibly and convincingly that I ever heard, and his personality will appeal to any judge or jury hereabouts. I heard him first at the waterways convention here in Chicago back in 1847, when we were after President Polk's scalp for vetoing as unconstitutional the bill which Congress had passed for the improvement of rivers and the construction of harbors in our Lake Michigan."[20]

Returning to Springfield, Lincoln proceeded to clear up the accumulation of office matters before setting out on the circuit for the fall term. The summer session of the Sangamon Circuit Court, scheduled to commence July twenty-sixth, was dispensed with, which gave him more time to prepare and file pleadings in the different Springfield courts.

CHAPTER IX

The Matson Slave Case

1.

A s the year 1847 drew to a close, Lincoln, in the interval between election and taking his seat in Congress, was retained to serve as co-counsel in the "Matson Slave Case" in Coles County,[1] his involvement in which constitutes one of the oddest anomalies in the life of this man of paradox. It may safely be said that few events in Lincoln's career as a lawyer have so long remained wrapped in an impenetrable fog of mystery. The picture presented by his defense of Matson, the slaveholder, is hardly an edifying one, for all the considerations by way of justification (which some of his biographers have gone to excessive lengths to show) cannot outweigh the simple fact that he argued for a result which could only have meant sending a family of hapless Negroes back to Kentucky, there to be sold for labor on plantations in the Deep South. It is not to be wondered at that Angle, in referring to this least loudly proclaimed event of Lincoln's law career, has termed the case "one of the strangest episodes in Lincoln's career at the bar."[2] His biographers have told us little of the case, and that little, in this veritable blind spot of Lincoln literature, has not been too free from special pleading in his behalf.

In 1843, Robert Matson, an unmarried Kentuckian of aristocratic background, who had served in his state's legislature, purchased a tract of farmland in Coles County, known as Black Grove, which he worked with the aid of slaves brought from his plantation in Bourbon County, Kentucky, each spring, to be returned there after the harvest. In this manner Matson preserved their legal status as slaves, not permanently situated in the State of Illinois, and hence in no danger of acquiring the status of free men. According to Orlando B. Ficklin, one of the attorneys who opposed Lincoln in the litigation, Matson, in order to make certain that there would be no confusion on this score, "invariably" called a witness to "his solemn declaration that the slaves were here temporarily and to be returned shortly to his plantation in Bourbon."[3] There was one exception: Anthony Bryant, a former slave, who remained continuously on Black Grove, acting as overseer of the others, and who thus became, in contemplation of law, a free man.[4]

All went well with the arrangement until the spring of 1847, when Matson brought a group of slaves from Kentucky to perform the farm work for the season; among them was Bryant's wife, Jane (reputedly the daughter of Matson's brother), accompanied by her four children. Matson's "housekeeper," Mary Corbin, a white woman whom he had brought from Kentucky, becoming enraged at Jane one day, threatened to have Matson ship her and her brood off to Kentucky forthwith, to be sent from there to plantations in the far South. Jane, who was an intelligent mulatto, had apparently seen enough to convince her that Mary Corbin was living in more or less respectable sin with the master and hence was in a position to carry out her threat.[5] Panic-stricken, the husband went to the town of Oakland, where the keeper of the local inn, Gideon M. Ashmore, from (strangely enough) Tennessee, and Hiram Rutherford, a young physician born in Lancaster County, Pennsylvania, and graduated from Jefferson Medical College, Philadelphia, lent ears sympathetic to his story.[6] They instructed him to bring his wife and children to Ashmore's inn that night, which done, they proceeded to round up other antislavery men to have on hand in the event of an attempt by the planter to retake the slaves.

Ashmore and Rutherford were of that order of intrepid men who have been dealt with somewhat less than adequately by historians—antislavery sympathizers who stood ready at all times to aid Negroes in escaping to the North. Though it was a criminal offense to harbor or secrete a slave owing service to a resident of another state,[7] there was no lack of volunteers to help those who sought freedom; many leading citizens, among them lawyers, doctors and ministers, regularly braved imprisonment, heavy fines and great personal danger, in giving aid and comfort to Negro fugitives.

Not untypical was the case of Owen Lovejoy, incarnate aider and abettor of runaway slaves and brother of Elijah Lovejoy, who was foully murdered at Alton by a pro-slavery mob in 1837. Owen Lovejoy's home at Princeton, Illinois (still standing), was a station on the Underground Railway—the popular name for the route taken by runaway slaves into Canada. He was repeatedly threatened by slaveholders with physical violence. Among those who were not active participants in effecting the runaway slaves' escape to freedom, but nonetheless staunch champions of their cause, was Henry Wadsworth Longfellow, who wrote: "The fugitive slave is surrendered to his master. . . . Dirty work for a country that is so loud about freedom as ours."

When his efforts to persuade the slaves to return peaceably proved unavailing, Matson went to law. He engaged the services of Usher F. Linder, prominent Charleston attorney, who had served with Lincoln in the Legislature. A skillful lawyer and fine orator, Linder, who was an exact contemporary of Lincoln, having been born the same year, was attorney general of the state at twenty-eight. Despite this auspicious beginning, he never realized on his seeming great potentialities in the field of politics, partly because of his excessive drinking and partly because of his inability to remain rooted in one party, having shifted from the Democratic party to the Whig party and back to the Democrats. Linder, who aspired to be the Boswell of Illinois lawyers, spent his declining years writing his *Reminiscences*; they are, for the most part, inconsequential, but completely charming. Like his eighteenth-century counterpart, he loved conviviality, sharing with Herndon, Lamon, Lamborn and others of the early Illinois bar a deep appreciation for bourbon.

Linder's first move, acting under the provisions of the in-famous Black Laws,[8] was to procure a writ from the local justice of the peace, calling for the production of the Negroes, where-upon they were lodged in the Charleston jail as runaway slaves.[9] After a hearing before Justice of the Peace Gilmore, in which Ficklin, another of Lincoln's former colleagues in the Legislature, and a lawyer of the first rank, appeared for the Negroes, it was held that the court lacked jurisdiction, but since the Negroes were in Illinois without certificates of freedom, Gilmore ordered that they be turned over to the sheriff and by him kept and ad-vertised "untill discharged by A due course of law."[10]

While the slaves were confined in jail, Ashmore and Ruther-ford sued out a writ of *habeas corpus*,[11] that ancient remedy provided by law to inquire into the cause of a person's detention and, where the confinement is found to be unlawful, for his de-livery therefrom.

By the time the *habeas corpus* proceeding came on to be heard in the Circuit Court,[12] the matter had attracted widespread interest. Chief Justice Wilson of the Supreme Court, accompanied by Judge Treat, traveled from Springfield to Charleston, the county seat, to hear the case. It was not because of the importance of the litigation that Wilson presided; Supreme Court justices at this time were required to perform circuit duty, and Wilson had been assigned to the Wabash (Fourth) Circuit, which em-braced the county near the Wabash bearing the historic name of Coles (after Edward Coles, second Governor of Illinois). The presence of Judge Treat from an adjoining circuit (the Eighth) was, however, an indication of the interest which the case had generated and its importance in the eyes of the Chief Justice. According to Ficklin, Treat sat at the invitation of Wilson.[13]

With them came Lincoln, who was well known in and had been a frequent visitor to Coles County, the home of his father and stepmother, Thomas and Sarah Bush Lincoln. Here lived, also, his stepbrother John and his stepsisters, Sarah Elizabeth and Matilda, with their families. Here lived his second cousin and boyhood companion, Dennis Hanks, husband of Sarah Elizabeth. Nothwithstanding that Coles, in the east-central portion of the state, was never a part of the Eighth Circuit, Lincoln practiced there fairly frequently from 1841 (following the change which added Shelby County to the Eighth Circuit on February 23, 1841, making Shelbyville the closest county seat on that circuit to Charleston) to 1846, and occasionally thereafter until 1857. The addition to the Eighth Circuit of Moultrie County in 1843 brought another county seat, Sullivan, within easy traveling distance of Charleston.

The records disclose that Lincoln had two other cases at the fall term, 1847, of the Coles Circuit Court. In *Linder* v. *Fleenor*, a slander action in which, appearing for the defendant, he was opposed by Linder and Ficklin, the jury returned a verdict in favor of the plaintiff for $1,000.[14] Two days later Lincoln secured a plaintiff's verdict for $215 in *Watson* v. *Gill*.[15] The noteworthy fact is that the two cases were not holdovers from any previous term of court. The writer cannot put down a suspicion that, despite Lincoln's fairly numerous court appearances in Coles County from 1841 to 1846, he went to Charleston in October of 1847 solely because of the Matson case, and in anticipation of being retained in the matter. Busy in Springfield winding up matters before going on to Washington, Lincoln had passed up the fall session of the Vermilion Circuit Court, commencing October fourth, and that of the Edgar Circuit Court, commencing October eleventh. Why, then, should he have taken time out from attending to pressing matters in Springfield to go to Charleston, ninety miles away, where he had no continued cases to finish? Knowing that Lincoln (in common with Herndon and most lawyers of his day) had no qualms about injecting himself into important cases, the suspicion intrudes that he went to Charleston in order to get in on the Matson case, and for no other reason.

The confidence and esteem of his fellow practitioners is the highest compliment which can be bestowed upon a lawyer, and in Lincoln's case it was abundantly evidenced by the fact that a substantial part of his business came from attorneys in other towns, who retained him to handle matters for them in Springfield or, as in the Matson case, enlisted his services as co-counsel on their own home grounds. Linder probably approached Lincoln upon his arrival at the Union Hotel, the local inn where visiting lawyers customarily stopped,[16] and, after listening to a recital of the facts, Lincoln, in one of his less intuitive moments, accepted the assignment. In what is perhaps the most significant utterance on the slavery question, Lincoln once characterized it, in a now-famous passage, as the basic issue of whether one man should live by the sweat of another's brow. With his acceptance of the defense of Matson, Lincoln became the devil's own advocate, arraying himself on the side of the affirmative of that proposition.

Beveridge, who steeped himself in virtually (but not quite) everything written about the case, states that, after Linder had engaged his services, Rutherford importuned the Representative-elect to appear in his behalf, but that Lincoln reluctantly declined to do so, explaining that he had previously been retained by the other side. Lincoln later intimated that he would be willing to withdraw from the Matson retainer, in order to represent Rutherford, but the mischief had been done; Rutherford was so annoyed with him that he spurned the offer and proceeded to engage State Senator Charles H. Constable, an influential Whig who hailed from the eastern shore of Maryland, and a lawyer of considerable ability.[17]

No one can guess what went on in Lincoln's mind when he accepted the defense of the Kentucky planter; his motives will probably always remain open to conjecture and dispute. It may be, as Beveridge suggests, that he had misgivings about taking the case—certainly one may imagine that such a sensitive man as Lincoln had soul-searching moments of doubt, when the promptings of his heart urged him to an opposite course; yet, there is no contemporary evidence to prove it. Not given to precipitate action (witness the fact that it took him two years to get around to joining the newly formed Republican Party),[18] Lincoln might reasonably have supposed that in a case of such importance he would eventually be approached by both sides, for his services were by then widely sought after; granted that he knew Linder from their days in the Legislature, the fact remains that, according to Rutherford, he and Lincoln were also well known to each other.[19]

If Lincoln entertained any moral reservations about accepting the Matson retainer, it would seem that *at the very least* he could have held off committing himself until after Rutherford had had an opportunity to consult with him, or until he had himself communicated with Rutherford. Lincoln was never timid about taking the initiative to insure getting his share of whatever business was lying around.[20] This was considered perfectly proper and permissible at the time. Herndon, too, was forever on the prowl for new clients and new cases; never noted for his subtlety, he was not above bluntly advising one or the other of the parties that, unless retained, he and his partner would offer their services to the other side. This fact was strikingly demonstrated on the occasion (October 6, 1857) when he sought from his friend Richard Yates, an official of the Tonica & St. Petersburg Railroad, "a permanent Engagement" for the purpose of bringing actions looking to the collection of unpaid stock subscriptions; when the hoped-for retainer did not materialize, he followed up with a reminder, adding the not-so-gentle hint that he was "put up on the other side well enough to defeat you."[21] Lincoln would have worded it more adroitly; just the same, the threat worked. (It is interesting, in this connection, that both of the test cases which Herndon argued in the Supreme Court were decided against the company.)

The fat was in the fire now. In a situation charged with great emotion, the hearing on the writ of *habeas corpus* was had, as are such proceedings, before the Court without a jury. How very odd that Constable and Ficklin, appearing, respectively, for Rutherford and Ashmore, should have been pro-slavery men. Linder, Lincoln's associate,[22] who viewed the institution from the perspective of a Southern upbringing, having been born and raised in Kentucky, was the only actor in the drama who was completely in character.

The proceeding got under way on October sixteenth (a Saturday night), in the charged atmosphere of the crowded courtroom in the little county-seat town of Charleston, in central Illinois near the Indiana border. For weeks, politics and the weather had been shelved as folks talked only of the coming trial. The melancholy little courthouse, built in 1835 in the center of the village square, was the first brick house erected in Charleston; in the prevailing style of architecture, it was perfectly square, with the roof running up to a point where it met the tower, which was topped, in turn, by a cupola. Charleston was later to be the scene of the fourth of the series of Great Debates with Douglas.[23] It was to Charleston, where he went to bid goodbye to his stepmother, that Lincoln made his last trip from Springfield before leaving for Washington in 1861.

Ficklin argued that the Ordinance of 1787 and the Constitution of the State conferred freedom upon the former slaves. No novel rule was being thus asserted, Lincoln having advanced the same argument in *Bailey* v. *Cromwell* six years before; yet, strangely, neither Ficklin nor Constable referred to the case, even though it furnished authoritative support for their contention. Constable went off on a long dissertation on Anglo-Saxon concepts of freedom.

Linder's argument, which did not particularly illuminate the issue, was the somewhat pedestrian one that every citizen must be protected in the possession of his property. This, however, did not by any means exhaust the arsenal of Matson's defense. Lincoln was yet to be heard.

At this point it is essential to dismiss a myth which has become part of the consecrated folklore of the near-deification of Lincoln, one which has been paraded with all the solemn authority of a self-evident truth. For all that Beveridge suffered from a willingness to swallow whole and uncritically everything that

Herndon wrote, his two-volume work must be numbered among the indispensable studies of Lincoln's life, as well as one of the classics of American literature. Nevertheless, the distinguished writer is on untenable ground when he indicates that Lincoln, having no heart for the affair, was something less than energetic in his efforts in behalf of Matson.[24] Whatever one's reservations about the fastidiousness of conscience involved in his acceptance of the case, one may be certain that, once in it, Lincoln tried it to the hilt. Few judgments can be more shallow than the one which would have us believe that Lincoln in effect threw in his hand and simply went through the motions of a *pro forma* defense of his client. This nonsense should get short shrift, for the claim not only has no basis in known fact, but controverts everything that is known of him. It is part of the understanding of Lincoln the lawyer to realize that, for all his strange and unaccountable ways, and despite the contrarieties of his nature, he was a man of uncompromising integrity, and nothing could be more out of keeping with his character and alien to his regard for professional ethics than the thought of rendering indifferent service to a client whom he was committed to serve. If there is one indisputable fact about Lincoln's work in the courts, it is that from the moment of his retainer he played for keeps. He may not have been the best of Illinois lawyers, but he has a strong claim to be considered the most conscientious.

The whole pattern of Lincoln's career at the bar constitutes a towering rebuttal of any implication of insensibility to his sworn duty as a member of the legal profession. The most diligent scrutineer of his conduct as a lawyer will search in vain for evidence of unconcern where a client's interests were involved. In connection with his defense of persons charged with crime, the consistency (almost, one might say, the cussedness) with which, in case after case, he moved for a change of venue, attests to the fact, to which recurrent reference is made in this work, that Lincoln left no stone unturned in invoking every defense available to a client. The writer knows of no case which Lincoln handled in his arduous practice for nearly a quarter of a century at the Illinois bar, in which it could not be said of him that, once his services were enlisted, he spent himself without stint, laboring with indefatigable zeal for the interests of the client he represented. If you hired Lincoln, you got your money's worth.

More than a touch of the advocate characterizes the approach of one of the most devout apologists for Lincoln's acceptance of the Matson retainer: "Lincoln was pitiably weak. His arguments in behalf of a cause his conscience detested were spiritless, half-hearted, and devoid of his usual wit, logic and invective."[25] "Half-hearted" indeed! The same writer is later heard to register what is certainly an inconsistent, if not exactly opposite conclusion: "Loyal to his clients and faithful to his ideals, Lincoln fought for whatever cause he enlisted in, to the best of his ability."[26] We have the word of Ficklin (one could hardly ask for a more authoritative one) that Lincoln's presentation was featured by "trenchant blows and cold logic and subtle knitting together and presentation of facts favorable to his side of the case. . . . The fact that General Matson had at such a time when he placed a slave on his Illinois farm, publicly declared that he was not placed there for permanent settlement, and that no counter statement had ever been made publicly or privately by him, constituted the web and woof of the argument of Mr. Lincoln, and these facts were plausibly, ingeniously and forcibly presented to the court, so as to give them all the effect and significance to which they were entitled and more."[27] It is a fact, for whatever it is worth, that most writers who have discussed the case have been inhibited from mentioning the article in which Ficklin's appraisement of Lincoln's argument appeared.[28]

Ficklin tells us that the main thrust of Lincoln's contention went to the fact that the Bryant woman came to Illinois as part of a group of *seasonal* workers, who were to be returned to Kentucky after harvesting of the crops, in accordance with their master's annual custom, and that therefore she and her children never, at any time, acquired the status of permanent residents. One does not have to be a lawyer to recognize that there was legal force in Lincoln's contention; moreover, it was the only sensible argument which he could have advanced. Certainly, from the facts before the Court, the only rational conclusion that could be drawn was that the slaves were not domiciled, were not "meant to remain permanently" in the State of Illinois;[29] only by stretching definition past its elastic limits could any other finding have been arrived at. Lincoln's argument was predicated on good sense and good law. He was in there pitching, and the fact that the decision went against his client does not detract one whit from the force of his argument.

Like every active trial lawyer, Lincoln may have had his bad days, but this was decidedly not one of them. No person wise in the ways of lawyers will criticize him for seizing upon the one tenable point in Matson's favor, and laboring it, to the exclusion of everything else. Lincoln, as usual, knew what he was doing; far from having given a lackluster performance, he displayed legal generalship of a high order. Just as he was later to prove a great natural strategist as director of the war effort, a better one, it has been said, than any of his generals, including Grant,[30] so in the trial of a case he was a superb tactician.

Indeed, of the four counsel appearing in the case, Lincoln would certainly seem to have presented the most cogent and convincing argument. Linder's was neither edifying nor particularly helpful to the court or his client; while Ficklin and Constable missed the boat, inexcusably, by failing to cite *Bailey* v. *Cromwell*, the very authority which lent to their contention the sanction of established precedent. Theirs, it would seem, was a performance of astounding ineptitude. How very devastating it would have been to confront Lincoln with the argument, advanced by him so forcibly in that case, that the slave girl, Nance, had been made free when her master took her into the State of Illinois, where slavery was forbidden!

Examination of the *Beveridge Papers* discloses that his evaluation of Lincoln's work on the Matson case is somewhat of a piece with the importance, or, rather, lack of it which he attached to Lincoln's legal career. Something of his attitude may be gleaned from a revealing letter which he wrote to Henry M. Bates, Dean of the Law School of the University of Michigan, on January 9, 1926, in which he observed that all of Lincoln's "law cases, little and big, put together do not, on their merits, deserve a line in history and not more than a paragraph in any biography, . . ."[31] Beveridge's uneven, almost haphazard, treatment of Lincoln the lawyer is reflected in the fact that almost all of his material in connection with Lincoln's circuit activities deals with his work after his return from Congress, whereas he was on the circuit just as much, if not more, before that time as after it. One finds no persuasive reason to disagree with the view of John M. Zane, one of the leaders of the Illinois bar and an authority on the subject of "Lincoln the Constitutional Lawyer," who wrote in 1932 that "Beveridge does not seem in the slightest degree to understand Lincoln's legal power, . . ."[32]

The attempt to gloss over Lincoln's acceptance of the case by having it appear that he was halfhearted in protecting the interests of a slaveholder, even though his own client, is pure hogwash—another instance of the fantastic lengths to which some authors have gone to render immune from any slight dispraise the name of Abraham Lincoln. Abounding in the field of Lincoln literature, as in the case of no other historical figure, are the myths so assiduously propagated by the Lincoln sanctifiers, who regard as almost indecent anything short of adulation of one whom they would present as a candidate for sainthood.

2.

The Bench was comprised of two men well known for the comprehensiveness with which they grasped the controlling facts of a case or features of an argument, and (fortunately for the Bryants) the ability to see that substantial justice was meted out. Samuel Hubbel Treat, his mind unsullied by formal education, but with a superior native intelligence, had studied law in the office of a lawyer in the county seat of his native Otsego County, New York. In 1834, at the age of twenty-three, he came to Springfield and entered upon the practice of his profession; in 1840 Governor Carlin appointed him to fill a vacancy on the circuit bench. He was one of the five judges chosen by the legislature in 1841, when the membership of the Supreme Court was increased to nine justices.

To Treat is due the credit (or discredit) for having introduced Lincoln to the bewhiskered chestnuts to be found in *Joe Miller's Jest Book* (originally published in 1739 in London). "The Judge loaned Mr. Lincoln the book," a clerk in Treat's court recalled, "and afterwards the Judge charged Mr. Lincoln with drawing on this book for some of his anecdotes. Mr. Lincoln's only reply was that he had the right to use a good story wherever he found one."[33]

William Wilson was elected chief justice of the Supreme Court in 1825, when he was barely twenty-nine years of age, and held that office until 1848. Though, like Treat, a man of little education, he was rich in human resources. Prior to his election as Chief Justice, he had been an Associate Justice of the Court since the adoption of the first Constitution in 1818. In thirty years on the Supreme Court, during the formative period of the state's juridical processes, Wilson sat in judgment on many important issues that arose out of that eventful era.

Distilled to its essence, the judgment of the Court was that the slaves should "be and remain free and discharged from all servitude whatever to any person or persons from henceforth and forever."[34] The basis of the decision is wholly uncertain; from all that appears, Wilson and Treat did not see fit to rationalize their finding by reference to *Bailey* v. *Cromwell*, and so it is that one is moved to wonder what imponderable part public policy, rather than the compulsion of *stare decisis*, may have played in the outcome.

3.

Legend has it that Matson lit out for Kentucky immediately upon learning the verdict, and never did square his account with Lincoln.[35] Ashmore went on a barnstorming tour with the freed Negroes, in order to raise funds with which to send them to Liberia, collecting money at Springfield, Jacksonville and other stops. It is not at all surprising that one of the contributors, back in Springfield, should have been Herndon,[36] who must have blinked in dismayed unbelief upon learning of his partner's participation on behalf of the slaveholder; it takes no great effort of the imagination to picture him revelling in the reflection that there was something akin to poetic justice in the fact that Lincoln had been cheated out of his fee.

Though Herndon, in the summer of 1865, visited east-central Illinois in quest of material for a life of his former law partner, and accumulated a rich store of information in Charleston, there is a curious omission of any mention of the Matson litigation. Nor is there any evidence that Lincoln, who had a way of keeping his own secrets, particularly those secrets that were contained in emotional conflicts that lay beneath the surface, ever left any written word concerning it. While he was probably just as pleased to dismiss the whole business from his mind, Lincoln was always, in fact, somewhat reticent about divulging details of his work as a practicing lawyer. Apart, of course, from pleadings and other legal documents, and incidental correspondence, Lincoln wrote practically nothing which might have assisted biographers in arriving at a satisfactory *critique* of the one interest from which he earned the living that supported Mary and their sons and which, time-wise, occupied the greater part of his adult life.

An unhappy aftermath of the case remains to be recorded. With funds raised in Illinois and Missouri, the Bryant family (Anthony, his wife and the four children) was given passage to Liberia. Elder S. S. Ball, of Springfield, an investigator for the Colored Baptist Association of Illinois, saw them at Monrovia,

Liberia, in the spring of 1848. He reported that they were without funds and living "truly in a deplorable condition." Anthony requested of Ball that money be provided for their return to the United States. The money was not forthcoming.[37] On this melancholy note ends the tale of the Matson slaves.

4.

As to Lincoln's reason for accepting the case, which comes close to being the most profound mystery ever to confound Lincoln specialists, one can but observe that the inscrutability of this "extremely uneven man"[38] has long been legendary. Never has a President possessed a more complicated personal character. The "apparent reluctance"[39] with which he informed the other side that he had already been retained by Matson, followed by his vigorous defense of the latter, affords a particularly apposite example of that paralysis of doubt in making decisions which has so frequently been imputed to him, and his fortitude in acting on them once they were made. One has the feeling that his ultimate judgments were perhaps the more real for the initial hesitancy that had to be overcome.

In Lincoln's defense, it is only fair to note that the practice of law is, in a sense, a cruel calling, entailing as it does a certain essential duplicity. Most individuals have an inherent or emotional bias which predisposes them in favor of one side or the other; yet lawyers, their talents for hire, are constrained to repress their own sometimes deep-seated convictions and become, at times, articulate advocates of ideas and clients abhorrent to their own inner feelings. Realistically speaking, it would be hard to find, this side of Heaven, the degree of self-immolation which a refusal of a retainer under such circumstances calls for; the harsh facts of life at the bar simply do not jibe with the precept of complete objectivity. Having said that much, one is compelled to add that even after large allowance has been made for the undoubted right of every lawyer to represent persons suspected of crime or political unorthodoxy, or anyone else whose cause is unpopular, the nagging thought remains that Lincoln chose to represent the master against the slaves in a case where he might, if he wished, have been aligned on the other side, simply by putting Linder off and waiting for Rutherford to get in touch with him, an event which he might reasonably have anticipated. A lawyer, like a lady, must learn the art of saying no.

In the process of "softening" anything which might in any way reflect upon Lincoln, effort has been made to explain away his acceptance of the case on the ground of his firm belief in the enforcement of the law "and the obedient acceptance of every law until in response to public opinion it was changed."[40] This apologia, which is in line with the stained-glass concept of Lincoln, entails a considerable assumption, and is the more remarkable in view of his subsequent dealings with wartime problems, in particular his suspension of the writ of *habeas corpus*,[41] where Lincoln was certainly not wedded to the correctitudes of law observance. Evidence is not wanting that during the war years constitutional impropriety held no terrors for him. Among numerous instances where Lincoln, anxious to get on with the war, stretched the Constitution past the breaking point, was the occasion when the Sixth Massachusetts Infantry, marching across Baltimore en route to Washington, became embroiled in a street fight with a secessionist mob.[42] Lincoln acted swiftly and in an extremely highhanded manner, and with none too much reverence for constitutional limitations. The Mayor of Baltimore and nineteen members of the State Legislature were promptly clapped in jail. When the Chief Justice of the United States Supreme Court issued a writ of *habeas corpus*, Lincoln ignored it. He sent troops into Baltimore, placing the ruthless Ben Butler— "Butler the Beast"—in command. "There were irregularities under Lincoln," wrote Professor Randall, "which have not become sound precedents, procedures which have not set the pattern for later executives."[43] The plain fact is that Lincoln flouted the Constitution; he flouted the Supreme Court; he countenanced the disregard of legal amenities and the invasion of due process of law—at times indefensibly, even on the ground of the exigency of a great national emergency.

In October, 1847, Lincoln had yet to witness the disgraceful spectacle of slaves shuffling through the streets of Washington, bound together by chains, and it was not until his Peoria speech of 1854 that he publicly commented on this, recalling the domestic slave trade carried on in the nation's capital, "where droves of negroes were collected, temporarily kept, and finally taken to Southern markets, precisely like droves of horses." Probably Benjamin P. Thomas, never one to indulge in rubber-stamp conclusions, came closest to the truth when he observed that in 1847 "the slavery issue had not yet seared itself into his conscience to the point of inducing him to place the plight of a few hapless Negroes above the abstract legal aspects of the slavery question."[44]

To attempt to depict Lincoln as one possessed of a lifelong abhorrence of involuntary servitude is to falsify the record. A number of tales in this area have been somewhat toned down by present-day Lincoln scholarship, which questions, for instance, whether Lincoln, seeing the slave auction in New Orleans, said what John Hanks, who wasn't present, said he said. Lincoln's eventual policy touching slavery was a matter of slow development. It was to take him several years of intellectual solitude, during which his mind turned inward on the question, to put his thoughts in order and think his way through to his settled attitude toward the wrong of slavery in a free society. Even then he would have been willing, as he told Horace Greeley, to let the South keep its slaves in order to preserve the Union. That he abolished slavery and saved the Union is a measure of his greatness.

Granted that his own personal feelings were not yet deeply engaged, there is something mystifying in the fact that Lincoln, a politician with an attentive ear to public opinion, should have taken a case his identification with which, he must have known, would make him appear so strangely out of harmony with the mood of the times in his own part of the state. Though the great majority favored a less extreme manner of solving the problem than did the Abolitionists, the climate of thought in central Illinois was becoming increasingly hostile to slavery, most persons feeling that it was morally, socially and economically wrong.

Whatever the inmost feelings of this enigmatic and infinitely complex man, one cannot but suppose that—for one who believed in the rights of all men, and yet enlisted three times in the Black Hawk War (later recalling that Black Hawk "only fought after his flags of truce had been fired upon"); who chose the Whig party, the party of the gentry and the well-born; and who, for all his commemoration of the sacrifice of the Gettysburg dead, kept his son Robert in a safe berth in order to save the unstable mind of Mrs. Lincoln—taking the Matson case may have presented no incongruity. Perhaps no man is ever really consistent.

5.

Probably the last legal matter which Lincoln personally handled before leaving Springfield was the extradition proceeding instituted by the executive authority of the State of New York seeking the rendition to that state of Joseph Thornton, Andrew Pringle, Samuel Stead and John Davidson. Lincoln had been retained by the relators' (supposed fugitives') attorneys, Bucker S. Morris and John J. Brown, of Chicago. In a letter to them dated October 19, 1847, six days prior to his departure for Washington, Lincoln wrote that he would "try . . . to have the only objection that can be made, presented to the Governor. I suppose it is the true construction of the act of Congress, for the Governor, on whom the requisition is made, to look to the sufficiency of the affidavit; otherwise the provision of the act, that a copy of the indictment or affidavit, shall accompany the requisition, is mere foolishness."[45] Lincoln's conception of the law of interstate rendition was well founded, and the Governor of Illinois declined, upon the grounds urged by Lincoln (the insufficiency of the affidavit from the demanding state), to issue a warrant for the apprehension and return of the men.

6.

With his departure for Washington, a chapter in the law career of Abraham Lincoln came to an end. He had much to look back upon, and so, as he prepared to make his entry upon the national scene, he may have paused to take stock of himself. The Lincoln of 1847 had come a considerable distance since the days of the fledgling lawyer who left New Salem ten years before, to seek his fortune in the newly designated state capital of Springfield. Ten years at the bar had had a profound influence in shaping the already maturing, if not yet fully realized Lincoln. Since the Anderson-case fiasco he had acquired mental discipline and balance; he was calm and self-possessed, with a disposition to deliberation best expressed in his own aphorism: "Nothing valuable can be lost by taking time."[46] His success as a lawyer was in a fair way of being established; he had made his mark at the Sangamon bar, as well as in the circuit courts of central Illinois, a section of the state that boasted many competent attorneys. Notwithstanding his almost-continuous political activity, Lincoln had appeared, during the preceding decade, in many of the important causes heard in Springfield and on the circuit. The cases covered virtually every conceivable subject of litigation at that time, and comprised a vast panorama of human problems.

Though years of intensive circuit practice were still ahead of him, he had had more than a taste of it, and already knew what it was to appear almost daily before juries. He knew, too, what it was to plead before an appellate court, braving the sometimes withering barrage of questions from the Bench. Close contact with men of the high caliber of Stuart, Logan, Douglas, Bledsoe, Linder, Browning, Treat, Wilson, David Davis and a few others of that Olympian roster—which, in retrospect, seems to constitute the golden age of Illinois advocacy—was also a factor in bringing about the growth and development which marked the Lincoln of 1847 and made him a lawyer to be reckoned with. He was no accident; he constantly grew.

Before leaving Springfield, Lincoln wrote out a lease, in duplicate, renting his home to Cornelius Ludlum, a brick contractor of nearby Jacksonville, for one year, commencing November first, at a rental of ninety dollars for the year, payable "in quarter yearly payments, [the lessee] to be especially careful to prevent any destruction by fire. . . ."[47] For most of the period that he was away, however, the house was occupied by Mason Brayman, a young Springfield lawyer who, though a political opposite, became Lincoln's close personal friend. Shortly after the Illinois Central Railroad received its charter, Brayman became the road's general solicitor, and was responsible for Lincoln's representation of the road in connection with important questions arising upon the construction of the company's charter, including the well-known McLean County tax case, as well as the question of the right of common carriers to limit their liability for damages.

The house rented, and final instructions given Herndon concerning the completion of pending matters, Lincoln and the family set out for Washington—Washington and an experience which all but ruined his political career.

CHAPTER X

In Congress and Before the United States Supreme Court

1.

E N ROUTE to Washington, the Lincolns visited the aristocratic Todd relatives in Lexington, where they stayed for three weeks. Arrived at the center of the national political arena on December 2, 1847, Mary and Abe, and their sons Robert and Eddie, took up temporary residence at the marble-fronted Brown's Hotel (later known as the Metropolitan), on unpaved Pennsylvania Avenue. Several days later they moved into the more moderately priced and congenial quarters of Mrs. Ann Sprigg's boardinghouse, located on Capitol Hill, on the present site of the Library of Congress (the old building, across from the Annex).

The only street lighted in Washington in the year 1848 was the section of Pennsylvania Avenue between the Capitol and the White House. The oil lamps in use were lighted only during the time Congress was in session. Though the sprawling, dusty city boasted a population of about 40,000, there were no police during the day, and a night force of but fifteen men.[1] Withal, it was an entirely new and vastly different *milieu* into which the relatively obscure Springfield lawyer was thrust. Cabinet members, ambassadors and attachés of the different foreign governments, business leaders and socialites entertained on a grand scale. As a teetotaler, a prairie lawyer from Illinois who loved simple things, Lincoln avoided most of the functions of the Washington social whirl, the superficiality and vapidity of which probably bored him. For

WITH MALICE TOWARD NONE

PRESENTED TO THE STATE OF ILLINOIS

This nine-foot statue by Avard Fairbanks, near the entrance to the restored New Salem village, depicts Lincoln as he is about to leave to take up his law career in Springfield. It shows him laying aside the frontiersman's axe and holding in his right hand a large book intended to represent a copy of *Blackstone's Commentaries*.

Statue "Lincoln the Circuit Rider," in Lincoln Monument, Oak Ridge Cemetery, Springfield.

Sangamon County Courthouse (former State House), in Springfield, where Lincoln made numerous appearances before the Illinois Supreme Court. Here, in the spring of 1858, Lincoln delivered his "House Divided" speech, and here, in 1865, his body lay in state.

Tazewell County Courthouse, in Pekin, where Lincoln appeared frequently until 1857, when Tazewell was removed from the Eighth Circuit.

The question with-
in propounded
is one which I
could not an-
swer without
liability to mis-
understanding,
and, as I fear,
doing harm

A. Lincoln

Memorandum in Lincoln's hand. Original in The Lincoln National Life Foundation, Fort Wayne, Indiana.

Trail Marker on the Old Eighth Judicial Circuit.

Printed summons filled in by Lincoln and signed by Bowling Green as Justice of the Peace in New Salem, in May, 1833. This is one of the first legal documents known to have been drawn by Lincoln. Original in possession of James T. Hickey, Elkhart, Illinois.

Reverse side of summons. The top six lines are in Lincoln's hand.

John Todd Stuart, Lincoln's first law partner (1837-1841) and a cousin of Mary Todd. The aristocratic Stuart served with Lincoln in the Black Hawk War, where he met and took a liking to the rough-hewn youth from New Salem.

Stephen T. Logan, Lincoln's second law partner (1841-1844), and one of the best jury lawyers in the State of Illinois. He served as judge of the First (later Eighth) Judicial Circuit from January, 1835, to March, 1837.

William H. Herndon, nine years Lincoln's junior, was the third and last of his law partners (1844-1861). The partnership continued nominally until Lincoln's death, the latter telling Herndon, "Give our clients to understand that the election of a President makes no change in the firm of Lincoln & Herndon."

Woodford County Courthouse, in Metamora, where Lincoln tried the Melissa Goings Murder Case in 1857. The building is preserved as a state memorial.

McLean County Courthouse, in Bloomington, where, for a week in 1857, Lincoln and Leonard Swett were opposed in the trial of the Wyant Murder Case.

Judge of the Eighth Judicial Circuit from 1848 to 1862, when he was appointed by Lincoln to a vacancy on the bench of the United States Supreme Court, David Davis was one of Lincoln's closest friends and played a leading part in securing his nomination to the presidency in 1860. He was administrator of the Lincoln estate.

Ward Hill Lamon was associated with Lincoln in practice in Danville from 1852 to 1856. As President, Lincoln appointed him Marshal of the District of Columbia.

Exterior view of the first Logan County Courthouse, in Postville, in which Lincoln practiced until removal of the county seat in 1848. The building, which is still intact, is included in the collection of The Henry Ford Museum and Greenfield Village, Dearborn, Michigan.

Courtroom in which Lincoln tried cases in Postville Courthouse. Courtesy of The Henry Ford Museum, Dearborn, Michigan.

Second Logan County Courthouse, in Mt. Pulaski. Furnished as it was in Lincoln's time, the building is preserved as a state memorial.

DeWitt County Courthouse, in Clinton, where Lincoln and Stephen A. Douglas appeared as co-counsel in the county's first murder trial (1840).

Leonard Swett, who bore a strong physical resemblance to Lincoln, was both opposed to and associated with the latter in the trial of cases on the Eighth Judicial Circuit.

Orville Hickman Browning, one of Lincoln's contemporaries at the Illinois bar, was a lawyer of distinction. He was appointed by Governor Yates to fill the unexpired term in the United States Senate caused by the death of Stephen A. Douglas in 1861.

Albert Taylor Bledsoe, a graduate of West Point and an ordained minister of the Episcopal Church, practiced law in Springfield from 1839 to 1847. He occupied, at one time, an office adjoining that of Lincoln. During the war he served as Assistant Secretary of War in Jefferson Davis's Cabinet.

Stephen A. Douglas, as special prosecutor, opposed Lincoln in the Truett Murder Case in Sangamon County in 1838, and was associated with him, for the defense, in the Spencer Turner Murder Case in DeWitt County in 1840. Lincoln and the "Little Giant" later (1858) opposed each other in the most famous debate in American history.

Piatt County Courthouse, Monticello, erected in 1843 and destroyed by fire in 1856.

Champaign County Courthouse, Urbana, where Lincoln practiced extensively.

the most part, he divided his spare time between listening to the concerts given twice a week on the White House lawn, and reading, either in his room or in the Library of the United States Supreme Court. According to the librarian, he frequently borrowed books from the library to take to his room.[2]

On December fifth we find Lincoln writing Herndon concerning an item of unfinished business which he had neglected to take up with him before leaving Springfield. The letter sheds revealing light on the slipshod manner in which the firm records were kept. The year before, "a man by the name of Wilson" had paid the firm twenty dollars as an advance fee, and left ten dollars with Lincoln to pay for certain abstracts. Lincoln had forgotten to leave the ten dollars with Herndon and, upon reminding himself of it, sent the money to him "so that the case may go on this winter; . . ."[3]

Also, there was the matter of certain fees which remained outstanding; when Herndon advised him that he had succeeded in collecting one of them, Lincoln replied: "Your letter, advising me of the receipt of our fee in the bank case, is just received, and I don't expect to hear another as good a piece of news from Springfield while I am away."[4] The money did not come amiss, as Lincoln had several small bills outstanding in Springfield, which he directed his partner to pay with his portion of the fee.

The first session of the Thirtieth Congress had scarcely gotten under way when the freshman Representative, who occupied a back-row seat on the Whig side of the House, took his political life in his hands by plunging headlong into the mounting controversy over the war in Mexico. Early in 1845, Texas was annexed by joint Congressional resolution; the following year Polk ordered American troops under Zachary Taylor to advance through territory claimed by Mexico, to the Rio Gande. Negotiations for the purchase of the northern provinces of that country having collapsed, American and Mexican troops clashed on April 24, 1846.

Except for parts of New England, where the war was viewed

as a plot to extend slavery, a spirit of rampant imperialism soon was abroad in the land, as Americans, now become jingoistic in their thinking, thrilled to the prospect of adding a new empire to the Republic. "It is for the interest of mankind," wrote Walt Whitman, then editor of the Brooklyn *Eagle*, "that its [America's] power and territory should be extended—the farther the better."[5] Especially in the midlands, where the nation first outgrew its colonial status, did men entertain the hope that, in the magnetic phrase coined in 1845, "manifest destiny" would be fulfilled.

As a good party man, Lincoln was committed to the Whig policy of opposing the conflict, even though this meant flying in the face of public sentiment back in Illinois, where most people believed the war to be just and necessary. On December twenty-second, a never-to-be-forgotten date in the chronicle of Lincoln's involvement in this explosive issue, the Representative from the Seventh Illinois District risked his political neck by presenting a series of shrewdly worded resolutions calling upon the President to advise the House whether the "spot" on which American blood was first shed was not within the territorial limits of Mexico. Three weeks later (January 12, 1848), in a speech of great force, which was widely published in central Illinois and widely damned, he defended his "spot resolutions," and challenged Polk to answer his charges. The President disdained to reply.

It cannot be said that, aside from his unpopular stand on the war, Lincoln played a conspicuous role in the deliberations of the House; as a first-term man his opportunities for distinguishing himself were decidedly limited. He served on the Committee of the Post Office and Post Roads and the Committee on Expenditures in the War Department, and was conscientious in the performance of his tasks as a committeeman. He cheerfully complied with the endless demands of an insatiable constituency, running errands for passports, land-grant pensions, patents and postmasterships. The *Robert Todd Lincoln Collection*, for the period of Lincoln's service in Congress, discloses a voluminous stream of communications from importunate office seekers. Herndon thus sums up the nature and extent of his service: "He attended to the duties of the Congressional office diligently and with becoming modesty. He answered the letters of his constituents, sent them their public documents, and looked after their pension claims."[6]

2.

Though the second session concluded on March 4, 1849, Lincoln lingered in Washington for almost three weeks after Taylor's inauguration, during which time he argued the first of the two cases in which his name appears in the reports of the United States Supreme Court. On March seventh, Lincoln was admitted to practice before that august tribunal. Admitted at the same term of court were other notable persons, among them Hannibal Hamlin, then a United States Senator from Maine, later to be Lincoln's running mate on the 1860 ticket; Albert Pike, famous lawyer and explorer of the Southwest; Joseph P. Bradley, known to history for his vote on the Electoral Commission of 1877 which elected Hayes to the Presidency over Tilden; and Judah P. Benjamin, who later served as Attorney General and Secretary of War in the Confederate cabinet of Jefferson Davis.

That same day, appearing before the nine justices seated in high-backed chairs, just beyond the railing, and nearly on a level with the floor in the Court's modest quarters immediately beneath the Senate chamber, Lincoln, in his thin, high voice and Kentucky accent, opened his oral argument in the case of *William Lewis, for use of Nicholas Longworth v. Thomas Lewis, administrator of Moses Broadwell*.[7] The action, which posed a complicated legal problem (too involved to be detailed here) concerning the question of the Illinois statute of limitations, as applied to nonresidents, originated in the United States Circuit Court for the District of Illinois, where a verdict had been rendered in favor of the plaintiff. Upon the appeal, Lincoln represented the defendant-appellant. Although there is no record of

Lincoln having tried the case in the court below, it is quite possible that he may have done so, and the file and docket book been consumed by the flames of the Chicago fire of 1871, the records of the United States Circuit Court for the Illinois District having been removed there in 1856, upon the splitting up of the district into a northern and southern division.

In Lincoln's day a lawyer could appeal his client's cause to the highest court in the land almost as a matter of course, no matter how picayune the claim or devoid of public interest.[8] This is not to say, however, that the case of *Lewis* v. *Lewis* was unimportant, either from the standpoint of the subject matter of the litigation or the question of law involved. In the early days of the Republic, when large areas of procedural and substantive law remained uncharted, cases which today might be held to involve no question of wide public or governmental interest were the necessary and proper subject of review by the nation's court of last resort.

It is a singular piece of good fortune that, among the great mass of letters, manuscripts, documents and other papers left by Lincoln, and now preserved in the nation's archives, are to be found the outline notes, written in his own hand, for use as a guide in his oral argument before the Court. These notes, long the property of Robert, were turned over, after his death, to John Flannery, a Washington lawyer. On June 29, 1948, Flannery strengthened the resources of the nation's primary Lincoln source material by presenting the original manuscript summary to the then Chief Justice Fred M. Vinson of the Supreme Court, to be placed in "some safe and suitable repository" as part of its archives. The following day the yellowing Lincoln manuscript was put in a display case in the foyer adjoining the main reading room of the Court's library, where it still attracts the attention of many thousands of visitors annually.

It is a fact well known to lawyers that, while advocacy before appellate courts, with its relative absence of rhetoric, seldom if ever earns for an attorney the plaudits of the crowd, it does test his mettle as a lawyer as no other phase of practice does. These notes show Lincoln—the "mast-fed lawyer," as he called himself —to be the possessor of a clear legal mind, with the power of documentation and analytical reasoning which is the mark of the true appellate advocate.

Heading the notes is a "History of the case, and the statutes bearing on it—," which shows at a glance the sequence of relevant events. There follows a brief analysis of the pleadings, after which the divergent opinions of the members of the court below are summarized. Lincoln's faculty for putting his finger on the nub of the question appears in his concise statement of the issue: "Did the Legislature intend it [the statute involved] to be retrospective? and, if so . . . Had they constitutional power to do so?" Even though not on all fours with the case at bar ("the exact point is not in any of them"), Lincoln proposes to show the applicability, in principle, of precedents closely analagous. Among those listed are cases from the appellate courts of Massachusetts, New York, Connecticut, Illinois and Vermont, as well as one from the United States Supreme Court. In addition, we find two references to *Angell on Limitations*. In his comprehensive examination of the law, Lincoln covered what was, for those early days of our jurisprudence, a wide range of authorities. If the notes are at all reflective of the substance of the points relied upon in the oral argument, it is fair to surmise that Lincoln, pursuing the tack indicated, made out a reasoned case for his client.

The Bench before which Lincoln appeared was headed by a brilliant lawyer, one of the truly monumental occupants of that office, in the person of Roger Brooke Taney, of Maryland (and of subsequent Dred Scott disrepute), who in 1836 had been appointed Chief Justice by Andrew Jackson. Of the other members,[9] only John McLean of Ohio, possessed of an insatiable ambition to become President,[10] stood out. (Like Taney, his name is immediately associated with the Dred Scott decision [1857], in which he wrote a sharp dissent.)

After hearing oral argument, the majority of the Court,

speaking through the Chief Justice, rendered its decision on the thirteenth, holding against Lincoln's client. McLean, a frequent if not chronic dissenter, noted his disagreement with the views of his colleagues, pointing out that the position of the majority represented a shift in judicial interpretation from the rule enunciated in *Ross, et al.* v. *Duval*,[11] in which he had written the Court's opinion ten years before. Even in the early days of its existence, the Court apparently experienced no difficulty in upsetting the rule of *stare decisis*.

3.

It has often been erroneously asserted that *Lewis* v. *Lewis* was Lincoln's "only case before the Supreme Court of the United States." It is, rather, the only one which he *argued* before that Court, for his name appears in the reports in connection with one other case—*Forsyth* v. *Reynolds*,[12] decided at the December term, 1853. The report of the case shows that "The cause was argued by Mr. Williams for the appellant. Briefs were filed by Mr. Lincoln and Mr. Gamble. Mr. Chase argued the case for the appellee and a brief was also filed by Mr. Purple." (The latter is readily identifiable as Norman H. Purple, of Peoria, by way of New York, an associate of Lincoln on the judicial circuit and one of the outstanding personages of early Illinois legal history.)

The reasonable limits of this work preclude a detailed discussion of the circumstances leading up to the litigation. Suffice it to say that by two acts, passed in 1820 and 1823, Congress granted a lot in the village of Peoria to each settler who had not "heretofore received a confirmation of claim or donation of any tract of land or village lot from the United States." The claimants' assertion of title to a tract of land in Peoria, granted under these acts of Congress, was contested on the ground that they had been the recipients of land grants in Michigan prior to the surrender of the Western posts by the British Government.

The case came to the Supreme Court from the United States

Circuit Court for the District of Illinois, sitting as a court of equity. This time Lincoln, representing the claimants, had the satisfaction of having his contention adopted—and by a unanimous bench. The Court's conclusion, written by Justice John Catron, of Tennessee, was that lands granted to settlers in Michigan before the surrender of the Western posts by the British, which grants were made to carry out Jay's treaty in 1794, were not "donations" so as to exclude a settler in Peoria from partaking of the benefit of the two acts of Congress.

Search among public archives (including, of course, the Supreme Court), as well as among numerous other sources— probable and improbable—has brought to light no trace of the appellants' brief which, according to the published report of the case, Lincoln submitted. And, not having argued the appeal, there were no notes for argument, as in *Lewis*.

While, therefore, little evidence survives of Lincoln's work in connection with the two cases in which his name appears in the Supreme Court, there is enough, in the *Lewis* notes for argument, to show him as the same painstakingly thorough lawyer we know him to have been in connection with his appellate work before the Illinois Supreme Court. One may fairly surmise that the clarity of thought, the organization of material and searching analysis which he displayed before the State's highest court, where his trained legal mind enabled him to state the facts clearly, to leave nothing out and to add nothing extraneous, were present in the Supreme Court of the United States.

4.

It was not long before Lincoln came to know his way about the Patent Office.[13] Several months after assuming his Congressional duties, he looked into a matter, involving the transfer of a patent on an "improved iron pump," for Benjamin Kellogg, Jr., an attorney of Pekin;[14] later, he forwarded to Amos Williams, resident of Danville and clerk of the Circuit Court of Vermilion

County, a "document of 'Information &c.'" outlining the procedure to be followed in obtaining a patent on Williams' invention, together with a request for twenty dollars filing fee.[15]

Despite the lack of success of his own venture into the field
of mechanical innovation (a device for buoying vessels over
shoals), a fair case might be made out for Lincoln as a frustrated
inventor, whose career was sidetracked by the demands of an
ever-jealous mistress—the law. Lincoln always displayed a considerable curiosity and informed judgment concerning the scientific and intricate problems of this branch of jurisprudence, which
proved of great help in connection with that phase of his practice.
Patent litigation invariably excited his lively interest. One of the
more curious of his cases involving scientific inventions was the
"horological cradle case," having to do with a patent on a cradle
which, when wound up, would supposedly rock itself until run
down. Another was the "tombstone case," so-called,[16] in which
the practicability of a tombstone made of cast iron was called into
question.

Charles S. Zane, once a member of the firm of Herndon &
Zane, successors to the firm of Lincoln & Herndon,[17] and one of
the dwindling few, after the turn of the century, who remembered Lincoln in the courts, recalled some incidents illustrative of
the latter's curiosity about such matters and his grasp of the
mechanical processes involved: "After Mr. Lincoln had left the
office, I started to the post-office. When I reached the street I saw
Mr. Lincoln a short distance ahead, going in the same direction.
Something seemed to attract his attention; he stopped and walked
out to a self-raking reaping machine on exhibition. It was then
[1856] a new invention, and quite intricate in its construction. I
had caught up with him and stopped to listen. It was the first
self-raker that he had seen. He examined it with much interest,
and then I listened to him explaining, in the fewest words but
with great clearness, how power and motion were communicated
to the different appliances, especially to the sickle, the revolving
rake, and the reel. His faculty for comprehending and under-

standing machinery I afterward saw exemplified when I heard him argue a patent case in the United States Court at Springfield. A number of models representing different machines had been introduced in evidence and they were upon the floor before the jury. During his argument, to get a better view of the different parts of the invention, he knelt down, and several of the jurors for the same purpose came to where he was and also got upon their knees."[18]

Lincoln's bent for gadgets was understandable. His father was a competent carpenter and cabinetmaker, and as a boy Lincoln helped him in this work. There are letters and accounts of lawyers who rode the judicial circuit with him that tell of his habit of pausing to inspect and draw his own shrewd judgment on any new piece of farm machinery he happened to come across. He was even known to have delivered a lecture in 1859, at the Congregational Church in Jacksonville, on the subject of "Discoveries and Inventions."[19]

His consuming interest in the subject was later to prove of great service to the nation. Countless communications were received at the White House from inventors, promoters and cranks with sure-fire devices for destroying the Confederate armies. Lincoln studied many of them carefully, and in a number of instances personally supervised the testing of new weapons in back of the White House. But for Lincoln's insistence, John Ericcson's *Monitor*, the ironclad which defeated the *Merrimack*, would never have been built. On the whole, his judgment regarding the technology of warfare was sound, even though there were occasions when his support was enlisted on behalf of contrivances backed by crooked politicians.

5.

As his term in Congress drew to a close, Lincoln began to give some thought to planning for the future. The "spot resolutions," as they came to be known, had gotten him into hot water with the folks back home, who considered them unpatriotic. As Herndon and his friends in Illinois viewed the situation, Lincoln had so offended his constituency that his political career was at an end. Albert T. Bledsoe, Lincoln's one-time friend and political associate, observed that Lincoln, after his one term in Congress, was "in such low repute among his neighbors, and with his former political friends, that he could not have been elected a constable or a justice of the peace."[20] (Bledsoe's statement must be discounted somewhat. Since he was by then bitterly antagonistic to Lincoln, it seems possible that he may have been moved by a desire to discredit him. Furthermore, Bledsoe had left Springfield several years before Lincoln's return from Congress.) The reaction of the voters to his stand on the war, as interpreted in the stunning defeat of Stephen T. Logan, Whig candidate to succeed Lincoln in Congress, in a district ordinarily impregnably Whig, was hardly the sort of thing that commends itself to politicians in search of a winning candidate for anything, and Illinois Whigs were an intensely practical breed. Logan lost eight of the district's eleven counties. By all the rules, Lincoln was washed up as a political figure.

And so, on the eve of the half-century mark, with his own party about to take over the reins of government in Washington, a federal appointive post seemed highly desirable. Of all the jobs awaiting distribution to the hungry Whigs, the Commissionership of the General Land Office, paying three thousand dollars a year,[21] appeared to offer the solution to his problem, but, having promised to support Ninian Edwards's son, Cyrus, for the post, he refused at first to heed the urging of his friends and become a candidate.[22] While Edwards and J. L. D. Morrison, of St. Clair County, another aspirant, were killing off each other's chances, a boom was started for Justin Butterfield, of Chicago, who was backed for the office by both Clay and Webster. Lincoln was considerably disturbed over Butterfield's candidacy, for while, as he stated, Butterfield was his personal friend and "qualified to do the duties of the office," he possessed "less claims" than any of a hundred other Whigs in the State of Illinois. What made the Butterfield entry especially galling to Lincoln was the fact that the former had "voted for Clay and against General Taylor to the bitter end."[23]

With the growing intensity of the Butterfield bid, and the corresponding diminution to the point of hopelessness of the chances of Edwards and Morrison, Lincoln decided to enter the lists as a candidate; by June 1, 1849, the contest had narrowed down to him and Butterfield. Lincoln worked furiously in his own behalf, pulling wires, writing letters requesting recommendations from persons he thought might have any slight influence with the new administration. On June twenty-first, however, while both candidates were in Washington, Butterfield received the appointment.

It was a bitter pill to swallow. Learning the news, Lincoln returned to his room and flung himself on the bed, where he lay for an hour or more.[24] To his keen disappointment and humiliation, he was obliged to add the expense of his futile trip to Washington, and the loss of legal fees which he would otherwise have received back in Springfield. If he didn't already know it, Lincoln now realized that politics is an uncommonly cruel business, a ruthless disposer of careers.

6.

Coming home to Springfield, Lincoln, though a saddened and disappointed man, proceeded to put the disillusioning experience behind him and, with a singleness of purpose which brooked no distractions, plunged again into his law practice— partly to make up for time lost away from it and partly, no doubt, to help push the memory of the rebuff from his mind. The vigor with which this repudiated politician returned to the law, at the age of forty, was living disproof of the maxim that nothing is so abject as a disappointed office seeker. In the autobiographical sketch prepared by Lincoln for the guidance of Scripps in 1860,

Lincoln said: "Upon his return from Congress he went to the practice of the law with greater earnestness than ever before."[25]

Whatever his inner thoughts, outwardly he took his reversal in good part, never once displaying the slightest bitterness. His hopes dashed, and with political oblivion a virtual certainty, Lincoln, with his customary grace, and the peculiar genius for resiliency which was his inner resource, made the best of matters. Certainly, as regards his practice, it was to prove a blessing in disguise, for, as he stated in the Fell autobiography, from 1849 to 1854 he "practiced law more assiduously than ever before." The life and career of Abraham Lincoln abound in ironies; it is ironical that, in his hour of disillusionment, Lincoln should have sought solace in the calling for which he had at first had no great heart and which he embraced simply as an avenue to a public career.

The interlude during which Lincoln renounced politics was to prove the period of his emergence as an important lawyer, and of some of his finest work in the courts. It has been well said that to come of age as a lawyer is in part a deliverance, but more a challenge. Case by case, Lincoln met the challenge, growing steadily in stature until, at the time of his re-entrance upon the political scene, he had gained a deserved reputation as one of the ablest lawyers in central Illinois, a section which boasted not only a high percentage of the best lawyers in the state, but some of the finest legal minds in the country.

And what a range of cases! It would be both impracticable and undesirable to attempt to cover the entire field of litigation in which Lincoln took part during his remaining eleven years of practice at the Illinois bar. One need make no more than a casual examination of his cases during this most intensive period of his activity in the courts to realize why he stood high among his contemporaries and was widely hailed as a superb all-round lawyer. Nor did his achievements owe anything to contrasted mediocrity, for most of his fellow practitioners were lawyers of the first rank. While the Lincoln of the 'fifties was a legal star of the first magnitude, such was the caliber of the Illinois bar of those days that he was only one of a constellation.

The period covering the years 1849 to 1854, from his "retirement" from politics to his championship of the doctrine of free territories, is not stressed by Lincoln's biographers, and yet it was, in some respects, the most important preparatory stage of the pre-presidential years. Years in political limbo were to be spent not only in close attention to his practice, but in deep thought on public questions, which in due course gave birth to the attitude which he gradually evolved toward slavery, as expressed in the debates with Douglas and his subsequent public utterances. As in the days which followed the shattering emotional experience of his broken engagement to Mary Todd—"the fatal first of January"—Lincoln went into retreat with his cases and his thoughts. Gone, soon, was the winter of his discontent, as he burned his bridges behind him and came to have a firmer grip on life and himself than ever before.

According to Herndon, Grant Goodrich, of Chicago, one of the most prominent members of the Cook County bar, offered to take Lincoln into partnership with him, but the latter rejected the idea, assigning as his reason the fact that he disliked the confinement of an office, preferring life on the circuit, for "even if he earned smaller fees he felt much happier."[26] Giving himself none the worst of it in the telling, Herndon states that Lincoln, realizing that much of the Lincoln & Herndon practice (as of the time of the senior member's return to Springfield) was due to his (Herndon's) efforts, offered to step out of the partnership. Herndon claims to have replied that he was not unmindful or unappreciative of the fact that Lincoln had aided him when he "was young and needed it," and he "could afford now to be grateful if not generous." "I therefore," continued Herndon, "recommended a continuation of the partnership, and we went on as before."[27]

In relating the incident, Herndon was probably a little carried away. He was rather apt to be carried away. What he was at pains not to tell us, however, is something of which he must have been only too unhappily aware—that the staid and proper Mary would have preferred that her husband seize this convenient opportunity to start anew by dropping the bumptious junior member, the "earthy tavern keeper's son" whom she so cordially detested. To one of Mary's genteel upbringing, it must have been embarrassing, indeed, to have her husband called upon in the middle of the night to bail out of the local lock-up his drunk and disorderly law partner who, in the company of some companions in mischief, "had broken in almost the entire front of a grocery or saloon and otherwise committed acts of such vandalism that before daylight the sheriff was forced to apprehend them."[28] Springfield's upper-crust society did not view with favor bizarre deviations likely to invite the attention of the sheriff.

The common notion is that Herndon was able to maintain only a fractional part of the clientele while Lincoln was in Congress, resulting in an evaporation of the firm's practice almost to the vanishing point. This theory badly needs revision. Even though there was a certain inevitable defection of some who preferred an older, more experienced practitioner, the Lincoln & Herndon daybook, perfunctory as it is, reveals that if the firm was not exactly deluged with retainers, Herndon was able not only to retain a substantial part of its business, but, in addition, to bring in new clients. Making allowance for a certain amount of characteristic overstatement, one is made to realize, reading through the daybook, that there may have been something to Herndon's claim: "I retained all the business I could, and worked steadily on until, when he [Lincoln] returned, our practice was as extensive as that of any other firm at the bar."[29] Entries disclose that he was engaged in the trial or other disposition of circuit court cases in Sangamon, Menard, Christian and Logan counties, and that the fees which he took in suffered not by comparison with those charged by Lincoln.

One should be chary about drawing any large inferences

from the fact that Herndon had but two cases, involving trifling amounts, in the Supreme Court during the period that the senior member was in Congress. In 1848 he began serving as deputy clerk of that court, and consequently, apart from the impropriety of habitually appearing before it in the role of attorney, had little time to engage in a field of practice which entailed intensive preparation. Moreover, Lincoln, as noted, was a "lawyer's lawyer," his services in the Supreme Court being frequently solicited by other attorneys, so that, strictly speaking, the falling off in cases, represented by matters which would otherwise have been forwarded by outside lawyers, did not mean a loss of "clientele" as such.

7.

The matter of landing a political plum being over and done with, the old partnership was not long in re-establishing itself in Springfield, which, quite naturally, had always furnished the nucleus of the firm's practice. One can picture Mr. Lincoln on the hot, humid morning of August 27, 1849, putting on his tall headgear, leaving his home on Eighth Street and walking the nearly seven blocks, four of them north and three west, to the public square, across from which was the three-story brick building which furnished the address for the dilapidated Lincoln & Herndon office. On the way, he doubtless exchanged a salutation or a few friendly words with the neighbors he encountered. Lawyer Lincoln was back in the swing of things, and far happier, one may be sure, than he ever was in Washington.

After having ascended the dusty, creaky stairs to the second floor, he proceeded down the hall to the firm's two-room law office at the rear, where he gathered his papers for court. Returning to the street, he walked the short distance to the Sangamon Circuit Court where, on the convening of the fall term that day, the partners took up where they had left off in October, 1847. They had three cases on the calendar; business soon picked up, for the following day they had sixteen. By 1850 they were handling roughly twenty per cent of the cases tried in the Sangamon Circuit Court, a figure exceeded only by Logan.[30] From that year on, Lincoln was so busy, what with his numerous court appearances and, during the last six years of his practice, his labors in opposition to the repeal of the Missouri Compromise, that he had no time for drawing deeds, mortgages and other documents not having to do with actual litigation. This phase of the practice he usually left to the other half of the combination.

Even though their practice embraced a wide variety of cases, the general run of it, at that stage, was of no great significance—prosecutions for minor offenses, such as gambling and selling liquor; and, on the civil side, appeals from rulings of justices of the peace; slander suits (in which early Illinois abounded); actions involving small claims and petty suits for trespass, assault and similar grievances. Much ado about nothing marked much of the litigation of that day, when folks went to law far more readily than they do now. Although early Illinoisans may have had few neighbors, they very often found cause to invoke the machinery of the law against them. To settle these differences in court was a pleasant divertissement from the monotony of life on a prairie farm, with all its ennui-provoking drabness.

Among the criminal matters handled at that term was *People v. Sullinger,* involving a charge of operating a bawdy house. On September seventh, Lincoln & Herndon entered a plea of guilty to the first count of the indictment, to cover the indictment, the remaining two counts being dismissed on consent of the District Attorney. On September eleventh, the defendant got off with a twenty-five dollar fine. On the other hand, there were cases involving the important question of title to real estate; also tort actions seeking substantial damage awards. In addition to their business in the courts of original jurisdiction, they soon built up an active appellate practice in the Illinois Supreme Court.

After several brief sorties to the circuit courts located in Bloomington (McLean County) and Mt. Pulaski (Logan County), Lincoln, accompanied by the family, went to Lexington, Kentucky, in connection with the settlement of the Robert S. Todd estate. Returning, he remained in town for the balance of the year, being largely occupied in the Federal and Supreme Courts. On March 18, 1850, he started on the round of circuit courts.

CHAPTER XI

The Eighth Judicial Circuit

1.

HERE WE well may pause, on the threshold of the resumption of Lincoln's law career, for a look at that colorful pattern of practice and life, known as traveling the circuit, with which the name of Abraham Lincoln is so inseparably linked. It was, for him, more than a system of state courts of original jurisdiction; it was a way of life, and as important a part of the man as anything could be.

The most distinctive and picturesque institution in the recorded legal annals of this country, circuit travel has importance in any depiction of American legal history. But its larger significance lies in the fact that it subjected the future preserver of the federal Union to a discipline which tested his mettle and brought out all his latent powers. The Lincoln of the war years may be understood only as the product of what Benjamin P. Thomas refers to as "the cunning of the Illinois circuit."[1] Facing each day new problems, which at times necessitated heroic improvisation, Lincoln had to develop the capacity to think under fire and acquire the knack of adjusting himself quickly to changed situations; confronted with a type of practice which required a legal mind quick to find expedients, he found himself relying, not on precedents, but on his wits and native shrewdness. In this toughest of competition, a man's true ability was bound to be disclosed.

Something of what John Dean Caton, Chief Justice of the Illinois Supreme Court and a product of the Fifth Circuit, which took in his own Cook County, characterized as the "quickness of thought and rapidity of action"[2] required of members of this ambulatory bar, may be gathered from the procedure followed. Arriving in the county seat town on Saturday or Sunday, with no clients and no cases, except, perhaps, one or two left over from the previous term six months before, the phalanx of legal talent was soon approached by those desirous of engaging their services. After the litigants and/or their local counsel had completed their shopping, each would proceed, in turn, to state his case. One would require a bill in chancery to be drawn, another an answer, another an action commenced for the redress of some grievance, for another a demurrer must be interposed—all to be done before the opening of court on Monday. Then, likely as not, the still travel-weary wayfarer would be called upon to assist in or conduct the trial of a case of which he knew little or nothing before the jury was chosen. This required of one the ability to think quickly and to act promptly in taking advantage of the mistakes of his adversary.

The overriding impression one receives from a study of Lincoln's work on the circuit is that he was possessed of more than ordinary talent for it, and that Herndon was not even remotely accurate when he characterized him as "a third-rate attorney" in this phase of practice. Elsewhere in this study, the writer has expressed something of Lincoln's way with a jury, craftsmanship which called forth the highest praise of his professional brethren. Herndon notwithstanding, it can be said with perfect accuracy that, for all his awkwardness of manner, Lincoln had courtroom finesse to an extraordinary degree; for all his sincerity, he had a shrewdness not apparent on the surface. No artless, wide-eyed country lawyer, he was a match for the best of them in wiliness, presenting his cases to circuit court juries in a manner that stood up year after year.

Herndon's snide estimate leaves him open to a just rebuttal from Leonard Swett, himself an accomplished advocate, who felt that Lincoln had "few equals" as a circuit lawyer[3]—which, in the writer's opinion, is not an overstatement. Swett declared that he had listened to Rufus Choate, and many others of equal standing before the bar, in the trial of cases, but that Lincoln was more impressive than any of them, and that what Lincoln could not accomplish with a jury no other need try.[4] Lawrence Weldon, who frequently rode the circuit with Lincoln and was associated with him in numerous cases, rated him "above and beyond them all" in this type of practice.[5] Judge Caton considered him "equally potent before the jury as with the court."[6] Of particular interest is the statement of Douglas, his great antagonist, that Lincoln had, in his day, no equal before a jury.[7]

Any evaluation of Lincoln as a circuit lawyer, trying cases day in and day out, while taking on all comers, must include the unqualified admiration of Isaac N. Arnold, himself a lawyer of no mean ability, who considered Lincoln "the strongest jury lawyer in the state."[8] Another extremely capable jury pleader, who had both the opportunity and the perception to judge, was Usher F. Linder. In a letter to Joseph Gillespie, Linder had this shrewd comment to make: "But you speak of our mutual friend Lincoln—What a strange and marvellous career he had, he was a man of singular, but a large minded man. I think his greatest fort [sic] was, as a lawyer—and I don't know whether he was strongest before the Judge or the Jury, I certainly never asked to have him against me."[9]

All this, and more, has served to confirm for the writer the impression that, in the type of practice with which his name has become so thoroughly identified, Lincoln was a superior attorney, toiling alongside some of the best legal minds in the country. Though he may not have been the most consistently winning lawyer on the Eighth Circuit, he was among the two or three most sought after by the various local practitioners, a testimonial of the high esteem in which he was held by those best qualified to judge. He was, indeed, as the saying goes in the trade, a "lawyer's lawyer." In this, as in other aspects of Lincoln's life and career, Herndon was either without the insight to appreciate his deceased partner's greatness, or else deliberately set out to create a false picture.

Much has been written about Lincoln's connection with this itinerant form of law practice which, regrettably, has completely disappeared from what we sometimes call the American scene. In 1892, a generation after Lincoln had quit the circuit, Henry C. Whitney (1831–1905), of Urbana, an attorney who came from the same world that produced Lincoln, wrote a contribution to the greater understanding of the human side of both Lincoln and circuit life, and gave to it the promising title *Life on the Circuit with Lincoln*. Unfortunately, Whitney's title suggested more than he delivered. The limitations of content intrinsic in an account written by one whose acquaintance with Lincoln covered only seven years,[10] and whose firsthand knowledge of circuit travel was limited to its final stages, are readily evident. Moreover, from the point of view of style this loosely written work leaves much to be desired, requiring of one the patience to separate the wheat from the chaff, for much of the discursive potpourri is cluttered with digressive anecdotes and subjects completely extraneous to the book's central theme. (Like Herndon, Whitney liked to talk and write about everything under the sun.) And yet, for all its shortcomings, Whitney's book, with its vivid glimpses of Illinois lawyers in their native habitat, is indispensable to an appreciation of Lincoln the lawyer and "life on the circuit."

Despite the difference in their ages, Whitney was one of the few men who came to know Lincoln well; during seven of the twenty-three years that the latter spent at the bar, Whitney was intimately connected with him in law-circuit practice, and enjoyed his professional esteem to a degree noticeably greater than most of Lincoln's colleagues. There is preserved, in the Illinois State Historical Library, a letter to Joshua F. Speed, in which Lincoln, declining a retainer because of a prior commitment, wrote: "I think H. C. Whitney, of Urbana, would be a very proper person to entrust the business to." The original edition of

Whitney's book contains facsimiles of eight letters, from Lincoln to the author, which clearly demonstrate the trust which Lincoln reposed in him, and the high degree of understanding which existed between the two men. With the exception of Herndon, and possibly Swett, no lawyer was associated with Lincoln in more circuit-court litigation than was Whitney.

In its realistic portrayal of contemporary legal life a century ago, and for the warm, rich flavor and the "feel" of its period, Whitney's colorful account of the later years of Lincoln's nomadic practice remains incomparably the best. One comes out of the experience of reading it with the instinctive feeling that this is the way lawyers talked, worked and amused themselves while on circuit; here is Lincoln as he actually appeared, in pursuit of his calling, traveling up and down the rigorous circuit, from county seat to county seat, "behind his own horse, which was an indifferent, rawboned specimen, in his own blacksmith-made buggy—a most ordinary looking one";[11] at the rude hostelries at which he stopped, where "the lawyers slept two in a bed and three or four beds were located in one room";[12] at the nightly gatherings around the fireplace of the public room, with the swapping of stories (many of them tall), and the friendly badinage and high jinks and protracted discussions of shop and politics; or in court, where Lincoln was always one of the principal attractions in the most entertaining of the town's free shows. Whitney has had many successors who, in one way or another, have written of the affinity between Lincoln and the Eighth Circuit. None has re-created the latter years of that practice with more evocative power.

In 1905, Frederick Trevor Hill, a New York lawyer, undertook to write a study of Lincoln's career at the bar, with primary emphasis on his practice in the circuit courts. Finding the information then available in published sources, in connection with his special field of inquiry, to be incomplete, and realizing that a writer's great need is someone to talk with who knows intimately the people and scenes he is describing, Hill set out for Illinois.

He traveled over the circuit, soaking up the locale and plumbing the recollections of a number of residents of Springfield, Decatur, Bloomington and other cities in central Illinois, men who had been Lincoln's clients or who had been otherwise associated with him in his practice as lawyers, witnesses, jurymen and the like. With that conscientiousness for which there is no good substitute in a biographer, he dug endlessly and successfully for fact, anecdote and illuminating example touching Lincoln's activities in the courts. Among the individuals whom Hill interviewed was Lawrence Weldon, of Clinton, in his day a well-known lawyer and judge, and one of the last surviving lawyers who had traveled the circuit with Lincoln. They spoke of his experience at the bar with Lincoln and of much that pertained to circuit practice in those days; after Hill returned to New York, Weldon continued to provide reminiscences out of his own capacious memory, in several letters written shortly before his death.

In 1906, Hill traced the results of his inquiry in a series of articles written for *Century Magazine*, entitled "Lincoln the Lawyer" (later published in book form),[13] in which, limiting himself to a relatively small number of typical cases, he wrote engagingly of Lincoln's activity as "one of the equestrian retinue."

Good books in their day, these two major attempts at evaluation of Lincoln's work on the circuit need to be re-examined in the light of the material now at hand. It is safe to say that there is to be found today, in public documents, private diaries and the gamut of primary and secondary sources, fifty per cent more material on Lincoln as a circuit lawyer than was available to Hill, and a much larger percentage than was at the disposal of Whitney.

2.

The judicial circuit system was not peculiar to Illinois, having prevailed in some of the older states; the procedural plan, as Lincoln found it, was much the same as that of Kentucky. The

1825 session of the General Assembly created, as a separate entity in the state's judicial system, the first circuit courts, five in number, each to be presided over by a circuit judge, at an annual salary of six hundred dollars. Prior to then, the four Supreme Court Judges, each of whom received a yearly salary of eight hundred dollars, held circuit court sessions. The public sense of a wise economy was apparently shocked at the expenditure of sixty-two hundred dollars each year for judicial salaries, and at the next session of the General Assembly the circuit judges were legislated out of office. In 1835 another act was passed by the legislature, providing for eight circuit judges, to be chosen by the people. Again, in 1841, the circuit judges were, by act of the legislature, deprived of office, the same act providing for an increase in the Supreme Court to nine judges, each of them to hold circuit court sessions in addition to two terms each year of the supreme court.

The shrewdly conceived move of the Democrats to pack the court by increasing the number of Supreme Court Judges from four to nine was led by that other great son of Illinois, Stephen A. Douglas, then a young man of vaulting ambition; by a not-altogether-peculiar coincidence, the crafty Little Giant was, at the age of twenty-eight, one of the five judges newly chosen by the General Assembly. Another who gained by the creation of the new justiceships was Samuel H. Treat. Lincoln practiced before him extensively until 1848, when David Davis succeeded him. Under the Act of 1841, Lockwood was assigned to the first circuit, Breese to the second, Scates to the third, Wilson to the fourth, Douglas to the fifth, Browne to the sixth, Smith to the seventh, Treat to the eighth and Ford to the ninth circuit.

It was not until adoption of the 1848 Constitution that provision was again made for a disjoined circuit-court judiciary, consisting of a separate judge for each circuit, to be elected, by popular vote, for six years. The circuit court was authorized to entertain civil and criminal cases and act as appellate tribunal for cases decided by the justices of the peace.

At the time of Lincoln's admission to practice there were seven judicial circuits in the state. The First Circuit took in the counties of Sangamon, Morgan, Greene, Macoupin, Tazewell, McLean and Macon, as then bounded. During the first two years of his practice Lincoln may have traveled this circuit in Morgan, Greene (Hardin) and Macoupin; it is to be doubted that he made periodic rounds of them, the first positive evidence of his circuit work appearing after the creation of the historic Eighth Circuit. In 1837 and 1839, twenty-one new counties were created by the legislature, necessitating a reorganization of the system and the creation of two new circuits, the Eighth and Ninth. Under the Act of 1839 Sangamon became a part of the Eighth Circuit. As originally organized, the circuit included, in addition to Sangamon, seven other counties—Macon, McLean, Livingston, Tazewell, Dane (whose name was changed to Christian the following year), Logan and Menard. On March 1, 1839, before the circuit commenced functioning, DeWitt County was organized and added to it, thus bringing the total number of counties to nine.

From time to time, until 1845, Lincoln's legal stamping ground was enlarged by the addition of other subdivisions; at the time of its greatest number, it embraced fifteen counties. When the growth of population and the increase in the volume of the courts' work necessitated longer terms, counties were dropped from time to time, and in 1853 only eight remained. In the matter of territory covered, the circuit, as originally defined, comprised an area one hundred and twenty miles long and about eighty-five miles wide—approximately ten thousand square miles. A complete swing around the circuit, as laid out in 1839, entailed a journey, on horseback or by buggy, of over two hundred miles, much of it over difficult, muddy roads, many of them mere bridle paths or prairie trails created by wagon ruts, across a land of wide spaces and long silences—an untamed terrain, with only an occasional house or inn to relieve the vast loneliness of the Illinois plains.

On February 11, 1847, the General Assembly made changes

in the composition of the circuit by transferring Menard County to the First Circuit, Livingston to the Ninth, and Shelby back to the Eighth. And so, as it existed at the time of Lincoln's return to practice, the sprawling Eighth Circuit, comprising virtually a quarter of the entire area of Illinois, included fourteen counties, a complete traversing of which meant a grueling 400-mile trek of about eleven or twelve weeks. Many of the lawyers, depending on the distance to be traveled, returned to their respective points of departure on Saturday night; others left home—some, like Lincoln, spiritually as well as physically—to take the vows of circuit life for the duration. It is, of course, true that some of the counties were so distant from Springfield as to render it inconvenient, if not impossible for him to return home on weekends. (David Davis attributed Lincoln's failure to return to Springfield to spend Sunday with his family to an unpleasant home life. ". . . as a general rule," Davis declared, "when all the lawyers of a Saturday evening would go home and see their families and friends, Lincoln would find some excuse and refuse to go. We said nothing, but it seemed to us all he was not domestically happy.")

Lincoln alone, among lawyers on the "Old Eighth," was unremitting in attendance on the entire circuit, which he knew from end to end. Even in the latter years of his practice, when he had more than enough business to keep him occupied in Springfield, he continued to make the rounds. Mary is said to have been resentful of the fact that he devoted more time to the judicial circuit than any of his fellow lawyers. According to James Gourley, who lived next door to the Lincolns for nineteen years, "She always said that if her husband had stayed at home as he ought to that she could love him better."[14] Robert, when asked for details of his father's early life, wrote: "My Father's life was of a kind which gave me but little opportunity to learn the details of his early career. During my childhood & early youth he was almost constantly away from home, attending courts or making political speeches—."[15] One is tempted to say, without meaning to cast reflection on the most maligned of First Ladies, that Lincoln's true home at that time was the circuit, with its freedom from domestic strife. For this, one is prone to think, was Lincoln's big love affair. Even though he was a devoted husband and father, through all these years (1839–1859) the love of his life, which he never succeeded in banishing from his heart, was —the circuit.

Until 1853 the court commenced its spring term about the middle of March and its fall term about September first. Duration of the sessions of the individual counties varied from three days to a week. In Sangamon County the regular spring and fall terms were of two weeks in length; as early as 1837 and until 1849, a third term, lasting a week, was held in July despite the withering heat of Springfield. As of the spring of 1850, the peripatetic bench and bar visited the counties in the following order: Sangamon, Tazewell, Woodford, McLean, Logan, DeWitt, Piatt, Champaign, Vermilion, Edgar, Shelby, Moultrie, Macon and Christian.

Leonard Swett and others who rode the circuit with Lincoln have given descriptions of various of the early temples of justice which, according to them, were rather primitive affairs. The seamy old backwoods courthouses, with their drab façades, were —until the 'forties, at least—mostly glorified cabins. County seats, the centers of population of sparsely settled counties, were, with the exception of Springfield, little more than hamlets. According to the census of 1840, Sangamon had a population of 14,716. Tazewell had 7,222 inhabitants, McLean 6,565, Menard 4,431, DeWitt, 3,247, Macon 3,039, Christian 1,878. Springfield had a population of 2,500, but the census shows most of the county seats to have been villages. Bloomington, in McLean County, numbered approximately 800, while Postville, the county seat of Logan County, boasted in 1837, according to J. M. Peck's *Gazetteer of Illinois*, only three stores and three or four families, and it was not much larger in 1839.

Not all county seats boasted regularly enrolled attorneys, and those which did had insufficient business, despite the disputatious propensities of Illinoisans, to keep them busy full time. Many lawyers supported themselves through agrarian and other side occupations. It is surprising how many callings could be combined with the practice of law—farming, journalism, real estate, storekeeping, insurance, office holding. Even in Springfield, where the higher courts met, there was an insufficiency of business to support the members of the bar. The Supreme Court sat for only a few days annually, while the sessions of the Circuit Court, even though three in number each year, as compared with two in the other counties, lasted but a total of five weeks. The semiannual sessions of the United States District Court in Springfield, being brief in duration, consumed little of a lawyer's time. In other counties, where there was only the circuit court, there was, in all, less than a month of court business each year. So it was that for those like Lincoln who preferred to concentrate on the law rather than eking out their lawyers' earnings by farming, editing a small-town newspaper or engaging in some form of business on the side, the slim pickings offered by the law, locally, had to be supplemented by practice in the outlying counties.

Some of the county-seat practitioners, especially in the less populous communities, were essentially office lawyers, who rarely went into court for the trial of cases unaided by experienced trial counsel. In those cases where litigants engaged local counsel, the latter frequently aligned themselves in association with the traveling lawyers, digging up business during recess of court, perhaps drawing up the necessary pleadings and other papers involved in bringing the cases on for trial, and then awaiting arrival of the more experienced trial lawyers at terms of court.

It is an interesting fact that, while for the most part the visiting attorneys had their court papers prepared for them by the local lawyers, Lincoln apparently preferred drawing his own. Hundreds of pleadings in Lincoln's hand have been found in the courthouses of the county-seat towns of the Eighth Circuit. (Hundreds of others have doubtless disappeared from the files.) Drawn, always, with meticulous care, they are usually signed by

Lincoln with his own last name and that of his associate. Reading through them, one is appalled not only by the vast number of cases which Lincoln tried on the circuit, but by the labor which he poured into them.

Lincoln became associated with resident attorneys in every county on the circuit, as well as in counties outside it, which fact has given rise to the belief that he formed numerous partnerships. Such was not the case; these combines were, in fact, nothing more or less than arrangements of convenience, known as legal associations. It is to be noted that not all of Lincoln's associates on the circuit were inexperienced in trial work; many of them were themselves capable trial lawyers, who nevertheless felt better about entering upon a court contest with Lincoln on their side.

In the tough scramble for law business, the members of the peregrinating bar at first rode from county to county on horseback, with saddlebags, containing a clean shirt or two, slung across the animal's back. In Lincoln's case an oversized, cheap cotton umbrella, green with age, with his name sewed on the inside with white thread, and tied with a strand of twine to keep it from falling open, together with a law book or two, completed his travel impedimenta. (For all the eccentric picture which this figure under the plug hat presented as he rode along, his feet not much removed from the ground, it may be said that Lincoln was an uncommonly fine horseman, one of the best ever to be elected to the presidency.)

When better roads came (they were poor at best), the one-hoss shay, one of the nation's most famous contraptions, came into use, though at times these were rendered useless by the liquid mud. The soil of the old Eighth Circuit ("the mud circuit," as it was appropriately called) was rich black loam, and when dampened by rain or melting snow, it was hardly conducive to easy travel with vehicles. Until the railroad had dislodged the horse as the favorite means of getting from place to place, horseback riding was still the most trustworthy means of conveyance. Prairie travel by any means of equine locomotion was, in wet weather, a nightmare. We have a glimpse of its hazards in a letter written by Jesse W. Fell, one of Lincoln's closest friends: "I came pretty near to losing a horse. . . . We came to a slew that looked too deep for safety and I detached a horse and rode in to ascertain the depth. I had gone but a little way till we plunged into a deep hole and with great difficulty my horse got through, having swam some distance."

Cynical laymen may wax witty over the fact that in those early days when horse thieves, as clients, were rather common, lawyers were well mounted—though Lincoln's steed, be it noted, was in a condition of constant deterioration. Possibly Lincoln felt, regarding the matter of accepting the proceeds of a larceny, somewhat as did Clarence Darrow when a young man facing a charge of theft begged the famous criminal lawyer to defend him, offering to obtain a substantial retainer fee that very night. Darrow accepted the case but declined the immediate retainer, saying he did not care to accept money "that has been stolen—so recently."[16]

3.

So much for the general picture. A vicarious "swing around the circuit," as it existed at the time of Lincoln's return to practice, should prove of interest to the reader. Those, more fortunate, who are favored with the opportunity to retrace in person the historic route of the "Old Eighth"—through a prosperous farming country, along a paved highway, in sharp contrast to the same section a century and more ago—will be aided in following Lincoln's trail by granite slabs which still appear at some of the county limits, bearing the inscription:

ABRAHAM LINCOLN
Traveled This Way as he
Rode the Circuit
of the
old Eighth Judicial Circuit
1847   1859
Erected 1921

A more formal marker, consisting of a bronze tablet, with the medallion head of Lincoln at the top, and bearing the same inscription, appears in each county seat. It was designed by Henry Bacon, who was chosen by Congress to erect the Lincoln Memorial, at Washington, D.C. Additional indicators formerly appeared on telephone poles at all cross and diverging roads along the route, before their removal by souvenir hunters.

In 1914, Joseph O. Cunningham, in his day one of the leading lawyers of Urbana, whose association with Lincoln went back to the time (1840–41) when they were fellow members of the State Legislature, interested the Daughters of the American Revolution in the work of marking the Lincoln circuit.[17] "It was the trail over these roads," Cunningham said, "and the mingling with and associating among the people dwelling here that gave him [Lincoln] his deep insight into human character. Here in the primitive courts of the people and within their simple and artless homes, he learned and perfected the language which in his speeches moved and still moves the hearts of men; which shines forth in his official declarations, and will ever influence human action while language lasts."

As befitted the largest town on the circuit and the capital of the state, Springfield, one of the circuit's pivotal points, furnished the situs of the initial spring session of each term, after completion of which Judge David Davis took the show on the road. The small but rapidly growing community in the prairie wilderness boasted a two-story brick courthouse of Grecian-style architecture, with stone portico supported by six Ionic columns, on the east side of the public square; built to house the Sangamon Circuit Court, it was commenced in 1845 and completed a year later. The first floor was given over to rooms for the county officers, which opened off a long, wide hall extending from the building's entrance to the rear. On the second floor was the courtroom, which was as barren of appointments as it was large. The second brick courthouse to be erected in Springfield, it remained in use until 1876.

The first term of the Sangamon Circuit Court was held in

1821.[18] John Kelley was commissioned to build a log courthouse, which cost $42.50;[19] an additional $30.00 was spent to install a fireplace, and for sundry miscellaneous items. In 1831 a square two-story brick courthouse was erected in the center of the square, at a cost of $6,841.[20] Nearby was the county jail, also a brick structure. In 1837, upon the conveyance of the public square to the State, the courthouse was razed to make way for the State House, the cornerstone of which was laid on July 4, 1837. After such transfer to the State, the county leased a store on Hoffman's Row, which served as county courthouse until 1840. Thereafter court was held for one term in the Campbellite Church and for another in the Methodist Episcopal Church, after which the store on Hoffman's Row was rerented and remained in use until April, 1846.[21]

Springfield's leading hotel, at the time of Lincoln's return to practice, was the American House, a three-story brick structure, with forty rooms, a spacious lobby and a fine dining room. Generally considered one of the best hotels in the Middle West, it remained a favorite stopping place for lawyers from other parts of the state until the late 'fifties, when the Chenery House and the St. Nicholas Hotel supplanted it in public favor.

At midpoint of the nineteenth century Lincoln's home town boasted a population of about 4,500 persons, but in Chicago there were nearly 30,000. Though rapidly being surpassed in importance by the stretch of prairie at the end of Lake Michigan, Springfield was not without evidence of civic consciousness. In June the Illinois State Medical Society was formed in the state's capital, and the first annual exhibit of the Springfield Horticultural Society took place in the fall.

4.

The Eighth Circuit, during the period of Lincoln's association with it, knew but two judges—Samuel H. Treat, of Springfield, who served from the organization of the circuit, in

1839, to 1848; and David Davis, of Bloomington, who succeeded him. Here we must pause to become more intimately acquainted with the man who, in any true picture of those whose lives touched Lincoln's at significant points, must hold a center place. Davis, six years Lincoln's junior, hailed from the eastern shore of Maryland. After having read law in the office of a friend of the family in Lenox, Massachusetts, and attended lectures for a year in the Yale Law School, he headed for the pioneer country of Illinois in the fall of 1835; he was examined for admission to the Illinois bar by Judge Theophilus W. Smith, of the Supreme Court, and soon admitted to practice.[22]

After first hanging out his shingle in Tremont, and then Pekin, he moved to Bloomington at the urging of Jesse W. Fell. In 1844 he formed a partnership with Wells Colton, and in a short time the firm of Davis & Colton had built up a considerable collection practice. Their office, at 102 East Front Street, was in the same block wherein Lincoln made his famous "Lost Speech" in May, 1856. Davis traveled the Eighth Circuit with Lincoln from 1839 to 1848; his home was a port of call for the latter when in Bloomington. After a term in the legislature, he served as circuit judge from 1848 to 1862, when Lincoln appointed him to the United States Supreme Court. Herndon, never one to bestow praise on an unworthy recipient, was favorably impressed with the new judge of the Eighth Circuit. On March 26, 1849, he wrote Judge Caton, at Ottawa, that "Judge Davis makes quite a good and agreeable Judge, and I hope he may continue to give genuine satisfaction."[23] Davis was the administrator of Lincoln's estate, and upon his resignation from the Supreme Court in 1877, served one term in the United States Senate.

A dedicated Whig and later faithful Republican wheel horse, Davis played a leading role in the horse trading that led to Lincoln's nomination at Chicago in 1860. In Illinois history he is known as one of the "three musketeers" who groomed Lincoln for the Presidency, the other two being Jesse W. Fell (former Governor Adlai E. Stevenson's great grandfather on his mother's side) and Leonard Swett—both men, like Davis, residing in Bloomington.

In the *Beveridge Papers*, in the Library of Congress, is a letter from Kellogg Fairbank to Beveridge, under date of April 7, 1926, which gives an amusing and revealing picture of the lengths to which Davis and others of Lincoln's supporters went to secure the nomination for him. "My father, the late N. K. Fairbank, was a great admirer of David Davis, of Illinois," wrote Fairbank, "and when he was a boy Mr. Davis paid a visit one summer to our house at Lake Geneva. There was a large dinner party in his honor. Mr. Wirt Dexter, one of the leaders of the Chicago bar and an adept in the conversational art, drew Mr. Davis out to tell the story of the Convention which nominated Mr. Lincoln. The company was a congenial one and Mr. Davis talked freely. He told how they lacked votes to nominate Lincoln, and how they caught the Seward people napping and adjourned the Convention to the next day. How that night Mr. Lincoln's friends, Norman B. Judd, Leonard Swett, Davis and others, went from delegation to delegation, arguing, finding out what the delegation wanted, and making promises to bring them into line. Sometimes the promises overlapped a little, as in the case of the office of the Secretary of War. As the tale drew near its close, Mr. Dexter turned a quizzical smile on Davis's huge bulk and ventured the remark, 'Brother Davis, you must have prevaricated somewhat.' 'Prevaricated,' replied Davis in his high voice, raising his right hand which still grasped his table knife, and gesturing towards Mr. Dexter, 'Prevaricated, Brother Dexter? We lied, lied like hell.' "

Davis's stature as a judge has been the subject of differing opinion. Beveridge, with his penchant for going overboard in his judgment of men, refers to him as "a really great lawyer and one of the foremost Justices who ever sat on the Supreme Bench of the United States."[24] That, one is inclined to think, is at the very least exaggerated. As Harry E. Pratt, long known as one of the most indefatigable scholars in the Lincoln and contiguous areas, has pointed out: "There is no record of Davis appearing on either side of a case in the Supreme Court of Illinois."[25] Whitney, who reproduced with candor the contemporaneous judgments he formed of his colleagues, was certainly qualified in his regard for one he felt "had not great erudition and no brilliancy,"[26] and who he believed Lincoln "did grudgingly place on the Supreme Bench, not on his merits, but on the earnest importunity of Swett."[27] Closing a twelve-page discussion of Davis in his *Life on the Circuit with Lincoln*, Whitney caustically remarked: ". . . his name occupies but a few inches in local, and none in general history."[28]

Contemporary estimates of a public figure, whether favorable or the reverse, are apt to be overdrawn. Whether Whitney's evaluation of the man is true or untrue, it is certainly no overstatement to say that David Davis was more intimately woven into Lincoln's personal life than almost anyone else with, perhaps, two or three exceptions. In the winter of 1836, Davis visited Vandalia while the legislature was in session. One day John T. Stuart introduced him to the lanky assemblyman from Sangamon County, then serving his second term in the General Assembly.[29] The introduction soon ripened into a friendship which was life-long in duration.

That Davis should have developed, as he did, such a profound admiration, almost amounting to affection, for one who never bowed or scraped to him, is no small tribute to Lincoln, for it was said of the Judge that he was an autocrat "who ruled over the circuit riders like a potentate of old,"[30] and woe to the lawyer who failed to do obeisance to his majestic self, or even disagreed with him. "Leonard Swett dared do it once, and the unfair rulings that his clients suffered during that trip over the circuit was a scandal to be whispered about by the other lawyers."[31] Another who had the gumption to stand up to Davis, though also at the expense of his clients, was Asahel Gridley. In the middle of a summation, Davis broke in on him to say: "You don't call that law, you are talking to the jury, do you?" "My clients hired *me* to try this case, and if we need *your* help, we will call on you," retorted Gridley. This was *lèse majesté* of a high order. Grandly hauling his bulk up, the Judge rejoined: "All right: I'll instruct the jury directly; and then we'll see who rules this court."[32] Lincoln, like Swett and Gridley, had no talent for unction.

Tyrant though he may have been, Davis was capable of extreme consideration where not only Lincoln, but the members of Lincoln's family were concerned. Robert Lincoln, a singularly smug, bumptious and self-centered individual, an odd fish if ever there was one, had this to say concerning his father's friend: "I cannot remember when I did not know Judge Davis, first as the Circuit Judge of whom I heard as a boy everything good from my father, and who was very kind to me. Upon my father's death I went to Judge Davis as a second father, and this he was to me until his death. I am deeply indebted to him for counsel and affectionate help on many occasions and revere his memory."[33]

As in the case of the Lincoln & Herndon partnership, there were few affinities between the two men. The soberly clad Lincoln, with his long, sweat-stained linen duster, or shawl and hat of doubtful age, didn't put much stock by fancy clothes; most of the time he was just functionally dressed. Davis, on the other hand, was impeccably correct about his clothes and personal appearance. His beard, which extended around his throat and the lower part of his face, was always immaculately clipped. Lincoln was a man of limited finances. Davis, who was acquisitive in the extreme, found the law "not profitable," and so, as a side line, entered the merchandise business in 1844, with a store across the street from his law office. This solid citizen acquired large land holdings, and in his later years erected a palatial mansion in Bloomington, which survives, in a perfect state of preservation, as one of the outstanding historical sights of the central Illinois city. By virtue of his business sagacity, Davis died a millionaire. Many early Illinois lawyers acquired, as did Davis, large fortunes which were the result of foresight and judicious investments in real estate, rather than their efforts at the bar.

The Judge was a person of quick and inflexible determination, while Lincoln, a man of pedestrian judgment, came to conclusions slowly and carefully and only after due deliberation and sober, second thoughts. In their views on the subtle quality that men call "justice," one has no doubt that they differed somewhat. The coldly judicious Davis, whose judgments did not often err on the side of charity, expressed in a letter to a friend something of the sterner side of his nature: "If any wanton attack is made on them then they should have a fair defense, nothing more. They are in common with the rest of mankind entitled to justice, not to generosity."[34] One may be sure that Lincoln, with a working knowledge of human venality, and at the same time more prone to mercy than strict justice,[35] entertained no such narrow concept; basic to everything he did and thought was an abiding curiosity and affection for the strengths and weaknesses of all men. A lawyer who, like Lincoln, spends any considerable part of his time poking around the criminal courts, develops an understanding for those caught in the many snares of living and a view of human nature which is, one might say, tinged with an acute, almost an affectionate awareness of human weakness. Something of the essential humanity of the man was compressed into a statement which he made, as wartime president, in discussing a pardon for some boys who had deserted, were recaptured and had been sentenced by a courtmartial to be shot: "All I can say is that I have always found that mercy bears richer fruits than strict justice." One of the most convincing impressions which the writer has received in connection with his study of Lincoln's law career, is that his first, his essential characteristic as a lawyer was an understanding of the foibles of men and a vast tolerance for the infirmities of humankind.

Despite their divergences, the two men had certain things in common. Both were solid Whigs; both were shrewd professional politicians; both were gregarious, alike in their companionable qualities. Even Whitney was moved to describe Davis as, "on first acquaintance, one of the most genial and companionable men I ever knew."[36] Davis's home was a center of gracious hospitality for lawyers away from home, where "court parties" were regularly held whenever court was in session in Bloomington.

Circuit life made for a sharing of experiences which brought the two men ever closer together. If the prairie in solitude is grand, human beings drawn together by a sense of their fewness in the presence of its majesty are especially warm. "There is some fun and a good deal of excitement in practicing law in this *prairie* state, but not much profit or personal comfort," wrote Davis to a relative during the period when he and Lincoln were riding the circuit as lawyers, and at a time when travel must have been a particular tribulation to one of his bulk. "We have been deluged by rain this spring. The windows of heaven are certainly open. Bad roads, broken bridges, swimming of horses and constant wettings are the main incidents in Western travel."[37] For all its adverse conditions, circuit travel, with its atmosphere of comradeship and relaxed informality, became an inherent part of both men, and the impressions and friendships of those years were never effaced.

5.

A few days prior to commencement of the spring term in Springfield, Davis set out from Bloomington on his judicial rounds, riding majestically in his buggy, drawn by a spanking team of gray mares. The day of horseback travel for lawyers was not yet over, but for Davis, a Brobdingnagian of a man, standing over six feet tall and weighing, by 1850, more than three hundred pounds, it was—so much so that a *two-horse* buggy was required to haul this mountain of flesh over the rugged terrain.

Arrived in Springfield (usually on a Saturday night), after a sixty-mile ride with an overnight stop at Hoblit's tavern, run by Lincoln's old friend, John Hoblit, situated roughly equidistant between Bloomington and Springfield, the Judge prepared his charge to the Grand Jury, for delivery on opening day. Davis was, in the beginning, a poor speaker, with a dread of speaking extemporaneously. His charge was directed not only to calendared causes, but to general conditions in the county. On Sunday, Davis attended the Episcopal Church where the Reverend Charles Dresser, who had married the Lincolns, officiated.

Monday, the first day of court, was a general meeting day. People flocked in from the surrounding countryside to engage in horse trading or attend the auction sales of cattle, hogs and farm implements. Others came to watch the most diverting of the town's free shows. Come two o'clock in the afternoon, the bailiff opened court in the usual manner; proceeding to the open windows of the courtroom, he announced to all and sundry the convening of court. Lawyers, litigants and spectators strolled in leisurely, until the courtroom was filled. By then many of the sight-seers were three sheets in the wind. Lincoln's old law clerk, Gibson W. Harris, tells how "The most common annoyance in the court-room came in the form of loud talking and braggadocio from spectators half seas over."[38]

One useful approach to a study of Lincoln's law career is to consider, as the writer has endeavored to do, his close professional relationship with those lawyers who most frequently practiced in Springfield. It was an arresting cast of characters which, in that heroic age of Illinois law, regularly appeared at the counsel table of the Sangamon Circuit Court—Lincoln, Logan, Stuart, Dummer, Baker, May, Linder, Browning, Dickey, Shelby M. Cullom, "the man who looked like Lincoln," James H. Matheny, who was the best man at Lincoln's wedding, and others of the eminently able Illinois bar, all then in their prime.

It would appear, at first notice, singularly strange that the surviving records disclose very few cases in which Douglas, who was active in the social life of Springfield and a member of Springfield Masonic Lodge No. 4,[39] appeared as attorney. There was, of course, an interregnum during which he served as associate justice of the Illinois Supreme Court, from 1841 to the time of his resignation, in 1843. (Here he earned the title of "Judge"; for the rest of his life he was "Judge Douglas" to friend and foe alike.) He was elected, on December 14, 1846, to the United States Senate, in which he served until his death, though his service in that body would not have prevented his appearing in court during the time when Congress was in recess. After 1847 he maintained a law office in Chicago, where he practiced desultorily for a while, and eventually not at all.

Douglas, who was ambitious for high place, played the game of politics for all it was worth—so much so that, as his biographer, Frank E. Stevens, states, "whatever of attention the law business received, it came, most likely from his partner, Mr. [John D.] Urquhart."[40] He did, however, gain considerable trial experience, as well as enhancement of reputation, when, as a brash young prosecutor on the make, he served for two years as State's Attorney for the First (later Eighth) Judicial District, the most populous in the state, "prosecuting offenders without fear or favor."[41]

Isaac N. Arnold, a transplanted New Englander living in Chicago, who was for many years president of the Chicago Historical Society, and who knew both Lincoln and Douglas intimately, and, as an attorney, had firsthand knowledge of their work in the courts, had this to say regarding their comparative effectiveness as jury pleaders: "Both Lincoln and Douglas were strong jury-lawyers. Lincoln, on the whole, was the strongest jury-lawyer we ever had in Illinois. Both were distinguished for their ability in seizing and bringing out, distinctly and clearly, the real points in a case. Both were very happy in the examination of witnesses; I think Lincoln the stronger of the two in cross-examination. He could compel a witness to tell the truth when he meant to lie."[42] This assessment was no afterthought of reminiscence from one whose admiration of Lincoln's qualities as a lawyer was always unstinted.

Spring of 1850 was a busy period for Lincoln. Opening day of the term (Monday, March eighteenth) found Lincoln & Herndon with eleven cases on the Sangamon Circuit Court calendar, in five of which, representing plaintiffs, they took default judgments aggregating $1,906. On March twenty-third Lincoln's client, Henry McHenry, charged jointly with one Martha Graves with the crime of adultery, posted bond in the sum of two hundred dollars. Lincoln managed to have the trial of the case put over until the fall, when he again secured a continuance, this time to the March term, 1851. His delaying action availed the defendant nothing, however, for came the day of judgment on March 19, 1851, when the defendants were forced to trial. The result was never in doubt, the jury promptly convicting. For his amorous adventure, Lincoln's client was fined fifty dollars and costs.[48]

CHAPTER XII

The Eighth Judicial Circuit
(continued)

1.

AFTER TWO WEEKS of attendance at the Sangamon Circuit Court, the journeying bar sallied forth in search of business; without so much as a day's respite from their labors in Springfield, Judge Davis and his supporting company set out on the first leg of the long, grueling journey. Leading the parade across the prairie's vast, for the most part untenanted, reaches was Davis. Following, in all manner of rattletrap "rigs" and nondescript conveyances, was a somewhat forlorn-looking group consisting of the state's attorney and some twenty-five or thirty lawyers. (Browning, in his *Diary*, states that lawyers practicing in western Illinois frequently traveled by stage, but it would appear that the lawyers of the Eighth Circuit did not.)

Sometimes Lincoln accompanied the Judge in the latter's buggy; more often, he went it alone in his own rickety contraption.[1] When he first began to stalk the provinces in search of law business, Lincoln was too poor to own a horse and was obliged either to rent one[2] or borrow from friends. In time, however, he became the proprietor of a nag which had seen better days— "Old Buck." Dispensing with the saddlebags of his early horseback days, Lincoln now carried his books, papers and a spare shirt in a carpetbag.

For all his gregariousness, much of the time Lincoln, whose temperament required a certain amount of solitude, preferred being alone. To one of his inbred melancholy, the pensive loneliness of prairie travel exercised a special fascination; while the intellectual climate of the frontier towns and villages may have been unkind to abstract thought, traversing the solitary plains, on horseback or by "rig," made for contemplative reflection and tended to turn men inward upon themselves. Riding oftentimes past sundown, during nights in the late fall when the bright moonlight shone on a sea of untrodden snow, it was quiet, prairie quiet, with only an owl or a fox speaking, or a distant dog. (The scene is sensitively evoked in an oil painting hanging in the Lincoln Room at Lincoln Memorial University, in Harrogate, Tennessee, in which the artist, Louis Bonhajo, has pictured the lonely Lincoln, with his law books in his saddlebags, making his way across the Illinois prairie in an early winter snow.) In those days and nights of circuit travel, when the scene breathed the very essence of solitude, Lincoln became a man of deep cogitation.

On Sunday the assembled circuit riders set out for Tremont, roughly fifty miles northeast of Springfield, which gave them a day in town to gather their forces and prepare for the opening of court on Wednesday. Proceeding along the vast stretch of prairie country at the rate of about four miles an hour (assuming favorable weather), they made Tremont by nightfall Monday, after an overnight stop en route. Converging upon the town, the weary, travel-stained caravan shopped around for accommodations, either at the local inn or in private boarding homes. Linder, one of Lincoln's circuit companions, recalled: "Lincoln and myself generally put up at the same hotel, and not unfrequently Lincoln and I occupied the same bed. Judge Davis was too large to take either of us for a bed-fellow."[3] Came morning, the lawyers were up betimes, in order to hustle up business for the forthcoming term of court.

The 40' x 60' courthouse, erected in 1839, was constructed of red brick, topped with an octagonal cupola with a copper-covered dome, and surmounted by a weather vane. The building had a huge bell to summon the lawyers to court.

On the site of the old Tremont courthouse is a marker, the inscription on which reads:

TREMONT COURTHOUSE
1839–1850

Abraham Lincoln Attended Court in the Fine Two Story Rectangular Brick Courthouse With Four Grecian Columns and Copper Dome on This Site. Here in 1842 He was Challenged to a Duel by James Shields. Lincoln Last Spoke Here August 30, 1858. Erected by the Illinois State Historical Society 1956.

The Circuit Courthouse for the County of Tazewell, during the years when it was located at Tremont, was among the busiest on the circuit. In addition to the members of the Springfield and local bars, Lincoln customarily encountered there Asahel Gridley and Wells Colton, of Bloomington; Norman H. Purple, Charles Ballance, Onslow Peters and William Frisby, of Peoria, and a score or so others of the small, intimate world of the traveling bar of the Eighth Circuit.

Lincoln enjoyed a rather large practice in Tremont. It was here, in April of 1841, that he obtained the most sizable judgment of his career up to that time—$16,058.22.[4] Here *Bailey* v. *Cromwell* was tried, though, as has been noted, there is no clear proof of Lincoln having appeared as trial counsel.

Lincoln figured in the litigation which grew out of the removal, in 1850, of the county seat from Tremont to Pekin, when the donor of the public square sought to recover the property, upon the ground that the gift was conditional upon the county seat being permanently located in Tremont. Lincoln did not represent the plaintiff in the circuit court, where judgment was rendered in favor of the county. Upon the appeal, the plaintiff engaged the services of Lincoln, Logan and the firm of Stuart & Edwards, while the county was represented by Norman H. Purple. In affirming the holding of the lower court, Judge Trumbull, at the December term, 1851, of the Supreme Court, rejected the contention of Lincoln and his associates that the deed from Harris to the county commissioners was not absolute in its terms.

The daughter of the editor of the *Tazewell Telegraph,* a resident of Tremont at the time of removal of the county seat to Pekin, has left a delightfully moving account of the farewell gathering of the visiting bench and bar upon the occasion of the final session in Tremont. "I recall," she wrote, "during the last session of the eighth judicial circuit court held in Tremont in April, 1850, an interesting and what was to me a memorable gathering of the prominent attorneys of the state, at their last Sunday night supper at the 'Red Brick' as our place was called. . . . On that Sunday afternoon, I heard my mother ask my father to drive to Col. Pierre Menard's (he lived two miles southwest of Tremont), to bring the Colonel, Mr. Lincoln, and Judge Davis to our home for Sunday evening supper with the other lawyers who were attending court. My mother had a long table loaded with appetizing food for the gentlemen. It was placed on the lawn, under a row of blooming locust trees. In these days only coffee and milk were served, rarely tea. . . . The lawyers were seated in true Methodist form on one side of the lawn, and my mother, not far off, was seated at another table with her lady guests. . . . And thus the session ended with good cheer, toasts, and Auld Lang Syne, as the lawyers went the rounds shaking the hand of each guest in farewell. As Mr. Lincoln bade my mother good night, he apologized for his shabby coat, saying: 'You know, Mrs. Jones, that travelling is very laborious.' "[5]

The story of the origin of the Pekin courthouse, which was torn down in 1914, goes back to 1849, when construction was commenced. Among the attorneys whose names one frequently encounters in connection with Lincoln's appearances there, was Benjamin S. Prettyman, leader of the local bar, who enjoyed a wide reputation as an able lawyer. Like Lincoln, he had, early in his professional life, come under the severely watchful eye of Stephen T. Logan, from whom he received much of his legal training. (It is worth a note, in passing, that apprenticeships in Logan's office were much sought after by young law students and fledgling lawyers, and numerous of the leading attorneys of the state, including four United States Senators and three Governors of States, received their training under him.) Prettyman was one of the few lawyers on the circuit who possessed a law library.

Among Lincoln's cases in Pekin, one must mention *Pearl, et al.* v. *Graham, et al.*, an action in trespass arising out of the acts of the defendants, a group of twenty-one self-constituted vigilantes, in raiding the premises of the plaintiffs and destroying a quantity of liquor found there. On May 4, 1854, Lincoln wrote and filed, under the name of Bush & Gridley, attorneys of record, a plea on behalf of the defendants, setting forth that the trespass complained of was against a disorderly house in which "drunkenness, idleness, quarreling, profane swearing, obscenity" and other offenses were permitted, and that in destroying the complainants' liquor the defendants were acting lawfully and in the public interest. On May eleventh, on application of the plaintiffs, the action was ordered removed to Woodford County. It is amusing to note that on September twenty-eighth, Lincoln, not to be outdone in this, his field of special competence, obtained a change of venue back to Tazewell. On May 4, 1855, the action was dropped as against four of the defendants. The remaining seventeen went to trial, with Lincoln as their attorney. The jury returned a verdict of fifty dollars damages against six of them, dismissing the complaint as to the others.[6]

On February 11, 1857, Tazewell, by act of the Legislature, was transferred to the Twenty-first Circuit; Lincoln did not attend in Tazewell after 1856.

2.

With adjournment of court for the last time in Tremont, Davis, Lincoln and the rest of the touring company took to the road again, setting off across the prairie land of north-central Illinois to Metamora, county seat of Woodford County, about twenty miles away. Lincoln attended the first circuit court in Woodford, held in a schoolhouse at Versailles, then a rude and straggling settlement, September 23–25, 1841. All the lawyers were from outside the county; they included Baker, Logan and Stuart, of Springfield, and Davis and Gridley of Bloomington.

The Metamora courthouse, construction of which was completed two years after the county seat was moved there from Versailles in 1843, was built of bricks burned in local kilns and hardwood timbers hewn from trees chopped down near the village. Since 1921 the venerable old building has been a State Memorial; retaining its nostalgic charm, it is substantially the same today as it was in Lincoln's time, a 40' x 50' structure, with a corridor, lined with offices, running through the center. In 1870, the stairway was moved from the back to the front of the building, and in 1884 wings were added, but no other changes have been made. On the second floor is the old Eighth Circuit courtroom, with original furnishings, in which appeared not only Lincoln, but Douglas, Adlai E. Stevenson, later to become Vice President under Cleveland, and Robert G. Ingersoll, the renowned orator and noted skeptic. Among the jurists who presided here were Davis, Purple and Treat.

At the time of Lincoln's appearance at the spring term 1850, Metamora, in the heart of the Illinois prairies, was a quiet little village, one of the smallest on the circuit. A description of the rustic frontier town reveals that there were a tavern, a courthouse whose brick façade looked out on the village square, a few stores and a handful of homes. The county, too, was small, and its rural population generally orderly and peaceable, and so the criminal business was light. The earliest docket, from which the names of the attorneys in the different cases must usually be obtained, is dated 1856. For this reason it is, except in rare instances, difficult to determine those cases in which Lincoln appeared prior to that year. In 1857 Woodford was severed from the Eighth Circuit and placed in the Twenty-first Circuit; Lincoln did not attend court in Woodford after 1856.

3.

After two or three days in court, and nights spent sharing the rigors of "Traveller's Home," the picturesque, though primitive local tavern where, like most hotels of the time and section, the beds were hard and the food poor,[7] Lincoln and the rest of the nomadic practitioners took off for Bloomington, thirty miles southeast of Metamora. The inconveniences of country taverns, irregular hours of sleep and irregularity of meals, poorly prepared, were all part of the exacting life on the circuit; a man had to be uncommonly healthy to stand the wear and tear of it. Whatever may have been its compensating joys, circuit riding was to Herndon a "soul's sore trial." Years later, he wrote: "No human being would now endure what we used to on the circuit. I have slept with 20 men in the same room—some on bed ropes—some on quilts—some on sheets—a straw or two under them; and oh— such victuals—Good God." To quote Swett: "I have travelled with him [Lincoln] on the circuit. Now, travelling on the circuit in the olden times meant pretty rough accommodations. . . . We would get up in the morning and have our breakfast; pretty tough coffee—pretty mean. Now, I have never heard Lincoln complain of anything in my life on the Circuit. I never heard him complain that his food was not good."[8]

Gibson W. Harris expressed the general opinion when he said that "Mr. Lincoln was not given to complaining." "As I look back over it," he recalled, "the equanimity with which he accepted the rougher features of traveling the circuit seems astonishing. Chief among these features were the wretched hotel accommodations. The taverns, invariably so called, were almost always cheerless and uncomfortable. . . . The 'transient' of those days could not be sure of finding his hostelry so much as waterproof; more than once I have slept with tiny eddies of snow drifting in upon my bed. The furniture in the guest-chamber rarely comprised more than the bedstead, one or two split-bottom chairs, and possibly a spittoon. The bedding was usually abundant, perchance the bedbugs superabundant. The guests performed their ablutions in a tin basin on the back porch, or on a bench out by the well in the yard, using soft soap, if any soap at all, and wiping on a crash towel that late risers were sure to find too wet for effective service. I distinctly remember washing at the well one morning when the thermometer was thirty degrees below zero, the water freezing on the basin-side as it dropped from my hands. It was either this or postponing the rite to another day. As might be expected, tavern charges were ridiculously low."[9] (One of Lincoln's fellow circuit riders recalled that for supper, lodging and breakfast for Lincoln and himself, and the feeding and stabling of their horses, the bill was seventy-five cents.)[10]

It was, to Judge Davis, a constant source of amazement that, while others were loud in their complaints, Lincoln not only never appeared bothered by the intolerable conditions, but, adapting himself to their challenge, seemed to thrive on them. His strong physique, which had stood him in good stead in a quarter-century of circuit travel, was the subject of comment by attending physicians at his death. With all its unspeakable food; rest for night unknown; cold, often dirty, quarters; and all the other almost primitive conditions which marked circuit practice, this was the life for which Lincoln, in his years in the White House, was to feel nostalgic yearning.

To portray, within the confines of a paragraph or two, the place which Bloomington occupies in the law career of the man who went from the Illinois courtrooms to become an almost legendary figure in the hearts of men everywhere, is plainly impossible. Here, in the county seat of McLean County, he suffered, at the very outset of his career, a humiliating experience. In 1837 Stuart sent him to Bloomington to handle a case for an Englishman named Baddely, giving him a letter of introduction. So indignant was Baddely over the appearance of substitute counsel that he curtly dismissed the ungainly, rumpled young lawyer with the coarse boots, innocent of polish, and the baggy pants too short for his long legs.[11]

The circuit court records of McLean were lost in the courthouse fire of 1900. From various other sources, however, such as the collected papers of his contemporaries, newspaper files of the Bloomington *Pantagraph*, and the firsthand impressions of old residents, a considerable mass of data has been garnered concerning Lincoln's cases there. While many of them were routine and thus devoid of any great material interest, there were other, important ones in which he played a significant part. Here Lincoln, representing the plaintiff, filed the suit in equity brought by the Illinois Central Railroad against McLean County to restrain the collection of certain taxes claimed by the county. Upon appeal to the Supreme Court, Lincoln, in one of his most signal victories, succeeded in reversing the lower court. Here, in June, 1857, a year and a half after the reversal, Lincoln's suit against the railroad for his five-thousand-dollar fee was brought. Here, for a week in 1857, he participated, on behalf of the prosecution, in the sensational murder trial of *People* v. *Isaac Wyant*, in which he was pitted against his friend, Leonard Swett, who advanced, in one of the first cases in which it was invoked on an indictment for murder in Illinois, the defense of insanity.[12] In addition to Swett, McLean numbered among its distinguished lawyers Asahel Gridley, John M. Scott and William Ward Orme.

Lincoln attended every spring and fall term of the McLean Circuit Court, from the fall of 1849 until a month before his nomination for President in 1860, with the exceptions of April, 1851, and September, 1859. Throughout the decade of the 'fifties, McLean was regarded as a happy hunting ground for lawyers in search of cases. So great had the volume of business become by December, 1859, that a six-week session was held, in order to eliminate the backlog of calendared cases. Judge Davis, in an effort to clear the court docket, instructed the Grand Jury to confine their deliberations to matters of a serious nature—"something worthy of penitential honors or hempen promotion—grave subjects only."[13]

No architectural gem, the McLean County courthouse, situated atop a knoll in the center of town, was of the drab "coffee mill" type. The building, resembling nothing so much as a livery stable, in which Lincoln practiced (the site now marked by a bronze tablet), was erected for the then substantial sum of $8,500, and was in use from 1836 to 1868. The bell in the cupola was rung to convene court, and again at seven o'clock in the evening. In one of the ground-floor rooms Jesse Fell turned out the short-lived *Bloomington Observer and McLean County Advocate* (1837–1839).

Lincoln was a frequent visitor at the homes of Fell, Davis and Swett, and their law offices were used by him at different times. He also availed himself of the facilities of the office of the local justice of the peace, Zachariah Lawrence, who served in that capacity from 1846 to 1881. The Squire, as he was known, recalled Lincoln coming to his office one day, sitting at a table, taking half a sheet of paper and proceeding to write out a declaration. When the Squire remarked on the fact that it was a mighty small piece of paper on which to write a declaration, Lincoln replied "that he had always found it best to make few statements, for if he made too many the opposite side might make him prove them."[14]

By common consent, without dissenting voice, Jesse W. Fell (1808–1887), reputedly the first lawyer to settle in McLean County, was known as Bloomington's first citizen. He came to Illinois in 1832; in 1833 he began the practice of law in Bloomington, then engaged in real estate and a variety of other business enterprises, as well. He was an early friend of Lincoln—in fact, one of his very closest. In politics he was a staunch Whig, who assisted in the birth of the Republican Party. He founded the *Pantagraph*, which under his guidance soon became one of the leading newspapers in the state.

Fell it was who suggested the idea of a joint discussion between Lincoln and Douglas, and though at first he met with discouragement from the Douglas forces, he continued to urge it from 1854 to 1858. To this nineteenth-century Warwick, more than to any other man, is due the credit of suggesting and bringing about those great debates, the influence of which on Lincoln's fortunes and the events of history was so tremendous. It was at the earnest request of Fell that in 1859 Lincoln, in the courthouse in Bloomington, wrote his autobiography,[15] which he for-warded to Fell with the note: "There is not much of it, for the reason, I suppose, that there is not much of me." (The one-page note accompanying the "little sketch," formerly in the Barrett Collection, is dated Springfield, December 20, 1859.)

Lincoln numbered, among his many friends in Bloomington, William McCullough, who was, from 1840, sheriff and clerk of the McLean County Circuit Court. His deputy clerk recalled that "Judge David Davis, who was the Circuit Judge, had his office in the same room with McCullough, and Mr. Lincoln was very inti-mate with both. That office was his [Lincoln's] waiting room mornings before Court opened."[16] As Lieutenant Colonel of the Fourth Illinois Cavalry, McCullough was killed while leading a night charge near Coffeeville, Mississippi, on December 5, 1862. To lighten her overwhelming grief, Lincoln took time out from his presidential tasks to write a comforting letter to his daughter Fanny; for tenderness and sensitivity, it bears favorable compari-son with the more famous Bixby letter.

> Executive Mansion,
> Washington, December 23, 1862.
>
> Dear Fanny
> It is with deep grief that I learn of the death of your kind and brave Father; and, especially, that it is affecting your young heart beyond what is common in such cases. In this sad world of ours, sorrow comes to all; and, to the young, it comes with bitterest agony, because it takes them unawares. The older have learned to ever expect it. I am anxious to afford some alleviation of your present distress. Perfect relief is not possible, except with time. You can not now realize that you will ever feel better. Is not this so? And yet it is a mistake. You are sure to be happy again. To know this, which is certainly true, will make you some less miserable now. I have had experience enough to know what I say; and you need only to believe it, to feel better at once. The memory of your dear Father, instead of an agony, will yet be a sad sweet feeling in your heart, of a purer and holier sort than you have known before.
> Please present my kind regards to your afflicted mother.
> Your sincere friend
> A. Lincoln
>
> Miss Fanny McCullough.[17]

One is constantly moved at the wisdom and grace of expression of this prairie lawyer and politician.

4.

After a week spent in Bloomington, the group traveled thirty-five miles southwest to Mt. Pulaski, seat of Logan County. Lincoln, as chairman of the Eleventh General Assembly, reported favorably on the bill which carved Logan County out of sprawling Sangamon in 1839. At his suggestion, the new county was named in honor of his old friend Dr. John A. Logan, then a member of the House; he was the father of General John A. ("Black Jack") Logan. The prairie community of Postville, with a population of less than 100, was selected as county seat. The first term of court in the newly created county was held on June 13, 1839, in a makeshift courtroom in Deskins' Tavern, a renowned hostelry where travelers sought refreshment and where Lincoln was a frequent guest.

Later that year a two-story frame structure was erected to house the Postville courthouse; this building, in which Lincoln undoubtedly made a number of appearances, was 28' x 38', and cost slightly more than one thousand dollars. Its interior provided offices for the county officials, as well as a courtroom. Here Lincoln practiced until the removal of the seat of justice to Mt. Pulaski in 1848. Consumed in the fire which destroyed the Logan County records in 1857 were most of the files of cases in which Lincoln participated in Postville; those surviving are not especially rewarding.

Over the protests of a group of leading citizens, the old Postville courthouse was purchased by Henry Ford and removed, in 1929, to Dearborn, Michigan, for inclusion in the collection of Americana in Greenfield village. On the site of the original Postville courthouse, where the State of Illinois has built a replica of the building removed to Dearborn, there is a plate mounted on a heavy boulder which reads:

In memory of
Abraham Lincoln who practiced law from 1840
to 1848 in Logan County's first court
house on this site
Erected by
Abraham Lincoln Chapter—Daughters of
the American Revolution

Deskins' Tavern, just south of the courthouse, furnished food and lodging for the judge and the lawyers. Together with the litigants, jurors and prisoners out on bail, they occupied the same table, with the judge seated at the head. A ball was customarily given during the period when court was in session; it was the social event of the season, "looked forward to by gentlemen and the fair sex alike."

Logan County, in late 1848, was excited by a controversy over the removal of the county seat to Mt. Pulaski which, with a population of three hundred, was somewhat larger than Postville. Lincoln played a leading role in the court battle touched off by the transfer. At the time of the original location of the county seat at Postville, the proprietors of the town agreed, in order to secure the designation, to erect a courthouse on a block owned by them and deed the land and building to the county, which they did. The deed was in the usual fee simple form, without reservation. Upon removal of the county seat, the county commissioners sold the land and building to private parties, whereupon the Postville proprietors, contesting the right to sell, sued for damages.

The lawsuit came to trial before Judge Davis, at Mt. Pulaski, in August of 1849. Lincoln, Herndon and Charles Emerson (with whom Lincoln was often associated, in Decatur and on the circuit, from 1838 until 1853, when Emerson became a circuit judge) appeared for the county; they were opposed by Stuart, Logan and a son of Ninian Edwards, for the proprietors. It was Lincoln's contention that the owners, in deeding the land without condition or reservation, had taken their chances on the people later changing the situs of the county seat. Davis, adopting

Lincoln's argument that the deed was absolute on its face, found for the county; on appeal, the Supreme Court sustained him.[18]

This is, perhaps, as good a time as any to take notice of the oft-repeated assertion that Lincoln secured an unfair advantage over his opponents, in that he commanded the Judge's private ear. The negative view finds distinguished support in the person of Paul M. Angle, who points out that of eighty-seven cases tried by Lincoln before Davis without a jury, in only forty cases were judgments rendered in favor of Lincoln's clients.[19] Many of the appeals which Lincoln was obliged to take to the Supreme Court were from adverse decisions which he had sustained at the hands of Davis. That the great panjandrum of the circuit was "a friend at court," in any derogatory sense, hardly squares with the facts.

In the center of the business district of Mt. Pulaski stands an attractive two-story red-brick building which, unlike most early Illinois courthouses, has escaped being sacrificed on the altar of rising real-estate values. This State Memorial, which housed the Logan County courthouse from 1848 to 1853, was erected at a cost of $2,700, raised by popular subscription. The building, which is three-quarters intact, has been restored to its original appearance, after having been used for years as a schoolhouse, city hall, firehouse and post office. The Logan County Historical Society has furnished it as it was in Lincoln's time. An interesting exhibit is the gavel used by Judge Davis when he held court there.

From 1849 to January, 1856, years of active practice on the legal circuit of which Logan County was a part, Lincoln appeared regularly in Mt. Pulaski, as did Stuart, Logan, Swett, Emerson, Baker, Lamborn (who carried into his private practice the skill he developed as a cross-examiner during his career as Attorney General), Weldon, Clifton H. Moore and Samuel C. Parks— titans all. Most of the circuit riders stopped at the Mt. Pulaski House, constructed in 1844 and dismantled in 1902. Parks, who sent Lincoln his copy of the Howells campaign biography to read and correct, was frequently associated in the trial of cases with Lincoln, for whose nomination he worked at Chicago. At the

Congressional convention which nominated Logan as Lincoln's successor in Congress, he was one of the two delegates favorable to Lincoln's renomination.[20] (Even Herndon advocated Logan over Lincoln.) Parks made his home in Mt. Pulaski, and his office there (as well as that later occupied by him in Lincoln) was used by Lincoln as his legal headquarters while in town. It was Parks who wrote: "I have often said that for a man who was a quarter of a century both a lawyer and a politician he [Lincoln] was the most honest man I ever knew." Something of the same thought was expressed (even though in a perverse sort of way) by Douglas when, speaking of the man who opposed him in the most famous debate in American history, he said: "Of all the damned Whig rascals about Springfield, Abe Lincoln is the ablest and the most honest."

At the beginning, the lawyers who tried cases at the Logan County bar were, for the most part, from outside the county, principally from Springfield and Bloomington. In John M. Palmer's splendid recapturing of the county's early legal history, one reads that it "was seemingly regarded as an out-post of Springfield and Bloomington lawyers, who claimed it as part of their bailiwick and monopolized or 'gobbled up' all the paying practice; but a time came when the lawyers here were not only able to sustain themselves and hold their practice at home against all comers, but were able to retaliate upon the enemy by carrying the war into their own camps and 'foraging' upon them; . . ."[21]

Nominally, Mt. Pulaski ceased to be the county seat in 1853, when the seat of justice was transferred to Lincoln, laid out in August of that year. Actually, because of pending litigation, complete transfer did not occur until 1856. The first courthouse in Lincoln's "namesake town," the only city in the United States named for Abraham Lincoln before he became President, burned down on April 14, 1857, a year after its construction. The September term of court was held in the Christian Church. Lincoln did not attend, being busy in Chicago with the Rock Island Bridge Case. The county fathers outdid themselves when they built the second Lincoln courthouse in November, 1857, at a cost of fifteen thousand dollars, on the site of the one that had burned.

The town of Lincoln was formed after the coming of the railroad, and consequently Lincoln's circuit trips there, in the spring of 1858 and the spring and fall of 1859, were by rail.

Standing on the site of the original courthouse in Lincoln is an excellent reconstruction, built by the State of Illinois as a part of the city's centennial celebration in 1953. Enclosed in a state park, it is visited yearly by thousands interested in the Lincoln story.

The first hotel in the young town, where many famous men of that day stayed while in Lincoln, was the Lincoln House. Jacob T. Randolph, a justice of the peace in Lincoln, recalled: "When Lincoln attended court in Lincoln he always stayed at the Lincoln House." Once, according to an unverified legend, Randolph and other friends of a man who had been indicted for murder, the defense being the unwritten law, "sought Mr. Lincoln at the Lincoln House to defend their friend and Lincoln, being convinced that their friend was justified in his act, took the case, secured an acquittal, and charged them $15 for a fee."[22]

5.

The next sitting of court entailed a twenty-mile trip northeast to Clinton, county seat of DeWitt County (named for De Witt Clinton, a former New York governor). Here, the reader will recall, Lincoln and Douglas, appearing as co-counsel in the county's first murder trial (1840), successfully defended Spencer Turner. Here Lincoln served as judge, acting for Davis. Here, in 1853, he was to defend Moses Loe on a charge of murder, a case which had the roads alive with countryfolk hastening to the trial. It was here, in 1858 or 1859, according to Weldon, that he first met George B. McClellan, in connection with the trial of a case in which the latter appeared as a witness on behalf of the Illinois Central Railroad, by which he was then employed as chief en-

gineer, later becoming vice president and general manager of the
road. Lincoln, at the time, was retained by the railroad to try
damage suits for them.[23]

Among the cases occupying Lincoln's attention in the Clinton courthouse was the defense, on May 18, 1854, of nine overly
zealous women crusaders from Marion, DeWitt County, charged
with riot. These early counterparts of Carry Nation had swept
through the complainant's saloon, or "doggery," armed with
clubs, destroying the saloon keeper's stock and reducing the place
to so much broken glass and splintered wood, upon his refusal
to voluntarily close up his business. When the defendants appeared in court, they were attended by a horde of women fellow
workers in the crusade to save men from the drunkard's fate; they
came from far and wide. Moral support availed the defendants
nothing, for the jury convicted; their bar-smashing escapade cost
the ladies two dollars each.[24]

The *Swett Papers* contain an interesting letter written by
Lincoln's colleague while awaiting the jury's verdict in a case
tried in Clinton, at the October term 1850:

Court room Clinton
Oct. 10, 1850

My dear sister
    Our circuit court is now in session. the room is crowded, I have
just closed an important case and while I am waiting the verdict of
the jury I will scribble a few lines to you. A few weeks since I received a letter from Danville stating that you were married in August
and in these few lines therefore I will most earnestly wish for yourself and your husband bountiful and continued blessings of joy, peace
and prosperity. . . .

Affectionately your Bro
L. Swett

P.S.   My jury have come in and I am badly whipped.[25]

6.

Twenty miles southeast lay the then tiny town of Monticello, county seat of Piatt County. Architecturally undistinguished

both inside and out, its first courthouse, erected in 1843, has been likened to the little red schoolhouse. It served the county until 1856, when it was moved to the west side of the square, where it was soon destroyed by fire. Piatt's next courthouse was erected on the site of the old one, and was in use until 1903, when it was sold to the highest bidder for $138.03. Though Lincoln is known to have practiced in Piatt County, the distressing meagerness of the extant records precludes any discussion of his trials there.

7.

From Monticello northeast to Urbana, seat of Champaign County, was a trip of some twenty miles. With its wooded, unbridged streams, and roads that were little better than wagon tracks, Champaign, which boasted a population, in 1854, of but 6,565, was the most bucolic of the circuit's fourteen counties.[26] The two-story brick courthouse in which Lincoln most frequently appeared was erected in 1848, at a cost of $2,744, which brought down denunciation upon the heads of the authorities, for their extravagance.[27] Their lives prosaic, with few ecstasies, the folks of Urbana and the farmers of the back country almost never failed to attend at court sessions. The Urbana *Clarion* of October 29, 1854, observed that "during the past week, nearly every resident of the county has been in our beautiful city— Courting."

Until 1840 the county was without a jail. The first to be erected was a two-story affair, with an outside stairway to the second floor where, by the only door of the building, prisoners were admitted. By means of a trap door, those who showed symptoms of being refractory were lowered by ladder to the ground floor, after which the ladder was raised to the upper level.[28] It was from this supposedly escape-proof jailhouse that Lincoln's client, the convicted murderer William Weaver, took his departure in 1845.

In a five-column report of the spring term 1850 of the Champaign Circuit, the Danville *Illinois Citizen* gives a good description of Lincoln as a lawyer, and reveals something of the high regard in which he was held in counties making up the Eighth Circuit ten years before his nomination for the presidency:

> In his examination of witnesses, he displays a masterly ingenuity . . . that baffles concealment and defies deceit. And in addressing a jury, there is no false glitter, no sickly sentimentalism to be discovered. In vain we look for a rhetorical display. . . . Seizing upon the minutest points, he weaves them into his argument with an ingenuity really astonishing. . . . Bold, forcible and energetic, he forces conviction upon the mind, and, by his clearness and conciseness, stamps it there, not to be erased. . . . Such are some of the qualities that place Mr. L. at the head of the profession in this State.

It was in Urbana that Lincoln tried his first case (*McGinnis v. Illinois Central Railroad*) for the Illinois Central, in May, 1853. The trial resulted in a jury verdict for the plaintiff of $37.50 for damages sustained by reason of the construction of a roadbed over his lands. For his services Lincoln received a fee of $25.[29]

Though life on the circuit may have been, at times, somewhat dull, the lawyers must have found Urbana particularly genial. As Whitney tells it, "The counties of Champaign and Vermilion were closely identified and bound together; and, socially, segregated from the rest; while the business in those counties seemed to produce less strain on the bench and bar than in the rest of the circuit. Certain it is, that the social circle which revolved around the Judge was larger and more active there than elsewhere."[30]

8.

The scene shifts to Danville, seat of Vermilion County, where, in the fifty-foot square, two-story brick courthouse which served the county from 1833 to 1872, Lincoln did an extensive business. This important county seat town sustained three hotels. When in Danville, Lincoln usually stopped at the McCormick

House, the leading inn in that bustling community; if it was filled upon arrival, he and the other lawyers joined the overflow of guests at the more pretentious but less dignified Pennsylvania House, around the corner, or at nearby Bailey's Tavern. After a thirty-mile trip due easterly from Urbana, across the "Grand Prairie" region of east central Illinois, Judge Davis led the way to the McCormick House, where, as befitting his station, the parlor had been fitted up for him as a bedroom. (The room set aside for Davis was often the only decent one in the tavern.) Come dinnertime, the Judge, no inconsiderable trencherman, led the procession to the dining room where, on a long table, the evening meal was soon laid out. After dinner the group betook themselves to the porch, there to be serenaded by Reynolds' Brass Band, in celebration of the opening of court week.

It is narrated of Lincoln in Danville that, at one of the 1850 terms of court, he and Ward Hill Lamon (whom Lincoln always addressed by his middle name) were in attendance, as spectators, while court was in session. Something which occurred in the case on trial reminded Lincoln of a story, which he proceeded to whisper to his friend, who was convulsed with loud laughter, bringing down upon himself the ire of Judge Davis and a five-dollar fine for contempt of court. At the same time, the magisterial Davis turned to Lincoln and inquired: "Is this my court or yours?" Later in the trial, Davis called Lamon to the bench and asked him to retell Lincoln's story. When Lamon had finished the rib-tickling yarn, the Judge laughed quite as heartily as had Lamon and promptly remitted the fine.[31]

In the day-to-day grind of circuit practice, Lincoln, who was a man of infinite jest, found not only pastime, but a certain utility in humor. As Whitney acutely noted, his broad streak of fun withdrew his mind "from brooding melancholy, and from the severe mental strain which, unless relieved, would have broken him down; . . ."[32] (In the same manner, he was later to relieve his distress over military reverses with rueful quips.) Lincoln demonstrated that tribulation and humor are not altogether incompatible. "In our walks about the little towns where courts were held," wrote Whitney, "he saw ludicrous elements in everything, and could either narrate some story from his storehouse of jokes, else he could improvise one; . . ."[33]

Among the striking personalities associated with Lincoln was Lamon, with whom he entered into a working arrangement, in Danville, which lasted from 1852 to 1856, when Lamon was elected prosecuting attorney of the circuit.[34] The frequently stated thesis that Lincoln's business relationship with Lamon bore all the characteristics of a bona fide partnership, does not bear the test of the record. While it is true that a newspaper notice of November 10, 1852, carried the announcement that "Lincoln & Lamon, Attorneys at Law, having formed a co-partnership will practice in the courts of the Eighth Judicial Circuit, and the Superior Court, and all business entrusted to them will be attended to with promptness and fidelity,"[35] the extant evidence indicates that the "co-partnership" was not that all-embracing. There is a lurking suspicion in the writer's mind that Lamon was solely responsible for insertion of the advertisement; Lincoln's co-laborer, though a likable chap, was, like Herndon, possessed of a pronounced tendency toward exaggeration. John M. Zane wrote of him: "He does not seem to be a naturally truthful man."[36]

It would have been decidedly unfair to Herndon for Lincoln to have become involved in another, separate partnership, with the conflicting loyalties and overlapping of interests implicit in such duality. For all the advertisement's proclaiming that the "co-partnership will practice in the courts of the Eighth Judicial Circuit," in but a single instance does one find them associated outside of Vermilion, and in that case (in McLean County) they were joined in interest with two other attorneys, Clifton H. Moore and Harvey Hogg. Nor, for that matter, is there any evidence that they ever appeared together in the Illinois Supreme Court or the Federal Court. During the period commencing with Lamon's opening of an office conveniently situated over a saloon in the Barnum Building in 1852, and ending with his election as state's attorney in 1856, there were instances of Lincoln appearing in association with other Danville attorneys.

Taken all in all, this is hardly the record of a partnership. In the writer's opinion, it all adds up to the fact that the term, when used to describe their business relationship, is a misnomer—that Lamon was nothing more than a resident attorney, who engaged Lincoln in connection with a great many cases in Vermilion County. Weik, writing in this connection, stated that "Mr. Lincoln had but three law-partners: John T. Stuart, Stephen T. Logan and William H. Herndon in the order named. He was frequently associated with other lawyers in certain cases, but there was no partnership or union of interest beyond the case at bar. In this way has developed the notion that Ward Lamon and others were his law partners."[37]

Whatever the business relationship between this unlikely pair, one thing is certain: Lincoln had taken unto himself, in the swashbuckling Lamon, another two-fisted drinker, a big, burly, outgoing man who, as befitted a Virginia gentleman, "always took them standing." This lusty character, boisterous in manner and with a penchant for bending the elbow on the slightest provocation, was redolent of Midwestern ebullience. With the notable exception of Lincoln and Herndon, probably two personages more sharply contrasted than Lincoln and Lamon could not have been brought together; yet the remarkable fact is that they hit it off well.

Despite the fact that Lamon, a man of modest abilities whose qualities were the opposite of intellectual, was certainly no great shakes as a lawyer, their joint appearances were for the most part successful. With his liking for good company and strong whiskey, the rollicking, convivial "Hill" enjoyed immense local popularity. In what proportion the fees were divided is not known, but it would seem reasonable to believe they were split down the middle. The *Robert Todd Lincoln Collection* contains but one letter bearing on the subject of their joint practice. Lamon wrote: "I have commenced about fourteen suits against the Great Western Rail Road Company . . . for damages, in the next circuit court—You will be here if you are well, will you not?" Elsewhere in the letter he mentions "Our Clark vs Hoxworth *et, al,* suit" and seeks Lincoln's advice concerning information given under oath. And in a postscript he asks another question having to do with procedure.[38] It is quite apparent that Lamon depended on Lincoln for guidance in connection with the handling of their cases.

As President, Lincoln appointed him Marshal of the District of Columbia, and though an antagonistic Senate sought his removal, Lincoln went with him right down the line, standing firmly by the man who, by the attraction of opposites, had become his trusted friend. Lamon, for his part, was utterly single-minded in his devotion to the President, whom he admired unstintingly; he it was who, armed with two pistols, two derringers, two large knives and a set of brass knuckles, accompanied the President-elect on his secret night ride from Harrisburg, Pennsylvania to Washington. Though he thought less with his head than his heart, Lamon possessed great personal magnetism, and that capacity for loyalty which forges the bonds of friendship more surely than any superiority of intellect can do.

As was usually the case on the circuit, Lincoln drew up most of the pleadings. Lamon's aversion to paper work might charitably be ascribed to the distracting sounds of brawling and merriment coming, respectively, from the saloon below and the house of sin immediately adjoining his office;[39] a more likely explanation lies in the fact that he was not overly given to cerebration.

From the 1840's on, Lincoln had a large volume of business in Vermilion County, a fact the more remarkable since, being at the extreme eastern terminus of the circuit, it was the farthest away from Springfield of any of the courts he attended. Among the resident attorneys, other than Lamon, who engaged Lincoln's services in Danville was Oliver L. Davis, whom Judge Davis consulted on the eastern end of the circuit whenever "puzzled about the law."[40] (On the western end it was Clifton Moore.)[41]

In Danville, Lincoln incurred the disapproval of his fellow attorneys through having committed the unforgivable sin in law of returning part of a fee, in a case involving conservation of the assets of a feeble-minded young lady. Her brother, suspecting that a suitor had his sights set on the ten thousand dollars of which the girl was possessed, engaged Lamon to bring a proceeding looking to the appointment by the court of a conservator of her assets. Lamon brought Lincoln into the picture. Upon completion of the work, the former charged and received $250 for their services. When Lincoln learned of what he considered an unconscionable fee, he prevailed upon the reluctant Lamon to return one half. Lamon, relating the incident, said: "I protested that the fee was fixed in advance; that Scott was perfectly satisfied, and had so expressed himself. 'That may be,' retorted Lincoln, with a look of distress and of undisguised displeasure, 'but *I* am not satisfied. This is positively wrong. Go, call him back and return half the money at least, or I will not receive one cent of it for my share.' I did go, and Scott was astonished when I handed back half the fee."[42]

Judge Davis, hearing of this shocking departure from one of the profession's most sacred precepts, chided Lincoln with the observation: "Lincoln, you are impoverishing this bar by your picayune charges of fees, and the lawyers have reason to complain of you." That evening, at the hotel, his fellow attorneys charged him with having broken one of the unwritten rules of the trade, and, after a mock trial, "fined" him for what they considered an act inimical to the best interests of the bar.

Lincoln's last appearance in the Vermilion Court was at the November term, 1859. In Danville, at that time, he accepted an invitation to speak in New York the following February, where he made the famous Cooper Union speech that made him a national figure. "I will be on hand and in due time will notify you of the exact day," he wrote James A. Briggs, of New York City, on the stationery of the McCormick House. "I believe, after all, I shall make a political speech of it."[43]

The Lincoln Circuit Marking Association had its home in Danville where, during the life of the association, its annual meetings were held. The day following the meeting, a hardy group of enthusiasts for the old circuit-riding days joined in a pilgrimage over the course linking the various county seats of the "Old Eighth."

9.

From Danville the route lay south thirty-five miles across the Illinois plains to Paris, seat of Edgar County, one of the middle tier counties lying on the eastern border of the state, where prairie and woodland met. The sleepy little prairie hamlet was a charming place, which Lincoln and the others always looked forward to visiting, even though the accommodations were typically bad. No appreciable amount of information is available concerning Lincoln's practice there.

Lincoln first attended the Edgar County Circuit Court in May of 1842, at the request of Linder, whom he assisted in the trial of *Samuel Nolan* v. *John Hunter*. Appearing with Linder on behalf of the defendant, Lincoln drew the pleadings in the case and participated in the trial before a jury—all for the sum of five dollars.[44]

Edgar County is one of the counties in Illinois that never had a log courthouse. The contract for the first temple of justice, erected in 1823, called for a frame structure 22 x 32 feet. In 1832 the county fathers decided that a better building was needed, and so erected a brick "coffee mill" for $4,250, which, like the present courthouse, stood in the center of the square. Erected as a display of local pride when most counties were still in a pioneer state, it remained in use until 1891.

10.

Fifty-five weary miles separated Paris from Shelbyville, seat of Shelby County. This represented the greatest distance between

county-seat towns on the route of the Eighth Circuit. The ex-
hausting trip southwesterly took two days, and sometimes three,
depending on the weather. Nights, the tired travelers stopped at
wayside inns or at the homes of prairie settlers who, living in
isolated segments of society, heartily welcomed them to share
their modest lot. The frontier was hospitable; it took in the wayfarer as a matter of course.

When Shelby became a part of the Eighth Circuit in 1842,
Lincoln commenced attending the circuit court each spring and
fall, and continued doing so until 1852. He was often associated,
in law as in politics, with Anthony Thornton, the leading Whig
lawyer in Shelbyville; upon dissolution of the Whig, and forging
of the Republican Party, they parted political company.

One of Lincoln's more interesting cases in Shelby County
was the slander action brought by Sarah Alsop against Lincoln's
client, John Sturgeon. According to the declaration, the defendant had accused the plaintiff of having committed adultery. The
defense may be gathered from the following extract from the
motion in arrest of judgment, in Lincoln's hand, filed May 21,
1850:

> 1st. Because each and all of the counts of the declaration charge
> that at the time of speaking the words the plaintiff was an unmarried
> woman; and that the defendant, by the words, imputed to her the
> crime of adultery; whereas an unmarried woman can not be guilty
> of Adultery—[45]

While, as a proposition of law, there may have been some
merit in Lincoln's contention, the judgment for the plaintiff was
permitted to stand.

Shelbyville's second courthouse, a forty-foot square brick
edifice with cupola, and two outside stairways leading to the
courtroom on the second floor, was erected in 1832, at a cost of
$1,094. The most attractive of the square courthouses that were
so popular from 1830 to 1850, it remained in use until 1881.

11.

With the clearing of the docket in Shelbyville, the caravan moved on fifteen miles northeast, to Sullivan, county seat of Moultrie County, which was added to the Eighth Circuit in 1843. The courthouse, which served the county for two decades, was a square, two-story brick building of no great architectural merit, measuring thirty-eight feet on each side. The courtroom occupied the entire upper story. Moultrie County was formed from parts of Shelby and Macon Counties, and was named for William Moultrie, a soldier of the Revolutionary War.

Upon its organization, the leading legal talent of the neighboring counties commenced practicing there. Foremost among them were Lincoln, Linder, O. B. Ficklin, Emerson and Thornton. It was in Sullivan that Richard J. Oglesby, a significant figure in Illinois history, first hung out his shingle as an attorney. His dalliance with the law, which commenced in 1845, was of brief duration. A bedrock Whig and later black Republican, Oglesby, who came on the scene by way of Kentucky, became so immersed in politics and public life that his interest in the law diminished in proportion as his political activity increased. Writing, in after years, to John M. Palmer, he said: "Then I went to war, and when I returned from it, in 1864, . . . I slipped in to be a governor, and that finished my fooling with the law,—a noble profession, but one that will not be trifled with."[46]

A fire in 1865 burned the courthouse to the ground, destroying all records of cases prior to 1849; thus, little information on Lincoln's early practice there is available. While he made a number of court appearances in Sullivan in the 'fifties, none of the cases in which he appeared can be said to have a commanding claim on the reader's attention.

12.

From Sullivan northwest to Decatur, seat of Macon County and penultimate stop on the "swing around," was a trek of twenty miles. Lincoln had a very special affection for this town, not far from the Sangamon River in central Illinois, with which his name is so unforgettably linked. Here it was that he spent his first year in Illinois, made his first recorded political speech (1830), and met Denton Offutt and Richard J. Oglesby, both of whom were significant in his later career.

The first courthouse, erected in 1830, which served the county until 1838, once had the distinction of being the oldest of the courthouses of the Eighth Circuit, then standing, in which Abraham Lincoln practiced law. Enclosed in a site in Fairview Park, Decatur, is a log replica, 18' x 24', one-and-a-half stories in height. Known as the Lincoln Courthouse, it is the closest link with the Decatur which Lincoln knew. When the Lincoln family arrived there in 1830, on the way from Indiana, the building was then in the course of construction on the west side of the square. Whitney tells of the occasion, in May, 1856, when Lincoln, en route to the Bloomington convention, stopped overnight in Decatur. On the afternoon of his arrival, he strolled about town, talking with others bound for the convention. To Whitney he said, as they approached the open space in front of the old courthouse: "Here on this spot, twenty-six years ago, I made my first halt in Illinois; here I stood, and there our wagon stood, with all that we owned in the world."[47] The building has been kept in excellent repair, intact as built, except for the roof.

It was in Decatur, in 1860, that Illinois Republicans endorsed Lincoln as their successful candidate for President.

13.

Last stop on the circuit,[48] after a journey of thirty miles southwest from Decatur, was Taylorville, county seat of Christian, named after the Kentucky county whence came many of the residents. The first courthouse, completed in 1840 at a cost of $2,350, still stands on the Christian County fairgrounds, a mile west of its original location on the public square. A two-story frame building, it possessed a courtroom but no jury room, so that deliberations of the jury had to be conducted outside under a tree.[49] It was in this building that Lincoln practiced while Christian County formed part of the Eighth Circuit. Because of the sparse data available, not very much is known of Lincoln's practice there.

14.

A final leg of twenty-five miles brought the circuit's travellingest lawyer to the end of the journey. As "Old Buck" came trotting down familiar Eighth Street, Lincoln was happy in the thought that Robert and the cherubic little woman then expecting the arrival of a third son (Eddie had passed away the previous February first), would be waiting for him. For dinner she may have prepared his favorite dish of stewed chicken "and small biscuits with thick cream gravy poured over it, all on one platter;" for dessert, the "yellow cake" of which he always was so fond. Later he could sit back in the rocking chair and tell Mary, who was so very proud of her "Mr. Lincoln" and discerning of his greatness, of amusing things that occurred the latest time around.

CHAPTER XIII

In the Federal Court

1.

THE United States District Court for the State of Illinois was established on March 3, 1819, about a year after the state's admission to the Union, at which time Nathaniel Pope was appointed, by President Monroe, the first United States District Judge for Illinois, an office he held until his death in 1850, when he was succeeded by Thomas Drummond. Linder's sprightly collection of character sketches of coeval figures of the Illinois bench and bar describes Pope as an "eminent lawyer," who "was pretty severe upon the lawyers who practiced in his court, and was not very choice as to the words he used when he saw fit to reprimand them."[1] The Quincy *Whig* described him as an "able jurist and distinguished lawyer."[2] He was the father of John Pope, the pugnacious general selected by Lincoln as commander of the Army of Virginia, only to be later relieved of his command and sent back to the West because of ill feeling existing between him and McClellan. Judge Pope was somewhat abrasive in manner, but his gruffness toward Lincoln had a touch of tenderness in it. He greatly admired the lanky Springfield lawyer, as did a few others of perception who, at a time when some people were writing him off as a buffoon, given to coarse jokes and moth-eaten homilies, saw the true quality of this exceptional man.

It will be recalled from an earlier chapter that Lincoln's earliest contact with the federal courts was at Vandalia where, while serving as a member of the lower house of the Legislature, he found time to visit the Illinois Federal District Court, which held two annual sessions at the then state capital. In 1839, when the state offices were moved to Springfield, the Federal Court also removed to the new capital, setting up temporary quarters in the Christian Church. In 1840 it began holding sessions in rented quarters on the second floor of the Tinsley Building, at the southwest corner of Sixth and Adams streets, where for fifteen years Lincoln tried his federal cases. Although the records of his earlier cases there are incomplete, sufficient data is at hand to show that even during the early years of his practice Lincoln received his fair share of business in the United States courts.

When Lincoln was admitted to federal practice on December 3, 1839, there was no Federal Building in Springfield. A search of the old records of the Interior Department shows that on August 17, 1855, the Government moved from the Tinsley Building and rented new quarters—seven rooms in the three-story building on the northeast corner of Sixth and Washington Streets, belonging to Stephen T. Logan, and known as the Logan Building. The rooms provided, in addition to a courtroom heated by a great "cannon ball" stove in its center, accommodations for the judges, juries, clerks, marshal and the prosecuting attorney, all at an annual rental of eight hundred dollars. With some slight increase in the rental, these quarters were occupied by the court until February 15, 1870, when the Federal Building was ready for occupancy.

During the years 1855 to 1860 Lincoln & Herndon appeared in ninety-one of the approximately one thousand cases tried in the Logan Building before Samuel H. Treat, United States District Judge. In his appearances in the Federal Court, Lincoln was associated with and opposed by, at different times, Stuart, Logan, Purple, Goodrich, Archibald Williams, Joseph Gillespie, Browning and the latter's partner, Nehemiah Bushnell, John A. McClernand, Isaac J. Ketcham, E. D. Baker, Palmer, Bledsoe and Onslow Peters—all of them top-flight lawyers.

It does not appear that Herndon did very much, if any, of the firm's work before the federal judges. The extant pleadings of Lincoln & Herndon, in connection with their cases in the Federal District Court, range from *praecipes* written on small slips of paper to declarations and bills of complaint pages in length. Taken as a whole, they furnish important information on this phase of Lincoln's practice. Roughly ninety per cent of them are in his hand. Of course, there is no sure way of knowing which member of the firm bore the brunt of oral argument, though it seems virtually a certainty that Lincoln, having done the paper work, also handled the cases when they came up in court.

A number of Lincoln's cases in the United States Court for the Southern District of Illinois involved important questions of law and considerable sums of money. On a single day at the March term, 1856, of the United States Circuit Court in Springfield, Lincoln, representing the Chicago, Alton & St. Louis Railroad, appeared in three actions involving claims against the road totaling over four hundred thousand dollars.[3] Not only did he enjoy an extensive practice in the lower federal courts—equal, in importance if not in volume, to that in the state courts—but the fees which he received for work performed there during the late 'fifties represented no small part of the income of Lincoln & Herndon. In one case, *Beaver* v. *Taylor and Gilbert,* involving title to a tract of land adjoining the city of Cairo (pronounced "Kerro"), in southern Illinois—"Egypt," as it has been called—Lincoln & Herndon, Logan and Stuart & Edwards represented the defendants. Of the three-thousand-dollar fee paid by the latter, Lincoln & Herndon received fifteen hundred—a princely sum, especially considering the then value of money. In 1859, when Lincoln was engaged extensively in the federal courts, where the fees were somewhat larger than those in the state courts, his account with the Springfield Marine and Fire Insurance Company (then engaged in the banking business) shows his total deposits for the year to have been $2,739.25.

However all of that may be, it seems safe to conclude that whatever money Lincoln was enabled to save as a result of his practice reflects, for the most part, the sheer volume of cases handled, rather than instances of juicy fees, which were few and far between. A digression may be permissible, at this point, in order to discuss something of Lincoln's peculiar sense of values in connection with the matter of legal fees. It is no part of the purpose of this book to encourage resistance on the part of clients to the payment of adequate fees for legal services, through citing the example of one with whom all lawyers feel a certain kinship. The writer quite naturally inclines to the view of David Davis and the others of Lincoln's contemporaries in this important matter of fees, yet complete candor compels the disclosure that, while he was not altogether indifferent to tangible rewards for his services, there were *numerous* instances of Lincoln's extremely modest charges—modest even when judged by mid-nineteenth century standards.

"One of the first things I learned," observed Lamon, "after getting fairly under way as a lawyer was to charge well for legal services,—a branch of the practice that Mr. Lincoln never could learn."[4] Laymen will note with pleasure, lawyers with horror, the case where Lincoln collected a debt of six hundred dollars due a client and charged a fee of $3.50—much to the disgust of his companions on the circuit.[5]

At a time when he was in practice almost twenty years, a client in Quincy sent him twenty-five dollars for drawing certain legal papers in connection with the leasing of a hotel. Lincoln's letter to the client, returning ten dollars, reads:

Springfield, Illinois
February 21, 1856

Mr. George P. Floyd
Quincy, Illinois

Dear Sir: I have just received yours of 16th, with check on Flagg & Savage for twenty-five dollars. You must think I am a high-priced man. You are too liberal with your money.

Fifteen dollars is enough for the job. I send you a receipt for fifteen dollars, and return to you a ten-dollar bill.

Yours truly,
A. Lincoln[6]

Lincoln's colleagues may have been riled, as well they might, upon learning that he charged the County of Menard only twenty dollars for his services in a case involving, in all, ten court appearances, including a successful application for change of venue to Sangamon and a trial.[7]

The fees which Lincoln charged for work performed on the circuit did not increase greatly from 1839, when the circuit was formed, until the close of his practice. Ten and twenty dollars were the charges customarily made. Thus we find him writing to James F. Joy, attorney for the Illinois Central Railroad, on September 14, 1855, that he had, within the past year, taken care of "at least fifteen cases (I believe, one or two more)" for the road, in the counties of McLean and DeWitt, and that he had decided to "lump them off" at ten dollars a case. At the bottom of his letter Lincoln had Judge Davis certify to the facts and the reasonableness of the charge of one hundred and fifty dollars.[8]

His somewhat preposterous conception of values where compensation for legal services was concerned, is amply confirmed by a receipt in Lincoln's hand for twenty dollars, representing his half of a "joint advance fee," *retention of same being contingent upon the successful outcome of the case.*

Received May 16, 1855. of W. H. Hanna twenty dollars, my half of our joint advance fee, in a case we are to bring in McLean County, for some people by the name of Whitelock, and others, perhaps, which fee we are to refund, in case we have no success in their case—[9]

Lawyers, like gossipy washerwomen, have a nose for the tidings of the trade. It takes no imagination at all to envision the mental anguish of Lincoln's colleagues upon learning of his charge for handling a Supreme Court appeal at a time when he was already a seasoned lawyer and in a position to demand substantial compensation for his services. In 1856 there lived in Greenville, Illinois, a blacksmith and buggy maker by the name of Moffatt. A few days after the November presidential election of that year, Moffatt and his friend Isaac Smith became embroiled in a dispute over how the State of New York had cast its vote. Finally Smith offered to—and did—bet him one hundred dollars against a buggy which Moffatt had in his shop that the election had gone as he claimed. When Smith won and went to collect the buggy, he was advised that Moffatt had sold it to one John A. Smith, whereupon Isaac Smith brought an action in replevin against the vendee.[10] The trial, which was held at the September term, 1857, of the Bond County Circuit Court, Judge Gillespie presiding, resulted in a judgment for the plaintiff. The attorney for the defendant, Salmon A. Phelps, an *émigré* from Cooperstown, New York, and Greenville's leading attorney, then wrote to Lincoln, with a view to retaining his services on the appeal. The first and second pages of the Phelps letter were given over to a discussion of the facts; at the top of the third page Phelps concluded: "My client wishes to know whether you can and on what terms you will attend to this case in the Supreme Court. Yours respectfully, S. A. Phelps." At the top of page three appears Lincoln's answer:

[November, 1857]
If the case is as stated within, I will attend to the case in the Supreme Court for ten dollars.   A. Lincoln.[11]

The case, cited in *Clark on Contracts*, went against Lincoln.[12]

For arguing a case in the Supreme Court[13] for Samuel D. Marshall, of Shawneetown, Lincoln asked for five dollars and a two-year subscription to Marshall's newspaper, the *Illinois Republican*.[14]

Something of Lincoln's very definite ideas on the subject may be gathered from his "Notes for a Law Lecture"[15] (July, 1850?), in which he said: "The matter of fees is important far beyond the mere question of bread and butter involved. Properly attended to fuller justice is done to both lawyer and client. An exorbitant fee should never be claimed. As a general rule, never take your whole fee in advance, nor any more than a small retainer. When fully paid before hand, you are more than a common mortal if you can feel the same interest in the case, as if something was still in prospect for you, as well as for your client. And when you lack interest in the case, the job will very likely lack skill and diligence in the performance. Settle the *amount* of fee, and take a note in advance. Then you will feel that you are working for something, and you are sure to do your work faithfully and well. Never sell a fee-note—at least not before the consideration service is performed. It leads to negligence and dishonesty—negligence, by losing interest in the case, and dishonesty, in refusing to refund, when you have allowed the consideration to fail."

Taking note of the general opinion of members of the legal profession (Horace Greeley once said that the only good use a lawyer could be put to was hanging), Lincoln went on: "There is a vague popular belief that lawyers are necessarily dishonest. I say *vague*, because when we consider to what extent *confidence*, and *honors* are reposed in, and conferred upon lawyers by the people, it appears improbable that their *impression* of dishonesty, is very distinct and vivid. Yet the expression is common, almost universal. Let no young man, choosing the law for a calling, for a moment yield to this popular belief. Resolve to be honest at all events; and if, in your own judgment, you cannot be a honest-lawyer, resolve to be honest without being a lawyer. Choose some other occupation, rather than one in the choosing of which you do, in advance, consent to be a knave."

It was probably from his custom of charging ridiculously small fees for his services that many of Lincoln's biographers concluded that he could not possibly have accumulated very much from his years of law practice. Some have described him as being extremely careless in the matter of his personal finances and constantly on the verge of bankruptcy. Reference is frequently made to the fact that after his death his widow appealed to Congress for a pension.

Some of these specific allegations are true, but the general inference drawn from them is false. Simple, frugal and abstemious in his habits, and altogether without predilection for ostentation, Lincoln, who was always rather secretive as to his personal affairs, managed to save a goodly portion of what he earned—so much so that he was able to invest substantial sums in notes and mortgages at ten per cent interest (then the legal rate). As Herndon so aptly put it, while Lincoln had "no avarice of the get,—yet he had the capacity of retention, or the avarice of the keep."[16]

It is interesting to note, in this connection, that at the time of the 1855 state census Lincoln declared his assets to be: Livestock $200; real estate $5,000; personalty $12,000. The census also shows "two household helpers living in house."[17] (It is also interesting to note that in the 1850 census Mrs. Lincoln gave her age as twenty-eight, instead of thirty-one, which she was. In the 1860 census she gave it as thirty-five instead of forty-one.) With all that his fees were, in so many instances, absurdly small, at the time of his election to the Presidency Lincoln was worth, at a conservative estimate, twenty thousand dollars—a substantial accumulation for those days. Far from having to borrow money for the inaugural trip to Washington—a popular delusion, oft repeated—he withdrew four hundred dollars from his account in the Marine Bank, which still left a balance of six hundred.[18] At the same time he deposited with the bank certain securities for safekeeping and collection. These consisted of eleven notes representing sums he had loaned to Springfield residents, varying in amounts from $150 to $3,000 and totaling $9,337.90. In addition, he turned over a Springfield City Bond for $1,000, reduced by two payments to $666.67; a certificate for six shares of Alton and Sangamon Railroad stock, and a fire-insurance policy on his home. (The document listing the foregoing items, written by Lincoln and receipted by Robert Irwin, was discovered in the old files of the Marine Bank by Harry E. Pratt; the discovery resulted in Pratt's interesting and important book, *The Personal Finances of Abraham Lincoln*.)

With the increase of legal business in the northern part of the state, especially in Chicago, lawyers from that section found it inconvenient to come to Springfield to dispose of cases in the Federal Court; accordingly, on May 9, 1848, Congress provided for the holding of an annual session in Chicago on the first Monday of July. Later, on March 3, 1851, provision was made for the holding of two terms at Chicago—on the first Monday of October and the third Tuesday of April. Eventually, it became necessary to divide the state into two districts, known as the Northern and Southern Districts.

2.

To attempt to catalogue all of Lincoln's cases in the Federal Court would be tedious and not particularly fruitful. A fair percentage of them were collection suits, brought, for the most part, on behalf of Davis & Co., a St. Louis wholesale house. Most of these actions were on promissory notes, brought in that court by reason of the diversity of citizenship of the parties, Lincoln's client being a Missouri concern, and the defendants residents of Illinois. In time, Lincoln came to have his fill of collection practice; some evidence of the dislike which he developed for this form of drudgery is to be found in a lengthy letter which he wrote his St. Louis client, some sentences from which will give its spirit and tone:

Springfield,
Novr. 17, 1858

Messrs S. C. Davis & Co

Gentlemen
      You perhaps need not be reminded how I have been personally engaged the last three or four months [in the historic series of debates with Douglas]. Your letter to Lincoln & Herndon, of Oct. 1st. complaining that the lands of those against whom we obtained judgments last winter for you, have not been sold on execution has just been handed to me to-day. I will try to "explain how our" (your) "interests have been so much neglected" as you choose to express it. . . . we employed a young man to visit all the localities, and make as accurate a report on titles and values as he could. He did this, expending three or four weeks time, and as he said, over a hun-

dred dollars of his own money in doing so. When this was done we wrote you, asking if we should sell and bid in for you in accordance with this information. This letter you never answered.

My mind is made up. I will have no more to do with this class of business. I can do business in Court, but I can not, and will not follow executions all over the world. . . . I believe we have had, of legal fees, which you are to recover back from the defendants, one hundred dollars. I would not go through the same labor and vexation again for five hundred; . . .

Yours &c
A. Lincoln[19]

It would appear to have been more or less established practice among lawyers, where action had to be instituted to collect delinquent accounts, to charge five per cent on claims under two hundred dollars, and a smaller percentage on more sizable claims, which, as one Logan County attorney complained, often did not "more than pay for the writing & making out of papers."[20]

3.

The Bankruptcy Law, which was passed by Congress in the summer of 1841 and took effect March 1, 1842,[21] furnished a fairly fertile field of activity for the firm of Logan & Lincoln. The second system of national bankruptcy regulation, it was designed to cover a period of business stress following the panic of 1837. As in the case of its predecessor, it was of short duration, politics bringing about its repeal on March 3, 1843.

It will be recalled that the records of many of Lincoln's cases in the federal courts of Illinois were lost in the fire traditionally attributed to Mrs. O'Leary's cow. A number of the surviving files may be found in the Federal Records Center in Chicago; the case files extant have, unfortunately, been rifled of much of the most important and valuable information. From newspapers and various other sources, however, an inconsiderable amount of data has been secured concerning the Lincoln federal-court records. For the most part, the *Sangamo Journal* constitutes the principal source of material concerning Lincoln's bankruptcy cases. The law required publication in a Springfield paper of notice of the preliminary and final hearings, from which notices it is possible to arrive at certain conclusions concerning the volume of business which the new law brought to the lawyers of Springfield.

Judge Pope ordered that all notices to creditors be published in the Whig *Sangamo Journal*. (With the entry of Pope's Order, the Democratic *Illinois State Register* commenced a campaign of opposition to the bankruptcy law which continued until its repeal.) A large list of such notices appears in practically every issue, commencing February 4, 1842. The name of virtually every Springfield lawyer appears among the names of attorneys for the petitioners. The issue of March 4, 1842, contains an entire page, filled on both sides with petitions in bankruptcy. The edition of July 29, 1842, contains three whole pages of bankruptcy notices; two extra pages were inserted in order to accommodate them.

Lawyers used the medium of the Springfield newspapers to advertise their availability for this type of practice. One Springfield attorney, Levi Davis, who became a specialist in the field, made his headquarters in the room of the Clerk of the United States Court—which, one supposes, is another way of saying "in his hat." His advertisements appeared regularly in the *Sangamo Journal*, usually on page one, column one:

> LEVI DAVIS, Attorney at Law.
> Will give particular attention to any
> bankrupt business which may be en-
> trusted to his care.—Office in the room
> occupied by the Clerk of the United
> States Court. July 6, 1842.[22]

Logan & Lincoln, for their part, led the Springfield lawyers in number of cases handled, with seventy-seven, and were tied for fourth place in the state.[23] Among the Springfield bar, Shields & Conkling ranked second, with seventy-three. Cook County was in the forefront, among the counties, with one hundred cases, while Hancock County, small in point of population, had sixty-five, most of them Mormons following the example of their leaders, Joseph and Hyrum Smith and Sidney Rigdon.[24]

The customary attorney's fee in bankruptcy cases was ten dollars a case, which, with the cost of publication and filing fees, ran the total expense of the proceeding to around twenty-five dollars; those attorneys who had a volume of the business found it fairly profitable. On the other hand, attorneys who lived any distance from Springfield could hardly afford to handle them at that figure, and thus it was that many of them turned these matters over to Springfield lawyers. A large percentage of Lincoln's bankruptcy matters were referrals from attorneys in other counties. Lincoln had the ability of making a powerful impression upon many of the ablest men he met, both in the legislature and in the courts, and the great number of instances where he was retained by other counsel, many of them lawyers of distinction, attests to this fact.

Something of the manner in which this newly created branch of law practice, which put money in lawyers' pockets, was handled by Logan & Lincoln is outlined in a letter written by Lincoln to G. B. Shelledy, a Paris (Edgar County) attorney, on February 16, 1842. Lincoln wrote:

Springfield, Ills., Feby. 16— 1842—

G. B. Shelody: Esqr.
    Yours of the 10th is duly received. Judge Logan and myself are doing business together now, and we are willing to attend to your cases as you propose. As to terms, we are willing to attend each case you prepare and send us for $10 (when there shall be no opposition) to be sent in advance, or you know that it is safe. It takes $5.75 of costs to start upon, that is, $1.75 to clerk, and $2 to each of two publishers of papers. Judge Logan thinks it will take the balance of $20 to carry the case through. This must be advanced from time to time as the services are performed, as the officers will not act without. . . .
    . . . . The schedules too, must be attended to. Be sure that they contain the creditors *names*, their *residences*, the *amounts* due each, the debtors *names*, their *residences*, and the *amounts* they owe, also all *property* and *where* located. . . .

A. Lincoln[25]

Lincoln's rule of insisting upon receipt of expense money in advance is perhaps best illustrated in a letter to Frederick A. Thomas, a Lawrenceville attorney. On April 21, 1842, Lincoln wrote: "One thing bear constantly in mind; that is, that unless I am furnished with money to pay cost as the case progresses, I can not move an inch—and State Bank paper will not do, at that. The whole cost, exclusive of lawyer's fees, will be, as we think, about $20. in something at least as good as Shawnee."[26]

It frequently happened that the bankrupt person was so destitute of funds that lawyers were obliged to accept promissory notes in payment of fees and expenses. On March 17, 1842, Lincoln filed a petition on behalf of James Gambrell, of Sangamon County, from whom he had taken a promissory note, as follows:

Springfield, Feb. 24, 1842

On or before the first day of November next I promise to pay A. Lincoln twenty dollars in good fire wood about four feet in length, at the selling price when delivered, to be delivered at any place designated by said Lincoln, in the city of Springfield—for value received.

James Gambrell[27]

4.

Not all of Lincoln's cases in the Federal Court were of the dull, humdrum sort. The trial of Charles H. Chapman, a Chicago merchant, in the United States District Court, in Springfield, on a charge of perjury in obtaining his discharge under the bankruptcy act, attracted considerable attention in December of 1844. It was the last case tried by Logan & Lincoln as partners; together with Norman Judd, they represented the defendant, though it does not appear that Judd participated in the actual trial. In the roster of the bench and bar of early Illinois there was a towering figure—Justin Butterfield, of Chicago, who prosecuted the case for the Government (the same individual who was later to win out over Lincoln in the bitter contest for Commissioner of the General Land Office). A contemporary described him as "one of the greatest lawyers of his time," one who "belongs to that early group who attained national distinction."[28]

After a four-day trial, which the Alton *Telegraph* reported had been "conducted with great ability on the part of Justin Butterfield, Esq., United States Attorney, and Messrs. Logan and Lincoln on behalf of the prisoner,"[29] the defendant was convicted on December 14, 1844, the jury being "out but a few moments, when they returned into court a verdict of GUILTY against the prisoner. . . ."[30] On December twenty-first, Lincoln argued the motion for a new trial.[31] Decision was reserved, and on the twenty-third, Judge Pope denied the motion and sentenced the defendant to a term of five years in the federal penitentiary.[32]

David Davis, who was at the time a member of the Legislature, then in session, "was so fascinated by the intellectual struggle" that he heard the trial through, to the neglect of his official duties. "Chapman was convicted," he later wrote, "but I thought at the time the result would have been different had not the judge charged so strongly against the prisoner."[33] Although the learned Judge Pope had much respect for Lincoln's ability as a lawyer, one wonders if the latter, whom judicial arrogance never did overawe into servile submission, entertained similar regard for some of the methods employed by Pope. Lincoln had little use for "hanging" judges. He liked to repeat an anecdote concerning a strict judge he knew: "He would hang a man for blowing his nose in the street, but he would quash the indictment if it failed to specify what *hand* he blew it with."[34] Lincoln felt strongly, we may be sure, that a judge who embraces his high office to force a verdict in accordance with his own caprice is false to his oath.

5.

Patent suits afforded Lincoln an opportunity to put to practical use his love of inventions. On July 7, 1850, he arrived in

Chicago for his first case in the Federal Court there— Z. *Parker* v. *Charles Hoyt*, involving an alleged infringement of a patent in the construction of a water wheel, in which Lincoln represented the defendant. The trial got under way on July tenth, and was not concluded until the twenty-fourth. None of the available records of Lincoln's practice in the federal courts contain any evidence of his connection with this case, and the Chicago press is strangely silent concerning it; apart from statements by Herndon, the "master myth-maker" of all Lincoln literature, we are entirely in the dark concerning the case. If one can take the word of the junior partner, who was probably not present, Lincoln summed up "in a manner so clear and intelligible that the jury were enabled to comprehend the points and line of defense without the least difficulty." Apparently Lincoln sought to exculpate the accused device by showing that the defendant, in constructing his water mill, had simply availed himself of ordinary basic means, within the public domain and outside the scope of the plaintiff's patent. According to Herndon, the jury found for the defendant.[35]

6.

Lincoln appeared at the December term, 1851, of the United States District and Circuit Courts, the opening of which was delayed several days by the absence of Judge Drummond, who left Chicago by stage on Friday, December twelfth, but did not arrive in Springfield until late at night the following Tuesday.[36]

In the United States Circuit Court, which then had original jurisdiction, Lincoln's services were engaged on behalf of the plaintiff in connection with *Columbus Insurance Co.* v. *Curtenius, et al.*,[37] known as the Peoria Bridge Case. The plaintiff insurance company, having paid out on the claim of their assured, whose steamboat had been sunk by striking a pier of a railroad bridge over the Illinois River near Peoria, was subrogated to the rights of the shipowner.[38] Lincoln was associated with William Chumasaro, of Peru, Illinois, who later removed to Montana, where he served as territorial judge. Opposed was Logan.

The lawsuit, which turned on the power of the state to authorize the obstruction of navigable waters within its territorial limits, was a forerunner of the notable *Effie Afton* case (otherwise known as the Rock Island Bridge Case), involving the right of a railroad to bridge a navigable stream, which Lincoln was to try at Chicago in 1857, the facts being somewhat the same. The defendants pleaded immunity under an act of the Legislature authorizing the construction of the bridge. Lincoln's line of argument was that the building of a bridge constituted a nuisance— a serious hazard to navigation—and that, in any case, the legislative act in question was unconstitutional.

The river interests, who foresaw in the creation of the bridge the diversion of much traffic from the river, were solidly arrayed behind the plaintiff. That Lincoln was nevertheless dubious about the outcome of the suit is evident from a letter written by him to Hezekiah M. Wead during its pendency. "They are pressing me very hard on one or two points," he wrote. "I should not wonder if the case is decided against us."[39] In charging the jury, Judge Drummond instructed them that the Legislature had the right to authorize obstruction of a navigable stream running within its territorial limits for the purpose of erection of a bridge, provided it did not constitute a material obstruction to navigation. The two days trial resulted in a hung jury, after which the action was settled out of court. As it happened, in this case Lincoln opposed the bridge interests, whereas in the *Effie Afton* case he defended them. No doubt the knowledge and experience which he here acquired were of tremendous help to him in the more famous suit.

7.

That prolific and punctilious diarist, Browning, refers to several cases in the federal courts in the trial of which he and

Lincoln were associated. Under date of July 12, 1852, he records: "Attending [U.S.] Court. Commenced trial of [William] Williamson, formerly Post master at Lacon who is indicted for robbing the mail. I am assisting Lincoln at his request—"[40] Williamson was accused of having stolen a package containing fifteen thousand dollars in bank notes. On the following day Browning notes: "Argued case agt Williamson. The evidence was very strong. Almost conclusive. I was so discouraged that I wished to decline a speech, but at the persuasion of Lincoln addressed the jury for something over two hours. The case was given to them at 4 P M & they are yet out at 9. The Defendant is a young man, who lost a leg in the Mexican war, and does not look to be very bright. Is a total stranger to me, & I believe him to be guilty, but wish him acquitted. My sympathies are awakened. I am sorry for the poor devil." The following day, the old war horse sadly noted: "Jury found Williamson guilty. Will yet try to arrest the judgment but have not much hope."[41] Williamson drew a sentence of ten years. It is interesting to note that the case furnishes one of the few known instances where Lincoln, reliant for the most part on his own devices, not only called in outside counsel, but relinquished to him the right to sum up.

On June 28, 1858, Lincoln appeared in the United States District Court, in Springfield, on behalf of Jonas D. Hartgen, of Danville, accused of stealing from the mails. The story of the case can be shortly told: The defendant, who had had a contract to carry mails from the trains to the post office, was detected by means of a decoy letter. The case for the prosecution was airtight, and Lincoln, in summation, spoke "in palliation of the crime." He was put to it to move the jury, which was out but a few minutes before returning with a guilty verdict. At this juncture, Lincoln, who was apparently prepared for the worst, read a letter to the Court from a number of Danville residents, speaking of the defendant in the highest terms and begging clemency for him. The Judge, in consideration, imposed a sentence of two years in the federal penitentiary, the shortest time to which the defendant could be sentenced under the law.[42]

The captious might question the wisdom of Lincoln's unorthodox gambit in virtually conceding the defendant's guilt, upon summation, and, as it were, playing for a sympathy verdict. The problem which confronted him was one which has plagued many a lawyer since his day; there is something to be said both for and against his strategy. There are times when boldness, in trial work as in everything else in life, pays off handsomely; at other times, it recoils. In the instant case, it would seem that Lincoln had nothing to lose by his resourcefulness and daring. As usual, he did his all-out best, but in view of the multitude of facts arrayed against his client, his best was bound to be not good enough.

Going over his cases, one finds more than enough evidence that Lincoln the lawyer did not always go by the book. Even so, he invariably had a very clear idea of what he was about. Take, for instance, the case where one of his own witnesses was, on cross-examination, so patently evasive that Lincoln felt his case slipping away from him. In a definite deviation from accepted practice, Lincoln arose and, showing his vexation, rebuked the refractory witness. "It was a dangerous experiment," said Anthony Thornton, Lincoln's associate in the case, "which might have brought discredit on our most important witness." Lincoln's action, however, had the desired effect, for the object of his displeasure proceeded to answer questions without evasion and thus rehabilitate himself in the eyes of the jury.[43] Like every good lawyer, Lincoln, who was an individualist in the most individualistic of all American professions and vocations, broke many a courtroom convention while taking his share of calculated risks. Moreover, he belonged to a time when individuality still counted for something.

A word about Judge Drummond, who served on the federal bench from 1850 until 1884. Born and educated in the State of Maine, he studied law in the city of Philadelphia, where he was admitted to practice in 1833. Two years later, feeling the pull of the West, he selected as his home the town of Galena, where he practiced law until his appointment to the United States District Court by President Taylor. Upon the state's division, for federal judicial purposes, into the northern and southern districts, Judge Drummond was assigned to the Northern District. In 1870, by appointment of his fellow Galenian, President Grant, he became Judge of the United States Circuit Court for the Seventh Judicial District, comprising the states of Illinois, Indiana and Wisconsin.

It is of interest to note that he became an avid fan of the new pastime reputedly devised by the ex-Union officer, Major General Abner Doubleday, and would, upon any plausible pretext, adjourn his court to attend a game.[44] When in Springfield, he doubtless was a frequent attendant at the home games of the "Springfield Reds," Springfield's first baseball team, organized in 1877.

8.

In the United States Courts, as in other courts, the range and variety of lawsuits handled by Lincoln is astonishing. An important test of a good lawyer in Lincoln's day was his ability to prosecute and defend any and all forms of litigation, on any subject and in any court. There is ample warrant for the view that in this respect Lincoln took second place to none. Even the nuances of maritime law, a dark continent to the general practitioner, were not outside the ken of this self-educated lawyer. On June 21, 1858, five days after delivering the famous "House Divided" speech, he appeared for the libelants, The Wiggins Ferry Company and John Trendly, in a salvage proceeding brought by them against the steamer "*Ocean Spray*" (suits for salvage are maintained *in rem* against the property saved, not its owner). The firm of Stuart & Edwards and James Conkling appeared for the owners of the vessel.

The complaint (or, as it is known in the jargon of the profession, the "libel") in the action, drawn by Lincoln in his own careful hand, reflects not only a working knowledge of the labyrinthian world of salvage law, but something of Lincoln's individual approach and creative ability in the matter of composing pleadings which were not of the run-of-the-mill variety.

District Court of the United States of America   Southern District of Illinois

In Admiralty.

To the Hon. S. H. Treat, Judge

The libel of the Wiggins Ferry Company owner of the American Steam Ferry Boat, "John Trendly of Illinois," and of John Trendly master of said boat for themselves and all others entitled against the Steamer Ocean Spray her tackle, apparel & furniture and cargo and against all persons intervening therein for their interest therein in a cause of salvage civil & maritime alleges as follows.

1. That on April 22, 1858 the said John Trendly being on a voyage in the said Steam Ferry Boat "John Trendly" from St. Louis to Illinoistown discovered the said Steamer Ocean Spray on fire deserted by her own crew and all other persons floating down the river Mississippi in a wrecked condition whereupon the said master approached the burning vessel at great risk to the said steam ferry boat and made fast to her and at immenent hazard to the safety of the said ferry boat he towed the said Ocean Spray to the Ill. Shore in the County of St. Clair and by means of the fire engine on said steam ferry boat and by great exertions of himself and crew he succeeded in extinguishing the flames and saved her hull and a large portion of the cargo consisting of iron, dry goods and other mdse. unknown as yet to the libellants. That in putting out the fire it became necessary to scuttle her at great risk and exertion. There she lies now. . . .

Therefore the libellants pray that . . . this honorable court will be pleased to decree to the libellants a reasonable and proper salvage in proportion to the value of said vessel and cargo and that it may be condemned and sold to pay said salvage with costs charges and expenses that libellants may have such other and further relief in the premises as in law and justice they may be entitled to receive.

John Trendly

April 29, 1858[45]

In addressing himself to the task of bringing to light, within the covers of one book, part of the great mass of material which has long existed in widely dispersed sources on the subject of Lincoln the lawyer, the writer has largely refrained from including samples of pleadings in Lincoln's handwriting. For the most part, they were copied from *Chitty on Pleadings* (the foregoing being one of the exceptions), the names of the parties and other pertinent data being filled in. Making, as they do, for somewhat arduous reading, and bearing nothing of the imprint of Lincoln's own originality, the writer has deemed them to be not only out of place in a work designed for the general reader, but of little, if any, historical significance. It was for this reason, too, that Logan Hay, the first president of the Abraham Lincoln Association (1920–1942), whose father had studied in Lincoln's law office, instituted the rule that pleadings in Lincoln's hand were not to be collected.

As was the usual procedure, the Court referred the case to one of the commissioners of the Court "to take testimony of witnesses and report with all convenient speed." The following day the matter was heard by the Commissioner, who reported to the Court that, the steamer being in great peril of becoming a total loss, the libelants had intervened and saved it from destruction, and hence were entitled to remuneration for salvage services. Accordingly, the vessel was ordered sold by the court; out of the proceeds realized, Lincoln's clients were awarded one third, or a little over six hundred dollars.

9.

One of Lincoln's last appearances in the federal courts was in connection with the inaccurately named "Sandbar Case," as it is usually called (*Johnston* v. *Jones and Marsh*), which was tried before Judge Drummond and a jury in the United States Court in Chicago about two months before Lincoln's nomination for the Presidency. The case involved the question of ownership of a valuable tract of alluvial land created by sand being washed in from Lake Michigan at the mouth of the Chicago River. Beveridge, relying on Whitney, incorrectly states that Lincoln represented the Illinois Central.[46] The railroad was in no way involved, the alluvial accretion being claimed by individuals, one of whom was the predecessor in title of the Chicago and Northwestern, which subsequently occupied the property. The case had been in the courts since 1855, although Lincoln did not figure in the two previous trials. On April 4, 1860, Lincoln and attorneys associated with him won a verdict for the defendants. The Chicago *Tribune* of April fifth reported: "The great Sand Bar Case. Verdict for defendants. The trial of the great North Side Sand Bar case, or rather the contest as to the title to the valuable accretions on the lake shore, north of the pier, which has been on trial in the U.S. District Court in this city, for the past two weeks, came to a conclusion yesterday. This is the fourth trial of the case. This most important case has engaged the services of a most distinguished array of counsel, among them Abraham Lincoln."

CHAPTER XIV

In the Illinois Supreme Court

1.

CONTRARY TO popular belief, it was in the Supreme Court, and not on the circuit, that Lincoln had his greatest impact as a lawyer. During the period when the outlines of the state's jurisprudence were being established upon an enduring basis, he helped to mold, in a significant way, doctrines of law laid down by the state's most authoritative court. If the principles evolved seem commonplace today, one needs to be reminded that Lincoln had no encyclopaedias of law, no digests to go by—only the maxims of the English common law as set forth in *Blackstone* and applied by a few adjudications in the older sister states. It would not be rash to claim for him that, in exploring areas that the Illinois courts had not yet clearly delineated, he hacked out important precedents in the law of that state and, more than any other Illinois lawyer of his generation, made a distinct contribution to law that governs today. Herndon's statement that Lincoln was "a great lawyer . . . in the Supreme Court of Illinois" is, for once, no exaggeration. He was an uncommonly fine appeals lawyer.

Lincoln was one of the foremost lawyers in practice before the Illinois Supreme Court in the 1840s and 1850s, both from the standpoint of the number and importance of the cases he handled, and the percentage of cases which he won. This volume is not large enough to anthologize in any comprehensive fashion the cases which Lincoln had in the state's highest tribunal. For more than a half century after his death it had been thought that his practice there was limited to something less than two hundred cases, but investigation indicates that he had 243[1]—a record few Illinois lawyers of his time could duplicate or even approach. Nor is it by any means a certainty that the number presently credited to him represents the complete list.[2]

No review of Lincoln's cases in that court has ever been made, using the original files, and because of their dispersal it is to be doubted that such a study could now be conducted. In only a dozen cases do the available files contain anything written by Lincoln, much of the most important information having been rifled therefrom; the looting, in fact, has been almost as thorough as in the courts of the Eighth Circuit. These are limitations which no compiler can hope to entirely overcome. Fortunately, the Official Reports contain, in many instances, rather full recitals of the facts and the essentials of the arguments advanced by Lincoln. At all events, a proper *critique* upon Lincoln's work in the Supreme Court can only be based on a reading of the Official Illinois Reports of all his cases in that court.

The general public, whose knowledge of Lincoln, the lawyer, is confined to a rather casual acquaintance with the "almanac trial," hardly thinks of Lincoln as a great advocate, but, rather, as something considerably less. No one can go over the record of his appeals without arriving at a very high opinion of the legal ability of this self-taught lawyer. One ought to begin by stressing the fact that appellate work is the most exacting and concentrated phase of the practice of law, for it involves the presentation of the essence of a trial, oftentimes protracted, within a relatively brief allotment of time. In contrast to his practice on the circuit, where, for the most part, cases were tried with a minimum of preparedness, Lincoln's work in the Supreme Court was marked by meticulous preparation, with the result that he knew each case in its every phase. The assiduity of his preparation was such that he was never taken off his guard. Quite frequently, no record of his activities can be found for the weeks preceding terms of that court; there is a very strong presumption that he spent the time at his office or in the State Law Library, preparing his records on appeal and his arguments for presentation.

In making up the record on appeal, the lawyer for each side stated the substance of his recollection of the testimony, and the trial judge, after correcting the two versions, certified the result to the appellate court, just as the clerk certified the pleadings to the court above.[3] Should counsel for either side feel that the transcript of the record sent up did not accurately reflect the substance of either the pleadings or the testimony, he had the right to move, in the superior court, to correct the transcript. Such a motion, in Lincoln's handwriting, appears in the *Herndon-Weik Collection*.

In the Supreme Court for the State of Illinois—December term A. D. 1841

Riley Averill, and
Alfred Lowell
   vs.
Spencer Field

Abraham Lincoln, being first duly sworn, states on oath, that he was of counsel for Averell & Lowell in the Court below, and drew up and filed the plea in the cause; that, on inspection of the transcript of the record in the cause on file in this court, he verily believes that a material part of said plea is omitted and left out of said transcript by the clerk in the court below— It is impossible for affiant to recollect the precise words so omitted from said transcript, but he believes them to be in substance and very nearly in language as follows to wit: "And the said defendants further aver that they have sold an amount of said lots equal to the amount of said notes, or any other amount of said lots"

A. Lincoln

The State Law Library, the only law library on the circuit (aside from scattered individual collections), in which Lincoln spent countless hours preparing his cases, conveniently adjoined the Supreme Court chamber, across the street from the Lincoln & Herndon office. This rather well-equipped workshop was apparently available to and used by lawyers 365 days a year. In his *Diary*, Browning records, under date of December 25, 1851: "No festivities of any kind in this dull Town [Springfield]. Spent the morning in the law library at work—dined at my boarding house."[4] Lincoln put in many evenings there, coming from home around seven or eight o'clock and working until midnight.[5] Another place of refuge when in need of solitude while preparing his more important cases was the office of his friend Governor Bissell, where, concealed in one of the recesses, he would think and write by the hour.

In fairness to Herndon, it should be noted that some of the drudgery of digging up and collating the authorities was performed by the junior partner. Bledsoe, who did not leave Springfield until 1847, recalled that Herndon "with creditable zeal and industry, would collect all sorts of cases for him. From these he [Lincoln] would make his selections, and prepare his arguments, to the great disgust often no doubt, of Mr. Herndon, who saw so much of the material collected by him thrown aside as useless."[6] (The value of Bledsoe's observations as a dependable source of information must, of course, be subjected to some discount in view of his bitterness toward his old friend.) Herndon, himself, complained rather dolefully: ". . . I made out his best briefs in the largest law cases and . . . Lincoln would argue his case from those briefs and get the credit for them while I was the power behind them."[7]

Even though his share in the winning of Lincoln's cases before the Supreme Court was not negligible, it may be questioned whether Herndon's plaintive bleats are entitled to complete credence. With his intellectual vanity, his readiness to embrace any opportunity to proclaim his own importance, and his pronounced bias in favor of the once junior partner, the Herndon of the post-Lincoln years was no exception to the rule that lawyers, as a class, are not devoid of professional jealousy. As has been noted, at least one of their contemporaries felt that Herndon "did not spend much time in the preparation of his cases. . . ."[8]

The first session of the Supreme Court in the newly designated state capital was held in St. Paul's Episcopal Church. After a brief tenancy there, it moved, in July, 1839, into permanent quarters in a room on the second floor of the State House. The space allotted soon proved inadequate to accommodate the Clerk of Court and his records, making necessary the renting of outside quarters. It was not unusual for the Court to avail itself, for this purpose, of rooms in private homes, as would appear from the following warrant for payment, the original of which is in the Illinois State Archives:

> To Sarah Raines in full for rent of
> one room for the Clerk of the Supreme
> Court from Oct 2 1840 to Mar 2 1841
> 5 mo. @ $8 $40
> Warrant No. 6586
> Mar. 3, 1841

Room 212 of the famous old building in the center of the square has historic significance, for it was there that the Illinois Supreme Court held its sessions until dedication of the Supreme Court Building, across Second Street from the State House, in 1908. A faded mural depicting the American eagle and a flag still can be seen on the wall of the old courtroom, directly above where the justices sat; the words "Supreme Court" are carved in black stone above the west door. (As this book is being written, the room, long vacant, is being converted into a hearing room for both the Illinois House and Senate.)

While Lincoln made a number of appearances in the Supreme Court in the early 1840s, most of his appeals during those years were of the dry-as-dust variety, virtually none of them of great importance—and so, because this work is not being written exclusively for lawyers, it has been deemed best to omit discussion of all but a few of them. (It is of interest to note that of the 103 cases which Lincoln had in the Supreme Court from 1840 to 1846, 54 were from counties outside the Eighth Circuit—further proof, if any were needed, that Lincoln was a "lawyer's lawyer" whose services were greatly in demand by the members of his profession.)

2.

Even though the issues were not stupendous, the case of *Scammon* v. *Cline*,[9] argued June 10, 1840, is noteworthy for the fact that it was one of Lincoln's first cases in the court in which he afterward became so constant a practitioner.

One of the early settlers in Boone County (Little Boone, as it was called) was Cornelius Cline, who in 1835 emigrated from New York to Belvidere, the county seat. The following year he issued a promissory note in the amount of $52.50, which was assigned to Jonathan Young Scammon, who had come to Chicago from Maine, also in 1835. Scammon became a lawyer, and in time (1839) was appointed official reporter of the Supreme Court, which position he held at the time of the suit. Authorized by the Court to report and publish its decisions, Scammon published four volumes, known as Scammon's Reports. Chief Justice Caton, speaking of them in his memoirs, says: "The syllabi of his cases are models of perspicuity and brevity."[10] After his admission to the Illinois bar, Robert Todd Lincoln served an apprenticeship in the Scammon law office, in Chicago.[11] The latter's son, Charles T. Scammon, was at the time of his death a law partner of the younger Lincoln.

Scammon sued on the note before a justice of the peace in Belvidere; after trial, judgment was rendered in favor of Cline. The records fail to disclose any reason why the instrument sued on should not have been considered valid and binding, and so one can only conclude that the finding was in the nature of a hometown verdict.

Scammon appealed the case to the Boone Circuit Court, which dismissed his appeal on the technical ground that, at the time when the notice of appeal was filed, Boone County was still a part of Jo Daviess County for judicial purposes, even though a clerk of court had already been appointed for Boone, and hence the appeal had been taken to a nonexistent court. Scammon's counsel was the prominent Chicagoan, Norman B. Judd, who appealed to the Illinois Supreme Court. At this stage of the proceedings Lincoln was brought in by James L. Loop, of Belvidere, Cline's attorney.

The case proved a tough nut for Lincoln to crack. Brushing aside all the chaff and technicalities advanced by him upon the argument, Chief Justice Wilson, speaking for a unanimous court, held that the appeal was improperly dismissed, the appointment of a clerk of court having constituted the court's inception. A facetious remark has been ascribed to Lincoln, at a later period of his career, on an occasion when he thought the Supreme Court had ruled against him without good cause, to the effect that the time had arrived when an appeal should be allowed from the Supreme Court to a justice of the peace. Whether or not Lincoln's criticism of the Court was justified, it certainly could not have been addressed to its ruling in *Scammon* v. *Cline*, for on the merits his client had no just cause for complaint.

The story of the case would not be complete without a postscript. Upon the retrial in Belvidere, in which Lincoln took no part, the court again found for the defendant—which only serves to emphasize the unhappy truism that Lady Justice can, at times, be as capricious as all get out.

3.

The December term of the Supreme Court, which opened on December 9, 1844, and ended on March 1, 1845, was an especially busy one, not only in the volume of cases handled by the court but, for Lincoln, in the number of appearances which he made. Among the well-known lawyers who attended from other parts of the state were Lyman Trumbull from Belleville; Justin Butterfield, Isaac N. Arnold and Norman Judd from

Chicago; Joseph Gillespie from Edwardsville; Josiah Lamborn from Jacksonville; Norman H. Purple and William L. May from Peoria; Orville H. Browning from Quincy, and Levi Davis from Vandalia.[12] Members of a dynamic bar which was shaping the law and life of the great Sucker State, they each contributed something to the growth of the law and the proper ordering of the affairs of all Illinoisans. It was a great period in which to live and be a lawyer: a time of expanding horizons, when law could be practiced with zest. Among those whom Lincoln opposed was Browning, in the case of *Martin* v. *Dryden, et al.*, an action for an injunction involving the title to real estate, on appeal from Madison County. On January 9, 1845, Lincoln, representing the defendant-appellee (respondent), was successful in having the judgment of the lower court affirmed.[13]

Like many another young man of that day, Browning (perhaps best remembered for his inimitable *Diary*, which he kept for over thirty years, until his death in 1881) mixed in Whig politics; his friendship with Lincoln dated from December, 1836, when both were in the Legislature. Despite his early ties with the Republican party, of which he was one of the builders, he left it in the postwar period; though he was appointed United States Senator by Governor Yates, to fill the unexpired term caused by the death of Douglas in 1861, and later fought the Radical Republicans of the Johnson administration, his great reputation was made in legal work, not in partisan politics.

While his preference for the law did not preclude his participation in public affairs, something of Browning's distaste for the stress and strain of political life and the campaigning leading up to elective office, is revealed in a letter which he wrote to Trumbull, then United States Senator from Illinois, on May 19, 1856: "Morris is the nominee in this district as successor to Col. Richarson. I am *teazed to the verge of desperation* to take the field against him—but I cannot do it. I always had uncontrollable repugnances to political life, and political contests, and situated as I am at present in reference to important professional engagements, it is impossible for me to be a candidate."[14] The Quincy *Whig* had occasion to comment editorially on his reluctance to sacrifice his practice in order to run for public office.[15]

Browning was a consummate advocate, equally effective in the criminal and civil courts. Such talent was—and is—unfortunately rare. As a practitioner before the latter, he was a lawyer of distinction, though his great satisfaction came from the defense of persons charged with crime and hapless Negroes in the act of being carried off to bondage (this despite the fact that, while opposed to the institution of slavery, he was a consistent and steadfast antiabolitionist), where his passion for the underdog and his keen sense of justice frequently impelled him to intervene without fee. A skilled master of criminal defense, Browning went far beyond that accomplishment to lead in over-all defense of human rights and personal liberties; posterity is, indeed, indebted to him as an early exponent of what would today be called civil liberties.

A genial man of culture and charm, Browning was, by any standards, one of the most striking and appealing characters in all the gallery of Lincoln contemporaries. Unfortunately, his reputation became somewhat tarnished during the war years, when he turned to influence-peddling in Washington and, together with James W. Singleton, another of Lincoln's old friends, sought to make a fortune speculating in contraband Confederate cotton.

In the last decade of his long career at the bar, Browning turned his massive talents from his civil rights and criminal practice to representing the Chicago, Burlington and Quincy Railroad in suits involving rates, taxes and charters of carriers, which, though more prosaic, he doubtless found more remunerative. Although he amassed a large fortune, most of it slipped out of his hands as a result of unsound investments.

An important Federal District Court matter in Chicago, in which Browning and Lincoln were opposed, was the case of *Forsythe* v. *Peoria*, tried in July, 1855. After a four-day trial, the jury returned a verdict against Lincoln's client—a verdict doubtless influenced by the charge of Judge McLean, who indicated his predisposition in favor of the other side.[16]

In an entry for April 20, 1853, Browning confided to his *Diary* his own reaction in a similar situation, one where the shoe was on the other foot. Commenting on the Court's remarks, heavily weighted against the defendants, in connection with Browning's defense of two clients charged with cattle stealing, he wrote: "I was indignant that remarks so calculated to create prejudice, forestall opinion & prevent a fair & impartial trial should have been thus publicly and causelessly made by one who should as zealously guard individual as public right."[17] (As any lawyer will attest, these observations are not without contemporary significance.)

Something of Lincoln's own formula for coming to terms with an adverse ruling, brought about (to counsel's way of thinking) through the judge's bias, is revealed in a humorous anecdote relating to his appearance in Danville Court. A fellow lawyer, Daniel Voorhees (afterward Senator from Indiana), complaining of a decision rendered against them in a case in which they had appeared as co-counsel, asked Lincoln "What can we do?" "Well," said Lincoln, "we can go over to the tavern and, just among ourselves, cuss the judge to our hearts' content."

4.

At the December term, 1846, Lincoln appeared before the Court in *Anderson* v. *Ryan*,[18] an appeal from Coles County. The essentials are to be found in the official report of the case in the Supreme Court. The action, which sought redress for loss of services, was filed against a client of Lincoln's who had inadvertently sired a child by the plaintiff's daughter. In the circuit court below, where Lincoln and Ficklin, appearing for the defendant, were opposed by Linder, a jury verdict had been rendered in favor of the plaintiff for $656.[19] In due course the case reached the Supreme Court, where it was elaborately argued by Lincoln for the appellant, and by those two worthies, Linder and Bledsoe, for the respondent. The issue which engrossed the attention of counsel and the Court was whether the judge below had erred in instructing the jury that they might *infer* a loss of services from the mere fact of the defendant having had carnal knowledge of the plaintiff's daughter. Nourished on *Blackstone*, Lincoln was well equipped to expound the common law doctrine that *actual* damage, in the form of loss of services, was indispensable to a cause of action for seduction.

The error of law to which Lincoln, on behalf of the appellant, attributed his mischance below, proved itself a phantom and the judgment was affirmed. It is an interesting fact in connection with this case that the Appellate Courts of Illinois,[20] in two subsequent decisions (*Bayles* v. *Burgard*, 48 Ill. App. 371, decided in 1892, and *Garretson* v. *Becker*, 52 Ill. App. 255, decided in 1893), came around to Lincoln's position and reverted to the rule that proof of loss of services *is* necessary to support an action for seduction, even though only slight evidence thereof is required.

5.

In the Supreme Court, Lincoln and Bledsoe confronted each other in connection with the argument of five appeals, in three of which the latter prevailed. In *Trumbull* v. *Campbell*,[21] in which they were opposed, the amount involved was relatively small, but the question settled was not without importance. Lyman Trumbull (afterwards a justice of the Illinois Supreme Court, later United States Senator from Illinois during three terms, 1855–1873) was appointed Secretary of State by Governor Carlin. With the election of Governor Ford, Trumbull, who opposed Ford's policy on the state banks, was dismissed from office and replaced by Thompson Campbell, of Galena, who brought suit for two hundred of the four hundred dollars which had already been paid Trumbull by the State Auditor, the plaintiff claiming that it was rightfully his, inasmuch as it represented an advance in salary for which Trumbull had rendered no services.

Campbell was represented by Bledsoe and Stephen T. Logan; Trumbull, by Lincoln. In the Sangamon Circuit Court, where the case had been submitted on an agreed state of facts, the plaintiff prevailed, but on appeal to the Supreme Court the judgment was set aside (December term, 1846), the Court, in an opinion by Judge Treat, adopting the rationale of Lincoln's reasoning that Campbell was not a proper party plaintiff. The decision turned upon the principle that, in the words of the Court, "the right of action is in the state," in whose name, as Lincoln had argued, any suit for recovery should be brought.

Trumbull, who later defeated Lincoln in the election showdown in the state Legislature, served as United States Senator during the turbulent times of the Civil War and the Reconstruction period. Though he had once been a most articulate proponent of Whiggism and Republicanism, he voted against the impeachment of Andrew Johnson, and in so doing separated himself from the Republican party. It was said of him that, as a logical thinker and debater, he was the peer of any public man of his day. In the Senate he was respected by all, not alone for his great intellectual qualifications, but for his splendid ability as a constitutional lawyer. Despite a certain austerity and a condescension of manner toward his senatorial colleagues, he enjoyed their immense esteem; though he was certainly conceited, he had the stuff in him to back up his pretensions.

That Trumbull, himself a lawyer of such superior attainments and marked intellectual ability, should have selected Lincoln to represent him, speaks exceedingly well for the latter's ability and reputation as an appellate advocate. Trumbull doubtless had been greatly impressed by Lincoln's argument, three years before, in *Dorman* v. *Lane*,[22] an appeal from Gallatin County, in which they were opposed before the Supreme Court. Justice James Shields, a native of Dungannon, County Tyrone, Ireland (the same fiery Celt who had once challenged Lincoln to a duel), in an opinion which was in effect a recital of Lincoln's argument, sustained the position of Lincoln's client. If it was not exactly a triumph of magnitude, the victory served to bring the name of Lincoln to the attention of Trumbull, one of the great figures in Illinois legal annals.

6.

A case which provided Lincoln with an argument he could get his teeth into was *Webster and Huntington* v. *French, et al.*, decided at the December term, 1849,[23] in which his shrewdly penetrating analysis nipped in the bud an ingenious scheme for circumventing the rule of competitive bidding.

Under an act of the Legislature, the Governor was authorized to sell certain property owned by the state in Quincy, to the highest bidder, after advertising. Sealed bids were to be received up to July 1, 1849. A comparison of the bids showed that various individuals had placed offers for the property, the highest specific bid being $21,100. Among the others were two which, if nothing else, had the virtue of simplicity. One was a proposition reading: "We, the undersigned, propose to pay the State of Illinois five hundred dollars more than any bid for the Quincy house property, up to 10 o'clock A.M., 2d July, 1849. Henry Root & Co." Another firm, possessed of the same ingenuity, hit upon the ruse of submitting a bid of "six hundred and one dollars over and above the highest bid of the highest bidder for said house and property, made according to the advertisement of the governor. Ash & Diller."

The Governor proceeded to add to the $21,100 bid of the plaintiffs the $500 excess proposed to be given by Root & Co., and to this aggregate sum he added the $601, making a total of $22,201, at which figure the "Quincy House" property was awarded to Ash & Diller.

The case was one of the first to come into the office after Lincoln's return from Congress. Representing the $21,100 bidder,

Lincoln & Herndon brought suit in the Sangamon Circuit Court to set the award aside. The defendants' demurrer was sustained by Judge Davis, whereupon Lincoln took an appeal to the Supreme Court, where he was opposed, on the argument, by his friend Browning. Lincoln argued that the offer of Ash & Diller was not a specific bid. Mincing no words, he said approximately this (as quoted by the official reporter): "This whole scheme is a gambling business—a stock jobbing transaction—an evasion of the law, and a total subversion of the manifest intention of the legislature." Lincoln's argument, which packed a lot of punch, struck a responsive chord in Judge Caton, who wrote a lengthy opinion completely sustaining the plaintiffs' position.

7.

In *Barrett* v. *The Alton & Sangamon Railroad Company*,[24] decided at the December term, 1851, an interesting question was presented to the Court concerning the right of railroads to enforce prior pledges for subscriptions of stock after change in the direction of the road, pursuant to act of the Legislature. James A. Barrett, who owned 4,215 acres in the vicinity of Island Grove, along the original course, subscribed for thirty shares of stock at one hundred dollars per share, on which subscription he made a down payment of five per cent. Thereafter, though the termini of the road remained the same, a change in course, consisting of a deviation of the road's trackage from the property of Barrett, was effected by legislative fiat. Upon Barrett's refusal to meet his commitment, the company retained Lincoln to bring suit on the pledge. Original documents in the Illinois State Historical Library show that Lincoln filed the *praecipe* in the Sangamon Circuit Court on February 22, 1851. Barrett engaged the services of Logan, who took the position that the change in direction was a material alteration in the original contract, which exonerated the defendant from the payment of his subscription.

On November 29, 1851, an order was entered providing that

the "cause be tried without jury . . . by consent of the parties."
That same day the Court found for the railroad, and assessed
its damages at $1,351, from which judgment the defendant ap-
pealed to the Supreme Court. Of interest are Judge Davis's original jottings of the testimony introduced by the parties, in
which he noted that Barrett "After promising to pay 15 or 20
times—refused. R.R. have expended $500,000 12 miles track
laid—Grading for upward of 45 miles nearly finished. Dir. have
located road in pursuance to the amendment to charter directly
from Carlinville to Spg. and not by New Berlin and saves 12
miles. Barrett did not object until road changed, however he
knew change was to be made." From these same judge's notes it
appears that "J. T. Stuart" testified as a witness for the railroad,
and "Said Barrett tried to keep him from passing amendment
while in Senate." Through another witness, one Virgil Hickox,
Lincoln established that Barrett expected to become treasurer of
the railroad, the inference being that his refusal to go through
with his pledge stemmed, at least in part, from his failure to secure
the appointment.

That Lincoln devoted a great deal of time and effort to preparing the case for trial is evident from the original file in the
Supreme Court, which contains a number of the papers from the
court below. On March 7, 1851, Lincoln sued out a commission
to take the testimony of Isaac Gibson, the secretary of the company, who resided in New York City. The interrogatories propounded by Lincoln, ten in number, and the answers given by
Gibson in the course of his examination before Edward C. West,
"Special Commissioner," at the latter's office at 35 Wall Street,
New York City, are contained in the deposition on file in the
Supreme Court. Lincoln proposed to, and did, show by the deposition that calls were duly made on Barrett for installment
payments, on the dates specified in the original contract.

In the Supreme Court, Lincoln drove home the argument
that the benefit which accrues to individual property, by the
location of a public road, does not, in contemplation of law, enter

into the consideration of the contract of subscription to stock of the railroad, and that subscriptions are made subject to the power of the legislature to change the location of the right of way. The higher court, in sustaining Davis, adopted Lincoln's argument in its entirety. The decision proved of the utmost importance, not only to the Alton & Sangamon, but, in its long-range impact, to all the other projected railroads.

8.

The Supreme Court docket for December, 1853, shows the listing of an appeal in *People* v. *Patrick Sullivan*, with the notation "Argued Mar. 4 [1854]; judgment affirmed Mar. 7."[25] The defendant, a tavern keeper, had been convicted in the Macon Circuit Court of selling spirituous liquors without a license and fined ten dollars, whereupon he sued out a writ of error to the Supreme Court. This was an important test case, involving the right of the state to regulate the sale of intoxicants and enforce its rules and regulations by fine or imprisonment. There is ample warrant for the belief that the wholesale grocers of Springfield, whose profits were largely derived from the sale of liquor to tavern keepers in central Illinois, were behind the appeal. Lincoln's client and personal friend, Jacob Bunn, was one of those wholesale liquor dealers.

Judge Treat's opinion, affirming the conviction, would indicate that Lincoln had set himself a stiff assignment in advancing the argument that there was no Constitutional basis for the statute under which the defendant was prosecuted, in that the declared aim of the Constitution to regulate the sale of spirituous liquors did not contemplate the power to impose punishment for violation of rules promulgated by the licensing authority. In the course of his opinion, Treat stated: "It was the design [of the Legislature] not only to restore the authority to grant licenses, but the power to inflict punishment for retailing liquors without license. . . . A different view of the case would impeach the wisdom of the legislature." Lincoln's was not, in all respects, a happy defense.

9.

One of the truly delectable footnotes of Lincoln's law career was the "horological cradle case," tried before Judge Davis at Mt. Pulaski at the fall term, 1854, and thereafter taken on appeal to the Supreme Court. Lincoln encountered, in his years of practice, many strange cases; not the least curious was the cause based upon a patent supposedly secured by one Alexander Edmonds upon an invention which Lincoln in his bill described as follows: "An horological cradle, rocked by machinery, with a weight running on one or more pulleys, the cradle constituting the pendulum, and which, being wound up, would rock itself until it run down, and so save the continual labor to mothers and nurses of rocking the cradle."

Edmonds, who operated a chair factory in Mt. Pulaski, sold the patent rights for the State of Illinois to George and John Myers of the same city, who caused to be inserted in the *Illinois State Journal* the following advertisement:

WOMAN'S RIGHTS
[picture of cradle]
Of Self-Rocking
Horological Cradle
Patented February 22, 1853

Mothers have the right to all the blessings of the day, and amongst our scientific men, Alexander Edmonds has invented the Self-Rocking Cradle, which forms a beautiful and ornamental piece of furniture for the parlor, and will be used more or less by all classes for its labor saving quality; it is of easy construction either of wood or iron, and extensive preparations are making east for manufacturing them of iron, which will add to their durability. No mother should be without one of these beautiful and essentially useful articles of furniture; it will work from eight to twenty-four hours as may be desired.

Ladies and gentlemen who are desirous of seeing this wonder of the age are respectfully invited to call on the under-signed, in this city, at the saloon of W. W. Watson & Son, where he will, with pleasure, exhibit a model of this grand and useful invention.

The undersigned being the owners of the above invention for the State of Illinois, offer the above for Sale

C. & J. Myers

N.B. All letters addressed to the undersigned, (postpaid) Mt. Pulaski, will receive prompt attention.[26]

It subsequently turned out that Edmonds' patent was not all it had been represented to be, inasmuch as it did not cover the cradle itself, but, rather, the ornamental design, as appeared from the concluding paragraph of his application for letters patent, a copy of which Lincoln obtained from the Patent Office in Washington: "What I claim as my production and desire to secure by letters patent is the design and configuration of the ornaments above described and set forth, forming together an ornamental design for a Horological Cradle."[27]

The situation was naturally productive of lawsuits, in one of which Lincoln represented the Myers brothers in an action brought in the Logan Circuit Court for the recovery of certain real estate conveyed by them in return for the patent rights in the State of Illinois.

While the action was pending, Lincoln, who was childlike in his love for gadgets he could tinker with, took a model of the cradle to his office where, with boyish eagerness, he exhibited it to all callers, explaining to them its operation. John W. Bunn, the local banker, while watching him operate the device, inquired of Lincoln how he managed to stop the darned thing once it was in motion, to which Lincoln, chuckling, replied: "It's like some of the glib talkers you and I know, John; when it gets going it don't know when to stop."

Lincoln's clients prevailed in the lower court. On behalf of the defendants, Archibald Williams, of Quincy, whom Lincoln pronounced to be "the most natural and most learned lawyer he ever knew,"[28] forthwith sued out a writ of error to the Supreme

Court. On February 3, 1855, the finding of the lower court was overturned,[29] the Court holding, in what would seem to be an altogether specious bit of reasoning, that the plaintiffs were presumed to know that a cradle was not patentable, and that when Edmonds represented that he had a patent for an "Horological Cradle," he was simply referring to the ornamentation.

There are grounds for thinking that Lincoln entertained no illusions about the fallibility even of judges of the state's court of last resort. "Squire" Lawrence, justice of the peace in Bloomington, recalled an occasion when Lincoln, while on circuit, stopped in at the Squire's office. When the latter asked him for his opinion in a justice-of-the-peace matter, Lincoln stated the law and then said that if the case went to the Supreme Court, the only advantage the judges there would have would be that they would have the last guess.[30]

10.

Lincoln's friend, Oliver W. Browning, sustained a broken leg as a result of a fall caused by an unrepaired street in Springfield, whereupon Lincoln commenced an action against the city, predicated on the failure of the municipality to maintain the street in good repair. Stuart & Edwards, representing the defendant, interposed a demurrer (objection to a pleading as being insufficient in law) to the declaration as drawn by Lincoln, which demurrer was sustained by Judge Davis. The case was thereupon brought up on appeal before the Supreme Court[31] where, at the December term, 1855, Lincoln made the notable argument that carried his reputation as a lawyer beyond Sangamon County and won for him the admiration of the ablest men at the Illinois bar.

At common law no remedy was provided for the failure of a municipality to repair city streets. Lincoln brought the action on the theory that it was the clear statutory duty of the city of Springfield to keep the city streets in repair, a duty imposed under the terms of its public charter (Article 5, Sections 9, 10 thereof, as amended 1839). The city having neglected its duty, it necessarily followed, reasoned Lincoln, that a cause of action lay.

The then Chief Justice, Walter B. Scates, whose decisions received and merited the commendation of lawyers throughout the state, wrote a lengthy and much-quoted opinion which has become a leading authority on municipal law. Adopting Lincoln's reasoning, Scates held that "Where a specific duty to repair is fully and completely enjoined, and full and adequate powers and means are provided . . . the obligation is perfect, . . ." Here, again, Lincoln played a significant role in the creation of decisional law in a highly important area of judicial interpretation. Though the principle enunciated is today a commonplace in the law of torts, it is well to remember that it was not always such; if, in retrospect, it seems to have been inevitable, there was nothing inevitable about it at the time.

11.

A case, the political repercussions of which far transcended the immediate issue determined, was *People ex rel. Lanphier and Walker* v. *Hatch*,[32] involving the veto by Lincoln's friend, Governor Bissell, of an apportionment bill passed by the Legislature in 1857. The decision climaxed an important political contest over the act's gerrymandering of the state, to the disadvantage of the Republican party. It seems that, through some unaccountable error, the Governor unintentionally approved and signed the bill. When the Republicans learned of the Governor's action, they strongly protested to Bissell, himself a Republican stalwart. At this juncture, the bill still being in the possession of the Governor, he sent a message to the Speaker of the House of Representatives, informing him that the measure had been signed through inadvertence. On the same day Bissell not only crossed out his signature to the bill, but returned it to the house with a veto message. The Democrats brought a mandamus proceeding to compel the Secretary of State to certify the act.

On February 2, 1858, John A. McClernand argued the case before the Supreme Court, for the Democrats. Lincoln and Jackson Grimshaw of Quincy, who represented the Governor (and the Republicans), contended, with much force, that the Governor had the inherent power to rectify an error, especially where, as here, the act of the General Assembly had not passed from his control by the customary modes of legislation.

A correspondent for the St. Louis *Republican* (a Democratic newspaper), who covered the proceedings, was quoted as saying of Lincoln's presentation: "He made one of the best arguments he ever made, and, although at the time, we differed with him in his positions, yet candor compels us to admit that he presented his case in a strong light and with much force."[33] The *Illinois State Journal*, commenting on the argument, said: "On yesterday, in the Supreme Court, the *mandamus* case, involving the validity of the Apportionment bill vetoed by the Governor at the last session of the Legislature, was called up. Col. McClernand argued the case on the part of the relators, and Messrs. Grimshaw and Lincoln on the other side. The argument of Mr. Lincoln was a most able and clear exposition of the law, and in the minds of the many disinterested parties who heard it, completely removed all doubt, as to the validity of the Governor's veto. The case was taken under advisement by the Court."[34]

On February sixth, the Court's mind, helped no little in its thinking by Lincoln, found for his client, holding that while a bill is in the possession and control of the executive, within the period limited by the Constitution, it has not the force of law, and the Governor may exercise a veto power and so return the measure to the house where it originated, with his name erased, notwithstanding he had once announced his approval of it. Thus, after a bitter fight, Lincoln won his case and had the satisfaction of knowing that his client, the Governor of the State, had been fully sustained by his sagacious pleading.

It is, perhaps, not irrelevant to mention that Lincoln's retention as counsel by Bissell was but one of a number of similar retainers. When, for instance, the city of Springfield was confronted with the question as to the legality of accepting its own script from a citizen in payment of a fine for violation of an ordinance, Lincoln went to bat for the city in the Supreme Court.[35] Such was the steadily mounting fame of his talents, in the 'fifties, that Lincoln was constantly being called upon to furnish legal opinions to public officials, state departments, municipalities, counties and other public bodies; an example in point was the time, in 1854, when the city of Springfield and the county of Sangamon jointly retained him to resolve the question as to the legal responsibility, as between them, for the support of an indigent person who had become a public charge. It says a great deal for Lincoln's reputation as a lawyer of probity and ability that both parties to the dispute should have been willing to confer upon him a power to interpret and decide which savored of the judicial function. As always, Lincoln's words were to the point:

> John Fitzgerald, eighteen years of age, able-bodied, but without pecuniary means, came directly from Ireland to Springfield Illinois, and then stopped, and sought employment, with no present intention of returning to Ireland, or going elsewhere—After remaining in the City some three weeks, part of the time employed, and part not, he fell sick, and became a public charge. It has been submitted to me, whether the City of Springfield, or the County of Sangamon is, by law, to bear the charge—
>
> It is my opinion, and decision, that the City is to bear it— I base this upon the construction I give the 4th Section of the 13th Article of the new City charter (Approved March 2, 1854) I think the Legislature intended that all public charges, arising from the indigence of persons, *resident* within the City, were to be borne by the City—and not by the County— I think it was not the intention that this class of charges was to be parcelled out between the City and county, by critical discussions on the words "citizen" "pauper" and the like—
> Dec: 18— 1854.
>
> A. Lincoln—[36]

That Lincoln was not one to render an opinion based upon insufficient knowledge, may be seen from the following brief memorandum, in his hand and over his signature:

> The question within propounded is one which I could not answer without liability to misunderstanding, and, as I fear, doing harm.
>   A. Lincoln[37]

12.

The 'fifties, which might accurately be termed the decade of Lincoln's greatness as a lawyer, saw the launching of the Illinois Central, that magnificent railroad running from the Mississippi River near Galena through the heart of Illinois down to Mobile, Alabama, on the Gulf of Mexico, as well as other systems of rail transportation whose early history was to touch his own at so many points. With the advent of the Iron Horse, new and important legal problems arose: The powers of the railroads under their charters had to be defined; the rights of individual landowners along the rights of way required determination, as did the rights and privileges of passengers and shippers and the corresponding duties and liabilities of the railroads. In the flood of new litigation which engulfed the courts—all part of the great romance of early railroading—it was given to Lincoln to contribute to the law of common carriers in the State of Illinois, and indirectly the law of the land, in a measure which is incalculable.

A case which proved his considerable stature was *Illinois Central Railroad Company* v. *Morrison and Crabtree*,[38] assuredly a landmark in Illinois railroad law. In a decision breaking new legal ground, the Court considered, for the first time, the right of a carrier to restrict its liability to a shipper by express agreement. The action originated in Coles County, where the plaintiffs brought suit against the defendant railroad for damage to plaintiffs' cattle by delay in transit while being transported by the defendant from Urbana to Chicago.

It is of interest to note that Lincoln had first been approached by James Steele and Charles Summers, Morrison's local lawyers, in Paris, Illinois, to represent Morrison, on the appeal, against the Illinois Central. At the time, Lincoln's claim for his fee in the McLean County tax case was pending against the road. On February 12, 1857, Lincoln wrote to Morrison's lawyers, stating that he had been "in the regular retainer of the Co. for two or three years," but that he believed they did not wish to retain him any longer. He further stated that he was going to Chicago on February twenty-first, and while there would ascertain if the company wished to continue using him, and if not, as Lincoln had reason to expect, then he would handle the case on behalf of Morrison. Instead of being discharged by the road, Lincoln was engaged by it to handle the *Morrison* case, as well as others which followed, some of them of far-reaching importance.

The evidence showed that the plaintiffs entered into a special contract with the defendant, whereby the railroad agreed to furnish cars sufficient to ship about four hundred head of cattle; that by the terms of the contract defendant was to furnish the necessary cars at a reduced rate, in consideration of which Morrison signed a release against loss by delay or escape, "and generally, from all claims relating thereto, except such as may arise from the gross negligence or default of the agents or officers of the said company, acting in the discharge of their several official duties." It was shown that, by reason of a breakdown of one of the engines, the shipment was held up en route, with a resulting shrinkage in the weight of the cattle considerably above that ordinarily sustained. On the trial below, in which Lincoln did not take part, the jury found for the plaintiff in the sum of twelve hundred dollars.

On the appeal, which was argued at the December term, 1857, Lincoln was associated with O. B. Ficklin and H. C. Whitney for the defendant-appellant railroad, while Charles Constable (previously encountered, as was Ficklin, in the *Matson* case) and

A. Green appeared for the plaintiffs-respondents. (From the surviving documents, it seems fair to assume that Lincoln handled the appeal for the railroad with little, if any, assistance from either Ficklin or Whitney.)

Lincoln's position, as reflected in his notes and in the opinion of Judge Breese, reversing the judgment below, deserves some analysis. Charting an unprecedented course, he conceded that the common law rule was rigidly opposed to exemption of common carriers from liability, but, pitching his argument on the high plane of a changing economy, reasoned that the new era in trade and transportation called for a modification of the old order of things. Transportation of livestock was attendant with great hazards, he pointed out, and if the railroads had no power of protection by special contract, disastrous consequences would likely ensue. Such was the largeness of his view, in the latter years of his practice, the period of his greatest intellectual growth, that in his appeals to the appellate bench Lincoln so often stressed the broad issue involved in the case, at times minimizing its importance in the case at hand. This was advocacy in the grand manner.

Lincoln's analysis brought about a ruling in his favor, one of profound significance to both the public and the railroad interests. The decision, which had the effect of cutting down the force of the old common-law rule that common carriers were in effect insurers, has been much cited in other courts, including the Supreme Court of the United States.

All told, Lincoln argued eleven appeals for the Illinois Central in the State Supreme Court, ranging in scope from cases involving freight claims, in which but a few hundred dollars were at stake, to the tax case (a detailed narrative of which must await treatment in another chapter) which involved the construction to be placed upon the Illinois Central's charter, and upon the result of which case depended the road's financial future.

It was, perhaps, only natural that Douglas should seek to make political capital of Lincoln's connection with the railroad.

"Can you Republicans deny," he asked, in a speech at Henry, Illinois, "that this day and this hour your candidate, Abraham Lincoln, is the agent and attorney of the Illinois Central, making stump speeches on its money?"[39]

13.

Momentous in its consequences was the case of *The St. Louis, Chicago & Alton Railroad Company*, appellant, v. *Joseph A. Dalby*, appellee, argued at the February Term, 1858, and involving the question of the responsibility of common carriers to the traveling public for the wrongful acts of their agents, committed within the scope of their employment. The appeal brought up for review a judgment of the Circuit Court of Logan County (Judge Davis presiding), rendered the previous September, awarding damages of one thousand dollars to the plaintiff, who had been assaulted by the road's employees while a passenger on its train, en route from Elkhart to Lincoln. The official report of the case[40] lists Stuart & Edwards as appearing for the railroad, Lincoln & Herndon for Dalby.

A search of the records discloses little of value in connection with this important case. The docket book shows that it was the fifty-ninth appeal listed on the calendar of the February term, that it was called and argued on February fourth, and that when court adjourned, the case was taken "under advisement." The jacket of those papers in the *Herndon-Weik Collection* which pertain to the case bears the pencil notation "59," from which one is led to conclude that Herndon helped himself to the actual Supreme Court file, as he did to so many others.

Although the opinion of Chief Justice Caton is a bit complicated by legal technicalities, it contains the essentials of the case. On the trial the plaintiff showed that, at the railroad station in Elkhart, he and his wife applied for tickets to Lincoln, and were told by the station agent that he was out of printed tickets to that point. In lieu thereof, the Dalbys were given a certificate or memorandum to show on the train, reciting that the passengers had applied for tickets, and that the same were not available. Upon being asked for their tickets by the conductor, the Dalbys showed him the memorandum and tendered the amount of the regular fare from Elkhart to Lincoln, at the rate of three cents a mile. The conductor informed them that his instructions were to collect four cents a mile from all passengers who did not have tickets. Upon the plaintiff's refusal to pay the extra fare, the conductor and the brakeman attempted to put him off the train; Dalby successfully resisted, though not without being, as one of the witnesses testified, "pounded in the face ten or a dozen licks."

Predicated on these facts, an action of trespass for assault and battery was instituted by Dalby. The defense interposed by the railroad consisted of the dual contention that an action for assault and battery could not lie against a corporation, and that the road "is presumed to have authorized its servants to use none but usual means for the purpose of enforcing the regulations of the company, and if, instead of using such means, the conductor, or other servant of the company, employed any unusual, unnecessary or unjustifiable measures, then, however culpable the servants of the company may have been, or whatever their liability to the plaintiff, the company, defendant, is not responsible for the employment of such excess means."[41]

On May 15, 1858, more than three months after the argument, the *Illinois State Journal* reported that "the Supreme Court . . . has affirmed the judgment." This highly important decision, which firmly established the liability of railroads for the wrongful acts of their duly authorized agents, formed the legal basis on which countless accident cases were later brought against the railroads. It was, for the firm of Lincoln & Herndon, a handsome victory.

One cannot say, with positive assurance, that Lincoln conducted the argument before the Supreme Court. Among the papers in the *Herndon-Weik Collection* is a penciled reference to Edwards's argument on behalf of the railroad, also the name "Herndon," with a listing of cases in precedence, and the further notation "Parks for Deft in Error"—in what was very likely the handwriting of the clerk of the court. Whether Lincoln or Herndon or Parks, or any combination of the three, made the argument on behalf of the Dalbys, this much seems certain: The collating of authorities in support of the appellee's position was done by Herndon. Items 47 and 48 in Reel 2, Group III of the *Herndon-Weik Collection* show: 1. a memorandum in Herndon's hand, citing authorities in other jurisdictions to show that "an action of assault & battery will lie against a corporation—R. Road Company"; 2. also in Herndon's hand, the point that "The agents of the Company have a discretion; and the Company are responsible when the agents act within their authority"—citing authorities, and 3. the further notation by Herndon: "However in this case there is no evidence that the Powers—the means were exhausted. On the contrary negligence is proved—" [with cases listed].

The assumption of some writers that Lincoln personally argued the case before the Supreme Court possibly derives from the mistaken belief that he conducted the trial, on behalf of the plaintiff, in the Logan Circuit Court. In Stringer's *History of Logan County* is a facsimile of instructions supposedly requested to be given the jury—"written in Lincoln's own hand," according to Stringer—on the basis of which the latter apparently took for granted that Lincoln tried the case. One does not have to be a handwriting expert to see that there is no resemblance whatever between the facsimile of the instructions and Lincoln's unmistakable handwriting. (The writing clearly is that of David Davis. The Illinois State Historical Library has some of the original papers in this case, and the Judge's hand is much in evidence.) Beveridge, citing Stringer, indicates that Lincoln tried the case in the lower court.[42] As a matter of fact, at the time of the trial in Logan County, Lincoln was in Chicago, trying the *Effie Afton* case.

While, on the basis of the existing evidence, no one can say

with certainty that Lincoln conducted the argument, the answer
to this question seems to be a slightly qualified "Yes." The records
show that he was in Springfield at the time, and that he appeared
at the same term of court and argued other appeals. As against
the undoubted fact of Herndon's elaborate research, and the
absence of any record of Lincoln's having made the oral argument, one cannot escape the feeling that the senior partner, with
his high sense of responsibility, would not have entrusted the
argument of this important appeal to Herndon, to whose defects
Lincoln could not have been blind. There appears to be little
doubt that, while Herndon was given a free hand in running the
office, Lincoln had the final say on matters involving court appearances. Gifted with a mind that never rattled or panicked, and
with his remarkable power of lucid exposition, the senior member
bore a deserved reputation, at the time, as one of the most skillful
appellate lawyers in the whole state. He thought straight and
spoke clearly; he did not, like Herndon, traffic in subtleties. How
very unlike Lincoln it would have been to have shirked the responsibility of arguing this case of extremely vital importance
and abdicated in favor of the sometimes brilliant, but notoriously
flighty and erratic Herndon!

That Samuel C. Parks should have figured in the case
strengthens the belief that it was Lincoln, with the armory of his
talents, and not Herndon, who conducted the argument. Parks,
who had an office (where Lincoln hung his hat when in town)
in Lincoln, where the case was tried, was not especially noted for
his work in the Supreme Court. His distinction lay elsewhere, for
he was generally acknowledged to be the best trial lawyer in
Logan County, which boasted a distinguished bar. That he entertained a very high opinion of Lincoln's ability as a lawyer is well
known. In turn, he enjoyed Lincoln's confidence, as is evidenced
by the fact that, as President, he appointed him a territorial judge
of the territory of Wyoming. Very likely the case was Parks's in
the first instance, and it was he who "briefed" Lincoln (as the
English would say). The notion that he would have chosen
Herndon, in preference to Lincoln, is almost beyond belief.

CHAPTER XV

Lincoln's Pardon Petitions

1.

Lincoln devoted a good deal of his time to assisting human beings in need of help. In the Archives Department of the Illinois State Library, in Springfield, are to be found a number of pardon applications, the first dated April 2, 1842, and the last August 8, 1860, which attest to his interest in prisoners serving sentences in the Alton and Joliet Penitentiaries, whose efforts at effecting release from further confinement had aroused his sympathy. Some of the petitions are in other handwritings, but with Lincoln's name appended thereto; others are in his hand, and now and then one comes across a letter or short statement by Lincoln, joining in the request for remission from further punishment.[1]

The first pardon petition known to have been drawn entirely in Lincoln's hand was presented to the Governor on April 2, 1842. It reads:

> To his Excellency Thomas Carlin, Governor of the State of Illinois—
> The undersigned, your petitioners, respectfully represent that Michael Hill has, at the March term (now in session) of the Sangamon Circuit Court, been tried on an indictment for manslaughter, and a verdict of guilty, and that he be confined in the penitentiary for the term of one year and ten days found against him, that your petitioners are the jurors that rendered the verdict; that, under their oaths, they felt it their duty to render such verdict as they did, but that, considering the circumstances, they deem Mr. Hill a most fit subject for the Executive clemency; that he is an elderly, respectable, and peaceful citizen with a large and respected family; that he was highly provoked by oft repeated and long continued abuse, to strike the fatal blow, and that when he did strike, it is agreed by all, he had no intention of killing, or very seriously hurting the unfortunate

deceased. They therefore respectfully request that your Excellency will grant him a full pardon of the entire punishment imposed by the law in the case.

Following the signatures of the petit jurors are those of ninety-two Springfield citizens. Appearing at the end of the list are those of Lincoln and Logan, his partner at the time, both of whom had represented the defendant upon the trial. Judge Treat, the sentencing judge, heartily endorsed the petition because of "an entire absence of any intention on his [Hill's] part to take the life of Lewis," and the lack of "moral guilt in this case, as requires corporal punishment. The law," wrote Treat, "has been fully vindicated by the conviction." Governor Carlin acted favorably upon the request five days after it was presented.

2.

In May, 1847, Lincoln was called upon to defend Sigler H. Lister on a charge of assault with intent to commit murder. The case originated in Coles County. Upon being retained, Lincoln proceeded typically to move for a change of venue, and the case was accordingly removed to Cumberland County in the eastern part of the state. Upon the trial, which was held in a log school-house in Greenup, Lister was convicted as charged, and sentenced to serve a year in the penitentiary. Lincoln thereupon proceeded to draw up and sign a petition for clemency, stating that "There are circumstances which in our opinion render it proper that the Executive clemency should be extended to him." The document, consisting of three and a half pages, contains the signatures of three hundred and fifty-three citizens of Coles County, including Lincoln's stepbrother, John D. Johnston, and his cousin, Dennis F. Hanks. After serving three months, Lister's sentence was commuted by Governor French.

3.

At the spring term, 1850, of the Coles County Circuit Court, William D. Davis, a one-armed veteran of the Mexican War, was indicted for murder. A change of venue was granted to Clark County. On July 1 and 2, 1850, Lincoln appeared in Marshall, the county seat of Clark, in defense of Davis, whose trial resulted in a conviction of manslaughter and his sentence to three years in the penitentiary. Two and a half years later, Lincoln addressed to Governor Joel A. Matteson (first occupant of the Illinois executive mansion) one of his strongest pleas for executive clemency, in the form of a letter which furnishes an outstanding illustration of that unique fusion of concision and felicity of statement which was his hallmark as a lawyer:

Springfield, Jany 10. 1853.

His Excellency, the Governor
of the State of Illinois—
    Sir:
    In July: 1850, a man by the name of William D. Davis, was tried and convicted of the crime of Manslaughter and sentenced to the Penitentiary for the term of three years, by the circuit court of Clark County, whither his case had been taken by a change of venue from Coles county—
    I assisted in his defense, and thought his conviction was right, but that the term fixed was too long under the circumstances— I told him that if he should behave himself well for a considerable portion of the time, I would join in seeking a pardon for the remainder— He has a young family, and has lost one of his arms— He has now served about five sixths of his time, and I understand, the Warden, who is now in Springfield, testifies that he has behaved well— Under these circumstances I hope he may be released from further confinement—

Your Obt Servt
A. Lincoln

The letter, addressed to Matteson on the day of the latter's inauguration, was ignored and the man served his full term. Lincoln, it is said, never quite forgave the Democratic Governor for his callous disregard of the matter. It is interesting to note that it was largely through Lincoln's influence that, in 1855, Matteson was defeated for United States Senator in the balloting before the Legislature.[2] On the first ballot Lincoln received forty-four votes, Shields forty-one, and Trumbull five. Realizing that Matteson, and not Shields, was the real choice of the Democrats, Lincoln threw enough votes to his friend Trumbull to elect him on the tenth ballot.

Though he was doubtless aware of Lincoln's action, Matteson, then in control of the St. Louis, Alton & Chicago Railroad, nevertheless engaged Lincoln in 1858 to handle certain litigation for the road. That the engagement was not carried through to a conclusion does not alter the fact that Matteson must have thought highly of the legal acumen and reputation of the man who had been mainly instrumental in wrecking his senatorial aspirations.

4.

In August, 1857, there was presented to the Governor a petition for the pardon of Moses Loe, the first person to be convicted of a homicide charge in DeWitt County. Appended to the original application is a sixteen-line statement by Lincoln, which reads: "I defended Moses Loe . . . and, with the exception of the assistance of a younger man at the trial, who volunteered merely to try his hand, the whole defense rested on me. I know Loe to have been a very young man at the time of the offence, and that more than half his time, (originally eight years) has elapsed since his conviction. As to his previous character, or his conduct in the State prison I know nothing; but willing to trust the numerous and very respectable gentlemen who speak on these points, I cheerfully join the request that he be pardoned for the remainder of his term." The petition was denied, and Loe served his full term.

The case itself, in which Lincoln seems to have been foredoomed to defeat, may have added nothing to his stature as a lawyer, but it is of more than passing interest for the reason that something of the way he went about handling a murder case may be seen in the documents which have survived. Loe was indicted by a Sangamon County Grand Jury for the murder of James Gray by stabbing. On September 4, 1852, the defendant was arraigned and pleaded not guilty, at which time Lincoln moved for a change of venue, submitting an affidavit drawn in his own hand and signed by the defendant with his mark, stating "on oath that he fears he will not receive a fair and impartial trial on said indictment . . . on account that the minds of the inhabitants of said county, wherein said trial is pending, are prejudiced against him, . . ."[3] The motion was granted the same day and the case removed to DeWitt County.

On October 8, 1852, the date set for trial, Lincoln appeared in Clinton and submitted an affidavit in which he requested a continuance, on the grounds that the defendant "cannot safely go to trial at the present term of the court, because of the absence of Thomas Blankenship and Elizabeth Grass, who, he is advised and believed, are material witnesses for him on such trial."[4] The case was accordingly put over to the following spring term when, to no one's astonishment, the defendant was, on May nineteenth, found guilty, though of a lesser crime than that charged in the indictment—manslaughter. He was sentenced to the maximum term under the law—eight years in the Alton Penitentiary, three months to be served in solitary confinement and the remainder of the sentence at hard labor. The result was generally regarded as a victory for the defense, as a determined effort had been made to convict for murder.

A most interesting summary of the evidence, in Lincoln's hand, presumably for use in summation, has come down to us.[5] It shows a comprehensive marshaling of the testimony on both sides, a circumstance the more remarkable in view of the fact that Lincoln was never known to have taken notes during the course of a trial, claiming that it distracted his attention.[6] It is no exaggeration to say that the retentive power of his memory was phenomenal, invoking comparison with that of the greatest American jury lawyer of his generation, Max D. Steuer of the New York bar, another who dispensed with the taking of trial notes. To Joseph Gillespie, veteran trial lawyer and judge, whose admiration for Lincoln's legal ability was unbounded, his power of recollection was "astonishing."[7]

It is possible to reconstruct the evidence from this somewhat detailed abstract of the testimony. On the part of the prosecution, it was shown that on the morning of the killing Gray and Loe met on the street; that the deceased inquired of the defendant if he had had his breakfast, whereupon the defendant proceeded to draw a knife; that Gray asked him to "put down" the knife, and Loe making no move to do so, Gray ran; that the defendant pursued him, caught up with him, knocked him down, stomped him and then bent over and stabbed him in the neck. The sheriff testified to an admission of guilt by the defendant, and the finding of a knife, containing traces of blood, on the latter's person. From this array of damning facts one gathers something of the dark picture which confronted Lincoln, who produced, as his sole witnesses, the aforementioned Blankenship, who testified to a conversation with Gray, in which the latter invited him to come along "if he wanted to see some fun," as he and Loe were going to engage in a fight, and Dr. Goodheart, who testified that the blood on the knife did not come from the cut on the decedent's neck.

In the same three-page summary appears a list of the jurors, with their ages. In the course of his closing remarks, Lincoln probably made it a practice to address the different veniremen by name. It is common courtroom knowledge that jurors react favorably to this form of flattery, a fact so well attested by experience that it has almost the force of an axiom in trial work. It is interesting to speculate on what he had in mind when he wrote, next to the names of the foreman and three of the other jurors, the word "Murder." Chances are that Lincoln, pitted against impossible odds and realizing that the outlook for his client was bleak, indeed, was aiming for a verdict in a lesser degree than murder, and, having tabbed these jurors as the ones most apt to vote a murder conviction, made note of them as requiring special attention. Lincoln seemed to have that rare faculty in a trial lawyer of sensing what the mental attitude of the twelve men would be toward the facts as developed on the trial.

5.

One of the cases in which Lincoln sought a pardon, where he had not appeared as attorney of record, was that of Samuel and James Jones, father and son sentenced to a term of confinement for stealing five pigs of the value of ten dollars each. Lincoln's letter, written while he was attending court in Logan County, is dated March 22, 1858. The trial had been held at Lincoln earlier in the month. Lamon, the prosecutor, joined in the request for clemency. A pardon would be satisfactory to the citizens of the county, wrote Lamon, "and strange to say they think that the end of public justice has been met by the mere conviction without the service." The remission was granted.

Another instance of Lincoln's interest in securing the release of a prisoner whom he had not represented upon the trial was the case of George High, who at the fall term, 1855, of the Champaign Circuit Court was convicted as a horse thief and sentenced to three years. High, a member of a notorious band of horse thieves, had been captured by a group of vigilantes. After the miscreant had been confined under the Court's sentence for over two years, having before that spent fourteen months in the county jail before trial (in those days there was no provision for a prisoner receiving credit for time served while awaiting trial), Lincoln drew up a petition reciting these circumstances and stressing the offender's youth. The document bears twenty-seven signatures, including those of the prosecuting attorneys, O. L. Davis and Ward H. Lamon. Judge Davis wrote an endorsement on the petition which is dated November 7, 1857. After apparently taking the petition to Springfield personally, Lincoln added his own endorsement: "I have been acquainted with the circumstances of George High's case from the time of his arrest;

and I cheerfully join in the request that he may be pardoned. Novr- 10- 1857. A. Lincoln-"[8] The prisoner was pardoned for the remainder of his term.

6.

In only one pardon petition does Lincoln flatly state that the conviction was contrary to the evidence. In April, 1856, he, Norman H. Purple, and John Clark represented David Thompson for murder in the Woodford County Circuit Court. The defendant was convicted of manslaughter, and sentenced to eight years. There was general dissatisfaction with the verdict, and on April 12, 1858, Judge Davis signed a petition for his pardon, to which Lincoln added: "I was appointed by the court to defend in part the above named David Thompson. I thought at the time his conviction was wrong, and I am now clearly of the opinion he ought to be pardoned. I have recently been at Woodford; and the universal sentiment there seems to be in favor of a pardon." Lincoln personally visited Governor Bissell and received the pardon.

It is to be noted that in not a single instance did he seek the pardon as a personal favor. In his notes and letters he endeavored to present to the Governor the bare facts. The closest Lincoln came to lending the weight of his name to the application were the several petitions for clemency, made on behalf of prisoners he had not represented, addressed to Governor John Wood after his nomination for the Presidency. In the case of Emanuel Fowler, sentenced to a year for an assault committed in Shelby County, he stated, on June 8, 1860: "Believing that Judge Emerson knows what is right in this case, I join in the recommendation he makes." On August 8, 1860, he wrote a similar note in connection with the petition of Patrick Cunningham, convicted of manslaughter and sentenced to eight years for the slaying of a Chicago policeman. "I think it is almost always safe," wrote Lincoln, "to pardon a convict, when, as in this case, the Judge before whom he was convicted, recommends it."

7.

Sometime in the last week of February, 1857, Lincoln was in Chicago for a conference with officials of the Illinois Central Railroad. While on the train en route from there to Clinton, where the spring term was set to convene on March second, Lincoln noticed a prisoner being taken from Chicago to the Alton Penitentiary. Possibly the word had gotten around that Lincoln had been quite successful with his pardon applications, for the man, whose "gentlemanly appearance" appealed to Lincoln, inquired of him concerning the chances of obtaining a pardon. Lincoln could not have been too sanguine, especially as the prisoner had not, at the time, even commenced serving his term of imprisonment. In the *Robert Todd Lincoln Collection* is a letter, written from the institution at Alton under date of April 25, 1858, and signed by the same prisoner, Alfred Hyde. "I was sentenced for 4 years," he wrote, "but I did not have a fair trial nor was I allowed time to get my Witnesses. I was indited for having fictitious money. . . . I am here *innocent*. Now what will you ask to obtain a pardon for me, cash *upon* my pardon?"[9] Probably Lincoln wrote, acknowledging receipt of the communication, though there is no evidence thereof.

On August 3, 1858, Lincoln took time out from his hectic campaign for the Senate to write to Daniel S. Dickinson, United States Senator from New York (1844–1851), enclosing the letter received from Hyde, in which the prisoner had mentioned Dickinson's name. "Do you really know him?" wrote Lincoln. "If our Governor could learn that he has been respectable, and is of respectable connections, perhaps he would pardon him. Please answer. Pardon the liberty I take in addressing you. Several years ago I knew you slightly at Washington."[10] On August ninth, Dickinson replied rather noncommittally that he had known

Alfred Hyde in a business way, but not personally. There the matter apparently ended, so far as Lincoln's interest in it was concerned.[11] While it is a virtual certainty that most of Lincoln's pardon applications carried with them no prospect of a fee, one feels that the overly smart prisoner did not help his cause any by the stipulation "cash *upon* my pardon."

8.

From Joliet Prison, the new penitentiary, came an appeal for assistance, after Lincoln's nomination for the Presidency, which he could not and would not turn down. The prisoner, with whose case Lincoln was very familiar, was Thomas Patterson, whose trial in Urbana in April, 1859, on a charge of manslaughter, was Lincoln's last important homicide case. The Lincoln-Douglas debates in the fall of 1858 and the engagement elsewhere of Leonard Swett, Lincoln's associate in the case, caused the postponement of the trial for six months when it first appeared on Judge Davis's calendar. A year ensued from the time of indictment before the case was brought to trial, the defendant having in the meantime been free on bail of three thousand dollars. From the indictment and other papers in the case, it is possible to reconstruct the case for the prosecution and something of the defense.

Patterson, who operated a general store in Sadorus, in Champaign County, was charged with having killed Samuel Dehaven, a local farmer, with a two-pound scale weight. The deceased had entered the defendant's store to purchase a hatchet, and upon being refused credit became abusive toward the defendant. It was shown that the deceased, who had a reputation for being violent when drunk, was in an intoxicated condition at the time. When Patterson ordered him out of the store, Dehaven left, but returned in a few minutes with a spade; approaching to within a few feet of the defendant, he raised the spade as though to strike the defendant, whereupon Patterson picked up the scale weight and threw it at him. Struck on the head, Dehaven slumped to the ground. Patterson and others picked him up and carried him into the defendant's house. The following day he died.

The defense was, of course, self-defense—that Patterson, knowing of the deceased's vicious proclivities when drunk, firmly believed, as he had every right to, that his own life was in danger, and threw the scale weight in order to protect himself from attack with the spade.

At the defense table, with Lincoln, were Swett, Whitney and William N. Coler, the latter two being among the leading trial lawyers of Champaign County.[12] The courtroom was jammed to capacity with residents of Sadorus. Throughout the county there was much sentiment against the defendant, the decedent having been an old resident; it was an open secret in Urbana that the cards were stacked against Patterson, who was a comparative newcomer to the county. One is prompted to wonder why the defense did not move for a change of venue; it would not be improbable to think that Lincoln, who subscribed so completely to belief in the efficacy of the remedy, was over-ruled by his three associates, who felt that the retention of local counsel in the persons of Whitney and Coler assured the defendant of a fair shake.

In a drawn-out trial, fourteen witnesses testified for the People; most of them were alleged eyewitnesses and, as came out on cross-examination, friends of Dehaven. Through them, Lamon sought to establish that the defendant, and not the decedent, was the aggressor. The defense called twenty-one witnesses, among them nine character witnesses from Vermilion county (from where the defendant originally hailed), who testified to the defendant's reputation for quiet and peaceableness.

Thanks to Whitney, one of the myths put out by the early Lincoln idolaters, concerning this case, was shown up for the fabrication it was. "I have noticed in most of the 'Lives of Lincoln' which have fallen under my notice," wrote Whitney, "this pretty story: that in the case of *Patterson*, who was tried for murder in Urbana, Lincoln said to Swett: 'The man's guilty—you defend him; I wont;' and Swett took the whole fee, Lincoln refusing any part of it, . . . The facts are these: I was the first lawyer employed in the case, and was instructed to employ any one I deemed needful for the best defense. I accordingly wrote to both Swett and Lincoln, and employed them. We each got $200.00, and each kept what he got. Lincoln remained in the case till the end, making the last speech."[13]

In his closing statement Lincoln made a determined effort to get the defendant off; the stolid jury remained unmoved, however, and in no time at all returned a verdict of guilty, whereupon Judge Davis sentenced the defendant to serve three years. Patterson, then thirty-four years of age, entered the penitentiary on May 3, 1859. One year later, at the time of Lincoln's nomination for President, petitions were circulated in Champaign and Vermilion counties, seeking a pardon for him. When 1,355 signatures had been obtained, the petitions were forwarded to Swett, who personally attended upon Governor Wood with them.

In addition to Swett's own formal written request, in which he stressed the element of self-defense and the fact that the prisoner had a sick wife and four small children who were in need of his support, there was addressed to the Governor a plea by Davis, written on the back of a letter signed by two citizens of Vermilion County. In it Davis said: ". . . The gentlemen who have written this letter, are as worthy men as there are in the state . . . and the opinion that I have expressed as to their character would be the universal opinion of all who know them." At the bottom of Davis's statement Lincoln wrote: "Considering the absence of a previous bad character of Patterson himself, the necessities of his family, the excellent character of all his family connections, and the very numerously signed petition of his neighbors, I recommend that he be pardoned at once." Sixteen days later Governor Wood issued the pardon.

An unpaid note for eighty dollars, being part of Lincoln's fee, was among his papers at the time of his death. Judge Davis, as administrator, turned the note over for collection to the firm of Sheldon & Jaques, of Champaign, who collected on it in February, 1866.[14]

CHAPTER XVI

Lincoln's Law Clerks

1.

S OON AFTER the partnership of Stuart & Lincoln was formed, Milton Hay came to work for them as a clerk and law student. Upon admission to practice in 1840, he moved to Pittsfield, Pike County, where he engaged in the practice of his profession. In 1858 he returned to Springfield, where he formed a copartnership with Stephen T. Logan, whose daughter he married, the firm of Logan & Hay occupying the front office on the same floor with Lincoln & Herndon.[1]

Joseph W. Fifer, speaking of Hay, recalled: "While I was governor of Illinois I was thrown in close contact with Milton Hay, who had read law for three years in the office of Lincoln in Springfield, when Lincoln was a practicing lawyer, before he became famous. Hay told me many anecdotes of Lincoln that I have never seen in print. Hay's duties as a law student was to go to the office each Sunday morning and sweep it out, put books back in their places and generally set it to rights. He said Lincoln did not go to church often, but he would find him in the office when he got there."[2]

In 1859 Lincoln was associated with Hay in the defense of "Peachy" Harrison, charged with murder. It was Milton Hay who recommended his nephew, John Hay, then studying law in his office, for the post of secretary to Lincoln, beside John G. Nicolay, whose connection with him was so intimate that they are seldom spoken of separately.[3]

Gibson W. Harris, the first law student to study under the aegis of Lincoln & Herndon, recalled[4] that "In September, 1845, through the kindness of our then State Senator, Mr. Charles Constable, it was arranged I should enter the law office of Lincoln & Herndon, at Springfield, as student and clerk." Arrived in Springfield after a three-day journey by stage from Albion, Harris went directly to the Lincoln & Herndon office, where he met Herndon, who told him that the senior partner was out on the circuit at the time but was expected back in Springfield in a few days. Returning several days later, Harris met Lincoln, who rose from his chair and gave him "a cordial handshake." "You are the young man Mr. Constable spoke to me about?" he asked, whereupon he proceeded to introduce the young man to Herndon. Then, motioning toward the office bookcase, Lincoln remarked: "You will need what that contains. Make yourself at home." Resuming his seat, Lincoln proceeded to "elevate his feet to a level with his head, litterally sitting on his backbone."

Harris did no reading that first day. "Mr. Lincoln was taking a rest after his tour of the circuit, and was in a chatty mood; . . . During my stay in his office I was the only student and only clerk in it. I . . . was soon made to feel the senior partner's kindly interest in me personally. Simultaneously the less pleasing fact dawned upon me that Mr. Lincoln was not an assiduous instructor in the technics of law (which, indeed, were always more or less irksome to him, his mind dwelling rather on its principles), and reluctantly I began to turn to Mr. Herndon for such explanations as I needed, or, as opportunity offered, discussed what to me were knotty points with various younger members of the local bar. But, while these developments could not but be a damper to the ardent youth unsatisfied until he could enter Mr. Lincoln's office, I never thought of admiring him less."

Harris served with the firm until 1847, when he moved to Cincinnati, where he became wealthy as a mattress manufacturer. Lincoln and his one-time clerk met on several occasions—in Cincinnati in 1859 and in Washington in the spring of 1861.

When Harris left the office, David A. Brown was taken on. Upon Brown's admission to the bar in 1848, he was appointed clerk of the circuit court of Menard County. Eventually he moved back to Springfield and, after practicing there for a while, quit the law and took up farming at Bates. Very likely Brown, like the others who succeeded him, was interviewed and engaged by Herndon. In 1858, Lincoln received a written application for leave to study in the Lincoln & Herndon law office from William H. Grigsby, a young man nineteen years of age, who was then employed in Pekin. In response, Lincoln wrote: "My partner, Mr. Herndon, controls our office in this respect, and I have known of his declining at least a dozen applications like yours within the last three months."[5]

Norman M. Broadwell was another who "read law" with the firm, serving from about 1849 to 1851, when he was admitted to practice. Broadwell went on to become a member of the state legislature, circuit judge and Mayor of Springfield.

Early in 1859 Milton S. Littlefield, prominent Republican lawyer of Illinois (dubbed "Prince of Carpetbaggers" by his biographer),[6] persuaded his friend Lincoln to take his younger brother, John H., into the Lincoln & Herndon law office, where he served as a law student until shortly before the President-elect left for Washington. John, who had some talent as an artist, eventually abandoned the law and opened a studio in Brooklyn, New York City, where he died penniless and obscure. In an interview with a reporter for the Brooklyn *Daily Eagle*, given while putting the finishing touches to a portrait of Henry Ward Beecher, Littlefield related how he applied at the Springfield office for admission as a student.[7] Turning the applicant over to Herndon, who was entrusted with the management of the office, Lincoln told the latter: "Whatever arrangement you make with him will be satisfactory to me." Herndon, in his *Life of Lincoln*, verifies the fact of Littlefield having served under him and Lincoln "for several years."[8]

The most colorful personality among the roster of clerks and law students who were exposed to the law in the office of Lincoln & Herndon was, by all odds, Elmer Ephraim Ellsworth.

Having experienced considerable difficulty in making up his mind "whether . . . to be a Lawyer—Soldier or Politician or a good for nought,"[9] Ellsworth did not get around to entering the Lincoln & Herndon office, where he studied for a short time, until the tail end of Lincoln's period at the bar—in the fall of 1860. The *Illinois State Journal*, recording the occasion, noted: "Col. Ellsworth. We are pleased to learn that Col. Ellsworth, late commander of the celebrated Chicago Zouaves, has reached this city [Springfield] for the purpose of making it his future residence. He has dissolved his connections with his company, and intends preparing himself for the practice of the legal profession. He is now completing his studies at the law office of Lincoln & Herndon.We wish him as much success and glory in his new profession as he has attained in the one he has left."[10]

Prior to establishing a connection with Lincoln & Herndon, Ellsworth had studied law for several months in the office of a Chicago attorney, John E. Cone. Upon the latter's being sold out for debt, in September, 1859, Ellsworth entered the office of E. Van Buren,[11] where he remained for a month or two.

Elmer's correspondence with his fiancée, Carrie Spafford, in Rockford, preserved in the Illinois State Historical Library, depicts something of his indecision "in reference to Mr. Lincoln's proposition, or rather Mr. Cooks. Mr. Cook told me that Mr. L—— *especially desired him to leave no means* untried to induce me to come to Springfield. I cannot but regard this as a very great compliment. I believe that the influence of Mr. L—— would do me great service. I mean the influence of his early example."[12] Two days later (January 31, 1860), this slightly pompous young man who would appear to have been a bit too pleased with himself again wrote Carrie, from Chicago, stating that he had been "offered very great inducements . . . to complete [his] studies, with Hon. Abram Lincoln—the matter remains open for me to decide upon at my leisure."[13]

Ellsworth's first letter from Springfield is dated September 15, 1860. In his communication to Carrie of November 18, 1860, he states: "I am working in the office of the State Auditor every day at the desk and studying and writing nights." Though by then he had seemingly more or less committed himself to the study of law, it would appear that his clerkship with Lincoln & Herndon was on a part-time basis. This conclusion is borne out, to some extent, by Littlefield's reference to Ellsworth as "nominally a student in Lincoln's office."[14]

Ellsworth participated in the campaign of 1860, making his first speech with Herndon on October twentieth. Among the sixty-six letters of Elmer to Carrie, contained in the Ellsworth manuscript collection, is one written the following day: "I made my maiden speech. (on political topics I mean) Mr. Herndon, (Mr. Lincolns law partner) & myself had the felicity of addressing a crowd of sovereigns on the 'all absorbing issues of the present campaign' . . . I believe it is arranged that I am to speak every day, until the election, in the country precincts. Hurray for the next President." On election day he, together with Herndon and Ward Hill Lamon, went with Lincoln to the polls. He was one of the Presidential party which accompanied the President-elect on his last departure from Springfield. Prior to that, he had definitely made up his mind as to his future course, for on January 18, 1861, he wrote Carrie from Springfield, stating that he was lobbying for his militia law, which he had written. "I have *decided* upon devoting myself to military matters hereafter to the exclusion of everything else."[15]

From the New York Fire Department Ellsworth recruited his regiment of dauntless Zouaves. In May of 1861 they embarked in transports and landed at Alexandria, Virginia. The rebels, when encountered, fell back, but the Stars and Bars still floated over the Marshall House, the city's leading hotel. Ellsworth, noticing it, raced up the stairs and rashly cut down the Confederate emblem; as he descended, the proprietor of the hotel discharged a double-barreled shotgun in his chest, before being himself obliterated by Ellsworth's men. Lincoln ordered a White House funeral for his young friend, who was the first Union casualty of the war. "In the untimely loss of your noble son," he wrote to Ellsworth's parents, "our affliction here, is scarcely less than your own. . . . In the hope that it may be no intrusion upon the sacredness of your sorrow, I have ventured to address you this tribute to the memory of my young friend, and your brave and early fallen child. May God give you that consolation which is beyond all earthly power."

Though our knowledge of them is decidedly meager, it has been established that at least three others served their apprenticeships in the modest quarters of the Lincoln & Herndon office. M. B. Church put in a year (1857–1858); Isaac Cogdale served for a brief period in the middle 'fifties, before his admission to practice. According to Herndon, Greek Crafton, who was stabbed to death by "Peachy" Harrison, whom Lincoln defended for murder, was another who "studied law with Lincoln & Herndon."[16]

In the material which Henry Bascom Rankin furnished for Who's Who after publication in 1916 of his first book, Personal Recollections of Abraham Lincoln,[17] he claimed to have been a student in the office from December, 1856, until February, 1861. Lincoln, Herndon and their more intimate associates had long been safely dead and buried, and no one was then living to contradict this "notoriously inaccurate" writer. Neither Herndon nor any of the clerks who served in the office during the four years that Rankin stated that he had been there, mentions him. It has been truly said that if all the lawyers who claimed to have been students in the Lincoln & Herndon office had actually served as such, there would seem to have been several times as many law students in that little office as ever before has been the case in any office anywhere.

Most Lincoln scholars view Rankin's claim to inclusion in the not-too-select group of Lincoln law students as being of dubious authenticity, due in part to the fact that Herndon's Life of Lincoln contains no mention of him. Possibly in a retaliatory effort to discredit the latter, Rankin, in his celebrated hatchet job on Herndon, launched and spread the notion that the once junior member of the firm, in addition to being a drunken sot, was a drug addict. December 16, 1916, he wrote to Lord Charnwood: "I would not consent to tell all the story for history, about his [Herndon's] shadowy decadence and incapacity for serious historical work while preparing with and for others the manuscripts for the 'Lives of Lincoln' with which his name was associated. His brain all through those lamentable years had been inflamed by alcoholic stimulants and his imagination distorted and made unreliable by his habitual use of opium."[18] Actually, there is no proof or reason to believe that Herndon, even in the period of his ultimate disintegration as a lawyer, ever took drugs. In his addiction to drink, which was decidedly a legal occupational hazard, he was not alone.

Rankin speaks of "papers I was expected to prepare."[19] Though the files of all the counties in which Lincoln & Herndon practiced have been combed for evidence of Lincoln's cases, not a single document in Rankin's handwriting has ever turned up.

Chief among the doubting Thomases was William E. Barton, who wrote *The Life of Abraham Lincoln, The Women Lincoln Loved,* and other books and articles on the subject of the most written-about American. Barton, "a great historical detective," never could understand just why Rankin, who came from a Democratic district, should have been so eager to serve a clerkship "in the intensely Republican office of Lincoln & Herndon."[20] But it was Rankin's statement that Lincoln read Walt Whitman's *Leaves of Grass,* a copy of which Herndon kept in the office, which aroused Barton's suspicions. The quotation from Rankin is of interest: "When Walt Whitman's *Leaves of Grass* was first published, it was placed on the office table by Herndon. It had been read by several of us, and, one day, discussions hot and extreme had sprung up between office students and Mr. Herndon concerning its poetic merit, in which Dr. Bateman engaged with us, having entered, from his adjoining office. . . . Time and again, when Lincoln came in, or was leaving, he would pick it up, as if to glance at it for only a moment, but instead he would often settle down in a chair and never stop without reading aloud such verses or pages as he fancied. His estimate of the poetry differed from any brought out in the office discussions. He foretold correctly the place the future would assign to Whitman's poems, and that *Leaves of Grass* would be followed by other and greater work."[21]

As Barton pointed out: "The only time when Lincoln's office adjoined that of Newton Bateman was in the busy period after Lincoln had been nominated for the Presidency. He was permitted courteously to share the Governor's office, and receive his visitors there."[22] (Bateman was, at the time, superintendent of public instruction, and as such occupied an office in the State House.) That Rankin waited until both Bateman and Herndon were dead before telling the story was, to Barton, a highly suspicious circumstance. As Barton further points out, Herndon, who owned a copy of *Leaves of Grass*, makes no mention of Lincoln having ever read it.

Almost alone among folks in the Lincoln field, Emanuel Hertz accepted Rankin unquestioningly—just as he did Herndon. "I disagree entirely with Barton's doubts and condemnation of Rankin," wrote Hertz (without stating the basis for his judgment), "and I think Rankin has done excellent work, and I take his word for it."[23] Though it is possible that Rankin may have served in the Lincoln & Herndon office, historical opinion has tended toward the conclusion that Barton's strong case in opposition remains unimpaired, and that the heavy burden of proof resting on Hertz has never been sustained.

Rankin rendered an inestimable service in connection with the marking of those Springfield sites which Lincoln made immortal. Largely through his efforts, the Lincoln law offices, the Globe Tavern, the store of Joshua Speed, and the Wabash Station from which Lincoln left for Washington and where he delivered his famous farewell address, have been suitably marked.[24]

Under the so-called preceptorial system, the transmitting of legal knowledge by means of regular instruction was virtually nonexistent. That Lincoln could have had no illusions about the benefits to be reaped from clerkships spent in law offices is plainly evident from a letter which he wrote to a young man residing near Chandlersville, Illinois, who had been a student at Illinois College: "I have just reached home, and found your letter of the 23rd ult. I am from home too much of my time, for a young man to read law with me advantageously. If you are resolutely determined to make a lawyer of yourself, the thing is more than half done already. It is but a small matter whether you read with any body or not. I did not read with any one. Get the books, and read and study them till, you understand them in their principal features; and that is the main thing. . . . Always bear in mind that your resolution to succeed is more important than any one thing."[25]

In a letter written several years later, Lincoln again described the method he pursued in studying for the bar. "When a man has reached the age that Mr. Widner has, and has already been doing for himself, my judgment is, that he reads the books for himself without an instructor. That is precisely the way I came to the Law."[26]

Considering the great number of papers in Lincoln's hand, it is hard to imagine just what were the duties of these undergraduates who, at one time or another, "studied" under the less-than-didactic Lincoln—other than occasionally sweeping out the office.

2.

Among the public services which Lincoln customarily rendered was that of acting as bar examiner. Until about 1850 oral examinations were, for the most part, conducted by Supreme Court judges. Thereafter and until 1897, examinations were given either by committees appointed by the circuit judges (1850-1858) or by examining boards appointed by the Supreme Court (1858-1897). The committees appointed by the circuit judges consisted of two or three practicing attorneys, one of whom was usually the prosecuting attorney of the circuit, while the boards appointed by the Supreme Court consisted of three members in each of a specified number of divisions of the state. Lincoln's work as a bar examiner was performed both as a Circuit Court and Supreme Court appointee.

Hiram W. Beckwith, after whose father, Dan Beckwith, the town of Danville was named, studied law in the office of Ward H. Lamon in Danville. On those occasions when Lincoln's work on the circuit brought him to that county-seat town, Beckwith and he probably saw much of each other, inasmuch as Lincoln made his headquarters, while in town, at the Lamon office. On May 27, 1854, while Lincoln was at Danville, he and Leonard Swett served as a committee to examine Beckwith and one George Lawrence concerning their qualifications to practice law, at the conclusion of which examination Lincoln wrote out a recommendation, which he and Swett signed:

> We have examined Hiram W. Beckwith and George W. Lawrence touching their qualifications to practice law; and find them sufficiently qualified to commence the practice, and therefore recommend that licenses be allowed them.
> Danville May 27, 1854.
>
> A. Lincoln
> L. Swett[27]

What the "examination" consisted of isn't of record. It seems safe to say it was not overly rigorous.

After Beckwith's admission he continued to associate himself with Lamon until the latter's election as prosecuting attorney, whereupon he succeeded to the practice. During the years of his active practice at the bar, he was associated, on one side or another, with nearly all the lawsuits originating in Danville. As first president of the Illinois State Historical Society, he was largely instrumental in getting under way the vast project of collecting and preserving data relating to the history of Illinois, disseminating the story of the state and its citizens, and encourag-

ing historical research, which has made this organization outstanding among its kind in the nation.

Not a great deal is known of Lawrence. Whitney wrote
that "Lincoln and George Lawrence, a worthless, drunken lawyer, used to play billiards together: one played as well as the
other."[28]

In 1856, Reuben M. Benjamin, fresh from Harvard Law
School, came to Bloomington to practice. On one of Lincoln's
periodic appearances in that city he examined, and certified as
having passed the examination, young Benjamin, who went on
to become a successful lawyer, county judge and first dean of the
law school of Illinois Wesleyan University.[29]

In 1906, Jesse W. Weik published a paper written by Jonathan M. Birch, in which the latter described in some detail his
examination for the bar, conducted by Lincoln, in which some
of the questions asked "bore but a faint relation to the practice of
law."[30] At the conclusion of the examination, Lincoln supposedly
wrote a certificate recommending the license. "The Supreme
Court," according to Beveridge, "at once issued the license on
Lincoln's recommendation."[31] Unfortunately for the tale, the
Illinois Supreme Court contains no record of Birch having been
admitted to the bar.

Lincoln's old student, Milton Hay, and Benjamin S. Edwards, who succeeded Lincoln as Stuart's law partner, were co-
signers with Lincoln of the certificate of admission for Henry I.
Atkins, found, years later, among the papers of Judge Pinkney
H. Walker of the Illinois Supreme Court.[32]

Others known to have been examined by Lincoln were
Josiah McRoberts and John H. Murphy on July 8, 1841, on
which occasion Josiah Lamborn and Schuyler Strong served
with Lincoln;[33] Benjamin F. James on July 21, 1841, the other
member of the examining committee being Albert T. Bledsoe;[34]
and Henry S. Greene on January 21, 1860, Orville Browning
and Lewis W. Ross serving with Lincoln.[35] Palmer, writing of
Ross, who practiced law in Illinois for close to half a century,

stated: "When a young man he was in sympathy with the Whigs, but, being a student and deep thinker, he became a Democrat and adhered to that party ever afterward."[36]

Though there can be no certainty about many matters connected with Lincoln's law career, it is a fair guess that, as a bar examiner, he was not very exacting, there being no known instance of his ever having turned an applicant down. Something of his general attitude may be gleaned from a letter which he wrote to the presiding judge of one of the circuits: "Your honor, I think this young man knows as much about law as I did when I began to practice, and I recommend his admission to the bar." On another occasion, he supposedly quizzed orally a candidate who dropped in while Lincoln was shaving. After a few perfunctory questions, Lincoln passed the young aspirant on with the dry observation, "This young man is smarter than he looks." The story probably is apocryphal, but it is in character.

CHAPTER XVII

Lincoln as Judge and as
Prosecuting Attorney

1.

DURING Lincoln's years at the bar, it was common practice throughout the Middle West for circuit judges, whenever called away by reason of sickness or for other cause, to designate attorneys to preside in their stead. This irregular practice, altogether without statutory sanction, entailed a bit of deception, inasmuch as the court records designedly did not show when an attorney sat for the regular judge. This, doubtless, was in order to prevent reversal upon appeal.[1] Consequently, the only means of determining those cases where court-appointed "judges" sat is through analysis of the different handwritings appearing in the Judges' Dockets.

Sandburg expressed a widely prevalent feeling when he wrote his harsh verses describing the lawyer's final journey, to the infernal regions. "Beware of lawyers" was (and is) almost an axiom. Yet, time and again we are reminded of the high repute in which Lincoln was held by all concerned—litigants, as well as his fellow attorneys. This, coupled with the trust and confidence reposed in him by Judge Davis, made Lincoln a natural and logical selection whenever that worthy decided to take a respite from his judicial labors. William H. Somers, who assumed office as Clerk of the Champaign Circuit Court in early 1857, recalled that "Judge Davis frequently called Mr. Lincoln to take the Bench, while he went out for exercise. A courtesy, I don't remember of seeing him extend to any other Attorney, of the twenty or more in attendance."[2] Lincoln's perception, his dogged integrity and his character were so outstanding as to inspire confidence in his findings and give weight to his judgments.

An old calf-bound, ledger-sized volume, its outer cover all weather-beaten from the rain, rested for years on a window sill of the Sangamon County Circuit Court, its contents unsuspected. Upon its close examination in 1950, this Judge's Docket for 1854 was found to contain, in addition to decisions in the handwriting of Davis, others entered by Lincoln, on the right-hand page under the heading "Remarks," where the judge customarily indicated the disposition of each case. The left-hand page carried the titles of the cases and the names of the attorneys for the parties, presumably in the handwriting of the clerk of court.

Among the three cases which thus came before "Judge" Lincoln in the latter part of 1854, were two in which the firm of Lincoln & Herndon appeared for one of the parties and Logan for the other. Even though the decisions which Lincoln was called upon to make involved the determination of what are known in the law as intermediate motions, and not the ultimate disposition of the case, it is a further attestation of the complete confidence which his contemporaries manifested in Lincoln's integrity, that Logan, always a tough and unyielding adversary, should have consented to the highly unusual arrangement. In *Edward Clark* v. *Henry Clark, et al.*, Lincoln ordered his clients, the defendants, "to answer by the 1st of Feby next." In the assault case of *Henry Perry* v. *Jesse Alexander*, where Lincoln & Herndon represented the plaintiff, he decided the motion against his own client by directing Perry to file security for costs.

Another volume, the Judge's Docket for 1856, shows Lincoln's notations in forty-six cases disposed of at the Sangamon County fall term. Among them was an uncontested divorce action, in which Lincoln granted the petitioner a decree. Two trials in actions on debt resulted in judgments of $1,105.11 and $1,526.58, and in two slander cases Lincoln dismissed the complaint. On December 1, 1856, he occupied the bench most of the day, entering routine decrees and orders in non-contested motions.[3]

By 1857, the counties comprising the Eighth Judicial Circuit had been reduced in number to five—McLean, Logan, DeWitt, Vermilion, and Champaign. The spring term of the Sangamon and Champaign courts meeting at the same time, Lincoln left the firm's business in Springfield in the care of Herndon, while he attended at Urbana. The Champaign County Judge's Docket A for that term reveals that on April twenty-second, twenty-third and twenty-fourth Lincoln took Davis's place on the bench. Notations in his handwriting disclose that he acted in a total of one hundred and thirty-eight cases disposed of during the spring session of that court.

One of the cases which came before "Judge" Lincoln on the last day of the term, *L. D. Chedden* v. *J. D. Beasley, et al.*, is of considerable interest. The defendants, twenty-one in number, had signed a note to enable L. G. Chase to begin publication of *The Spirit of the Agricultural Press* at West Urbana. Chase endorsed the note to Chedden, a holder in due course, who, after failing to collect, brought suit on the instrument. Sparring for time, the defense attorneys, Whitney, James W. and William D. Somers, William N. Coler, Joseph W. Sim and J. C. Sheldon, made a desperate effort to get the case continued over to the next term of court. Lincoln, himself a past master at the art of dilatory tactics, thwarted their efforts by holding a night session by candlelight, at the conclusion of which he rendered judgment for the plaintiff, at the same time denouncing the twenty-one defendants for trying to evade a legal obligation by advancing a lot of stuff and poppycock about "no moral obligation."[4] Though he was—or seemed—easygoing, Lincoln had his hands at all times on the levers of control.

A Judge's Docket of the Logan Circuit Court for 1859, found in 1952 among old files stored away and all but forgotten in the basement of the Logan County courthouse, shows Lincoln presiding as judge in thirty-four cases from March 21, 1859, to April 2,

1859.[5] The entries in Lincoln's hand included chancery, common law and criminal cases. In one divorce action captioned *Sherman P. Herington* v. *Hepsite Ann Herington,* Lincoln wrote: "Two years absence without reasonable cause fully made out. Divorce decreed." In the case of *The People* v. *Frederick Grosbernt,* the record written by "Judge" Lincoln reads: "Pleaded guilty on five counts [of selling liquor without a license], $50 costs and stands committed."

The DeWitt Circuit Court, at Clinton, had a heavy case load in 1858; thus we find Davis delegating his duties to Lincoln in twenty cases at the April term that year, and twenty-five at the October term. Lincoln also acted as *de facto* judge for a short period during the October, 1859, session. In one of the cases heard by Lincoln at Clinton, a merchant was suing a farmer for twenty-eight dollars for a suit sold to the farmer's minor son. The father, not having authorized the purchase, refused to pay. Lincoln, in holding that the charge was excessive, declared from the bench, "I have very rarely in my life worn a suit of clothes costing twenty-eight dollars."[6]

The practice of submitting cases, in the absence of the judge, to an attorney agreed upon, was in vogue in Illinois until 1876, when the Supreme Court, once and for all, put a stop to the practice, holding that "Judges are chosen as provided by law, and a stipulation that any other person shall exercise their functions is nugatory and void."

The belief once held that Lincoln never acted as trial judge, and that his acts while substituting for Davis were purely administrative, involving the exercise of no judicial powers. There is now so much evidence to the contrary, including written jury verdicts, containing such addenda in Lincoln's hand as "in manner & form as charged in the indictment," together with the notations "Granted" or "Refused," written by Lincoln on the margin of requested instructions to the jury, that this claim is no longer made.[7] As every lawyer knows, even uncontested motions very often call for the use of judicial discretion.

There is every reason to believe that the man who, as war President, exercised the power of review over the decisions of military courts, would have proved an outstanding full-time occupant of the bench. His intellectual integrity; his capacity for analysis and balanced decision; his practical, hardheaded approach to legal problems; his ability to strip away trivia and get to the heart of a matter; his sensitive consideration of others and his profound insight into the deep recesses of the human mind and heart, coupled with the gift of expressing himself in plain and pointed and unequivocal language, were precisely the essentials for success on the bench—in Lincoln's or any other day. And if ever the expression "judicial temperament" applied to anyone, it was Lincoln, whose simple dignity and infinite patience, even under great provocation, were impressive credentials. Judges like this don't grow on trees.

2.

Of no Illinois lawyer of that day could it be said as truly as of Lincoln that he was the archetype of a now practically vanished breed: the all-round lawyer. "Lincoln legals" which are still coming to light, one hundred and twenty-three years after his admission to the bar, demonstrate anew the diversity of his practice, a diversity which has been vouchsafed to but few lawyers in any period, anywhere.

Even a less-than-comprehensive examination of the extant records of the cases that came to him, in Springfield and on the circuit, must create in one the overriding impression that here, indeed, was a versatile lawyer, with an awesome capacity for work. When one tries to define the dominant characteristics as an attorney of this prairie lawyer who rose to high eminence at the Illinois bar, these qualities come quickly to mind.

Documents which have hitherto escaped attention constitute a significant increment to what has long been known of the range of Lincoln's talents as a lawyer and the informed craftsmanship which he brought to bear on whatever undertaking in the law he set about. These newly accessible source documents— yellowing court papers of an official nature, in Lincoln's unmistakable handwriting (even though not bearing his name or signature)—serve to place his law career in fuller focus, and affirm once more the ability with which he encompassed every aspect of his calling.

Though never elected to the office, Lincoln is known to have appeared in the unlikely role of prosecutor, actually trying cases on behalf of the People, and on occasions, drawing true bills for different of the state's attorneys. Our knowledge of this little-explored phase of his work as a lawyer has been enhanced by documents which have only recently emerged into the light of day, bringing fresh insight on the extent of the professional services which he rendered for the state in connection with the prosecution of criminal causes.

It was not uncommon in Illinois for state's attorneys to be replaced, temporarily, by outside counsel. While prosecutors on the political make were (and are) rarely beset with mistrust of their own abilities, it sometimes happened that the family of the deceased or injured person insisted upon retention of a more experienced or skillful lawyer to take the place of or collaborate with the regular prosecutor. A few state's attorneys, like Lincoln's friend Lamon, were not averse, whenever confronted with a difficult case, to calling in lawyers like Lincoln, Oliver L. Davis, Clifton H. Moore and Leonard Swett, men of outstanding competence in the handling of criminal matters. (It is worth a note in passing that Douglas, who was elected state's attorney for the First [later Eighth] Judicial District and served for two years, was never known to have stepped aside in favor of a prosecuting attorney *pro tem.*)

The clerk's docket of Menard County shows that Lincoln and that rather unattractive character, Josiah Lamborn, appeared for the People in connection with the prosecution of the brothers James and George W. Denton in June, 1846, on an indictment for murder. It was charged that the defendants had killed their brother-in-law, Cassius Brown, by hacking him to death with axes.[8] When the case came up for trial in Petersburg, one of the brothers moved for a severance and it was ordered that the defendants have separate trials. A jury was thereupon empaneled in the case of James Denton; the trial, which lasted two days (June eleventh, twelfth), ended in a hung jury.

Lincoln is credited with having prevailed upon Lamborn—who filled the office of prosecutor with much perturbation to the culprits who were tried under his direction—to drop further prosecution of the brothers, in view of the absence of eyewitnesses to the killing; apparently his suggestion was accepted, for the record shows no further proceedings to have been taken. What a considerable achievement this was on Lincoln's part may be gathered from what is known of Lamborn's obsessive zest for prosecuting, as noted in the *Trailor* case. That Lamborn should have availed himself of Lincoln's services was flattering recognition of the latter's capabilities, for, to do him justice, Lamborn was a highly competent trial lawyer.

At the May term, 1853, of the Tazewell Circuit Court, held in Pekin, Lincoln, while occupied with the usual miscellany of civil matters, was appointed by the Court to act as special prosecutor in *People* v. *Thomas Delny*, involving a charge of rape upon a seven-year-old child. A relevant item in the study of Lincoln the all-round lawyer is the indictment in the case, which he drew and prosecuted to conviction. Bearing the signature "Lincoln, Attorney *pro tem*," it recites ". . . that Thomas Delny, a male person above the age of fourteen years, on the seventh day of May in the year of our Lord one thousand eight hundred and fifty three with force and arms, . . . in and upon Jane Ann Rupert, a female child under the age of ten years, to wit of the age of seven years . . . feloniously did make an assault, and her the said Jane Ann Rupert, then and there feloniously did unlawfully and carnally know; contrary to the form of the statute in such case made and provided."[9]

Not for Lincoln the ornate, superfluous, oftentimes sanctimonious phraseology so dear to most prosecutors of that era—a sample of which is here culled from the true bill drawn by State's Attorney Elam Rust in *People* v. *Longnecker* at the May term, 1854, of the Piatt Circuit Court: ". . . that David Longnecker, . . . not having the fear of God before his eyes, but being moved by the instigations of the Devil . . ."[10]

Delny was sentenced to eighteen years in the penitentiary. According to the *State Register*, "A mob came very near getting possession of the base wretch and hanging him."[11]

Arrived in Bloomington on about March 28, 1857, Lincoln found the town in a state of unrepressed excitement over the approaching trial of Isaac Wyant, who had been held in custody since October, 1855, on a charge of murder.[12] Though the case originated in DeWitt County, it had been transferred to McLean on a change of venue.

In the summer of 1855, Isaac Wyant and Anson Rusk engaged in a dispute over a land boundary. After strong words had been exchanged, Rusk drew a pistol and shot Wyant in the left arm, necessitating amputation of that member. The affair occurred near Clinton. Seeing Rusk in October of the same year, Wyant, overwrought by the emotional and physical strain of all that he had been through, stalked him to the county clerk's office, in Clinton, and there, in broad daylight and in the presence of witnesses, blew his victim to kingdom come with four crashing pistol shots.[13]

Upon his indictment for murder, the defendant retained one of the outstanding figures that that period in Illinois law produced, in the person of Leonard Swett, of Bloomington, who was assisted by his law partner, William Ward Orme (later a brigadier general in the Union Army); while Lamon, for the prosecution, brought in Lincoln, Clifton H. Moore, of Clinton and Harvey Hogg, of Bloomington—though newspaper accounts of the trial would indicate that Lincoln conducted the prosecution almost singlehandedly, while Swett bore the brunt of the defense.

Mention of that colossus of the criminal courts otherwise known as Leonard Swett makes timely a discussion of one who was not only a brilliant trial lawyer but Lincoln's trusted friend and colleague. Any list of notable Illinois lawyers that did not include his name would seem curiously truncated, not alone because he earned an important place in the story of Lincoln's law career, but also because of his own success at the bar. One of the towering legal figures of his period, Swett, who had an extensive and lucrative practice, was connected with some of the most important litigation of his day. In both civil and criminal cases his almost unbroken record of success gave him immense prestige, and, as twilight settled on a career of distinction, it was this prestige that caused him to be employed, on behalf of the defendants, in the anarchist (Haymarket) cases when they were carried before the Supreme Court. This gallant war horse, who refused to be put out to pasture, was engaged in active practice virtually to the day of his death in 1889.

Although Swett was originally known as a general practitioner, criminal cases more and more engrossed his attention, to the exclusion of other departments of practice. Like Browning, he was equally proficient as a trial lawyer in the civil and criminal branches of the law, yet he preferred the latter, according to Herndon, "because it did not cramp his genius."[14] While Swett, who had a lively criminal practice, had never heard the word psychiatry (it had not then been coined), he advanced, in one of the first defenses of insanity interposed in the State of Illinois, toward truths that psychiatry would eventually establish. Many years before another great Illinois criminal lawyer, a Lincolnesque figure with Lincoln's gift for simple, eloquent prose, ready wit and apt illustration, would ask, "Is insanity so rare that men should deride that condition as a defense in a criminal case?"[15] Swett proclaimed the validity of the defense and deplored punishment for those who are mentally unbalanced. The impress of his thinking on the subject was more than local; it was national.

Though the circuit-court records of McLean County were

destroyed in the courthouse fire of 1900, the newspaper files of the Bloomington *Pantagraph* have furnished the writer with much information concerning Lincoln's cases there. Such was the interest manifested in this sensational murder trial, which lasted six days, that the *Pantagraph* gave it extensive coverage.

It was a gala occasion in Bloomington, March 30, 1857, when the case got under way. The hitching racks around the public square were filled as folks flocked into town to witness the mighty joust between Lincoln and Swett. There was nothing like a good murder trial to relieve the underlying melancholy of prairie life. According to the *Pantagraph,* "The court was constantly thronged."[16]

The *Pantagraph* reported that "Hon. A. Lincoln opened for the prosecution, and a clear *prima facie* case having been made out by the witnesses, the State's evidence closed the same evening."[17] The next morning Swett, over Lincoln's objection,[18] proceeded to establish through the testimony of neighbors that for some time prior to the trouble between Wyant and Rusk, the accused had acted in an irrational manner. Showing remarkable diligence in rounding up an array of witnesses, both lay and medical, to testify to the defendant's insanity, Swett's conduct of the defense was noteworthy. Throughout the trial, the outcome of which proved an enormous boon to bringing the law on the subject within reality and justice, he demonstrated a grasp of the problems of mental disease which was extraordinary for that day.

The physicians who attended upon him at the time of the amputation and during the post-operative period testified that brooding over the loss of his arm had further unhinged the defendant's mind. In an effort to show a taint of insanity in the defendant's family, Swett reserved for his final witness the accused's sister, who testified to an hereditary predisposition, citing the case of an uncle who went queer in the head "not getting a girl he had sparked."[19] The cumulative effect of all this testimony was telling heavily against the prosecution's case, and so, in rebuttal, the by-then-hard-pressed Lincoln proceeded to call sixteen witnesses, to combat certain features of the testimony for the defense and counter the stratagem of Swett. Lincoln never lacked staying power.

The defendant was found not guilty by reason of insanity, and on recommendation of the jury sent to the State Hospital for the Insane, at Jacksonville. Though the verdict went against him, Lincoln did a conscientious and eminently capable job. As in the *Matson* case, one wonders whether his sympathies were not with the other side. (There is reason to think that, with all his compassionate insight into human weakness, the duties of a prosecutor could never have been congenial to Lincoln.) Conforming strictly to his professional duty, he nevertheless presented the case for the People with vigor and skill. Lincoln never let a client down! He made both the opening and concluding statements to the jury, and, in addition to conducting most of the direct examination of the People's witnesses, took on the supremely difficult and complicated task of cross-examining the physicians who testified to the defendant's mental condition. (It is not improbable that he may also have drawn the indictment.) One who was present recalled that, on cross-examination of one of the doctors called by the defense, Lincoln observed: "You say, doctor, that this man picks his head, and by that you infer that he is insane. Now, I sometimes pick my head, and those joking fellows at Springfield tell me that there may be a living, moving cause for it, and that the trouble isn't at all on the inside. It's only a case for fine-tooth combs."[20]

Swett's able defense of Wyant, in a case which became a significant social document, made him conspicuous in legal circles, and it was not long before he was in demand in other jurisdictions. Most criminal lawyers are loath to risk leaving their own bailiwick to brave the unknown elements in strange communities. The audacious Swett was the exception to the rule.

Between Lincoln and Swett, who bore a strong physical resemblance to each other, there existed a mutual admiration.[21] Many persons wondered why Lincoln, intimate as he was with

Swett, who had labored effectively for the former's nomination at Chicago, did not appoint him to high office. When asked the reason why, as he often was, Swett preserved an unyielding silence, but in a letter to Herndon he explained that when David Davis and Orville Browning were being considered for appointment to the Supreme Bench, soon after Lincoln's election, Swett, who was a warm friend of Davis, went to the President and said: "If you will give that place to Davis, I will take it as one-half for him and one-half for myself, and never again will ask you for anything."[22]

It is of interest to note, in this connection, that Judge McLean of the United States Supreme Court died on April 4, 1861. Five days later Browning wrote Lincoln, asking for appointment as McLean's successor. He said:

> It is not without a great deal of embarrassment and hesitation that I have determined upon this course, but, having determined upon it, I do not propose to offer any apology for addressing myself to the task. You know me about as well as I know myself; and in regards to my fitness for the office you know me better—for you occupy a far better stand point for the formation of a fair and impartial judgment than I do. If, then, you shall think me competent to the duties of the office, and shall be at all inclined to gratify me in any thing, I say frankly, and without any sort of disguise, or affectation, that there is nothing in your power to do for me which would gratify me so much as this. It is an office peculiarly adapted to my tastes, and the faithful and honest performance of the duties of which would be my highest pride and ambition.

At the conclusion of the letter Browning asked Lincoln not to let it be known that he had "personally solicited the office," and expressed the hope that he might have "a line in reply."[23] There is no record of Lincoln having replied.

On June 8, 1861, Lincoln not having filled the vacancy, Mrs. Browning wrote him on behalf of her "Noble Husband." Browning had written, she said, at her own "earnest solicitations," and she was writing without his knowledge while he was attending court in Springfield.[24]

The Browning *Diary* contains no mention of the letter of April 9; it may be significant that there is a leaf missing from the original diary, covering the dates April ninth to eleventh. It may well have been that the diarist decided to remove all reference to the fact that he had so abjectly "personally solicited the office."

There have recently turned up two indictments from Vermilion County, written by Lincoln during the October term 1853, and signed by him "Swett, Atty."[25] There is no record of Leonard Swett ever having been elected to the office of prosecuting attorney for the circuit, and so one must assume that he was serving "*pro tem.*" One true bill, involving four defendants (John Armstrong, *et al.*), charged "Riot"; the other alleged that the defendants (Jesse Morgan *et ano.*) "set on fire a certain prairie, said prairie then and there being in the habitable parts of the state; ..." It says a great deal for Lincoln's ability as a draftsman of those important papers which form the starting point and foundation of any action or prosecution, that a lawyer of Swett's commanding talents should have called upon him to draw his indictments for him.

From another source comes newly uncovered evidence of Lamon's reliance on Lincoln in the matter of drawing up true bills. An assault indictment in the case of David S. Tucker, also in Vermilion, is dated May 26, 1856, and is drawn and signed by Lincoln for Lamon.[26] Not the least interesting feature of this document is the fact that it shows Lincoln following his own prescription in the matter of pleading. In a letter to Usher F. Linder, Lincoln wrote: "In law it is good policy to never *plead* what you *need* not, lest you oblige yourself to *prove* what you *can* not."[27] In preparing the indictment, Lincoln had set forth that the assault was committed in the presence of witnesses; on reading it over, he apparently thought better about pleading what he "need not" and drew a line through the allegation.

While Lincoln was in Chicago in the spring of 1860, in connection with the "Sandbar Case," he received a letter from Lamon in which the latter expressed his concern over a motion being made to quash an indictment which Lincoln had drawn for him.²⁸ The defendant was charged with having sent a threatening letter, and the basis for the motion to dismiss was the fact that the letter had not been set forth verbatim in the indictment. Lamon wished Lincoln to find authority to defeat the motion, since "Quashing an Indct. written by a prominent candidate for the Presidency of the U.S. by a *little court* like Col. [David] Davis' will not sound well in history."²⁹

Something of Lincoln's essential humility and his readiness to frankly concede his fallibilities (even though, in fact, Lamon's fears were illusory), may be glimpsed in his answer to Lamon, sent from Chicago March 28, 1860:

> Hon. W. H. Lamon.
>   My dear Sir: Yours about motion to quash an indictment, was received yesterday. I think I had no authority but the Statute when I wrote the Indictment. In fact, I remember but little about it. I think yet there is no necessity for setting out the letter in *haec verba*. Our Statute, as I think, relaxes the high degree of technical certainty formerly required.
>   I am so busy with our case on trial here, that I can not examine authorities near as fully as you can there.
>   If, after all, the indictment shall be quashed, it will only prove that my *forte* is as a Statesman, rather than as a Prossecutor.
>   Yours as ever,
>   A. Lincoln.³⁰

It seems not improbable to think that there were indictments, in Vermilion and other counties, in addition to those mentioned, which were drawn by Lincoln at the request of the regularly elected state's attorneys. The saturation point for new "Lincoln legals" has not been reached. Historians and researchers, in their unceasing quest for Lincoln source material, continue to turn up new documents in his handwriting,³¹ sometimes in the most improbable places. Old court records and the crannies of old houses are still being relentlessly ransacked in the never-ending search for Lincoln data; not long ago even the earth where the privy was situated in the rear of the Lincoln home, in Springfield,

Henry C. Whitney, of Urbana, author of *Life on the Circuit with Lincoln* (1892), was intimately associated with Lincoln, in circuit practice, from 1854 to 1860.

Edwin M. Stanton, who snubbed Lincoln in the "Reaper Case" in Cincinnati in 1855, and was responsible for his dismissal as associate counsel, was later appointed by Lincoln as his Secretary of War.

Jesse W. Fell, the first lawyer to settle in McLean County, was one of Lincoln's closest friends. It was Fell who first suggested the idea of a joint discussion with Douglas. He was one of the chief strategists of the little group which put Lincoln over at the Wigwam Convention in Chicago in 1860.

Norman B. Judd was associated with Lincoln in the trial of the *Effie Afton* case in Chicago in 1857. He made the speech placing Lincoln in nomination at the 1860 Convention.

John Fitzgerald, eighteen years of age, able-bodied, but without pecuniary means, came directly from Ireland to Springfield Illinois, and there stopped, and sought employment, with no present intention of returning to Ireland, or going elsewhere. After remaining in the City some three weeks, part of the time employed, and part not, he fell sick, and became a public charge. It has been submitted to me, whether the City of Springfield, or the County of Sangamon is, by law, to bear the charge.

It is my opinion, and decision, that the City is to bear it. I base this, upon the construction I give the 4th Section of the 13th Article of the new City charter (Approved March 2. 1854) I think the Legislature intended that all public charges, arising from the indigence of persons, resident within the City, were to be borne by the City—and not by the County. I think it was not the intention that this class of charges was to be parcelled out between the City and county, by critical discussions on the words "Citizen" "pauper" and the like—

Dec: 18-1854.

A. Lincoln—

A LEGAL OPINION WRITTEN BY LINCOLN.

Legal opinion written by Lincoln in connection with dispute between City of Springfield and Sangamon County regarding responsibility for support of an indigent person. Original in Illinois State Historical Library.

Vermilion County Courthouse, in Danville, in which Lincoln made frequent appearances in association with Ward Hill Lamon.

Edgar County Courthouse, Paris, on the eastern border of the state, in which Lincoln appeared. The courthouse, of the brick "coffee mill" type, cost $4,250.

Shelby County Courthouse, in Shelbyville, in which Lincoln practiced from 1842 to 1852.

. Lyle Dickey was associated ith Lincoln, in Carthage, Hanock County, in April of 1839, the defense of William Fraim, he only client of Lincoln's to ang.

William Wilson, Judge of the Illinois Supreme Court from 1818 to 1848, before whom Lincoln appeared as a lawyer. While performing circuit-court duty in 1847, he presided at the Matson Slave Case in Charleston, Coles County, in which Lincoln represented the slaveholder against his runaway slaves.

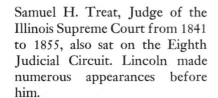

Samuel H. Treat, Judge of the Illinois Supreme Court from 1841 to 1855, also sat on the Eighth Judicial Circuit. Lincoln made numerous appearances before him.

Moultrie County Courthouse, in Sullivan. The county was named for William Moultrie, a soldier of the Revolutionary War. Drawing adapted by J. Kahane.

Nathaniel Pope, appointed a United States District Judge in March, 1819, presided over the "Bankrupt Court," the scene of some of the Logan & Lincoln practice.

Macon County Courthouse, Decatur. The building is still standing in Fairview Park, Decatur.

Henry B. Rankin, author of *Personal Recollections of Abraham Lincoln* (1916), was largely responsible for the marking of the Springfield sites associated with Lincoln.

Milton Hay served as clerk and law student in the office of Stuart & Lincoln. He was associated with Lincoln in the defense of "Peachy" Harrison, charged with murder in Sangamon County in 1859.

Christian County Courthouse, in Taylorville.

Morgan County Courthouse, Jacksonville, in which Lincoln appeared in 1854 in connection with the case of *Selby* v. *Dunlap*.

We the [Jury] find
The Defendant Not
Clinton May 23 1848 gilty
Henry Wilson
foreman

Jury verdict in Spencer Turner Murder Case. Original owned by James T. Hickey.

The county of Sangamon.
To Stuart & Lincoln Dr
To furnishing room for Grand an Petet juries
at July & October term of 1837 – and March
term of 1838 – $36-00–

Bill drawn in Lincoln's hand, addressed to the County of Sangamon, for use of Stuart & Lincoln law office as jury room. Original in Illinois State Historical Library.

Cass County Courthouse, Beardstown, where Lincoln cleared "Duff" Armstrong of murder in 1858. The building, still standing, is used as the town's city hall.

Coles County Courthouse, Charleston, in which the Matson Slave Case was tried in 1847.

State of Illinois }
Sangamon County } ss.

Moses Loe, the defendant to a
certain indictment for murder pending in the circuit
court of the county aforesaid, being first duly sworn
states on oath that he fears he will not receive
a fair and impartial trial on said indictment,
in the circuit court of the county aforesaid, where
the trial is pending, on account that the minds
of the inhabitants of said county, wherein said trial
is pending, are prejudiced against him; he therefore prays
the court to award him a change of venue to the
next nearest county where the causes aforesaid does
not exist—

                                        his
                              Moses X Loe
                                       mark

Subscribed and sworn to before me
this 4th day [illegible] 1852.
                    B. Talbott clk

Affidavit for change of venue, drawn by Lincoln and signed by Moses Loe with
his mark. Photostat in Illinois State Historical Library.

Menard County Courthouse, Petersburg, where Lincoln and Herndon made numerous appearances.

Hancock County Courthouse, Carthage, in which Lincoln unsuccessfully represented William Fraim on a charge of murder in 1839.

Clark County Courthouse, Marshall, where Lincoln defended William Davis on a charge of murder in 1850.

Peoria County Courthouse, Peoria, in which Lincoln frequently appeared. The brick courthouse was built in 1836 at a cost of $15,000.

Elmer Ephraim Ellsworth, who served as a clerk in the Lincoln & Herndon office, was one of the party which accompanied the President-elect on his last departure from Springfield. Lincoln ordered a White House funeral for Ellsworth, the first Union casualty of the war.

The Rock Island Bridge, first to span the Mississippi, figured in the *Effie Afton* case tried by Lincoln in Chicago in September, 1857. Photograph and permission to use kindly furnished by the Chicago, Rock Island and Pacific Railroad Company.

was dug up and minutely screened. There are, furthermore, any number of Lincoln letters and documents in the hands of private collectors that, for one reason or another, have never been published to this day. The Lincoln lode is so rich, and so dispersed in a hundred directions by the hazards of time and change, that it may be another century before it is completely worked out. One might justly assume, therefore, that not all the returns are in on Lincoln as prosecuting attorney.

CHAPTER XVIII

The McLean County Tax Case

1.

LINCOLN's appearance on behalf of the Illinois Central Railroad, in resisting the attempt by McLean County to levy a tax on the road's property within county limits, has taken its place among the memorable cases of his law career. It is surely understatement to say that this was no ordinary lawsuit. It was one of large importance—both pecuniarily and in the question of law involved. Here, in a case which reinforces his right to be rated among the top lawyers of the state, we see Lincoln in the plenitude of his powers as an appellate advocate, handling his assignment with great authority and persuasion.

In 1850, largely through the efforts of United States Senators Breese and Douglas, from Illinois, Congress passed a bill ceding to the state 2,595,053 acres of public lands in the State of Illinois, upon the understanding that the proceeds received from the sale of the land would be applied toward construction of a railroad. A charter to build the road was eagerly sought by, and eventually awarded to a group of Eastern capitalists who had organized the Illinois Central Company.

Still smarting under the effects of the state's ill-starred venture into the field of public works ten years previously, many people were opposed to the road's erection. There has long been some question as to whether Lincoln acted as a lobbyist for the company in its efforts to secure a charter from the legislature, though a report of his speech of October 11, 1858 at Monmouth, Illinois, furnishes rather convincing evidence that he *was* so employed.[1]

Under the terms of its incorporation,[2] the road was exempted by the legislature from all taxation, upon condition that it pay into the State treasury a "charter tax" of five per cent of its annual gross revenue for the first six years, and thereafter seven per cent (an arrangement still in effect). In May, 1853, the first section of the road, from LaSalle to Bloomington, in McLean County, was completed. That August the county authorities proceeded to assess a levy on the company's property, claiming that the State Legislature was without the power to exempt the road from county taxes. Clearly, if McLean succeeded in enforcing its claim, every one of the numerous counties through which the road passed would take its tax bite.

Lincoln, ever alive to the desirability of associating himself with important litigation, was anxious to participate on one side or the other, though, for no discernible reason, it would seem that his first preference was the side of the counties. On September 12, 1853, in a letter to Thompson R. Webber, Clerk of the Champaign Court, Lincoln revealed that he had discussed with some county officers the possibility of being retained by Champaign, whose interests were identical with McLean's, and the prospect of a substantial fee: ". . . The question, in its magnitude, to the Co. on the one hand, and the counties in which the Co. has land, on the other, is the largest law question that can now be got up in the State; and therefore, in justice to myself, I can not afford, if I can help it, to miss a fee altogether. If you choose to release me; say so by return mail, and there an end. If you wish to retain me, you better get authority from your court, come directly over in the Stage, and make common cause with this county."[3] How very odd that he who, in *Barrett* v. *The Alton & Sangamon Railroad Company*, *Illinois Central Railroad* v. *Morrison and Crabtree*, and the *"Effie Afton"* Case, showed himself to be so acutely aware of the importance of the railroad to the economy of the fast-growing young state, should have considered taking the side of those who would place an almost insuperable obstacle in the way of expansion by rail. If it is a total *non sequi-*

tur, it must be remembered that, for complexity among our presidents, Lincoln ranks with Jefferson and Franklin D. Roosevelt.

Having received no response to his letter, Lincoln, on October 3, 1853, wrote Mason Brayman, Solicitor of the Illinois Central (afterwards a general in the Union Army), from Pekin, where he was attending the circuit court: "Neither the county of McLean nor any one on it's behalf, has yet made any engagement with me in relation to it's suit with the Illinois Central Railroad, on the subject of taxation. I am now free to make an engagement for the Road; and if you think fit you may 'count me in.' Please write me, on receipt of this. I shall be here at least ten days."[4]

Four days later Brayman sent Lincoln his personal check for two hundred and fifty dollars, as a general retainer in the case. Thereupon Lincoln, Brayman and James F. Joy, of Detroit, the Central's general counsel and a leading railway lawyer, instituted a suit in chancery to enjoin the collection of the tax. In order to expedite matters and get the case before the Supreme Court at the ensuing term of court, the railroad consented to a *pro forma* decree of dismissal in the McLean Circuit Court.

The appeal of *Illinois Central Railroad Company* v. *The County of McLean*[5] first came before the Supreme Court at the spring term, 1854. The county, meanwhile, engaged eminent counsel in the persons of Logan, Stuart and Benjamin S. Edwards. Lincoln prepared the appeal with his usual thoroughness. It must be noted, however, that though his name does not appear in the printed report of the case, Herndon did much of the research work. Though "Mr. Lincoln was known alone in the case," Herndon wrote, "I was in it and recd my $2,500."[6] At the two sittings of the Court, Lincoln was thoroughly fortified and took the lead in presentation of the case for the road. At the conclusion of the arguments, upon the first hearing, the Court still entertaining doubts on the question involved, Chief Justice Scates ordered the matter to be re-argued.

After further argument had at the December term, 1855, Scates handed down a long opinion in behalf of the Court, sustaining the original contention of Lincoln that it was within the constitutional power of the Legislature to make exceptions from the rule of uniformity in taxation and commute the general rate in return for a fixed sum or proportion of the taxpayer's earnings. The opinion was profuse in citation of authorities, among them Pennsylvania and Massachusetts decisions exempting railroads from all taxation on the ground that they were public works. A number of these precedents are cited in the original brief, in Lincoln's own handwriting, and signed by Brayman, Joy and Lincoln, in the *Herndon-Weik Collection.*

2.

Lincoln's magnificent victory not only operated to the company's advantage, to the extent of hundreds of thousands of dollars, but was vital to its very existence. Considering the difficulty of the questions involved, the pecuniary interests at stake and the successful outcome of the litigation, Lincoln had every reason to feel that a fee commensurate therewith would be in order. There are conflicting accounts of what followed. As Herndon remembered it, Lincoln went to Chicago and presented "our bill" of two thousand dollars, which was rejected on the ground that it was as much as "Daniel Webster himself would have charged."[7] Joy, who received twelve hundred dollars for his services,[8] said that Lincoln wrote to him, asking that his fee be "a particularly beautiful section of land belonging to the company," which request was turned down.[9]

According to Herndon, Lincoln took counsel of Goodrich, Judd, Browning, Archibald Williams, and other attorneys, who prevailed upon him to increase his charge to five thousand dollars.[10] Eventually, Lincoln got around to rendering a bill in this amount, which the railroad refused to pay.

Even considering the then value of money, Lincoln's charge does not appear to have been unreasonable. As a matter of fact, the company has never since contended that it was, and very

likely did not then so regard it. The simple truth is that those were
days of financial stringency for the road, when every dollar
counted.

At the April term, 1857, of the McLean Circuit Court, Lincoln filed his complaint against the railroad, in which he demanded judgment for five thousand dollars. When the case came
on for a hearing on June eighteenth, Lincoln took a default judgment, no one appearing on behalf of the defendant. The railroad's
lawyer, John M. Douglas, who had been delayed en route from
Chicago, arrived in Bloomington that afternoon. Lincoln did not
oppose his application to vacate the judgment, and the case was
accordingly set down for the following week.

The story of the trial is briefly related: Lincoln told the
jury how he had been retained by the company, the work he had
done and the benefits accruing to the road from the successful
outcome of the litigation. The jury promptly returned a verdict
for the full amount asked, less the sum of two hundred dollars
already paid the plaintiff (as noted, the amount of the retainer
was really two hundred and fifty dollars).

There has come down to us, in Lincoln's hand, an outline
of his proof, containing the following clear statement of the elements which should be considered in the fixing of fees: "Are, or
are not the *amount* of labor, the *doubtfulness* and *difficulty* of the
question, the *degree* of *success* in the result; and the *amount* of
pecuniary interest *involved*, not merely in the particular case,
but covered by the principle decided, and thereby *secured*, to the
client, all proper elements, by the custom of the profession to consider in determining what is a reasonable fee in a given case?"[11]

Many writers have accepted the company view that the suit
was a mere formality, brought on by Lincoln at the suggestion of
John M. Douglas, who had succeeded Joy as the road's general
counsel. The wording of Lincoln's complaint, in which he
charged that ". . . the said defendant (although often requested
so to do) have not as yet paid the said sum of money or any part
thereof,"[12] leaves one with very little doubt of the fact that the

company was not disposed to pay the fee demanded, without a contest.

On the margin of the Judgment Record in the office of the McLean Circuit Clerk appears this entry: "Execution issued to Sheriff Moore, August 1, 1857." From this it is apparent that the company did not "promptly pay" the judgment, as has been so often stated, and which it doubtless would have done had the suit been a mere formality. Over a month after the jury returned a verdict in Lincoln's favor, the judgment remained unsatisfied, and it was not until execution had been levied by the Sheriff, preliminary to seizure of the company's property, that payment was made.[13]

Herndon's account of the case concludes on a humorous note: "Lincoln gave me my half, and much as we deprecated the avarice of great corporations, we both thanked the Lord for letting the Illinois Central Railroad fall into our hands."[14] From his own share of the fee, Lincoln was enabled to sustain his campaign against Douglas in 1858.

That the lawsuit for his fee did not seriously affect the relation of Lincoln and the Illinois Central, is shown by the fact that shortly after its conclusion Lincoln was again called upon to handle for the road two important cases involving the amount of taxes to be paid by the Illinois Central to the State.

In speeches in the 1858 campaign, Stephen A. Douglas accused Lincoln of being employed by the Illinois Central, at a salary of five thousand dollars, to help the railroad cheat the state out of what was due it for the charter tax. In a recently discovered speech at Carthage, October 22, 1858, Lincoln made a direct answer to the charge: "The decision, I thought, and still think, was worth half a million dollars to them. I wanted them to pay me $5,000, and they wanted to pay me about $500. I sued them and got the $5,000. This is the whole truth about the fee; and what tendency it has to prove that I received any of the people's money, or that I am on very cozy terms with the Railroad Company, I do not comprehend."[15]

3.

An interesting story having to do with Lincoln and the railroads concerns the opportunity reputedly offered to him by the New York Central Railroad to serve as its general counsel. While Lincoln was in New York City, in February of 1860, on the occasion of the Cooper Union speech, he was supposedly approached at the Astor House by Erastus Corning, then president of the New York Central, who had been deeply impressed by his speech. Corning's offer of an annual retainer of ten thousand dollars a year may have seemed rather tempting at the time, but Lincoln declined it.[16] The tale has never been verified by acceptable proof, and so one need not speculate overmuch on the intriguing question of what the effect of acceptance would have been on Lincoln's political future.

CHAPTER XIX

Law and Politics Again

1.

THE YEAR 1854 saw Herndon's election as Mayor of Springfield. It was the year of the founding of the Republican party, when a group of dissident Democrats, Free Soilers and others met in a little wooden schoolhouse, which now stands on the campus of Ripon College in Wisconsin, and decided to create a new party. It was, too, the year of the senior partner's emergence from political retirement. In the early part of 1854 Lincoln was engaged in his practice, traveling the circuit and appearing in the higher courts. On March twenty-first, the second day of the spring term of the Sangamon Circuit Court, he left the Springfield business in the hands of Herndon, while he attended in nearby Jacksonville, at the trial of *Selby* v. *Dunlap*. The preceding autumn, James Selby, a small-town editor, had, in his Morgan *Journal*, aspersed the integrity of James Dunlap, in connection with the latter's management of the State Institution located in Jacksonville. A day or two after publication of the item, Dunlap met Selby in the railroad ticket office and proceeded to administer a severe caning. Dunlap was arrested, charged with a breach of the peace, and fined twenty-five dollars. Selby, who later became an editorial writer for the Chicago *Tribune*, instituted suit for ten thousand dollars. Dunlap retained Lincoln as counsel.

Arriving in Jacksonville on the twenty-first, Lincoln, after registering at the Mansion House,[1] proceeded to the old Morgan County courthouse where, in the afternoon, the trial commenced. There was a parade of witnesses to testify to the defendant's violent assault upon Selby. The cumulative weight of their testimony was such that Lincoln must have realized that his best strategy lay in attempting to minimize the damage suffered. In his summation Lincoln put the whole affair, especially the demand for ten thousand dollars' damages, in such a ludicrous light that all the plaintiff's efforts to raise sympathy for his mistreatment went for nothing; after the jury had been out for several hours, it brought in a plaintiff's verdict of only three hundred dollars.

In the Illinois State Historical Library is Lincoln's request for instruction to the jury, which reads:

The court instruct the jury:

That, in case they find the issue for the plaintiff, they are then to consider *all* the circumstances in evidence before them, including all reasonable inferences, from the facts directly proved, and, on the whole case, give such an amount of damages, and such an amount *only*, as, in their common judgment, they think right between the parties.

GIVEN

2.

By all the rules Lincoln should have been washed up after his term in Congress. But the tough-minded Springfield lawyer had a way of defying the political laws of gravity. Lincoln wrote in 1859: "I was losing interest in politics when the repeal of the Missouri Compromise aroused me again." The Kansas-Nebraska Act, sponsored by Douglas and signed by President Pierce on May 30, 1854, provided for the repeal of the Missouri Compromise of 1820 which had excluded slavery from the Louisiana Territory. Within that region were the new territories of Kansas and Nebraska which, until their state constitutions were drafted, were to be open to settlement by slaveholders as well as non-slaveholders.

Lincoln, thoroughly aroused, made a number of speeches against the Nebraska Act. The Hall of the House of Representatives was the scene of his definite re-entry into politics on October 4, 1854, when in reply to Douglas he delivered one of the most profound speeches of his life. At Peoria, twelve days later, again in answer to Douglas, he delivered a speech which was the beginning of the series of fundamental discussions of which the Douglas debates of 1858 were no more than the climax.

His law work suffered to some extent as a result of his platform activities, and in the following year, August 11, 1855, he was to write to Owen Lovejoy that he was "quite busy trying to pick up my lost crumbs of last year." In his third-person autobiography, Lincoln says, speaking of the autumn of 1854, that "he did not abandon the law, but gave his attention by turns to that and politics." The proportion of his attention devoted to each cannot, in the state of the existing records, be exactly determined.

There is reason to think, however, that during the period in question Lincoln was necessarily obliged to pay something more than incidental attention to the firm's practice. Herndon, who was extremely busy carrying out his campaign promise to be a "reform" Mayor, was away from the office much of the time. During his tenure there were something like seventy-six meetings of the city council, and frequent sessions of the various standing committees. Mainly through Herndon's efforts, gas lighting was installed in Springfield, streets were graded and plank walks laid. As chairman of the council's committee on education, he strongly advocated a public school system, and though the schools did not commence operation until later, the project owed much to his powerful advocacy. Finally, the crusading Herndon pushed through a city-wide ordinance prohibiting the sale of intoxicating liquors, except for medicinal purposes. In committing his energies to the cause of prohibition, on which he was somewhat fanatical, Billy became a scourge to the wholesale liquor dealers of Springfield, among whom were Jacob Bunn and others of Lincoln's friends and supporters. What Lincoln's thoughts were as he viewed the bluenose activities of his frequently tipsy partner can only be a subject of conjecture.

3.

The year 1855 saw Lincoln, having failed of election to the United States Senate on February eighth, foregoing political activity and returning to his practice with his customary diligence. In the spring he attended the circuit as usual, and in the summer spent more than two weeks in Chicago, where he was engaged in handling several important cases in the United States courts then sitting in that sprawling, upstart city. It was a year of improved travel conditions for Lincoln, with rail transportation (at the average rate of twenty miles an hour) bringing better accommodations and new comforts to the fast growing state.

That fall his circuit work was interrupted by a trip to Cincinnati, where he suffered the indignity of being snubbed by associate counsel in the important "Reaper Case," *McCormick* v. *Manny, et al.*, before the United States Court in that city. The year before, Lincoln had been recommended by Ralph Emerson of Rockford, Illinois, to J. H. Manny & Co. of that city as a lawyer who might be of assistance to the company in connection with a suit to sustain a patent, brought against it by Cyrus H. McCormick, the original inventor of the mechanical reaper which, capable of doing the work of ten strong men, had revolutionized farming. Emerson's connection with Lincoln and the case is of interest on several counts. Their friendship dated from 1851, when Emerson was reading law with Kersey H. Fell of Bloomington, in whose office they met whenever Lincoln's circuit travel brought him to that city. It was in 1851 that Emerson asked Lincoln, while they were walking together in Bloomington: "Mr. Lincoln, is it possible for a man to practice law and always do by others as he would be done by?" It would be extremely interesting to know Lincoln's answer, which has not come down to us. Whatever it was, one thing is certain: Emerson soon dropped the law for business, becoming a partner of Manny.[2]

The case did not involve the original McCormick patent, which had expired years before the suit was instituted, but a subsequent McCormick patent, relating to certain improvements, which the plaintiff claimed Manny had infringed, to the former's damage in the sum of four hundred thousand dollars. Peter H. Watson, a patent attorney of Washington, D.C., representing the Manny interests, called upon Lincoln at the latter's home in June, 1855 and paid him a retainer of four hundred dollars.

It was the sort of case for which Lincoln, with his easy comprehension of things mechanical, had a particular aptitude. With his customary thoroughness, the lawyer-inventor set about familiarizing himself with the technical features of the reaper, interrupting his attendance at the United States Court in Chicago, in July, to spend half a day at the Manny factory, "examining and studying," as he wrote Watson, "Manny's Machine."[3]

To suit the convenience of Judge McLean, who was designated to preside, the case was removed from Chicago to Cincinnati, McLean's home city. Lincoln probably left Bloomington, where he had been in attendance at the circuit court, on September 17, 1855, arriving in Cincinnati on either the eighteenth or nineteenth. The trial commenced on the twentieth.

Both sides were represented by distinguished counsel—Edward N. Dickerson, a leading patent lawyer from New York City, and Reverdy Johnson, of Baltimore,[4] appearing for McCormick; George Harding, a well-known patent lawyer of Philadelphia, Edwin M. Stanton, then in his prime as a lawyer, and Lincoln for Manny & Co.

When Lincoln went to the Burnet House to confer with his fellow counsel, he was treated in a most discourteous manner. Stanton, who arrogated to himself the role of chief counsel, looked down his nose at the rumpled Midwestern lawyer, whom he treated as a person of no importance. Upon learning that Lincoln had been retained principally to make the closing argument,[5] Stanton flew into a rage and, with characteristic hauteur, dismissed him scornfully as "that long-armed baboon." Himself a superlative trial advocate, the nearsighted, asthmatic, ill-tempered Stanton did not fancy the prospect of relinquishing what he considered to be his definite prerogative, in favor of any backwoods lawyer from Illinois. To the ultimatum, "If that giraffe appears in the case, I will throw up my brief and leave," the Manny interests reluctantly bowed, and Lincoln was accordingly advised that his services would no longer be required.

It was a bitter pill to swallow. Though mortified, and his ego affronted, Lincoln showed commendable restraint. Suppressing his disappointment, he stayed in Cincinnati for a week, attending the trial and listening intently to Stanton's prodigious effort in summation.

For all that Lincoln took his rejection with remarkable dignity and self-control, he nevertheless "attached to the innocent city the displeasure that filled his bosom, . . ."[6] In an article by W. M. Dickson in *Harper's New Monthly Magazine* for June, 1884, reference is made to his leave-taking, when he stated to his hostess: "You have made my stay here most agreeable, and I am a thousand times obliged to you; but in reply to your request for me to come again I must say to you I never expect to be in Cincinnati again. I have nothing against the city, but things have so happened here as to make it undesirable for me ever to return here."

After his return to Springfield, Lincoln received a check from Watson for the balance of his fee. He returned the check, but Watson sent it back, insisting that Lincoln was entitled to be recompensed. This time Lincoln kept the check. It is not definitely known what the amount was, but the tradition is that it was for six hundred dollars.[7]

Evidence abounds of Lincoln's Christian forgiveness. Though Stanton had treated him with utter contempt, Lincoln appointed him Secretary of War because he was the best man for the job. When undecided whom he would appoint as Cameron's successor, Lincoln consulted, among others, George Harding, who had appeared in the case with Stanton. To the question "Whom, in your opinion, Mr. Harding, should I appoint Secretary of War?" Harding replied: "I have in mind only one man, but I know you could not and would not appoint him after the outrageous way he has insulted you and behaved towards you in the Reaper case, and while you were running for the Presidency." "Oh," said Lincoln, "you mean Stanton. Now, Mr. Harding, this is not a personal matter. I simply desire to do what will be the best thing for the country."[8] When Stanton's ego later grew too importunate, such was Lincoln's balanced judgment that he continued to regard him as an individual of real stature ("He's a great man, even if he does know it").

4.

Something of the almost incredible range of matters which found their way into the Lincoln & Herndon office may be gathered from the fact that, in 1855, Dr. Davis S. Smith, of Chicago, the pioneer homeopathic practitioner, together with Norman B. Judd, one of his patients, and Thomas Hoyne engaged Lincoln to draw up a proposed special charter granting them the right to establish a college of homeopathy. Lincoln presented the document to the Legislature, which approved of it and granted the incorporators permission to form the Hahnemann Medical College and Hospital. Smith, because of poor health, neglected to push the matter of the college, and it was not until October 15, 1860, that the first lectures were given to a group of twenty-five enrolled students.

5.

Examination of the probate records of Sangamon County fails to reveal much of importance in connection with the probate work done by Lincoln & Herndon. In the absence of any convincing reason why they should have passed up this phase of legal practice, while handling the trivial matters to which much of their time was necessarily devoted, one can only conclude that most of the estate papers which they prepared have somehow disappeared. It is true that, except in rare cases, the fees were not large. A typical receipt given by Lincoln, and dated October 15, 1838, reads: "Received of Moses M. Martin, as administrator of the estate of Isaac Martin, deceased, the sum of seven dollars and fifty cents, in full for services rendered said estate."[9] In view of their modest charges, generally, the prevailingly low rate of compensation for this type of legal work should not have deterred them.

Most of the Sangamon probate files were probably removed by Herndon, though not all of them found their way into the *Herndon-Weik Collection*. An examination of the probate papers in the latter group would indicate that Herndon handled most of the estate work, except for will contests.

On June 19, 1855, in the Sangamon Circuit Court, Lincoln appeared on behalf of the proponent of the will in the important will contest of *Correll, et. al.* v. *McDaniel, et. al.* The trial resulting in a disagreement, the matter was put over to the fall term. Upon the retrial, on November 30, 1855, the contestants succeeded in setting the will aside, the jury finding that the paper in question was not McDaniel's will.[10] The matter dragged its way through the courts until 1858 when, on February fifth, the Supreme Court reversed the finding of the Circuit Court jury and sustained the will. Lincoln successfully argued the appeal in the Supreme Court.

An interesting document has come down to us in connection with this case, in the form of an outline for the argument on appeal, in Lincoln's hand. The following portion contains the core of his line of reasoning:

> Show that, in this case, the Testator had such 'Sound mind and memory' at the time of making the Will—
> 1.   By his asking Dr. Randall to write his Will—
> 2.   His reply to Mrs. Henon, when she said he was too sick & weak to make Will.
> 3.   His saying his Will was already made, and getting roll of blank paper—
> 4.   His getting the package of title papers—

5. His making first provision for his Wife; and charge upon Sutcliff for her and his sisters—
6. His deciding correctly, as to the *'long way* of the land
7. His providing that James should pay rent to his mother—
8. His decision as to what to be done with the home place—
9. His reply when Correll proposed that all should leave the house—
10. His calling for Robert's widow, and describing the land to be given to her children.
10½. His recollection of his enmity to Cowell & McIntire—
11. His objection that any of his own family should be administrator.
12. His suggesting of Hamm for Administrator
13. His asking Cyrus Correll and Samuel Havener to witness the Will—[11]

6.

Any list of interesting trials in which Lincoln participated must include the Fleming "Chicken Bone" case, tried at Bloomington the week following the Wyant murder case.[12] The vitals of the case are largely missing; by some local research the writer has gathered some fugitive items of information throwing side lights on some of the personalities involved. It all started with a fire which burned to the ground the livery stable in back of the Morgan House, in Bloomington, on the night of October 16, 1855. Among the curious onlookers was Samuel G. Fleming, who was seriously injured when the spreading flames toppled the Morgan House chimney, which fell on him. Examination by Doctors Thomas P. Rogers, Jacob R. Freese, and Eli K. Crothers revealed that both legs had been broken.

The injured man was removed to the home of his brother, where the three physicians bound his legs in splints, which, after several weeks, they removed. Finding the right leg to be crooked and shorter than the left, the doctors proposed to Fleming that they rebreak and reset the limb. The injured man agreeing, the doctors set about their task. Dr. Freese, assisted by his medical student Isaac M. Small, administered the chloroform, after which Dr. Rogers began tugging at the leg. The anesthetic apparently had had little effect, for the patient cried out, "Hold on, hold on," declaring that he would rather have a crooked leg for the rest of his life than suffer such excruciating pain. Dr. Crothers begged him to go through with the rebreaking and resetting, but Fleming was unyielding. Months later, he was able to walk, but the leg was permanently shorter and misshapen.

Fleming lost no time in hiring a battery of legal talent, consisting of Leonard Swett and his partner, William Ward Orme; the partners William H. Hanna and John M. Scott; and the firm of Asahel Gridley and John H. Wickizer. On March 28, 1856, they filed suit for malpractice against Crothers and Rogers in the McLean Circuit Court, the complaint alleging that the defendants "not regarding their said duty but intending and contriving to injure the said plaintiff," did not "use due and proper care, skill or diligence."[13]

The defendants engaged the services of four Bloomington lawyers, who in turn brought in Lincoln and John T. Stuart. Lincoln and Stuart were probably retained in order to offset the advantage which the plaintiff enjoyed in having on his side the famed Swett, a recognized authority on medicine and anatomy. Lincoln, as usual, bore the main weight of the argument.

Dr. Crothers (whose wife took up the study of medicine at forty, becoming the first woman physician in that part of the state) had two daughters, Lulu and Rachel. (The latter, a well-known playwright, recently passed away, in July, 1958.) Lulu, recalling the case some years later, wrote that Lincoln, in the course of his cross-examination of the plaintiff, said: "Well! What I would advise *you* to do is to get down on your *knees* and thank your Heavenly Father, and also these two Doctors that you have any legs to stand on at all."[14]

Lincoln, an old friend of the Crothers family, had been coached by Dr. Crothers in the physiology of bone repair—in the young, when there is a plentiful natural supply of organic material in the bones, and in older persons (Fleming was a middle-aged man), when the bones become brittle. The better to illustrate his points to the jury, Lincoln hit upon the expedient of demonstrating with chicken bones—those taken from young pullets being pliant and supple, those from older chickens fragile and crisp.

The trial was protracted, a week being consumed in hearing the testimony of the parties and their witnesses, expert and otherwise—fifteen doctors and twenty-one other witnesses testifying for the plaintiff, whereas the defense subpoenaed the remaining twelve doctors in Bloomington. After eighteen hours' deliberation, the jury reported that it was hopelessly deadlocked, whereupon Judge Davis put the case over to the next term of court. After several further postponements, it was eventually, on March 15, 1858, dismissed by agreement of the parties.

7.

At the spring term, 1856, of the Champaign Circuit Court Lincoln took part in the trial of *Spink* v. *Chiniquy*, brought from Kankakee on a change of venue. The defendant, a priest, was sued for slander in having falsely charged that the plaintiff had been guilty of perjury. Lincoln and Swett represented Father Chiniquy. A number of followers of each side came to Urbana to hear the trial. "The hotels were monopolized," related Whitney, "and a large number camped out." It was a bitter legal struggle, lasting three days. Failing to reach a verdict after eleven hours' deliberation, the jury was discharged. Lincoln, realizing that nothing good could come from a renewal of the litigation, set about effecting an out-of-court settlement of this prickly case. In his practice, as in everything else, Lincoln was a man of consummate tact and good sense.

The formal decree prepared by him is a fine example of his unique facility for concrete expression:

Peter Spink
vs.
Charles Chiniquy

This day came the parties and the defendant denies that he has ever charged, or believed the plaintiff to be guilty of Perjury; that whatever he has said from which such a charge could be inferred, he said on the information of others, protesting his own disbelief in the charge; and that he now disclaims any belief in the truth of said charge against said plaintiff. It is therefore, by mutual agreement of the parties, ordered that the suit be dismissed, each party paying his own cost—the defendant to pay his part of the cost heretofore ordered to be paid by said plaintiff.[15]

Chiniquy, an indubitable eccentric, was subsequently unfrocked. After Lincoln's assassination he concocted the theory, which he never ceased advancing (to whoever would listen), that Lincoln's death was brought about as a result of plotting by the "perfidious Jesuits."

8.

A delectable dish for an avid public, composed largely of folks who led uneventful lives, was the Anderson case in Sangamon County. As he came out of the privy in his back yard, on the night of May 15, 1856, George Anderson, a long-time resident of Springfield, was brutally beaten to death. Prime suspects were his somewhat younger wife, Jane, and his nephew, Theodore Anderson, who were indicted, charged with the murder. There was intense excitement in regard to the case, many persons feeling that Jane had not only participated in the fatal beating, but had priorly attempted to poison her husband, by giving him strychnine in his medicine.[16]

A fund of two hundred dollars was raised for the purpose of hiring some outstanding lawyer to assist in the prosecution. It was first offered to Lincoln, who declined the retainer.[17] Instead, he took fifty dollars to represent the woman. Also retained in Jane's defense were Logan and John E. Rosette. The nephew was represented by Stuart & Edwards, Thomas Lewis and Antrim Campbell. Linder and A. McWilliams prosecuted.

The trial, which lasted ten court days, commencing November 19, 1856, was extensively reported in the *Illinois State Journal*, which devoted two or three columns daily to a résumé of the testimony. On the morning of the twenty-second, the jury visited the scene of the crime.[18] That afternoon, by way of establishing a motive for doing in the old man, the prosecution attempted to show that there had been improper relations between the defendants. In this they were blocked by objections on the part of Lincoln.[19]

There was testimony that a bottle of strychnine was found in Theodore Anderson's trunk; in addition, the prosecution called two doctors who testified that death was brought on, in part, by poison. The defendants both produced evidence of good character. Theodore called a sister of the deceased, who testified to an alibi for him. She also testified that on the night in question it was she, and not Jane, who gave Anderson his medicine. At nine o'clock on Saturday night, November twenty-ninth, the jury, after deliberating several hours, brought in a verdict of not guilty.

CHAPTER XX

The Effie Afton Case

1.

THE Saloon Building, in Chicago, where the Federal District Court for the Northern District of Illinois held its sessions in the late 'fifties, was the scene, in 1857, of one of the most celebrated cases in Lincoln's entire career and one which indirectly marked an important turning-point in the history of transportation. Pressed to name Lincoln's most famous case, the average person would probably reply, "The Armstrong case," but by more or less common agreement among those who have devoted any study to his law career, the lawsuit, known legally as *Hurd* v. *The Rock Island Bridge Co.*, but, popularly, as the *Effie Afton* case, shows him at his best. Out of the vast welter of cases, numbering in the thousands, which he handled in those busy, crowded years of practice, this one stands out as the highest point of his career at the Illinois bar. It can be said with absolute certainty that, though the outcome was, in a sense, legally indecisive, it nevertheless did more for his reputation as a lawyer than any other case he ever tried.

The coming of the railroad heralded the dawn of a new era in the history of the state. In the middle 'fifties, when Illinois railroading was in its first flowering, there commenced a contest for commercial supremacy between river and rail, which foreshadowed the doom of the golden days of steamboating. The story of this no-holds-barred struggle forms one of the romantic chapters in the history of American transportation. By 1857 the old Mississippi days of steamboat glory and grandeur and picturesque (at times picaresque) adventure—the stuff of which *Huck-*

leberry Finn and *Life on the Mississippi* were made—were on their way out; another generation would witness their virtual disappearance.

The completion in 1854 of The Chicago, Rock Island & Pacific Railroad (chartered as the Rock Island & La Salle) to the Mississippi River, and its continuation in Iowa as the Mississippi & Missouri, made highly desirable, if not imperative, a rail connection across the big stream. Despite the bitter antagonism of powerful river interests—who foresaw in the creation of through rail routes from east to west the diversion of much traffic from the river and the serious loss of prestige of the river cities as centers of trade and distribution, as well as the loss of ferry business—the State of Illinois granted a charter to The Rock Island Bridge Company, with rights to "construct, maintain and operate a bridge, in such manner as to leave unobstructed the navigation of the waterway, and furnish a connection with all railroads in Illinois and Iowa, which might have terminals at or near said bridge."

The construction of the bridge, the first to span the Mississippi, really involved three separate operations—a bridge across the narrow portion of the river between the Illinois shore and an island known as Rock Island, out in the channel; a line of tracks across Rock Island, and a long bridge between the island and the Iowa shore. The channel of the river passed near the west side of the island, and down the center of this channel ran the boundary line between the two states.

Upon commencement of the construction of the various termini of the bridges, and the more or less simultaneous laying of tracks across Rock Island in 1855, the river interests went into action. Notwithstanding the Act of Congress of 1852, granting "rights of way to all rail and plank roads or macadam and turnpike companies through the public lands of the United States," and despite the fact that Rock Island was government property, the river folks appealed to Jefferson Davis, Secretary of War, who forbade the Bridge Company to break ground on the island.

He went further and directed the United States Attorney for the Northern District of Illinois to apply to the courts to enjoin the construction of a railroad across the island and of a bridge over the river. The case (*United States* v. *Railroad Bridge Company, et al.*, 6 McLean 517) came before the United States Circuit Court in Chicago in July, 1855. The presiding judge, Associate Justice John McLean of the Supreme Court of the United States, in a decision the consequences of which it would be difficult to exaggerate, upheld the rights of the bridge company and denied the application for an injunction. And so, on April 23, 1856, the first train passed proudly over the first bridge ever thrown across the Mississippi, from Rock Island, Illinois to Davenport, Iowa.

In September, 1855, there was launched, at Cincinnati, the fastest side-wheeler of her draft on the Mississippi, a sleek craft which kept men and boys wide-eyed. With a deck two hundred and thirty feet long, side wheels thirty feet in diameter, and a capacity of seven hundred tons, the steamer was the last word in river packets. Christened the *Effie Afton*, she was owned by Captain John S. Hurd of Portsmouth, Ohio, who spent over forty thousand dollars on her construction.

On May 6, 1856, her flag flying at the jack staff, the fleet steamer headed upstream and, picking her way through the murky river, so full of snags and blind reefs, approached the newly built drawbridge; in the pilothouse Parker, the pilot, pulled the bell ropes, and was answered by faint jinglings in the engine room below, while the boat's speed slackened. The handsome river boat swung into the draw of the bridge, and then, as one of her side wheels stopped, struck one of the piers, was catapulted against another and bounced back onto the first. The collision overturned a cabin stove; the steamer took fire, and in five minutes was a total loss. The flames extended to the draw of the bridge, which also caught fire and, collapsing, fell into the river.

The disaster touched off a prairie fire of protest on the part of the river group; local feeling in the towns and cities on the Mississippi and Ohio Rivers ran high, as the press denounced the Bridge Company and its parent outfit, The Chicago and Rock Island Railroad, for their avariciousness and callous disregard of human safety. The St. Louis *Republican* pontificated editorially: "The Railroad Bridge at Rock Island is an intolerable nuisance. . . . It is utterly impossible for any man not an idiot to note the disasters at Rock Island and honestly ascribe them to any other cause than the huge obstruction to navigation which the Bridge Company have built there and insist shall remain, even though lives by the score and property by the millions are destroyed every year. . . . We have rarely seen such illustration of supercilious insolence, as have been presented by advocates of the bridge." The editor of a frontier newspaper was rarely a man to let a passion for objective news gathering or comment stand in his way.

For the defendant, the Chicago newspapers responded in kind. One Chicago paper went so far as to state that St. Louis, with the aid of other river towns, had raised a fund of half a million dollars for prosecution of a lawsuit.[1] The Chicago *Tribune* editorialized that "Facts . . . do not warrant the incessant clamor kept up by those who insist that that magnificent and necessary structure shall be torn down. . . . We trust that . . . the outcries of the St. Louis and river press may be silenced."[2] As one might expect, the newspapers of the river towns colored their news reports in favor of the owner of the *Effie Afton*, who brought suit for damages in the amount of fifty thousand dollars against the Bridge Company, while the Chicago papers quite naturally favored the defendant—a prime example of the penchant of the press for indulging in partisan speculation and comment on a case *sub judice*.

While the nominal parties in interest were Hurd and the Rock Island Bridge Company, the actual contest was between St. Louis and other communities on the Mississippi and Ohio rivers, on the one hand, and Chicago and inland railway centers on the other. The bill of complaint averred that the steamboat was at all times carefully and skillfully navigated, and that the boat "was forcibly driven by the currents and eddies caused by said piers against one of them," resulting in the destruction of the boat and cargo by fire. The bill further alleged that the bridge was an unlawful obstruction to navigation.

The plaintiff enlisted the services of an imposing array of counsel in the persons of Hezekiah M. Wead, of Peoria, formerly a circuit judge; Corydon Beckwith, of Chicago, and Timothy D. Lincoln, of Cincinnati. (Genealogical records indicate that the last-named was evidently not a descendant of Samuel Lincoln of Hingham, Massachusetts, the first American progenitor of the sixteenth President.) Wead, born in Vermont and admitted to practice in 1832 in Malone, New York, was among those who sought upon the prairies of the West a more compatible field for the practice of law than was afforded by the conditions of their native states. He was known as a lawyer of great competence, the last word of authority on "river practice." Timothy Lincoln was a seasoned and successful admiralty practitioner, while Beckwith, who was later (1864) appointed a Supreme Court judge by Governor Yates, was without question one of the ablest lawyers practicing at the Chicago bar.

Associated with A. Lincoln, for the defense, was Norman B. Judd, a transplanted New Yorker who ranked high in Republican circles, and Joseph Knox of Rock Island. While much of Judd's career was identified with politics and public affairs, he occupied a place of distinction at the Illinois bar. With the advent of the then virtually untried and untrusted means of transportation by rail (most folks still preferred the dreary, soul-wearying stagecoach), he had the foresight to cultivate this new field of practice and developed, in time, a better than local reputation as an able railroad lawyer. At various times he was attorney for The Chicago and Rock Island, The Michigan Southern and The Pittsburgh and Fort Wayne, and was associated, in one capacity or another, with other railways.[3] He nominated Lincoln at the wigwam convention of 1860[4] and accompanied the President-elect on his journey to Washington in February, 1861; a few weeks later the Senate confirmed his nomination as minister to Berlin, a post he held for four years.

Though, judged by rigorous standards, and compared to some of his contemporaries, he may not have been a lawyer of great stature, Joseph Knox was far from run-of-the-mill. It was said of him that when two farmers got into a dispute, the one who had the fastest horse won the case, for the reason that he got to Knox first.[5] He was the leading attorney of Rock Island. Judd and Knox were both directors and stockholders in The Chicago and Rock Island.[6]

Lincoln, who had a gargantuan appetite for facts, as well as the capacity to mobilize them, prepared the defense with his customary care and thoroughness. He collaborated with Judd and Knox in interviewing prospective witnesses and taking numerous depositions for use upon the trial. With his unerring sense of what was trivial and what was important, Lincoln's mind, as usual, went straight to the vital point (the winning point, if his client was to prevail)—that the accident could only have occurred through negligence in the handling of the *Effie Afton*. Lincoln had the ability, in the words of Matthew Arnold, "to see straight and think clear," which may be esteemed one of the most praiseworthy properties of a lawyer because it gives him a sure sense of discrimination and appraisal and the insight to detect and discard what is irrelevant. The ability to recognize and get swiftly to the basic issue, never once permitting himself to be lured into bypaths from the main road, was one of Lincoln's greatest skills as a trial lawyer, just as it was later to prove so effective in appealing to the American people.

2.

With the purpose in mind of mastering the facts—all the facts—as part of his prodigious preparation of the case for trial, Lincoln accompanied Benjamin Brayton, Sr., the Bridge Engineer, to Rock Island where, on September 1, 1857, he made an intense study of the rebuilt bridge, with its unchanged draw, as well as of the river currents and the effects of the latter on navigation. Oakleaf scouted the story of Lincoln's visit to the scene of the disaster, as told by Ben Brayton, Jr. in the Half Century Edition of the Davenport *Democrat and Leader* on October 22, 1905. A study of Beveridge's papers reveals that he even tried to convince Beveridge that it should be kept out of the latter's *Life of Lincoln*.

In undertaking to challenge the Brayton account, Oakleaf either was unaware of or chose to ignore a copy of a letter written by Judd to Lincoln on September fourth, in which reference was made to Lincoln's "inspection" of the bridge. In the files of the Rock Island Lines there was contained, at the time, in a letter copy book, a tissue-paper copy of the letter of Judd, inadvertently addressed to Lincoln at Springfield, Missouri.[7] It read:

September 4th, 1857.

Mr. A. Lincoln,
Attorney at law,
Springfield, Mo.
My dear Mr. Lincoln:—

I am pleased to hand you herewith Voucher drawn in your favor in the amount of fifty dollars, in payment for your services in connection with settlement out of Court of the Rathje case. The settlement was most satisfactory.

I sincerely hope you suffered no ill effects from your trip to Rock Island, and your inspection of the Mississippi river bridge last Tuesday. I also hope you were successful in securing the information of which you were in search.

I remain,
Your obed't servant,
N. B. Judd.

It is, on the other hand, more than passing strange that Judd should have written to Lincoln in Springfield at a time when the latter and, presumably, Judd, were in Chicago. (Lincoln's location in the city is based on a letter written by Mrs. Lincoln on

September twentieth, in which she stated that Lincoln had been in Chicago for four weeks.) Conceivably, Judd may not have known of Lincoln's presence there at the time, or may, merely as a matter of form, have written "Springfield" on the letter and then sent or delivered it to Lincoln in Chicago.

Young Brayton, then fifteen years of age, was, according to his narrative of the incident, present on the bridge at the time of Lincoln's inspection, and observed that "the explanations offered by the bridge master, bridge engineer, and others, did not seem to satisfy him [Lincoln] as to the currents, etc., and approaching me, he said, 'young man, are you employed here on this bridge? If so will you go with me to the head of the draw-pier and answer some questions' " Sitting down on the bridge, with his long legs dangling over the side, his young companion seated beside him, the tall stranger proceeded to question the youth at length concerning the currents of the mighty Father of Waters at that point, and their varying velocity. At the conclusion of the session, Lincoln expressed his satisfaction and, stating that he now "understood the situation," thanked the boy and returned with the elder Brayton to Chicago.

Even though there is no real proof in support of the thesis, there is some justification for thinking that there may have been still another occasion when Lincoln went over the "ground."[8] Charles Edward Russell, who wrote *A-Rafting on the Mississippi*, in which he reminisced expansively about his experiences on the river, cited a bit of river lore which he likely absorbed from talks with three local pilots based on the Iowa shore, near the scene of the accident. This genuine but little-known classic of Mississippi literature relates how the pilots were engaged by the defense to take Lincoln, in a chartered steamboat, back and forth, time after time, through the draw in both directions, until Lincoln "knew the bridge better than the man who made it."[9] He also doubtless knew the technical aspects of the river itself better than anyone else connected with the case. This was his "secret weapon." As an old river man, Lincoln could read the river and figure out the speed of the current in the draw as affected by the displacement of the *Afton*. The opposition contended that the effect of the increase in speed created by the vessel's displacement while in the draw was such as to constitute a hazard to navigation; Lincoln was able to demonstrate, with models prepared by the defense, that the effect was negligible.

For months preceding the trial, he was engaged in the most unremitting study of the case, in all its ramifications. With his infinite capacity for taking unlimited pains, Lincoln spent some time in Chicago, going over every aspect of it with his associates.[10] His pre-trial research into the facts was the sort of unlimited industry which Goethe said is the better part of genius; by the time the case came up, his knowledge of bridge construction, river currents, displacement and navigation of vessels, and other highly technical related matters was almost, one might say, encyclopedic. After years of experience as a trial lawyer, Lincoln must have realized that, the general run of circuit-court trials apart, cases are won or lost long before juries are impaneled.

3.

The battle lines drawn, the trial got under way on September 8, 1857, in a courtroom "not more than forty feet square, with the usual division for the judge, clerks, and attorneys occupying perhaps 20 feet on the farther side, and with the usual furniture. The rest of the room contained long benches for the accommodation of the public. Near the door was a large stove of the box pattern, surmounted by a drum."[11] Dominating the scene was the figure of Lincoln, even though Judd was nominally chief counsel for the defense.

A day-to-day account of the proceedings is to be found in the Chicago press, which gave the trial extensive coverage. The presentation of the evidence and argument of counsel consumed fifteen court days. Numerous witnesses were called by both sides, among them a number of "scientific experts."[12] In the course of the trial, which was highly technical and difficult in the extreme, numerous points of law arose, the argument of which, for the defendant, rested principally upon Lincoln. When the defense sought to establish that the volume of railroad traffic over the bridge exceeded that of the river, a lively discussion ensued over admissibility of the evidence. Lincoln, no longer a man who thought in terms that were merely local, argued the point with puissant wisdom, contending that the testimony was relevant as showing the demands of a changing economy. "The plaintiffs," he said, "held that their vested interests could not be interfered with, but the decisions of our courts are conforming, as they should do, to the nature of our country." Judge McLean held the evidence admissible. Showing great breadth of understanding and insight into the social significance of the new means of transportation, and drawing heavily on all the lessons he had learned through experience in many bruising courtroom battles, Lincoln's presentation of the defense—in particular, his masterful handling of the facts—was a brilliant *tour de force*. This was his finest hour as a lawyer.

The absence of an official record of Lincoln's summation (court stenographers were not yet employed)[13] is happily no misfortune, for it was taken down by a newspaper man who had acquired a certain skill in the new art of shorthand writing; his account, as carried in the Chicago *Daily Press* of September 24, 1857, probably represents a fairly accurate transcript. The argument, with its concise summarization of weeks of testimony, is worthy of consideration in some detail, for it clearly shows the acuity with which Lincoln grasped every implication of the evidence. Absent, here, were the *gaucheries* which crept into some of his jury appeals before the circuit courts; throughout, his self-restraint is manifest. Reasoning well and slowly, Lincoln defended his client's position with resourceful logic, assembling an arsenal of temperate, cogent arguments which had prophetic savor; he sensed that if the case were won by the river interests, the extensions of railroads westward and the liberation of the great

West would be seriously delayed, and, conversely, if the defendant prevailed, the cinder-strewn change would open the way to almost limitless possibilities of expansion.

The following remarks, excerpted from the rather full account of the Chicago *Daily Press*, constituted the meat of his argument: "What is reasonable skill and care? This is a thing of which the jury are to judge. I differ from the other side when it says that they are bound to exercise no more care than was taken before the building of the bridge. . . . it is unreasonable for him [the pilot] to dash on heedless of this structure which has been legally put there. The *Afton* came there on the 5th, and lay at Rock Island until next morning. When a boat lies up the pilot has a holiday, and would not any of these jurors have then gone around the bridge and gotten acquainted with the place? Pilot Parker has shown here that he does not understand the draw. I heard him say that the fall from the head to the foot of the pier was four feet; he needs information. He could have gone there that day and seen there was no such fall."

Warming to his task, he made a telling point of the fact that another boat, the *Carson,* had preceded the *Effie Afton* through the draw, and had done so without mishap, but the *Effie Afton* entered "so far wrong that she never got right. Is the defense to blame for that?"

After reviewing the growth of the West, he continued: "This particular railroad line has a great importance and the statement of its business during a little less than a year shows this importance. It is in evidence that from September 8, 1856, to August 8, 1857, 12,586 freight cars and 74,179 passengers passed over this bridge. Navigation was closed four days short of four months last year, and during this time while the river was of no use this road and bridge were valuable. There is, too, a considerable portion of time when floating or thin ice makes the river useless, while the bridge is as useful as ever. This shows that this bridge must be treated with respect in this court, and is not to be kicked about with contempt. . . . The proper mode for all parties in this affair is to 'live and let live,' and then we will find a cessation of this trouble about the bridge."

There were other points hammered home in the summation. In the final one, Lincoln neatly disposed of the at that time highly fanciful argument of the opposition that if the railroad had passed under the river by tunnel, or had been elevated high above it by suspension bridge, there would have been no obstruction to navigation. There was no practicability, he said, in building a railroad tunnel under the river, because there was no successful project of that kind anywhere in the world. (Today's advances in engineering skill were then largely unimagined.) "A suspension bridge," he logically argued, "cannot be built so high but that the chimneys of the boats will grow up till they cannot pass. The steamboat men will take pains to make them grow."

Finally, Lincoln reminded the jury that the burden of proof was squarely on the plaintiff to show that the bridge was a "material obstruction and that they have managed their boat with reasonable care and skill." He had a great deal more in mind which might be said, but "wished to close to save time." Verbosity is a sort of disease that seems to strike the legal profession with a particular virulence; it was among Lincoln's virtues as a lawyer that his chief aversion was to long-windedness.

In an editorial, after the verdict, the Chicago *Press*, commenting on the lucidity of Lincoln's summation, said: "Mr. A. Lincoln in his address to the jury was very successful, so far as clear statement and close logic was concerned."[14]

After a seven-hour closing argument by the other Lincoln, Timothy D., for the plaintiff, which the hostile Chicago *Press* was generous enough to characterize as "able, elaborate and ingenious," and the charge by Judge McLean, the case was submitted to the jury; after deliberating for some hours, it reported that it was hopelessly deadlocked (nine to three for the defendant), whereupon it was dismissed by the Court. So ended the *Effie Afton* case, the repercussions of which were transcendent. The denouement was especially noteworthy because it represented the second setback for the river interests in their campaign to prevent the building of bridges across navigable rivers.

Lincoln's conduct of the case was a performance of great stature. Throughout the trial he demonstrated an extraordinary grasp, not only of river navigation and all the other problems of fact and law involved, but of the long-range significance of the case itself, as well as a marvelous capacity for the logical, concise organization of material. Here was an occasion made to order for his peculiar gifts, and he made the most of it.

4.

For the sake of completeness, one further point calls for brief comment. Though most writers assume that it was somewhere in the neighborhood of five hundred dollars, according to the Rock Island Lines the fee paid Lincoln for his services by the Railroad Bridge Company was fifty dollars.[15] It seems a certainty that it was many times this figure. The case was absolutely vital to the defendant; if the action had been won by the river interests, the extension of railroads west would have been seriously delayed. It is hardly conceivable that Lincoln should have spent weeks in Chicago, in the preparation of the case for trial and in the trial itself, to say nothing of months of study back in Springfield—all for the insignificant sum of fifty dollars.

A few days after the termination of the trial, Lincoln deposited four hundred dollars in the bank. The Lincoln account with the Springfield Marine and Fire Insurance Company shows that several days thereafter he made out a check to Herndon for two hundred dollars. Assuming that this represented half of a four-hundred-dollar fee, the figure would still seem entirely inadequate to cover his services in the case. One doubts, furthermore, whether the matter of Lincoln's fee would have come up for consideration directly after the trial and without having been gone into more thoroughly. There is, of course, the possibility that the four hundred dollars was paid Lincoln, in September 1857, merely on account, with the understanding that the balance of his fee would be agreed upon when the litigation against the bridge company was finally passed upon by the higher courts.

On September 1, 1857, Lincoln is reputed to have loaned to Judd three thousand dollars and taken a mortgage on some land owned by the latter at Council Bluffs, Iowa. From all appearances, it would seem that Lincoln did not make this loan in cash; it may well have been that the mortgage was, rather, his fee, in whole or in part, in the Rock Island Bridge case, Judd having personally remunerated him for his services. The complete details of the private transaction with Judd have never come to light.

5.

One final observation remains to be made: It is another attestation of Herndon's superficial treatment of Lincoln's work in the courts and his inability to realize the scope of the latter's achievement as a lawyer, that his biography of Lincoln contains no mention of what was by all odds the most important case of Lincoln's entire career. Reading Herndon's *opus*, one has the feeling—indeed, the certainty—that, while making perfunctory acknowledgment of his capability in certain phases of practice, he was altogether without perception of the profounder levels of his partner's keen legal mind. His failure "to bring out . . . a searching insight into his [Lincoln's] activities as a lawyer" evoked the bitter disappointment of Leonard Swett.[16] Not without reason has Herndon been given his licks, by his contemporaries as well as by latter-day Lincoln scholars. John T. Richards, in his *Abraham Lincoln: The Lawyer-Statesman*, thought it clear "that Herndon did not comprehend his great law partner and that he underestimated his greatness as a lawyer."[17] Here, again, one is made to realize how very wide of the mark was Hertz in his adulation of the object of his adoration.

CHAPTER XXI

Final Years at the Bar

1.

Hardly had the smoke of the political battle of 1856 cleared away, when a new situation presented itself. On March 6, 1857, while Lincoln was in attendance at the DeWitt Circuit Court, in Clinton, the United States Supreme Court handed down, to a nation hopelessly divided on the issue of slavery, its decision in the Dred Scott case, a decision redolent of politics. The only ruling of that court that was ever reversed by a war, it furnished a new torch to a smoldering conflagration that erupted into civil war four years later.

The details of the case (*Dred Scott* v. *John F. A. Sanford*) are too complicated to be told here. Suffice it to say that Scott was a Missouri slave who, in 1834, had accompanied his master, an officer in the United States Army, from Missouri, a slave state, to Illinois, a free state, where he resided for a while. In 1836 he was taken to Fort Snelling, Minnesota, in territory that was a part of the Louisiana Purchase. By act of Congress, that was "free territory." In 1852, Scott was taken back to Missouri. He sought permission, as a citizen of Missouri, to sue for his freedom in the Federal Court, claiming that residence in free territory had struck off his shackles. Two days after Buchanan was inaugurated as President, the court, by a divided vote, held that Negroes were not citizens of any state and therefore were not citizens of the United States. Hence, Scott had no right to sue for his freedom. Although it was *obiter dicta*, the Court declared the Missouri Compromise unconstitutional because Congress had no power to exclude slavery from the territories.

On June 7, 1857, Douglas spoke in Springfield in support of the Dred Scott decision. On the night of June twenty-sixth, in the same hall where the Little Giant had spoken, a somber Lincoln, in his only political speech of the year, replied to Douglas. The essence of his view appeared in the statements that the Supreme Court must be respected and obeyed, but the decision was nonetheless "erroneous." The Court had "often overruled its own decisions, and we shall do what we can to have it overrule this."

Lincoln felt that Douglas's defeat for re-election in the senatorial contest of the coming year would be the most effective answer to the Court, and so, while he kept a close eye on his practice, he never overlooked an opportunity to promote his nomination to carry the Republican banner in opposition.

2.

An enumeration of all the cases, not previously discussed, which Lincoln handled in the last four years of his practice, would extend the limits of this book, but from the many a few have been chosen. In that rare combination of principle and flexibility which constitutes one of the marks of the wise advocate, Lincoln stood out among his contemporaries. Though some Lincoln idolaters may bristle at the thought, records of the Woodford Circuit Court, at Eureka,[1] indicate that, while a lawyer of scrupulous integrity, Lincoln, who had a great sympathy for those who were ill treated by the world or otherwise unfortunate, may not have been above winking an eye at the law's circumvention, in the interest of substantial justice. Ernest E. East, distinguished former president of the Illinois State Historical Society, and a long-time Lincoln specialist, is on record as saying, in discussing Lincoln's less than impeccably conventional course in the case of Melissa Goings: "That Abraham Lincoln was a practical lawyer who was willing to lean toward public sentiment when it disagreed with the strict letter of the law was demonstrated in a Woodford County murder case in which the defendant was a woman. In this course he appears to have had the tacit approval of law enforcing officers."[2]

The story of the Melissa Goings murder case has curious and dramatic overtones. It goes something like this: In Worth Township, in Woodford County in north-central Illinois, there lived in 1857 one Roswell Goings, aged seventy-seven, and his wife, Melissa, seventy. From all accounts, Goings was an irascible old codger, frequently in his cups, and the pair had many quarrels.[3] On April 14, 1857, according to the coroner's records, a dispute arising between them, Goings grasped his wife around the neck; struggling loose from his grasp, the old woman picked up a piece of stovewood and struck her husband two blows, one of which caused a skull fracture, from which he died four days later.

Melissa was arrested on the coroner's warrant, charged with murder. After a preliminary hearing, she was bound over to the grand jury. Bail, which was fixed in the sum of one thousand dollars, was furnished by two local property owners.

On October 8, 1857, the Woodford Grand Jury met in the little Metamora courthouse, with its Southern Colonial architecture, and returned an indictment against Melissa Goings on the charge of having murdered her husband. On October tenth, she was arraigned on the indictment, and directed to stand trial forthwith. Her bail was apparently ordered revoked and the defendant remanded to the custody of the sheriff, for the further proceedings show that that official was charged with the responsibility of producing her when the case was called for trial. The summary dispatch with which the old woman was being rushed to trial, and the revoking of her bail by the trial judge, doubtless caused Lincoln to take a dim view of the defendant's chances of receiving a fair trial at the hands of the latter. Nothing gives a lawyer a greater sense of futility than arguing before a judge predisposed in favor of guilt.

His client being in custody, Lincoln asked and received the

Court's permission to consult with her privately, on the lower floor of the courthouse. Presently the case was called for trial. Not seeing the defendant among those present in the court-room, the judge inquired, "Mr. Lincoln, where is your client?" to which Lincoln responded: "I don't know, Your Honor. I left her on the lower floor; she should be in the custody of the sheriff." A search of the lower floor revealed that Melissa Go-ings, like William Weaver, Lincoln's other disappearing client, had taken French leave, never again to be seen in the State of Illinois.

Apparently no serious effort was made by the authorities to apprehend her, and on May 24, 1859, the Court, on motion of the State's Attorney, ordered the cause stricken from the docket.[4] And though the prosecutor commenced a proceeding to collect on the bond of the two sureties, the case was dropped on October 5, 1858, the day after Lincoln visited Metamora for a political speech, and after, presumably, he had conferred with the State's Attorney.

Several versions of Lincoln's conversation with Melissa, just prior to her getaway, have come down to us. Robert T. Cassell, the court bailiff at the time, related this quaint story: "Mrs. Goings was brought into court that Lincoln might talk to her. After a while I was told by the state's attorney to bring her up for trial, but she could not be found. I asked Lincoln about her and he said he did not know where she was. I replied, 'Confound you, Abe, you have run her off.' 'Oh, no, Bob,' re-plied Lincoln. 'I didn't run her off. She wanted to know where she could get a good drink of water, and I told her there was mighty good water in Tennessee.' "[5]

Another tale has it that Lincoln, convinced that the de-fendant would receive all the worst of it from the judge, told her she would be far safer many miles away. He then left the room, whereupon the defendant took the hint and climbed to freedom through an open window.[6]

That Lincoln solved the old woman's problems by "running

her off" is quite unprovable, but there is enough plausibility about it to make it worth mentioning. Years later, Judge Stevens R. Baker, of the Woodford Circuit Court, thought enough of the story, as related by Cassell, to order it spread upon the court records.[7] Some of the sacred cows and cherished shibboleths concerning Lincoln, with which we have been regaled, hardly square with the versions of the Goings case given above. Whosoever will understand the lawyer who, as commander-in-chief of the nation's armed forces, went over Stanton's head to grant pardons, even when his Secretary of War was legally correct, before all things it is necessary that he comprehend that Lincoln placed humane considerations above the strict letter of the law. For Lincoln idolaters to claim otherwise does no service to his memory. Though his own pen was not invariably guided by strict regard for the facts, Herndon was indubitably right when he said, in the preface to his *Life of Lincoln:* "If . . . the story is colored or the facts in any degree suppressed, the reader will be not only misled, but imposed upon as well."[8] The most helpful evaluation is the product of love that is not blind.

3.

Isolated is the individual who has not heard of Lincoln's classic courtroom maneuver in the "Almanac Trial." Even though *Herndon's Life* devotes but a paragraph to the case, there is a considerable literature on this most widely proclaimed event of Lincoln's career at the bar, not all of it founded on unvarnished fact. (Indeed, one of the more fanciful versions has furnished grist for the Hollywood mill, in a picture[9] which contains some grains of truth, mixed with a good many grains of fantasy.) The story of this famous case has often been recounted, and the strange twists which have developed from the many tellings afford a perfect example of the unreliability of much so-called "honest" testimony.

Such has been the human interest in the case that it has

tended, inevitably, to obscure more important, though less picturesque litigation with which Lincoln was associated. Writers
have devoted so much space to it, and a few similarly spectacular
trials, that many of his other achievements at the bar have been
crowded from their proper places. This is not for a moment to
suggest that the trial is undeserving of prominence in the story
of Lincoln's law career, for it not only called out his agility and
resourcefulness as a trial advocate, but showed him to be a
skilled craftsman in that nightmare of lawyers—the art of cross-
examination. Such ability is not to be shrugged off. It is an
elusive and unique power, given to few.

The story of *People* v. *Armstrong* really had its beginning
in the New Salem days, when Jack Armstrong, leader of the
Clary's Grove Boys, and his wife Hannah, befriended Lincoln
and gave him a home in their humble cabin. More than a score
of years later, their son "Duff" (whose baptismal name was
William), aged about twenty-four, while embarked on a Saturday night spree, became involved in a brawl which ended in
tragedy.

In August of 1857, long years after Lincoln's departure
from New Salem, a religious camp meeting was being held in a
glade, known as Virgin's Grove, in the vicinity of Salt Creek,
near the old site of New Salem in what is now Mason County.
These religious gatherings were annual affairs which lasted about
two weeks. There was preaching, day and night, by a team of
circuit-riding evangelists possessed of the gift of exhortation,
which was one of the distinguishing features of pulpit power of
that time. Though these revivalist meetings were frequently productive of great moral results, with hundreds of sinners being
converted, they often attracted a tough element, bent on mischief. It hovered on the edge of the camp and frequently in-
dulged in rowdyism and drinking.

As a means of protection to the meetings, a statute was
passed prohibiting the sale of "ardent spirits" within a mile of
such gatherings. The result was that makeshift bars were set

up just outside the mile limit. At the meeting under consideration, there were three such bars in operation.

On Saturday night, August twenty-ninth, a trouble-seeking group of rowdies, all somewhat under the influence of liquor, was milling around, from bar to bar. Among them were "Duff" Armstrong, a huge, good-natured oaf; James Norris and James Metzker. At one of the bars Metzker, a quarrelsome individual, became involved in altercations with Armstrong and Norris. Shorn of its verbosity, the indictment in the case charged that, while acting in concert, (1) Norris struck Metzker on the back of the head "with a certain piece of wood about three feet long," and (2) Armstrong, "with a certain hard metallic substance called a Slung Shot," struck Metzker in the right eye. The wounds inflicted were alleged to have been "mortal bruises from which Metzker died."[10] After the fights Metzker climbed on his horse and rode away, but on the way home fell from his mount several times.

Norris and Armstrong were jointly indicted at the October term of the Mason Circuit Court, charged with murder. Mention has been made, at several points, of Lincoln's refusal to be rushed to trial when representing defendants in criminal cases, and his almost invariable resort to the application for change of venue. The precipitate dispatch with which Norris was tried and convicted at the same October term, in the emotional atmosphere of the county where indicted, is a fair sample of the sort of thing Lincoln was ever alert to avoid. Norris was convicted of manslaughter, and sentenced to eight years in the penitentiary. Without funds, and with a wife and four children, he was in no position to engage the services of an attorney, and so counsel was assigned in the person of William Walker, then a lawyer of but a few years' standing, who was opposed by three competent prosecutors. When the young lawyer permitted his client to stand trial in Mason County, within a month after indictment, he was, as Lincoln could have told him, asking for trouble. It is interesting and significant that Norris was sent to prison on the oath of a man who was afterwards proved to have given false testimony in the very same case, even though against a different party.

Armstrong's attorneys, Dilworth & Campbell, of Havana, Illinois, promptly sought a change of venue, the moving affidavit of Armstrong alleging that ". . . he fears that he will not receive a fair and impartial trial in this court on account of the minds of the inhabitants of said Mason County being prejudiced against him."[11] The application was granted, and the trial ordered removed to Cass County, of which Beardstown was the county seat. (Both Mason and Cass were outside the Eighth Circuit.) This resulted in what lawyers call a "severance," i.e., separate trials for the two defendants.

Meanwhile, acting on the advice of friends, Hannah Armstrong, who had mended Lincoln's trousers and buckskins in the New Salem days, drove to Springfield to enlist Mr. Lincoln's services on behalf of her son. Though it is a certainty that he neither received nor asked for a fee, Lincoln readily consented to lend his efforts toward getting him off. At the November, 1857, term of the Cass Circuit Court he tried unavailingly to have the defendant admitted to bail, and so, until the case was called for trial on May 7, 1858, the defendant was lodged in the nearby Beardstown jail.

On a spring morning a few weeks before Lincoln's nomination for the Senate, the trial commenced in the little building constructed by Thomas Beard for use as the Cass County courthouse. The structure, still standing, has been in use for many years as the Beardstown city hall. Its brick exterior is much the same as it was when Lincoln tried the Armstrong case. The courtroom, on the second floor, is preserved as it was then, and is maintained as a Lincoln shrine. Beardstown, founded in 1830, served as the county seat of Cass until 1870, when a group of citizens of the neighboring town of Virginia stole the public records from the courthouse and took them back to Virginia, where the county seat has remained ever since.

Lincoln arrived in the little town of Beardstown, on the Illinois River, on the sixth, on the eve of the trial. Appearing for the prosecution was Hugh Fullerton, State's Attorney for the district, who was assisted by J. Henry Shaw, special counsel employed by the Metzker family. Lincoln was assisted by Walker, who had represented Norris, and by Dilworth. Presiding was Judge James Harriott of Pekin.

As related by an eyewitness, Lincoln exercised great care in selecting the men who were to hear the evidence against the widow Armstrong's son. There are veteran trial lawyers who look upon a jury as so imponderable a compound that one does as well picking them by lot as by earnest sifting of the panel. However, Lincoln, who was something of a psychologist when it came to juries, had some rather definite ideas on the type of juror he preferred in a criminal case. He did not, for instance, want a blond, blue-eyed man in the jury box. This type was too nervous, he said, too apt to string along with the prosecution in any case involving violence. Nor would he have a man with a high forehead (what today, one supposes, would be referred to as the egghead type), unless he was certain beforehand that such a man leaned his way. A man like this, Lincoln figured, always had his mind made up in advance. A fat man was not only acceptable, but highly desirable; he was, to Lincoln's way of thinking, the ideal juror. Finally, all things else being equal, young men were to be preferred to older ones.[12] Lincoln scored his first point when he succeeded in getting a jury of young men, the average age being less than thirty years.

Lincoln knew from Walker's notes, taken at the Norris trial, that the prosecution's star witness, Charles Allen, who had testified against Norris, claimed to have seen Armstrong strike the deceased with a slung shot. Between the time of the Norris and Armstrong trials, however, Allen, who was a friend of the Armstrong family, had apparently suffered a change of heart about testifying, for it was necessary for the prosecution to send out and bring him in, by body attachment, from Virginia, Illinois, thirteen miles away, where he was hiding out.

Whatever his initial reluctance about testifying, Allen was, from all accounts, a crafty and nimble witness, swearing positively that he saw Armstrong strike the deceased with a slung shot. Without taking a note, Lincoln listened intently while Allen gave crucial testimony that, though it was eleven o'clock at night when the fight occurred, and Allen was 150 feet away from the combatants, he could see everything clearly, by reason of the fact that the moon was shining directly overhead at the time. He could not be mistaken. When the State's Attorney had finished with Allen, the outlook for the defendant appeared bleak, indeed, as the jurors leaned back in their seats as though the trial, except for the usual legal gymnastics by defense counsel, was for all practical purposes at an end. The case was soon to take a new turn, however.

Hooking his fingers under his gallus straps, which held up shapeless trousers, the cool, unruffled prairie lawyer took the chief prosecution witness over on cross-examination, pressing him with the most searching questions, asked with seeming casualness. He adroitly led him to commit himself irretrievably to the statement, repeated "a dozen or more times," that he could not be mistaken about what he had seen, because the moon was shining brightly at the time. Suddenly, dramatically, Lincoln fell upon the witness, riddling his testimony by confronting him with an almanac for 1857 which showed that at the hour of the alleged fracas the moon was not in the position stated by Allen, but, rather, was low in the sky, within an hour of setting. One can see the witness twisting and wriggling through the ordeal, like a sailfish coming to gaff, while the laboriously constructed case for the prosecution crumbled. As several jurymen later stated to Shaw, "The almanac floored the witness."[13]

As an experienced trial lawyer, Lincoln knew how to lay the foundation for Allen's ultimate annihilation. His most damning questions were asked conversationally, but he was ruthless withal. With no hint of what he had up his sleeve, he led the unsuspecting Allen on with disarming courtesy, in a manner more seductive than antagonistic. It was a deft performance, a devastating display of the art of cross-examination.

In the trial of jury cases the cross-examination of witnesses furnishes a fascinating study and, it goes without saying, is a most important factor. In this finest of the law's arts, Lincoln was a skilled craftsman. It was freely conceded by his contemporaries that, as a cross-examiner, he had few equals at the Illinois bar. One thing is clear: With that sixth sense which told him when he had reached dangerous ground, Lincoln knew when to stop. "Lincoln was a great cross examiner," declared James S. Ewing,[14] "in that he never asked an unnecessary question. He knew when and where to stop with a witness, and when a man has learned that he is entitled to take rank as an expert questioner."[15] A wise lawyer once said, speaking in this context: "When you strike oil, stop boring; many a lawyer has bored clear through and let the oil run out of the bottom."

On behalf of the defendant, Lincoln called as a witness Nelson Watkins, who testified that the slung shot found near the scene of the crime and produced by the State as the weapon with which Armstrong had struck Metzker, was, in fact, Watkins's; that he had had it in his home the night of the supposed murder, and that he had thrown it away, at the spot where found, the day after. Lincoln afterward said that the testimony of Watkins was as helpful to the defense as was the refutation of Allen's testimony by use of the almanac.

As part of the defense, Lincoln also produced a physician, Charles Parker, who testified, in answer to a hypothetical question propounded by Lincoln, that the falling off his horse by the deceased, and the striking of his head upon the ground, could have caused Metzker's death. Parker evidently made a good impression, for Judge Harriott maintained that it was the most persuasive testimony adduced on the defendant's behalf.[16] Dr. B. F. Stevenson, the physician produced by the State in rebuttal, was, like Allen, a reluctant witness, it being necessary to bring him in by court process.[17]

In a moving summation, which lasted an hour, Lincoln pleaded, with persuasive eloquence, for the life of the son of his old friends, Jack and Hannah Armstrong. He made telling use of the almanac incident, pointing out to the jury that if Allen was so badly mistaken as to the position of the moon, he could be, and very likely was, in error on other important matters. Writing of Lincoln's summation, in which he appealed to the heart as well as the intellect, Walker said: "I have never seen such Mastery exhibited over the feelings and emotions of men as on that occasion."[18]

Even though Armstrong's prospects appeared considerably brighter than they did at the conclusion of Allen's direct examination, Lincoln was careful to preserve the defendant's rights on appeal, in the event of a conviction. This he did by his requests for instructions to the jury, two in number, which the Court gave. They were:

> The Court instructs the jury that if they have any reasonable doubt as to whether Metzker came to his death by the blow on the eye or the blow on the back of the head, they are to find the defendant not guilty, unless they further believe from the evidence, beyond all reasonable doubt, that Armstrong and Norris acted in concert against Metzker and that Norris struck the blow on the back of the head.

> That if they believe from the evidence that Norris killed Metzker, they are to acquit Armstrong unless they also believe from the evidence, beyond a reasonable doubt, that Armstrong acted in concert with Norris in the killing or purpose to kill or hurt Metzker.[19]

The theory of Lincoln's defense is apparent from his requests to charge. His contention was that it was the blow on the back of the head that caused Metzker's death, a blow struck by Norris, and that, assuming *arguendo* that Armstrong administered a blow with the slung shot, there was no proof that the two were "acting in concert," as charged. In the absence of a showing of common design, it is difficult to see how a conviction could have been sustained on appeal. Even so, decisions of the Illinois Supreme Court being few at the time, with none whatever bearing upon the precise question raised by Lincoln, it was as well that the jury, after but an hour's deliberation, returned a verdict of Not Guilty.

After the trial a rumor was spread to the effect that, in destroying Allen as a witness, Lincoln had used a spurious almanac, *i.e.*, one for a year other than 1857. It is not certain just when the story originated, though it probably was during the presidential campaign of 1860, when the opposition circulated numerous slanders against him. The bogus almanac charge constitutes a very serious accusation. According to Shaw, who assisted in the prosecution, the story was that Lincoln, as he entered the courtroom, turned over to Sheriff James A. Dick an 1856 almanac, with instructions to hand it to him if he called for an almanac during the course of the trial. The story went on that when Lincoln produced the book the effect was so electric that, in the excitement, the judge, prosecutors and jury failed to examine its date.

A few months after the Armstrong trial, Lincoln's senatorial contest with Douglas commenced. It is reasonable to believe that, with feeling running so high, if there had been the slightest suspicion that Lincoln had been a party to a fraud in the production of the almanac, that fact would have been made known. On the contrary, there was, at the time, no intimation whatever of any such charge. What is more, however sensational may have been the effect of the almanac's production, it challenges belief that not only all twelve of the jurors, who voted to acquit, but the judge and the prosecutor, as well, should have been completely hoodwinked through use of an almanac which plainly bore, on its face, the year to which it referred.

Both Milton Logan, the foreman of the jury, and John T. Brady, another juror, stated emphatically that the almanac was one for the year of the killing. When interviewed, years later, Brady said: "There never has been a question in my mind about the genuineness of the almanac, that it was an up to date almanac; this I am sure of, as it was passed up to the Judge, jury and lawyers, who all examined it closely, and the State's Attorney said 'Mr. Lincoln, you are mistaken, the moon was just coming up instead of just going down at that time,' and Mr. Lincoln retorted: 'It serves my purpose just as well, just coming up or just going down, as you admit, it was not overhead as Mr. Allen swore it was.' "[20]

What more needs be said? The charge was unfounded and fantastic, with not a shred of evidence to support it. Unaccountably, it still persists in some quarters, even though repeatedly exposed.

In 1863, "Duff," who had served two years in the Union Army, was ill in a hospital in Louisville, Kentucky. In response to a plea for his discharge, Lincoln wrote Hannah:

Washington,
Sep. 18, 1863

Mrs. Hannah Armstrong
Petersburg, Illinois.
    I have just ordered the discharge of your boy William, as you say, now at Louisville, Ky.

A. Lincoln[21]

The roster of Company C, Eighty-fifth Illinois Volunteers lists William Armstrong as "Discharged at Louisville, Ky. by order of the President."

The records of the Illinois Archives show that, just a month before, James Norris, then thirty years of age, received a pardon and was discharged from the Illinois State Penitentiary; at the time, he was furnished five dollars cash and clothing of the value of fifteen dollars.[22] One cannot help reflecting that Armstrong might well have joined Norris in confinement, had he not been shielded by a stalwart defender.

4.

In the afternoon of June 16, 1858, the State Republican Convention met in the Hall of the House of Representatives, in the State House at Springfield, and unanimously resolved "that Abraham Lincoln is the first and only choice of the Republicans of Illinois for the United States Senate." The convention thereupon adjourned, to meet again at eight o'clock in the evening, when Lincoln delivered his famous "House Divided Speech," which many consider one of the greatest speeches he ever delivered. Here Lincoln the lawyer joined Lincoln the statesman, and in so doing achieved real grandeur.

The speech, in which Lincoln set forth his strong beliefs on slavery and defined the issues which were to split the nation, attracted national attention. In words so unmistakably Lincoln (almost everything he said seemed to bear his mark), he set the tone of the great series of debates, unparalleled in American history, which were shortly to follow: " 'A house divided against itself cannot stand.' I believe this government cannot endure permanently half *slave* and half *free*. I do not expect the Union to be dissolved—I do not expect the house to *fall*—but I do expect it will cease to be divided. It will become *all* one thing, or *all* the other."

The next two months were spent in attention to his practice and in marshaling his arguments and finances for the forthcoming Douglas debates. On July twentieth he wrote Henry E. Dummer of Beardstown concerning his fee in the case of *Charles Sprague* v. *Illinois River Railroad Co.*, tried by Lincoln and Dummer in the Cass Circuit Court November 21, 1857, and reviewed by the Illinois Supreme Court February 4, 1858. Like *Barrett* v. *The Alton & Sangamon Railroad Company*, also handled by Lincoln, the case involved the question of the effect of amendments to the company's charter on the liability of subscribers to its stock. "I am now in need of money," Lincoln wrote. "Suppose we say the amount shall be $50 . . . please get the money and send it to me. And while you have pen in hand, tell me what you may know about politics down your way."[23]

A century ago a tall, rumpled lawyer and a short, tireless orator set the prairies on fire, pulling no punches as they stumped Illinois in what history has called the Great Debate. Four exciting months these two contestants for United States Senator traveled nearly ten thousand miles, speaking in more than seventy-five towns. The first of the seven "joint discussions" was held at Ottawa, Illinois, on August 21, 1858. Subsequent debates were held at Freeport (August 27), Jonesboro (September 15), Charleston (September 18), Galesburg (October 7), Quincy (October 13) and Alton (October 15).

The issues were: the extension of slavery into the territories of Kansas and Nebraska; the power of the states to regulate the "peculiar institution" of slavery within their own confines; the Dred Scott decision, involving the status of the Negro. It was Lincoln's persistent theme that "There is no reason in the world why the Negro is not entitled to all natural rights enumerated in the Declaration of Independence, the right of life, liberty and the pursuit of happiness. I hold that he is as much entitled to these as the white man."

With the mastery of summarization which was his special stamp as a lawyer, Lincoln pithily recapitulated months of talking when the two faced each other for the last time: "I have said and I repeat it here, that if there be a man amongst us who does not think that the institution of slavery is wrong in any one of the aspects of which I have spoken, he is misplaced and ought not to be with us. Has anything ever threatened the existence of this Union save and except this very institution of slavery? That is the real issue. That is the issue that will continue in this country when these poor tongues of Judge Douglas and myself shall be silent. It is the eternal struggle between these two principles— right and wrong—throughout the world."

When the votes were toted up, it was found that though

Lincoln had received a majority, the gerrymandered legislative districts gave Douglas re-election to the Senate. It is curious to note that Lincoln carried Douglas's home county of Cook, while Douglas carried the county of Sangamon.

In the *Robert Todd Lincoln Collection* is a letter from Lyman Trumbull to Lincoln, written after the Ottawa debate, in which the former states: "I have just read & am delighted with the debate at Ottawa. In manner, temper, spirit, & every thing else you have obtained a complete triumph over the little pettifogger, for really that is all he is."[24] One could wish that Trumbull and others had not felt it necessary to imply that the differences between this most curiously neglected figure of mid-nineteenth-century American life and Lincoln represented such mutually exclusive views that we cannot praise the latter without deprecating the former.

We see the able Douglas in his true magnificence when, after Lincoln's election to the Presidency, he warned those who would embarrass the latter in his new office: "I shall be there and if anyone attacks Lincoln, he attacks me."[25] On April 25, 1861, less than six weeks before his death, Douglas delivered, in the State House in Springfield, his historic "Protect the Flag Speech," which became a rallying cry for Union Army volunteers. He died in the midst of his last great campaign to hold the Union, and particularly Illinois, behind Lincoln.

5.

Busy as Lincoln was in 1859, with his practice in the higher courts, and with politics claiming an increasing quota of his time, he was not too busy to handle a murder case and one of attempted murder. Abraham Nash, alias Yankee Sullivan, was charged in Logan County with assault with intent to kill. Appearing in Lincoln, the county's then county seat, on March 24, 1859, Lincoln moved on behalf of the defendant for a change of venue, which motion was granted, and the case removed to

Sangamon County. The Sangamon Judge's Docket for 1858–1859 shows that on April 30, 1859, Lincoln, who had just returned from the circuit, moved to quash the indictment, which motion was granted by Judge Edward Y. Rice, presiding.[26]

Early in the summer of that year, Quinn ("Peachy") Harrison, a grandson of Peter Cartwright, the Methodist circuit rider whom Lincoln had defeated for Congress in 1846, fatally stabbed Greek Crafton, a young lawyer who, according to Herndon, had studied law with Lincoln & Herndon. The killing, which was apparently without provocation, took place in the town of Pleasant Plains, outside Springfield, in Sangamon County. Because of the prominence of the two families, the case attracted much attention, and was fully reported in the Springfield press.

Upon Harrison's indictment for murder, his family retained Logan & Hay; Shelby M. Cullom, a young lawyer, later to become governor of the state; and the firm of Lincoln & Herndon to represent him. Appearing for the prosecution were J. B. White, John M. Palmer, Norman M. Broadwell and Isaac Cogdale, the latter a one-time law clerk of Lincoln & Herndon.[27]

As Herndon recalled, years later: "The case was opened and ably conducted on both sides; every inch of ground was contested and hotly fought."[28] On behalf of the defendant, Lincoln called as a witness his old political foe, the by-now aged Peter Cartwright. He told how he had visited the dying youth, who told him that he forgave his assailant and prayed that he would not be held accountable for his death. How Lincoln ever managed to slip this bit of evidence—hearsay of the rankest sort —past the judge and opposing counsel is a deep mystery, especially in view of the former's supposed prejudicial attitude toward the defendant. Lincoln pleaded feelingly, in summation, for the life of the young man. Though, at the outset, the trial may have seemed the merest formality en route to the nearest hanging tree, the defendant was, as Herndon put it, "honorably acquitted."[29]

According to Herndon, who apparently sat in on the trial, which was held in Springfield and lasted four torrid summer days

(August 31, 1859, to September 3, 1859), Lincoln encountered rough going throughout, because of the biased rulings of Judge Rice, a lifelong Democrat from Hillsboro. At one point a lengthy discussion took place between counsel and the Court, concerning a point of law raised by Lincoln. After receiving an adverse ruling, Lincoln begged leave of the Court to reargue the question, which application was granted. Lincoln, who had made a thorough study of the principle of law involved, argued the proposition with much skill, but to a mind hermetically sealed. Rice's ruling stood. Lincoln, who rarely lost his temper, found it difficult to suppress his indignation. According to Herndon, he addressed the Court, speaking "fiercely, strongly, contemptuously of the decision of the Court. Lincoln, in his anger and contempt, kept just inside the walls of the law, did not do anything, say anything, that would be a contempt of court; he was careful and yet the scoring that he gave the Court, through its foolish decision, was terrible, blasting, crushing, withering."[30] (Understatement was never a characteristic of Herndon's writing.)

6.

Fall of 1859 found Lincoln on the circuit for the last time, covering Logan, DeWitt, Champaign and Vermilion Counties. Because of the growth of the state's population, the Eighth Judicial Circuit had been greatly reduced in size—from fourteen counties in 1850 to five in 1857. Whereas in 1850 no two county seats were connected by rail, train service had become so extensive by 1854 that Springfield was within easy rail connection with all the county seats he visited, with the exception of Pekin and Metamora.

In spite of his growing political prominence, Lincoln nevertheless continued to attend to his practice. Returning to Springfield about the middle of November, he cleared up some pending matters in the United States Circuit Court on the twenty-fourth and the twenty-sixth, and on the thirtieth set out on a speaking tour which took him to Leavenworth, Kansas. Back in Springfield on December eighth, his professional work absorbed most of his time and energy throughout the remainder of the year.

During the month of January and the early part of February, 1860, Lincoln, now nearing the end of his journey as a practicing lawyer, was busy in the federal courts in Springfield. February twenty-seventh he delivered his famous Cooper Union Address in New York City. It was a calm, lawyer-like speech. Joseph Choate, who was among those present, observed: "For an hour and a half he held his audience in the hollow of his hand." That speech, which more than anything else prepared the Republicans of the effete east to accept the gawky Midwesterner, was a superb legal brief. It was Lincoln the lawyer who said, addressing his opponents: "You say we are sectional. We deny it. That makes an issue, and the burden of proof is on you."

In the Illinois State Historical Library is a demurrer in Lincoln's hand, in the case of *Laughery* v. *Heinrichsen*, filed in the clerk's office of the Logan Circuit Court on March 19, 1860. So far as the writer has been able to determine, this is the last circuit court case in which Lincoln's handwriting appears.

On June twentieth, a month after his nomination for the Presidency, the still clean-shaven Lincoln made one of his last appearances in the United States District Court. The *Illinois State Journal* of the following day reported: "The case of Charles Dawson v. H. M. and William Ennis for infringement of patent right in a double plow was up in the United States Circuit Court on yesterday, and was argued before the court by Messrs. Lincoln and Ketchum for the plaintiff, and Judge Palmer for the defendant. The Judge took the case under advisement." Five days after Lincoln's inauguration the Court found for the defendant.

According to Palmer, the last case in which Lincoln appeared in court was *David J. Baker* v. *Faculty of Shurtleff College* when, on behalf of the plaintiff, he opposed (unsuccessfully) a demurrer to the declaration, brought on by Palmer, appearing for the college faculty.[31] The date cannot be exactly fixed; Palmer states it as being "after the nomination of Mr. Lincoln for the presidency." The motion was heard by Judge Treat, who in June, 1860, was sitting in the United States Court, in Springfield. Though the court records are missing, the motion was probably brought on at the same term of court at which Lincoln appeared in connection with *Dawson* v. *Ennis and Ennis*.[32]

Thus Lincoln bade farewell to the law. Though he had been buffeted and bruised, and experienced his share of heartbreaking setbacks, he had, with that genius for picking up the pieces and going on which was one of his salient characteristics, left a profound imprint on a calling that has never been a stranger to greatness. Few lawyers have served their profession so well.

Even though Lincoln the lawyer had his faults as well as his virtues, it may be said, in all objectivity, that there were blended in him, in a fashion unmatched among his contemporaries, many, if not most of the qualities of greatness in a lawyer. It would be idle to suggest that, even in the later years of his practice, he was profoundly learned in the law. His strength lay, rather, in his extraordinary acuteness as a cross-examiner; in his great ability in summation, with his adroit mingling of wit and logic and insight, and his wonderful gift for language; in his resourcefulness in argument before the Illinois Supreme Court, where he was regarded as a lawyer of towering stature. These were the attributes which, in their total impact, combined to set him off somewhat from his contemporaries, lawyers of distinction though many of them were.

No Illinois lawyer of his day could do so many things so well, a fact which was ungrudgingly conceded by his colleagues at the bar. Every once in a while a lawyer comes along who attains that sure mark of greatness—the unstinted praise of his co-workers. Lincoln was supremely that kind of lawyer. "In all the elements that constituted a lawyer he had," according to David Davis, "few equals." Sidney Breese, Chief Justice of the Illinois Supreme Court, regarded him as "the finest lawyer I ever knew."

To Lawrence Weldon "He was the leader of the bar." Like estimates might be multiplied.

In coming to the conclusion that Lincoln was a great deal more than just a competent, successful lawyer, perhaps the writer has been too uncritical by modern standards of legal scholarship. Even though he encompassed with great ability just about every aspect of his craft, Lincoln's make-up as a lawyer was not without a flaw, but it was a minor one which scarcely detracts from the over-all estimate. That he could, and did, upon occasions resort to speciousness, in order to carry a point, cannot be denied. Inevitably, his almost capricious reasoning, in the *McCall* case and in others equally hopeless, will raise, in the minds of some, the question of his claim to greatness as a lawyer, and furnishes, perhaps, an argument in the negative, just as the McLean County tax case and the Rock Island Bridge case furnish a very strong argument for the affirmative. It is important to bear in mind, however, that the trial or appellate lawyer who takes every case that is thrown at him—even the ones where he seemingly hasn't a leg to stand on—enjoys a popularity and standing among his fellow lawyers unattainable by the practitioner who takes only those cases served up on a silver platter. It is well to remember, too, that when *McCall, et al. v. Lesher, et al.*[33] was argued, Lincoln's years of practice were mostly ahead of him. A splendid lawyer such as he came in time to be does not spring up from nowhere. He goes through a period of trial and error, of ripening and deepening through the years.

It was not without reason that, at the time of his accession to the Presidency, Lincoln's reputation was such that he was looked up to, by his contemporaries, as virtually the leader of the Illinois bar, which was noted for its lawyers of genuine stature. Moreover, if he seemed at times to be attempting to improve on the legendary ingenuity of Philadelphia lawyers, one must remember that Lincoln practiced within the framework of a time when Illinois law was still in its swaddling clothes, and the eventual outcome of a case was anyone's guess. Under those circumstances, functioning in a virtual statutory and decisional vacuum, Lincoln could hardly be blamed for taking his best shots (such as they were) and hoping for the best. (One is here reminded that, in this present age of legal sophistication, some quite distinguished lawyers have, often with conspicuous success, given voice to arguments equally weird, thus confirming the belief of many that the law is, to quote Dickens, an ass.)

It seems to the writer that historians have largely overlooked the importance of Lincoln's career at the bar, in many ways the most vital and significant part of the Lincoln story, in connection with his preparation for the great task which lay ahead. It was as a lawyer that he developed the judgment, the lucidity of expression and the unforgettable prose of our most eloquent President, one who wrote his own speeches and his own state papers. As wartime President, dealing with difficult individuals and even more difficult problems, Lincoln drew on all the craftiness which he had acquired in years of practice in the Illinois courts, and all the uncommon common sense of the prairie lawyer. While law was not his exclusive mistress, he devoted himself to her with assiduity, and his legal experience was an important asset in meeting the challenge of secession and war.

From 1837 to 1860 Lincoln was a practicing lawyer, one who faced and matched wits with thousands of witnesses, drawn from every segment of the community, and whose trials must number in the thousands. The gaunt Springfield lawyer with the tall top hat, old shawl draped about his shoulders, his head bowed in thought, who walked brooding through a cold and drizzly February rain to the Springfield depot of the Great Western Railroad as the journey to Washington began, had accumulated a vast knowledge of the ways of the human race, gleaned through almost a quarter of a century of practice at the Illinois bar. The law years were truly the most critical and the most important period of the life which carried him to the White House.

How very odd that his biographers, generally speaking, should not have sensed the law's tremendous influence upon his every act as President. The ability to create the immortal utterance at Gettysburg, the first and second inaugural addresses, and all the wonderfully expressive state papers with which his name is associated—literary masterpieces which will endure for all time—sprang in large part from his training in the law, which gave him the ability to think and write with precision. The knowledge of men and laws which he acquired in the practice of the law was repeatedly applied by him in administering the affairs of the government in the trying years of the nation's great crisis, when delicate legal and Constitutional questions were constantly presenting themselves for consideration. The importance of Lincoln's legal training in enabling him to meet significant Constitutional issues—the legal effect of the Emancipation Proclamation, the justification for conscription in advance of Congressional action, the problem of the conscientious objector, the matter of censorship, the use of martial law, and all the other potentially explosive questions of governmental powers in time of war—cannot be overstated. Though on occasion he may have deviated, for the most part his disciplined legal mind and lawyerlike prudence sustained the forces of reason in preventing the extreme use of power. Finally, it must always be remembered that it was Lincoln, the lawyer, who argued so cogently the indissoluble nature of the compact between the states. Few lawyer-statesmen, in Lincoln's or any other age, have had a more vital conception of the law, and in a real sense he was a great lawyer.

7.

Good Friday, April 14, 1865, was a gentle spring day. Late that afternoon Mr. and Mrs. Lincoln went for a ride in an open barouche driven by a team of matched black mares. The President, though tired, was in relaxed good humor. Gone were the cares of war. Though the task of reconstruction lay ahead, he had a vision of a generous peace that would help mightily in the process. With completion of his term of office, they would perhaps take a trip to Europe, after which "We will go back to Illinois, and I will open a law office at Springfield or Chicago, and practice law, and at least do enough to help give us a livelihood."[34] While they talked of a future that wasn't to be, a demented actor was surveying the layout of the State Box at Ford's Theatre.

NOTES

CHAPTER I

1. David C. Mearns, Arthur Bestor and Jonathan Daniels, *Three Presidents and Their Books* (Urbana, Ill., 1951), p. 58.
2. Isaac N. Phillips to James R. B. Van Cleave, Secretary Lincoln Centennial Ass'n., Apr. 26, 1909. Van Cleave Papers, Illinois State Hist. Lib., Springfield, Ill.
3. Herndon memorandum, Charleston, Ill., Sep. 8, 1865, copy Lamon MSS, referred to in David Donald, *Lincoln's Herndon* (New York, 1948), fn. p. 177.
4. William H. Herndon and Jesse W. Weik, *Herndon's Lincoln: The True Story of a Great Life*, Angle ed. (Cleveland, 1949), hereafter cited as *Herndon's Lincoln*, p. 40.
5. Jesse W. Weik, *The Real Lincoln: A Portrait* (Boston, 1922), p. 130.
6. Albert J. Beveridge, *Abraham Lincoln 1809–1858* (Boston and New York, 1928), I, p. 74.
7. *Herndon's Lincoln*, p. 40.
8. Emanuel Hertz, *The Hidden Lincoln:* From the Letters and Papers of William H. Herndon (New York, 1938), p. 177.
9. Thomas Ford, *History of Illinois* (Chicago, 1854), p. 82.
10. John L. Scripps to Herndon, June 24, 1865, *Herndon-Weik Coll.*, Lib. of Cong.
11. William E. Barton, "The Influence of Illinois in the Development of Abraham Lincoln," *Transactions* of the Illinois State Hist. Soc., 1921, p. 37.
12. Though it is perhaps an irrelevance, it is interesting to note that, for all that he was lacking the respectable parchment, Lincoln was honored with an honorary degree by Knox College in July, 1860. Columbia College followed in June, 1861 and the College of New Jersey (Princeton) in Dec., 1861.
13. R. B. Rutledge to Herndon, Nov. 18, 1866. Hertz, *The Hidden Lincoln*, p. 318.
14. *The Collected Works of Abraham Lincoln*, Roy P. Basler, ed., Marion

Dolores Pratt and Lloyd A. Dunlap, asst. eds. (New Brunswick, N.J., 1953), VI, p. 392. This work is hereafter referred to as *Collected Works*.

15. See, post, p. 125, for reference to Lincoln's summation in *Case* v. *Snow Brothers*.

16. Thomas P. Reep, *Lincoln at New Salem* (Petersburg, Ill., 1927), p. 64.

17. *Sangamon Co. Circuit Court, Record* A, pp. 139, 178–9.

18. The "Deep Snow" commenced some time between Christmas and New Year's Day, 1831, with a one-foot fall in the central part of Illinois, followed by rain, which, freezing, caused a firm covering of ice to form. This was followed by another fall of snow of several inches. Two weeks of sub-zero cold caused the whole to form a solid mass which, as Lincoln wrote in his *Autobiography*, failed to melt until "about the first of March, 1831."

19. Harry E. Pratt, "The Genesis of Lincoln the Lawyer," *Bulletin* No. 57 (Sep., 1939) of the Abraham Lincoln Ass'n., p. 9.

20. Benjamin P. Thomas, *Lincoln's New Salem*, rev. ed. (New York, 1954), p. 94.

21. Photostat, and permission to use same, kindly furnished the writer by James T. Hickey, of Elkhart, Ill., owner of original document.

22. Taken from speech of Edward D. Baker, made in reply to Judah P. Benjamin's speech on the right of secession, Jan. 2–3, 1861. *Journal* of the Illinois State Hist. Soc., Summer, 1954, p. 189.

23. George Alexander Dupuy, "The Earliest Courts of the Illinois Country," *Transactions* of the Illinois State Hist. Soc., 1906, pp. 47–8.

24. Harry E. Pratt, "The Genesis of Lincoln the Lawyer," *Bulletin* No. 57 (Sep., 1939) of the Abraham Lincoln Ass'n., p. 6.

25. *Sangamo Journal*, Feb. 18, 1842, referred to in Harry E. Pratt, *Lincoln Day-by-Day 1840–1846*, entry of Feb. 15, 1842, p. 112.

26. A related and long entrenched inaccuracy of popular tradition has been the notion that the edition of the *Commentaries* supposedly yielded up by the barrel of junk was responsible for Lincoln's resolve to make law his life's calling.

27. Original volume, with Lincoln's corrections, in Illinois State Hist. Lib.

28. Lincoln to James T. Thornton, Dec. 2, 1858. *Collected Works*, III, p. 344. Original in Illinois State Hist. Lib.

29. Lincoln to J. M. Brockman, Sep. 25, 1860. *Collected Works*, IV, p. 121.

30. Lincoln to Richard S. Thomas, June 27, 1850. *Collected Works*, II, p. 80.

31. The practice, which grew up among lawyers, of carrying legal papers in their hats continued, in some parts of the country, long after Lincoln's time.

32. Thomas, *Lincoln's New Salem*, p. 68.

33. *Herndon's Lincoln*, p. 96.
34. *Ibid.*, p. 96.
35. Helen Nicolay, *Personal Traits of Abraham Lincoln* (New York, 1939), p. 82.
36. *Collected Works*, I, p. 51. Original in Illinois State Historical Library.
37. Marquis James, *The Life of Andrew Jackson* (Garden City, N.Y., 1940), p. 612.

CHAPTER II

1. *Collected Works*, IV, pp. 60, 64–5.
2. Harry E. Pratt, "The Genesis of Lincoln the Lawyer," *Bulletin* No. 57 of the Abraham Lincoln Ass'n., Sep. 1939.
3. Herndon to Jesse W. Weik, Jan. 7, 1886, *The Hidden Lincoln:* From the Letters and Papers of William H. Herndon (New York, 1938), p. 126.
4. After the expiration of the twenty-one-year period stipulated in the deed of gift, the *Robert Todd Lincoln Collection* was, on July 26, 1947, opened to the American public.
5. William Dean Howells, *Life of Lincoln*, p. 48.
6. Bloomington *Pantagraph*, Feb. 6, 1886, p. 60, col. 2, clipping in *Leonard Swett Scrapbook*, in Illinois State Hist. Lib.
7. Jesse W. Weik, *The Real Lincoln* (Cambridge, Mass., 1922), p. 130.
8. Pratt, "The Genesis of Lincoln the Lawyer," *Bulletin* No. 57 of the Abraham Lincoln Ass'n., Sep. 1939.
9. "Judge Scott," cited in George Alexander Dupuy, "The Earliest Courts of the Illinois Country," Publication No. 11, *Transactions* of the Illinois State Hist. Soc. (1906), p. 45.
10. David Donald, *Lincoln's Herndon* (New York, 1948), pp. 357–9.
11. *Herndon's Lincoln*, p. 270.
12. *The Hidden Lincoln:* From the Letters and Papers of William H. Herndon (New York, 1938), p. 425.
13. Gibson W. Harris, "My Recollections of Abraham Lincoln," *Farm and Fireside*, Dec. 1, 1904.
14. William E. Baringer, *Lincoln's Vandalia* (New Brunswick, N.J., 1949), p. 31.
15. Thomas Lippincott's Recollections, Alton *Telegraph*, Mar. 17, 1865, cited in Baringer, *Lincoln's Vandalia*, p. 22.
16. Scripps "Autobiography," *Collected Works*, IV, p. 65.
17. *Herndon's Lincoln*, note, p. 145.
18. Robert was admitted to the Illinois bar on Feb. 25, 1867.
19. Mary Painter Randall, *Lincoln's Sons* (Boston, 1955), pp. 62, 177; *The Magazine of History with Notes and Queries*, v. 34, No. 1, extra no. 133, Lincoln No. 31, 1927, p. 57; The New York *Herald Tribune*, July 27, 1926, p. 5, col. 4.

20. Frederick T. Hill, *Lincoln the Lawyer* (New York, 1906), p. 59.
21. Paul M. Angle, *One Hundred Years of Law* (Springfield, Ill., 1928), p. 38.

CHAPTER III

1. Sep. 23, 1847, the name became *Illinois Journal*.
2. Actually, the office was situated directly over No. 5 Hoffman's Row, temporarily used as the circuit courthouse, though entrance to the building housing the Stuart & Lincoln office was only to be had through No. 4. See Angle, "Where Lincoln Practiced Law," *Lincoln Centennial Association Papers*, 1927, pp. 26–7.
3. Christopher C. Brown, "Major John T. Stuart," *Transactions* of the Illinois State Hist. Soc., 1902, pp. 111–2.
4. *Ibid.*, p. 112.
5. *History of Christian County* (Brink, McDonough Co., Philadelphia, 1880), p. 59.
6. *Collected Works*, I, p. 78.
7. "It would astonish . . . the older citizens to learn that I (a stranger, friendless, uneducated, penniless boy, working on a flatboat at ten dollars per month) have been put down here as the candidate of pride, wealth, and aristocratic family distinction. Yet so . . . it was." Lincoln to Martin S. Morris, Springfield, Ill., Mar. 26, 1843. *Collected Works*, I, p. 320.
8. Charles H. Coleman, "Spelling Bothered Lincoln, Too," *Journal* of the Illinois State Hist. Soc., Winter 1956, pp. 409, 410.
9. *Ibid.*, p. 408.
10. *Herndon's Lincoln*, p. 252.
11. David C. Mearns, *The Lincoln Papers* (New York, 1948), I, p. 38.
12. This book was retained by Lincoln upon the termination of his partnership with Stuart. When he went to Washington in 1861, he left it behind, in the office which he and Herndon had occupied. It remained there until 1877, when Herndon temporarily gave up his law practice, at which time it came into the possession of Alfred Orendorff, with whom Herndon had been associated. Upon the latter's death it became the property of his daughter, Mrs. Edna Orendorff Macpherson. Harry E. Pratt, *The Personal Finances of Abraham Lincoln* (Springfield, Ill., 1943), p. 26.
13. Joseph Gillespie, "Recollections of Early Illinois and Her Noted Men," 21 (*Fergus Historical Series*, 13).
14. Original in Illinois State Hist. Lib., having been among the extensive collection of Lincoln autographs which were transferred to the Library by the Abraham Lincoln Association in 1952.
15. The present whereabouts of the original complaint in the action are unknown, though it was apparently in existence in 1926 when the late

Albert J. Beveridge, discussing it, wrote: "It is curious that the bill is in three separate and distinct handwritings of which but six and one half lines—the description of the land by metes and bounds—are that of Lincoln, although there are eight pages of the bill." Beveridge, *Abraham Lincoln,* I, p. 214.

16. *Sangamon County Circuit Court, Record H,* p. 219.
17. Alton *Telegraph,* Aug. 26, 1843.
18. *Sangamo Journal,* Aug. 12, 1837.

CHAPTER IV

1. Moses Coit Tyler, writing in the New York *Independent,* Mar. 19, 1868.
2. James G. Randall, *Lincoln the President* (New York, 1945), I, p. 34.
3. *Sangamo Journal,* Mar. 17, 1838.
4. *Ibid.,* Jan. 27, 1838.
5. John M. Palmer, *The Bench and Bar of Illinois* (Chicago, 1899), I, p. 175.
6. *Ibid.,* p. 173.
7. George R. Gaylor, "The Mormons and Politics in Illinois: 1839–1844," Spring 1956 *Journal* of the Illinois State Hist. Soc., p. 56, citing Linn, *Story of the Mormons,* p. 247, and Smith, *History of the Church,* V, p. 95.
8. *Record D, Sangamon County,* 1838–1839, p. 95.
9. *Ibid.,* p. 74.
10. The list of Lincoln's applications for a continuance is long. There was, for example, the case of *People* v. *Samuel Brown,* involving an alleged assault with a deadly weapon, to wit, a gun. The defendant, hearing a rustling sound in his watermelon patch one night, ran out of his house and, firing a shot in the direction of the noise, struck the complainant. The indictment was pending in the Christian Circuit Court for over two years when, on Nov. 15, 1852, the state's attorney *nolle prossed* it. In the interim, Lincoln had obtained at least five continuances. (He was obliged to bring suit for his fee of ten dollars in this case.)
11. Photostat kindly furnished by Illinois State Hist. Lib., where original bill, in Lincoln's handwriting, may be seen.
12. Springfield *Republican,* clipped to the Peoria *Register and North-Western Gazetteer,* Oct. 30, 1838.
13. See, for example, statement in the Lincoln sketch in the *Dictionary of American Biography* (Vol. XI, p. 246) that Lincoln would "refuse to accept questionable cases" . . . where "his client's cause was unjust."
14. *Pearl* v. *Wellman,* 11 Ill. 352 (1849).
15. Photostat of motion to quash, in Lincoln's handwriting, in Illinois State Hist. Lib.

16. *The Hidden Lincoln,* p. 330.
17. *Daily Chicago American,* Apr. 18, 1840.
18. *Ibid.*

CHAPTER V

1. "Leonard Swett's Oration on the Life of the Late Judge Dickey," Chicago *Times,* May 10,1887. Clipping in *Leonard Swett Scrapbook,* Illinois State Hist. Lib.
2. Carthage *Journal,* Feb. 12, 1953.
3. Henry C. Whitney, *Life on the Circuit with Lincoln* (Caldwell, Ohio, 1940), pp. 43, 91. The old courthouse is now located in Fairview Park, Decatur.
4. *Rip Van Winkle, the Autobiography of Joseph Jefferson,* rev. ed. (New York, 1949), p. 23.
5. *Ibid.,* p. 23.
6. *Ibid.,* p. 24.
7. Paul M. Angle, *Here I Have Lived* (New Brunswick, 1935), p. 100.
8. Harry E. Pratt, "Lincoln and Douglas as Counsel on the Same Side," American Bar Association *Journal,* March, 1940.
9. From the original "Verdict of the Jury upon a Corroners inquest," dated April 18, 1840, found among the papers in the file of the case. Photostat in Illinois State Hist. Lib.
10. Photostat in Illinois State Hist. Lib.
11. Palmer, *The Bench and Bar of Illinois,* I, p. 174.
12. Frederic B. Crossley, *Courts and Lawyers of Illinois* (Chicago, 1916), II, p. 787.
13. *Journal* of the House of Representatives of the Twelfth General Assembly, pp. 10–11.
14. David Rankin Barbee to Harry E. Pratt, Feb. 9, 1934, in Illinois State Hist. Lib.
15. David Rankin Barbee, of the Washington *Post,* Washington, D.C., to A. H. Upham, Jan. 8, 1932. Copy in Illinois State Hist. Lib.
16. Amusing proof of the fact that not only Whigs and Republicans took their politics seriously, but Democrats, too, may be seen in the village of Carlock, in McLean County, Illinois, where, turning off U.S. Route 150, just east of the Congregational Church, one comes upon the Republican Cemetery first, and, a quarter of a mile up the road, the Democratic Cemetery, both established in Lincoln's time.
17. Emanuel Hertz, *The Hidden Lincoln* (New York, 1938), p. 112.

CHAPTER VI

1. *Herndon's Lincoln,* p. 209.
2. J. O. Cunningham, "Some Facts in the Judicial History of Illinois," *Transactions* of the Illinois State Hist. Soc., 1902, p. 98.

3. Charles C. Chapman, *County History of Tazewell County* (Chicago, 1879), p. 385.
4. *Herndon's Lincoln*, p. 209.
5. *Memorials of the Life and Character of Stephen T. Logan*. 1882. H. W. Rokker, Springfield, Ill., Printer and Binder, p. 18.
6. *The Hidden Lincoln*, From the Letters and Papers of William H. Herndon, p. 430.
7. Interview with J. H. Matheny, unidentified newspaper clipping in *Pasfield Scrapbook*, in Illinois State Hist. Lib., p. 37.
8. *Ibid.*, p. 37.
9. Mason H. Newell, "The Attorney-Generals of Illinois," *Transactions* of the Illinois State Hist. Soc. (1903), pp. 211, 218.
10. Quincy *Whig*, April 15, 1846; *Collected Works*, I, p. 373.
11. Usher F. Linder, *Reminiscences of the Early Bench and Bar of Illinois* (Chicago, 1879), p. 259.
12. From unidentified newspaper clipping in *Pasfield Scrapbook*, Illinois State Hist. Lib.
13. *Journal* of the Illinois State Hist. Soc., Oct., 1926, p. 170.
14. Harry E. Pratt, *The Personal Finances of Abraham Lincoln* (Springfield, Ill., 1943), pp. 31–32.
15. *Herndon's Lincoln*, p. 261.
16. Pratt, *The Personal Finances of Abraham Lincoln*, p. 31.
17. Bill of Exceptions, Tazewell Circuit Court.
18. *Ibid.*
19. In discussing the case, the writer has relied on two main sources—the Alton *Telegraph and Democratic Review* of Jan. 14, 1843, and Harry E. Pratt's illuminating article, "In Defense of Mr. Justice Browne" (*Bulletin* No. 56 Abraham Lincoln Association, June 1939). The *Sangamo Journal* of Jan. 12, 1843 carried an account of the trial, as well as an editorial on it. Other newspaper sources consulted were the *Illinois State Register* of Jan. 6 and Feb. 10, 1843, the *Sangamo Journal* of Jan. 5, 1843 and the Quincy *Whig* of Jan. 18, 1843.
20. *Illinois State Register*, Jan. 6, 1843.
21. *Sangamo Journal*, Jan. 12, 1843.
22. Affidavit of Bennett Abelle, in file of case, in Illinois State Hist. Lib.
23. Original jury verdict in file of case.
24. From file of case.
25. *Cabot* v. *Regnier*, 2 Gilman 34.
26. S. C. Parks to Herndon, Mar. 25, 1866. *Herndon-Weik Coll.*, Lib. of Cong.
27. Benjamin P. Thomas, *Lincoln's New Salem*, p. 47.
28. *Ibid.*, p. 18.
29. *Ibid.*, p. 47.
30. Photostatic copy of letter in Illinois State Hist. Lib.

31. *Records,* County Commissioners Court; David McCulloch, *History of Peoria County* (1902), p. 95.
32. Hertz, *The Hidden Lincoln,* p. 172.
33. *Herndon's Lincoln,* ed's note, p. 210.
34. 2 Gilman 47.

CHAPTER VII

1. "I generally say what I feel." Herndon to Lyman Trumbull, Mar. 4, 1857. *Lyman Trumbull Mss.,* Lib. of Cong.
2. *Herndon's Lincoln,* p. 211.
3. Herndon to Weik, Feb. 24, 1887. *Herndon-Weik Coll.,* Lib. of Cong.
4. *Illinois State Journal,* Sep. 24, 1883.
5. Original letter in Illinois State Hist. Lib.
6. *Illinois State Journal,* Nov. 16, 17, 1866.
7. The incredible quantity of hard liquor consumed was a startling feature of American public life during most of the nineteenth century. Drunkenness in Congress was so common that leaders found it hard to keep intoxicated members off the floor.
8. Thomas, *Abraham Lincoln,* p. 97.
9. Whitney, *Life on the Circuit with Lincoln,* p. 405.
10. *Herndon's Lincoln,* p. 239.
11. Joseph Gillespie to Herndon, Jan. 31, 1866. *Herndon-Weik Coll.,* Lib. of Cong. "He was the most indulgent parent I ever knew. His children litterally [sic] ran over him and he was powerless to withstand their importunities."
12. *Herndon's Lincoln,* p. 344.
13. Herndon to Weik, Nov. 19, 1885. Emanuel Hertz, *The Hidden Lincoln* (New York, 1938), p. 105.
14. *Herndon's Lincoln,* p. 256.
15. *Ibid.,* p. 268.
16. Albert J. Brooks to Lincoln, Dec. 16, 1858. *Robert Todd Lincoln Coll.,* Lib. of Cong.
17. Herndon to Henry Enoch Dummer, Apr. 11, 1847. *Dummer Mss.,* Illinois State Hist. Lib.
18. Herndon to Theodore Parker, Apr. 27, 1858 and Jan. 15, 1859. *Herndon-Parker Mss.,* Univ. of Iowa Lib., Iowa City.
19. Ralph G. Lindstrom, foreword to "Sifting the Herndon Sources," by Louis A. Warren (Lincoln Fellowship of Southern California, 1948).
20. Joseph Fort Newton, *Lincoln and Herndon* (Cedar Rapids, Iowa, 1910), pp. 252–3.
21. Quoted in Newton, *Lincoln and Herndon,* pp. 252–3.
22. Newton, *Lincoln and Herndon,* p. 252; interview of Weik with John C. Lanphier, Mar. 8, 1925, *Herndon-Weik Coll.,* Lib. of Cong.
23. Hertz, *The Hidden Lincoln,* p. 208.

24. David Donald, *Lincoln's Herndon*, p. 202.
25. Hertz notes on contents of "The Jesse W. Weik Collection of Lincoln Documents & Manuscripts." Copy in Illinois State Hist. Lib.
26. David Donald, *Lincoln's Herndon*, p. 13.
27. *Ibid.*, p. 13.
28. "Big Me," *Herndon Autobiography, Herndon-Weik Coll.*, Lib. of Cong.
29. Gibson W. Harris, "My Recollections of Abraham Lincoln," *Farm and Fireside*, Dec. 1, 1904.
30. Paul M. Angle, "Where Lincoln Practiced Law," *Lincoln Centennial Papers*, 1927, p. 32.
31. Herndon to Weik, Feb. 24, 1887. *Herndon-Weik Coll.*, Lib. of Cong.
32. Herndon to "Friend Weik," Oct. 21, 1885, Hertz, *The Hidden Lincoln*, p. 95.
33. Hertz, *The Hidden Lincoln*, p. 212.
34. Harry E. Pratt, "The Lincolns Go Shopping," Spring 1955 *Journal* of the Illinois State Hist. Soc., p. 68.
35. Frederick Trevor Hill, *Lincoln the Lawyer* (New York, 1906), p. 124.
36. Harry E. Pratt, "The Lincolns Go Shopping," Spring 1955 *Journal* of the Illinois State Hist. Soc., p. 68.
37. *Ibid.*, p. 68.
38. *Marine Bank Ledger;* also Angle, *The Marine Bank, the Story of the Oldest Bank in Illinois*, p. 12.
39. *Herndon's Lincoln*, p. 254.
40. Herndon to Weik, Oct. 29, 1885, *Herndon-Weik Coll.;* Hertz, *The Hidden Lincoln*, p. 97.
41. Newton, *Lincoln and Herndon*, p. 139.
42. *Ibid.*, p. 144.

CHAPTER VIII

1. J. R. Stewart, *History of Champaign County*, I, p. 179.
2. *Record*, Champaign Circuit Court.
3. Pratt, *Lincoln Day-by-Day 1840–1846*, p. 284.
4. Palmer, *The Bench and Bar of Illinois*, II, p. 627.
5. *Ibid.*
6. *Collected Works*, I, p. 371. As pointed out by the editors, Lincoln's authorship of the narrative, published anonymously, was well known.
7. *Lincoln File*, Menard County Circuit Court.
8. Paul M. Angle, "Abraham Lincoln: Circuit Lawyer," *Lincoln Centennial Papers*, 1928, p. 35.
9. Ida M. Tarbell, "Lincoln as a Lawyer," *McClure's Magazine*, July, 1896, p. 176.
10. Gibson W. Harris, "My Recollections of Abraham Lincoln," *Farm and Fireside*, Dec. 1, 1904.

11. Whitney, *Life on the Circuit with Lincoln*, p. 54.

12. Harry E. Pratt, "Lincoln in Bloomington," *Journal* of the Illinois State Hist. Soc., April 1936, p. 49.

13. See Osborne H. Oldroyd, ed., *The Lincoln Memorial Album Immortelles* (New York, 1882), pp. 187-9.

14. George W. Minier, Statement, April 10, 1882, *Herndon's Lincoln*, p. 492.

15. Lincoln to Samuel D. Marshall, Dec. 30, 1845, *Collected Works*, I, p. 352. Original in Illinois State Historical Library.

16. 11 Ill. 352.

17. 4 Ill. 26-28.

18. Original requests for instructions in Sangamon County Circuit Court. From photostat in files of Abraham Lincoln Ass'n., now in Illinois State Hist. Lib.

19. *Chicago Journal*, July 6, 1847.

20. From Seventieth Anniversary Brochure issued by the Rock Island Railroad, 1852-1922, marking celebration of seventy years of service, and containing an account of Lincoln's connection with the case, p. 19.

CHAPTER IX

1. *Circuit Court Record*, II, pp. 191, 196.

2. Henry C. Whitney, *Life on the Circuit with Lincoln*, fn. p. 315. Note by the editor, Paul M. Angle.

3. O. B. Ficklin, "A Pioneer Lawyer," *Tuscola* (Illinois) *Review*, Sep. 7, 1922, being reprint of an article which appeared in a Charleston newspaper of Jan. 15, 1885.

4. There is some question whether Bryant had secured the requisite "certificate of freedom," so in a technical sense he may still have been a slave.

5. Matson was arrested "on a charge of living in an open state of fornication with Marie Corbin." Original warrant in *Herndon-Weik Coll.*

6. It is of interest to note that Rutherford was Matson's physician for about two years, 1841-1843. *Journal* of the Illinois State Hist. Soc., Summer 1952, p. 169.

7. *Willard* v. *The People*, 5 Ill. 469.

8. The Illinois "Black Laws," enacted for the purpose of discouraging the presence of Negroes in Illinois, were not repealed until 1865.

9. Original writ of *habeas corpus*, and petition on which same was issued, are to be found in the *Herndon-Weik Coll.* (Item 1957).

10. From Order, dated Aug. 20, 1847. Beveridge, *Abraham Lincoln*, I, fn. p. 393.

11. Petition for writ in handwriting of Ficklin.

12. The Bryants, meanwhile, had been held in custody of the sheriff, whose bill to Matson for "keeping and dieting five Negroes forty-eight days at 37 cents each per day" is in the *Herndon-Weik Coll.* (Item 1958).

13. O. B. Ficklin, "A Pioneer Lawyer," *Tuscola Review*.

14. *Coles Co. Circuit Court Record*, II, pp. 167, 195; Thomas, *Lincoln Day-by-Day 1847–1853*, p. 42; *Herndon-Weik Coll.* The latter contains a written argument, in Lincoln's hand, for use in connection with a slander action in Coles County. The paper contains copious extracts from *Greenleaf on Evidence*. Though the names of the parties do not appear, it was probably written by Lincoln in preparation for the trial of this case.

15. *Coles Co. Circuit Court Record*, II, pp. 189, 196. In the *Herndon-Weik Coll.* is to be found the declaration, in Lincoln's handwriting.

16. According to Mrs. Amanda Hanks Poorman, daughter of Dennis Hanks, however, "In the spring of the year, when court was to be in session a week in Charleston, we always looked forward to the coming of Uncle Abe, who would be at our home and spend the week there, giving his days to his work in the court room and giving his nights to us in our home." Article appearing in St. Louis *Post-Dispatch,* May 26, 1901, clipping in *Joseph Wallace Scrapbook*, in Illinois State Hist. Lib. Mrs. Poorman was born in 1833, and hence was eight years old when Lincoln commenced to attend at the Coles Circuit Court in 1841. After sixty years, her recollection may have gained something in the telling.

17. In March, 1863, while a judge of the circuit court, Constable was arrested at Charleston by the Federal authorities, because of his obstructionist action in releasing four deserters and holding in bail, on a kidnapping charge, two Union officers who had arrested them. Though he was subsequently released by Judge Treat of the United States District Court at Springfield, the affair proved one of the contributing causes of the Charleston riot.

18. Lincoln remarked to Joshua Speed, Aug. 24, 1855: "I think I am a Whig; but others say there are no Whigs. . . ." *Collected Works*, II, pp. 322–23.

19. Beveridge, *Abraham Lincoln*, I, p. 394.

20. See letter, A. Lincoln to T. R. Webber, Sep. 12, 1853, *Collected Works*, II, p. 202; also, letter, A. Lincoln to Mason Brayman, Oct. 3, 1853, *Ibid.*, p. 205.

21. Donald, *Lincoln's Herndon*, p. 43.

22. There was a third appearance for Matson in the person of Thomas A. Marshall, attorney and banker of Charleston, who apparently only sat in on the case, taking no part in the oral argument. *Herndon-Weik Coll.* (Item 1951).

23. Sep. 18, 1858. Charleston is also known to history for the riot of Mar. 28, 1864 involving Copperheads and Union soldiers on furlough. See Charles H. Coleman and Paul H. Spence, "The Charleston Riot, March 28, 1864," *Journal* of the Illinois State Hist. Soc., March 1940, pp. 7–56.

24. Beveridge, *Abraham Lincoln*, I, p. 396.

25. Woldman, *Lawyer Lincoln*, p. 64.

26. *Ibid.*, p. 197.

27. Ficklin, "A Pioneer Lawyer," *Tuscola Review*.

28. A notable exception to the general avoidance of the article is Charles H. Coleman, *Abraham Lincoln and Coles County, Illinois* (New York, 1955), pp. 107–8.

29. Beveridge, *Abraham Lincoln*, I, p. 396.

30. T. Harry Williams, *Lincoln and His Generals* (New York, 1952), Preface, vii.

31. *Beveridge Papers*, Lib. of Cong.

32. John M. Zane, "Lincoln the Constitutional Lawyer," *Papers* of the Abraham Lincoln Association, 1932, fn. p. 29.

33. James T. Jones to James R. E. Van Cleave, July 6, 1908. *Van Cleave Coll.*, Illinois State Hist. Lib.

34. *Circuit Court Record*, II, p. 191. The order was dated Oct. 16, 1847. The case is not officially cited, for the reason that circuit court rulings were not published.

35. Jesse W. Weik, "Lincoln and the Matson Negroes," *Arena Magazine*, April, 1897, p. 757.

36. *Ibid.*, p. 758.

37. Paul M. Angle, "Aftermath of the Matson Slave Case," *The Abraham Lincoln Quarterly* (The Abraham Lincoln Assn., Springfield, Ill.), II (June 1944), pp. 147–8.

38. Whitney, *Life on the Circuit with Lincoln*, p. 124.

39. Beveridge, *Abraham Lincoln*, I, p. 395.

40. Woldman, *Lawyer Lincoln*, p. 65. The same writer speaks of "Lincoln's fidelity to the Constitution, which he was to display in the crucial days of the Civil War. . . ." *Ibid.*, p. 73.

41. Wendell Phillips remarked that Lincoln took about two months to abolish *habeas corpus*, but almost two years to abolish slavery.

42. April 18, 1861.

43. James G. Randall, *Constitutional Problems Under Lincoln*, rev. ed. (Urbana, Ill., 1951), Foreword, xxv.

44. Thomas, *Abraham Lincoln*, p. 112; Thomas, *Lincoln Day-by-Day*, 1847–1853, x.

45. From photostat of letter, Lincoln to Morris & Brown, Oct. 19, 1847, in Illinois State Hist. Lib. See *Collected Works*, I, p. 405.

46. First Inaugural Address.

47. *Collected Works*, I, p. 407.

CHAPTER X

1. Wilhelmus Bogart Bryan, *History of the National Capitol*, I, p. 295.

2. Allen Thorndike Rice, *Reminiscences of Abraham Lincoln by Distinguished Men of His Time*, New York, 1888, p. 16.

3. Lincoln to Herndon, Dec. 5, 1847. *Collected Works,* I, pp. 416–7.
4. Lincoln to Herndon, Dec. 13, 1847. *Collected Works,* I, p. 420.
5. Brooklyn *Daily Eagle,* Dec. 2, 1847, Whitman, "The Gathering Forces." See Bernard DeVoto, *The Year of Decision: 1846.*
6. *Herndon's Lincoln,* p. 233.
7. 7 Howard 776.
8. It was not until Feb., 1925 that Congress, in passing the Jurisdictional Act of that year, limited the right of appeal to those cases deemed by the Court worthy of review on writ of certiorari.
9. The membership of the Court was increased from seven to nine justices shortly after Taney took over as Chief Justice.
10. In 1856 Lincoln was favorably disposed toward the then seventy-one-year-old McLean for the presidency. See letter, Lincoln to Lyman Trumbull, June 7, 1856, *Collected Works,* II, pp. 342–3.
11. 13 Peters 57.
12. 15 Howard 350.
13. In Ruth Painter Randall's *Lincoln's Sons* (Boston, 1955), there is an interesting reference (page 20) to the fact that Robert recalled visiting the Patent Office on Sundays with his father during the period of the latter's service in Congress.
14. Lincoln to Benjamin Kellogg, Jr., Apr. 21, 1848, *Collected Works,* I, pp. 466–7. Original in Illinois State Hist. Lib.
15. Lincoln to Amos Williams, Dec. 8, 1848, *Collected Works,* II, pp. 14–15.
16. *Miller* v. *Whittaker,* 23 Ill. 453.
17. When Zane withdrew from the Herndon partnership in 1868, Alfred Orendorff, who was born in Logan County in 1845, became a partner of Herndon's, a relation that was maintained for fifteen years.
18. From Charles S. Zane, "Lincoln As I Knew Him," *Sunset Magazine,* v. 29, Oct. 1912, pp. 430–8, reprinted in *Journal* of the Illinois State Hist. Soc., v. 14, April–July, 1921, pp. 75–6.
19. Stephen R. Capps to James R. B. Van Cleave, Sec. Lincoln Centennial Ass'n., Springfield, Ill., July 17, 1908. *Van Cleave Papers,* Illinois State Hist. Lib.
20. Harry E. Pratt, "Albert Taylor Bledsoe: Critic of Lincoln." *Transactions* of the Illinois State Hist. Soc., 1934, pp. 153–83.
21. Roy D. Packard, *The Lincoln of the Thirtieth Congress* (Boston, 1950), p. 41.
22. David Davis to A. Lincoln, Feb. 21, 1849: "My dear Lincoln . . . my advise is worth nothing. Still were I in your place, could I get it, I would take the land office." *Robert Todd Lincoln Coll.*
23. Lincoln to J. M. Lucas, April 25, 1849, *Collected Works,* II, p. 43.
24. Thomas Ewing, "Lincoln and the General Land Office, 1849," *Journal* of the Illinois State Hist. Soc., Oct., 1932, p. 152.

25. *Collected Works*, IV, p. 67.
26. *Herndon's Lincoln*, fn. p. 247.
27. *Ibid.*, p. 247.
28. Interview of Jesse W. Weik with John W. Bunn, Oct. 15, 1914, *Herndon-Weik Coll.*; interview of Clinton L. Conkling with John W. Bunn, Nov., 1917, *C. L. Conkling Mss.*, Ill. State Hist. Lib.; Jesse W. Weik, *The Real Lincoln: A Portrait*, pp. 203–205; Ruth Painter Randall, *Mary Lincoln*, p. 117; Henry B. Rankin, *Intimate Character Sketches of Abraham Lincoln* (Phila. and London, 1924), pp. 64–6.
29. *Herndon's Lincoln*, p. 247.
30. At the March 1850 term 177 cases were docketed. Of these S. T. Logan appeared in 46; Lincoln & Herndon in 35.

CHAPTER XI

1. Thomas, *Portrait for Posterity*, p. 298.
2. John Dean Caton, *Early Bench and Bar of Illinois* (Chicago, 1893), p. 51.
3. Lecture, "Circuit Life With Lincoln," delivered by Leonard Swett in Grow's Opera Hall, Chicago, on Feb. 20, 1876, and reported in the Chicago *Times* Feb. 21, 1876, under the caption "What Leonard Swett Remembers of Life on the Circuit With Lincoln." Clipping in *Leonard Swett Scrapbook*, in Illinois State Hist. Lib.
4. John T. Richards, *Lincoln: the Lawyer-Statesman*, pp. 21–2.
5. "Judge Lawrence Weldon's Personal Recollections of the Great Emancipator," Bloomington *Daily Pantagraph*, July 21, 1882.
6. John T. Richards, Address Delivered Before the Chicago Bar Association, Chicago, Ill., Feb. 11, 1909.
7. *Ibid.*
8. Isaac N. Arnold, *Life of Abraham Lincoln*, p. 84.
9. Linder to Joseph Gillespie, Aug. 8, 1867, *Gillespie Letters*, vol. 14, p. 141, Chicago Hist. Soc.
10. Whitney, *Life on the Circuit with Lincoln*, p. 21.
11. *Ibid.*, p. 53.
12. *Ibid.*, p. 63.
13. Frederick Trevor Hill, *Lincoln the Lawyer* (New York, 1906).
14. Richard N. Current, *The Lincoln Nobody Knows* (New York, 1958), p. 49.
15. Ruth Painter Randall, *Lincoln's Sons* (Boston, 1955), p. 51.
16. Irving Stone, *Clarence Darrow, For the Defense* (New York, 1941), p. 169.
17. The work of marking the circuit and caring for the markers was subsequently taken over by the Lincoln Circuit Marking Association, acting under the auspices of the Daughters of the American Revolu-

tion. The maintenance of the markers has since been assumed by the Department of Highways of the State.

18. At the corner of Second and Jefferson Streets, once the heart of Springfield, stands a marker erected by the Springfield chapter of the Daughters of the American Revolution to mark the site of this first courthouse. The bronze tablet reads: "On this corner was built in 1821 the first Sangamon county courthouse, a log house one story high and 20 feet long, costing $72.50."

19. *History of Sangamon County* (Chicago, 1881), p. 554.

20. *Ibid.*, p. 555.

21. Paul M. Angle, "Where Lincoln Practiced Law," *Lincoln Centennial Papers*, 1927, p. 34.

22. Clipping from Chicago *Times*, June 27, 1886, appearing in *Leonard Swett Scrapbook*, Illinois State Hist. Lib.

23. Herndon to Caton, *John Dean Caton Coll.*, Lib. of Cong.

24. Letter, Beveridge to William E. Barton, Aug. 4, 1924. Copy in *Beveridge Papers*, Lib. of Cong.

25. Harry E. Pratt, "David Davis, 1815–1866," *Transactions* of the Illinois State Hist. Soc., 1930, p. 163.

26. Whitney, *Life on the Circuit with Lincoln*, p. 75.

27. Henry C. Whitney, "Abraham Lincoln: A Study From Life," *The Arena Magazine*, April, 1898, pp. 464, 472.

28. Whitney, *Life on the Circuit with Lincoln*, p. 85.

29. Clipping from Chicago *Times*, June 27, 1886, appearing in *Leonard Swett Scrapbook*, Illinois State Hist. Lib.

30. Henry Clay Tilton, "Lincoln and Lamon: Partners and Friends," *Transactions* of the Illinois State Hist. Soc., 1931, p. 180.

31. *Ibid.*, p. 180.

32. Whitney, *Life on the Circuit with Lincoln*, p. 78.

33. Robert Todd Lincoln to Thomas Dent, Manchester, Vt., Sep. 12, 1919. Referred to in Harry E. Pratt, "Lincoln in Bloomington," *Journal* of the Illinois State Hist. Soc., April 1936, p. 69.

34. Davis to William W. Orme, St. Louis, Mo., Jan. 19, 1861. *Orme Mss.* Illinois State Hist. Soc.

35. George Templeton Strong, the diarist, notes the observation of his father-in-law S. B. Ruggles that "The one consolatory fact connected with Lincoln's death is that he cannot pardon his murderer." *The Diary of George Templeton Strong*, ed. by Allan Nevins and Milton Halsey Thomas (New York, 1952), III, xiv.

36. Whitney, *Life on the Circuit with Lincoln*, p. 75.

37. David Davis to Julius Rockwell, May 14, 1844, in Harry E. Pratt, "David Davis," *Transactions* of the Illinois State Hist. Soc., 1930, pp. 162–3.

38. Gibson W. Harris, *Farm and Fireside*, Dec. 1, 1904.

39. Frank E. Stevens, "Life of Stephen A. Douglas," *Journal* of the Illinois State Hist. Soc., Oct. 1923–Jan. 1924, p. 323.
40. *Ibid.*, p. 324.
41. *Ibid.*, p. 292.
42. *History of Sangamon County* (Chicago, 1881), p. 94.
43. *Record*, Sangamon Circuit Court; Benjamin P. Thomas, *Lincoln Day-by-Day*, 1847–1853, pp. 221–2.

CHAPTER XII

1. It is known that Lincoln owned a buggy as early as 1843.
2. In the Stuart & Lincoln fee book, Lincoln recorded the expenses of a trip to the Tazewell Circuit Court. The total expenditure of $21.82½ was made up as follows: "Road expenses $2.82½; Tavern bill $9.00; Horse hire $10.00."
3. Linder, *Reminiscences of the Early Bench and Bar of Illinois*, p. 183.
4. Pratt, *Lincoln Day-by-Day 1840–1846*, p. 68.
5. Eugenia Jones Hunt, "My Personal Recollections of Abraham Lincoln and Mary Todd Lincoln," *The Abraham Lincoln Quarterly*, March 1945, p. 238.
6. *Record.*
7. The charges, however, were "modest, . . . $2.50 per week for board and lodging, washing and mending included." *The Letters of Robert G. Ingersoll*, ed. by Eva I. Wakefield (New York, 1951), p. 23.
8. "What Leonard Swett Remembers of Life on the Circuit With Lincoln," Chicago *Times*, Feb. 21, 1876.
9. Gibson W. Harris, "My Recollections of Abraham Lincoln," *Farm and Fireside*, Dec. 1, 1904.
10. Statement of E. M. Prince, no date. *Herndon-Weik Coll.*, Lib. of Cong.
11. Hill, *Lincoln the Lawyer*, p. 80.
12. This case is discussed at length in Chapter XVII.
13. Harry E. Pratt, "Abraham Lincoln in Bloomington, Illinois," *Journal* of the Illinois State Hist. Soc., April 1936, p. 61.
14. *Weekly Pantagraph*, July 23, 1897, cited in Pratt, "Abraham Lincoln in Bloomington, Illinois," pp. 47–8.
15. On Feb. 12, 1947 the Library of Congress came into possession of the original manuscript of Lincoln's three-page autobiography written for Fell.
16. Letter, Lyman Burr, Bloomington, Ill. to James R. B. Van Cleave, Jan. 25, 1909. *Van Cleave Papers*, Illinois State Hist. Lib.
17. *Collected Works*, VI, pp. 16–7.
18. *Adams* v. *County of Logan*, 11 Ill. 336.
19. Angle, "Lincoln, Circuit Lawyer," *Lincoln Centennial Association Papers* (1928), p. 38.

20. Lawrence B. Stringer, *History of Logan County, Illinois* (Chicago, 1911), I, p. 220.

21. John M. Palmer, *The Bench and Bar of Illinois*, II, p. 1010.

22. From unidentified newspaper clipping in *James T. Hickey Scrapbook*.

23. Weldon: Rice, p. 201, cited in Beveridge, *Abraham Lincoln*, I, pp. 595–6. The case referred to by Weldon was probably *Allen v. Illinois Central Railroad*, tried March 15, 1859.

24. *Illinois State Register*, May 27, 1854.

25. *Leonard Swett Papers*, Illinois State Hist. Lib.

26. In Urbana is a statue of Lincoln the Young Lawyer, by Lorado Taft.

27. *History of Champaign County*, ed. by Joseph O. Cunningham (Chicago, 1905), II, pp. 731–2.

28. J. R. Stewart, *History of Champaign County*, p. 146.

29. Thomas, *Lincoln Day-by-Day* 1847–1853, p. 335; Pratt, *Personal Finances*, p. 49.

30. Whitney, *Life on the Circuit with Lincoln*, p. 64.

31. Richard F. Lufkin, "Mr. Lincoln's Light From Under a Bushel—1850," *Lincoln Herald*, Dec. 1950, pp. 2, 7.

32. Whitney, *Life on the Circuit with Lincoln*, p. 175.

33. *Ibid.*, p. 174.

34. Jan. 21, 1861, Lamon was succeeded in that office by Joseph G. ("Uncle Joe") Cannon, of Danville, whom many still living recall for his long years of congressional service. He lived far beyond the Biblical three score and ten, to die at ninety-one.

35. Photostat of advertisement appearing in *Iroquois Journal*, of Middleport, July 6, 1853, is in Illinois State Hist. Lib.; referred to in Paul M. Angle, "Abraham Lincoln: Circuit Lawyer," *Lincoln Centennial Papers*, 1928, p. 32; Thomas, *Lincoln Day-by-Day*, 1847–1853, p. 307.

36. John M. Zane, "Lincoln the Constitutional Lawyer," *Papers* of the Abraham Lincoln Association 1932, fn. p. 30.

37. Letter, Jesse W. Weik, Greencastle, Ind. to A. H. Griffith, Fisk, Wis., Mar. 29, 1914. Photostat in "Menard County Folder," in Illinois State Hist. Lib.

38. Lamon to Lincoln, Danville, Nov. 21, 1854. *Robert Todd Lincoln Coll.*, Lib. of Cong.

39. Benjamin P. Thomas, *Portrait for Posterity* (New Brunswick, 1947), p. 30.

40. Whitney, *Life on the Circuit with Lincoln*, p. 238.

41. *Ibid.*, p. 238.

42. Lamon, *Recollections of Lincoln*, p. 18.

43. *Collected Works*, III, p. 494.

44. Pratt, *Personal Finances of Abraham Lincoln*, p. 38.

45. *Record*, Shelby Co. Circuit Court.

46. Oglesby to Palmer, July 8, 1898, Palmer's *Bench and Bar of Illinois*, II, p. 1155.

47. Whitney, *Life on the Circuit with Lincoln*, p. 43; *Transactions McLean County Hist. Soc.*, III, pp. 91–2.

48. At the spring term 1850, Lincoln left the circuit on June 2nd, proceeding directly from Decatur to Springfield, in order to attend the opening of the session of the United States District and Circuit Courts.

49. *History of Christian County*, ed. by Henry L. Fowkes, 2 vols. (Chicago 1918), II, p. 657.

CHAPTER XIII

1. Linder, *Reminiscences of the Early Bench and Bar of Illinois*, p. 215.

2. Quincy *Whig*, Dec. 14, 1839.

3. Angle, *Lincoln Day-by-Day 1854–1861*, pp. 114, 116.

4. Ward H. Lamon, *Recollections of Lincoln*, p. 18.

5. William H. Townsend, *Abraham Lincoln, Defendant* (Boston and New York, 1923), vii.

6. *Collected Works*, II, pp. 332–3.

7. *Lesure & Bliss* v. *County of Menard. File Box No. 38*, County Clerk's Office, Menard County. Cited in Pratt, *Personal Finances of Abraham Lincoln*, p. 37.

8. *Collected Works*, II, p. 325. Original in Illinois State Hist. Lib.

9. From file of photostats of papers taken from Christian County Circuit Court, and now in possession of Illinois State Hist. Lib.

10. The complaint and other papers in the action are to be found in the *Herndon-Weik Coll.*, Lib. of Cong.

11. Original in Illinois State Hist. Lib.

12. *Smith* v. *Smith*, 21 Ill. 244.

13. *Grable* v. *Margrave*, argued July 13, 1842.

14. Lincoln to Samuel D. Marshall, July 14, 1842, *Collected Works*, I, pp. 290–1. Original in Chicago Historical Society.

15. *Collected Works*, II, p. 82, taken from Nicolay and Hay, II, pp. 140–3.

16. *Herndon's Lincoln*, p. 279.

17. *State Archives*, Springfield, Ill.

18. Pratt, *The Personal Finances of Abraham Lincoln*, Foreword, viii.

19. From facsimile of original letter in Illinois State Hist. Lib., *Collected Works*, III, p. 338.

20. Lionel P. Lacey to John Williams, July 27, 1858. *Black-Williams Papers*, Illinois State Hist. Lib.

21. "An Act to Establish a Uniform System of Bankruptcy Throughout the United States." U.S. Statutes at Large, vol. 5, 27th Cong. Sess. I, ch. 9, 1841, pp. 440–9.

22. Advertisement of Levi Davis in *Sangamo Journal*, Aug. 26, 1842, p. 3, col. 6.

23. Harry E. Pratt, "Lincoln and Bankruptcy Law," *Illinois Bar Journal*, Jan., 1953.

24. *Ibid.*

25. *Collected Works*, I, p. 270. Original in Illinois State Hist. Lib.

26. *Ibid.*, I, pp. 285–6.

27. From photostat from Gordon A. Block in Illinois State Hist. Lib.

28. Palmer, *Bench and Bar of Illinois*, II, p. 613.

29. Alton *Telegraph*, Dec. 14, 1844.

30. *Ibid.*

31. Pratt, *Lincoln Day-by-Day*, 1840–1846, p. 260.

32. *Ibid.*, p. 261.

33. Palmer, *Bench and Bar of Illinois*, I, p. 168; *Memorials of the Life and Character of Stephen T. Logan* (Springfield, 1882), p. 30.

34. F. B. Carpenter, *Six Months at the White House with Abraham Lincoln* (New York, 1866), p. 254.

35. *Herndon's Lincoln*, p. 265.

36. *Springfield Register*, Dec. 16, 18, 1851; Thomas, *Lincoln Day-by-Day* 1847–1853, p. 260.

37. 6 McLean 77.

38. *Springfield Register*, Dec. 20, 1851.

39. Thomas, *Lincoln Day-by-Day*, 1847–1853, p. 265.

40. *The Diary of Orville Hickman Browning*, I, p. 57.

41. *Ibid.*, pp. 56, 57.

42. Chicago *Weekly Times*, July 28, 1858.

43. Anthony Thornton in Chicago *Tribune*, Feb. 12, 1900, p. 14.

44. Talk delivered by John N. Jewett. *Proceedings upon the Occasion of the Presentation of Portraits of Federal Jurists to the United States Courts for the Southern District of Illinois*, at Springfield, on June 2, 1903, p. 77.

45. From photostat in Illinois State Hist. Lib.

46. Beveridge, *Life of Lincoln*, I, p. 597.

CHAPTER XIV

1. See Donald, *Lincoln's Herndon*, p. 47.

2. Included in the roster of Lincoln's known cases in the Supreme Court are a number in which his name appears in the court record, but not in the published reports. The latter, far from being complete, do not always give the names of all the attorneys in each case, and sometimes incorrectly list the names of both attorneys and parties.

3. Hill, *Lincoln the Lawyer*, fn. p. 221.

4. *The Diary of Orville Hickman Browning*, I, p. 32.

5. Hertz, *The Hidden Lincoln*, p. 215.

6. Albert Taylor Bledsoe, *Southern Review*, XIII, p. 332.

7. "Ingratitude of Lincoln," undated Herndon monograph, *Herndon-Weik Coll.*, Lib. of Cong.

8. Charles S. Zane, quoted in Joseph Fort Newton, *Lincoln and Herndon* (Cedar Rapids, Iowa, 1910), pp. 252-3.

9. 3 Ill. 456.

10. John Dean Caton, *Early Bench and Bar of Illinois* (Chicago, 1893), p. 205.

11. Palmer, *Bench and Bar of Illinois*, I, p. 74.

12. Memorandum in the papers of Henry Eddy, cited in Pratt, *Lincoln Day-by-Day* 1840–1846, Appendix, p. 369.

13. 6 Ill. 187.

14. *Lyman Trumbull Papers*, Lib. of Cong.

15. Quincy *Whig*, May 10, 31 and June 21, 1843.

16. Peoria *Weekly Democratic Press*, July 25, 1855 (reprinted from Chicago *Times*): "Judge McLean delivered his charge to the jury somewhat strongly for the defense." In a diary entry for July 13, 1855 Browning states: "Concluded the case of Forsythe vs. Peoria. . . . Judge McLean charged strongly in my favour . . . & I think we must succeed." *Diary of Orville Hickman Browning*, I, p. 191.

17. *Diary of Orville Hickman Browning*, I, p. 100.

18. 8 Ill. 583.

19. *Record* of Circuit Court of Coles County, II, p. 66.

20. After July 1, 1877 the appellate work of the Illinois system of courts was, within prescribed bounds, shared with the Supreme Court by four Appellate Courts.

21. 8 Ill. 502.

22. 6 Ill. 143.

23. 11 Ill. 254.

24. 13 Ill. 504.

25. 15 Ill. 233.

26. *Illinois State Journal*, Aug. 15, 1853.

27. Duplicates of the original patent papers were recently recovered among a case file of old documents found in the Logan Circuit Clerk's Office.

28. Whitney, *Life on the Circuit with Lincoln*, p. 196.

29. *Edmunds* v. *Myers, et al.*, 16 Ill. 207.

30. Bloomington *Weekly Pantagraph*, July 23, 1897.

31. *Browning* v. *City of Springfield*, 17 Ill. 143.

32. 19 Ill. 283.

33. *Illinois State Journal*, Feb. 18, 1858.

34. *Ibid.*, Feb. 3, 1858.

35. *City of Springfield* v. *Hickox*, 7 Ill. 241.

36. Original in Illinois State Hist. Lib., which has kindly furnished the writer with a photostatic copy.

37. Photostat of memorandum, and permission to use the same, was kindly furnished the writer by The Lincoln National Life Foundation. On the reverse side appears the notation: "Answer to a letter from myself. C. H. Doll." Apparently Doll had written Lincoln, posing some legal question, to which Lincoln responded with the frank acknowledgement of his lack of knowledge.
38. 19 Ill. 136.
39. Chicago *Daily Times*, Oct. 5, 1858.
40. 19 Ill. 353.
41. 19 Ill. 353, 355.
42. Beveridge, *Life of Abraham Lincoln*, I, p. 574.

CHAPTER XV

1. In writing this chapter, the author has been greatly aided by discussions had with the late Dr. Harry E. Pratt and by his article "Lincoln's Petitions for Pardon," appearing in the *Illinois Bar Journal* of February, 1942. S. Ambrose Wetherbee, of the Illinois State Historical Library, whose "Lincoln Collection. Illinois State Archives" appeared in *Lincoln Libraries*, published by the Illinois State Libraries February, 1943, has also been most helpful.
2. Until the adoption of the Seventeenth Amendment to the United States Constitution in 1913, members of the Senate were chosen by the legislature of the states.
3. From photostat in Illinois State Hist. Lib.
4. From photostat in Illinois State Hist. Lib.
5. From photostat in Illinois State Hist. Lib.
6. Whitney, *Life on the Circuit with Lincoln*, p. 231: Beveridge, *Life of Lincoln*, I, p. 549.
7. Gillespie to Herndon, Jan. 31, 1866. *Herndon-Weik Coll.*, Lib. of Cong.
8. Harry E. Pratt, "Lincoln's Petitions for Pardons," *Illinois Bar Journal*, February 1942, p. 240.
9. *Robert Todd Lincoln Coll.*, Lib. of Cong.
10. From facsimile copy of letter in Illinois State Hist. Lib. *Collected Works*, II, p. 535.
11. Documents in the Archives Department of the Illinois State Library show that in July, 1858 Alderman Charles H. Abbott of Chicago interceded for Hyde with Governor Bissell, who on October 7, 1858 pardoned the prisoner on condition "he leave the State, never to return."
12. Coler's son, Bird S., was later elected Comptroller of the City of New York, and ran for Governor of the State on the Democratic ticket. *History of Champaign County*, ed. by Joseph O. Cunningham (Chicago, 1905), II, p. 901.
13. Whitney, *Life on the Circuit with Lincoln*, p. 466.

14. Harry E. Pratt, "Lincoln Defends Tom Patterson," *Illinois Bar Journal*, 1940.

CHAPTER XVI

1. *Herndon's Lincoln*, p. 255.
2. Interview in *The Kansas City Star*, Feb. 9, 1930.
3. Statement of John W. Bunn, in Jesse W. Weik, *The Real Lincoln*, p. 284.
4. "My Recollections of Abraham Lincoln," *Farm and Fireside*, Dec. 1, 1904.
5. Lincoln to Grigsby, Aug. 3, 1858. *Collected Works*, II, p. 535.
6. Jonathan Daniels, *Prince of Carpetbaggers* (Phila. and New York, 1958).
7. *Brooklyn Daily Eagle*, Oct. 16, 1887.
8. *Herndon's Lincoln*, p. 254.
9. Ellsworth to Carrie Spofford, Oct. 29, 1860. Ellsworth Mss., Illinois State Hist. Lib.
10. *Illinois State Journal*, Sep. 11, 1860.
11. Ellsworth to Carrie Spofford, Sep. 22, 1859.
12. Ellsworth to Carrie Spofford, Jan. 29, 1860.
13. Ellsworth to Carrie Spofford, Jan. 31, 1860.
14. Interview with John H. Littlefield, *Brooklyn Daily Eagle*, Oct. 16, 1887.
15. Ellsworth Mss., Illinois State Hist. Lib.
16. Herndon to Weik, Springfield, Ill., Nov. 20, 1885, *The Hidden Lincoln*, p. 106.
17. Published in New York City by the Knickerbocker Press.
18. Benjamin P. Thomas, *Portrait for Posterity*, fn. p. 213.
19. Henry Bascom Rankin, *Intimate Character Sketches of Abraham Lincoln*, fn. p. 59.
20. William E. Barton, *The Life of Abraham Lincoln* (New York, 1928), p. 93.
21. Rankin, *Intimate Character Sketches of Abraham Lincoln*, p. 54.
22. Barton, *The Life of Abraham Lincoln*, p. 94.
23. Original letter, Emanuel Hertz to Paul M. Angle, Springfield, Ill., Apr. 10, 1930, in Illinois State Hist. Lib.
24. *Transactions* of the Illinois State Hist. Soc. for the year 1920, p. 20.
25. Lincoln to Isham Reavis, Nov. 5, 1855. *Collected Works*, II, p. 327.
26. Lincoln to James T. Thornton, Dec. 2, 1858. *Collected Works*, III, p. 344. Original in Illinois State Hist. Lib.
27. Angle, *New Letters and Papers of Lincoln*, p. 129, where original certificate is copied from the papers of David Davis.
28. Whitney to Weik, Aug. 27, 1887. *Herndon-Weik Coll.*, Lib. of Cong.

29. Illinois Wesleyan *Argus,* Oct. 3, 1917. Robert A. Sprecher, "Lincoln As A Bar Examiner," *Illinois Bar Journal,* Aug., 1954, p. 920.
30. Jonathan M. Birch, "A Law Student's Recollection of Abraham Lincoln," *The Outlook,* Feb. 11, 1911, vol. 97, pp. 311–314.
31. Beveridge, *Abraham Lincoln,* I, p. 529, fn. 1.
32. Howard F. Dyson, "Lincoln in Rushville," *Transactions* of the Illinois State Hist. Soc., Pub. No. 8, 1903 (1904), pp. 224–5.
33. Pratt, *Lincoln Day-by-Day* 1840–1846, p. 80.
34. *Ibid.,* p. 82.
35. Robert A. Sprecher, "Lincoln As A Bar Examiner," p. 922.
36. Palmer, *The Bench and Bar of Illinois,* II, p. 1039.

CHAPTER XVII

1. Whitney nevertheless recalled that two cases over which "Judge" Lincoln presided were reversed by the Supreme Court because of the infringement of the rules involved in this practice. Whitney, *Life on the Circuit with Lincoln,* p. 241. The writer has not been able to determine the cases to which Whitney referred.
2. William H. Somers to James R. B. Van Cleave, Dec. 7, 1908. Van Cleave Papers, Illinois State Hist. Lib.
3. Angle, *Lincoln Day-by-Day* 1854–1861, p. 153; *Record* of Sangamon Circuit Court.
4. Harry E. Pratt, "Judge" Abraham Lincoln, *Journal* of the Illinois State Hist. Soc., Spring 1955, p. 35.
5. These entries, found by James T. Hickey, then vice-president of the Illinois State Historical Society, were transferred to the Illinois State Historical Library by order of the Board of Supervisors of Logan County.
6. Swett to Herndon, Jan. 15, 1866. *Herndon-Weik Coll.,* Lib. of Cong.
7. A number of these documents in the Illinois State Historical Library have been examined by the writer in the course of his preparation of this chapter.
8. *Missouri Republican,* Jan. 31, 1846.
9. Photostat in Illinois State Hist. Lib.
10. This is the case in which Lincoln, though not representing the defendant, drew and signed, together with fourteen other members of the bar, including Stuart, a petition to the Court praying for a *"Nolle Prossecui"* of the indictment, on the ground that there had been two trials, each resulting in a disagreement, ". . . in the first, the jury standing six for a conviction of manslaughter, and six for an acquital, and in the second 5 for a conviction of manslaughter, and 7 for an acquital, . . ." Photostats of indictment and petition in Illinois State Hist. Lib.

11. *Illinois State Register*, May 14, 1853; Thomas, *Lincoln Day-by-Day*, 1847–1853, p. 333.
12. *DeWitt Courier*, Oct. 19, 1855.
13. *Ibid*.
14. Herndon to Mrs. Swett, Feb. 28, 1890. Swett Papers, Illinois State Hist. Lib.
15. Clarence Darrow, *The Story of My Life* (New York, 1932), p. 240.
16. *Daily Pantagraph*, Apr. 6, 1857.
17. *Ibid*.
18. It may not be stretching things to say that Judge Davis, who presided, made a significant contribution to the law on this intricate subject by overruling Lincoln's objections to the introduction of this line of testimony and holding it to be relevant. The Illinois jurist may not have been versed in psychoanalytic theories, but his instincts were true to modern psychiatry.
19. *Daily Pantagraph*, Apr. 10, 1857.
20. *Chicago Tribune*, June 20, 1889.
21. It was appropriate that Swett should have been designated to make the official address on the occasion of the unveiling, on Oct. 22, 1877, of the famous statue, designed and executed by Augustus Saint-Gaudens, in Lincoln Park, Chicago.
22. A. T. Rice, *Reminiscences of Abraham Lincoln* (New York, 1888).
23. *Robert Todd Lincoln Coll.*, Lib. of Cong.
24. *Ibid*.
25. Photostats of both indictments in Illinois State Hist. Lib.
26. This document, in the possession of King V. Hostick, of Springfield, Ill., was kindly placed by him at the disposal of the writer.
27. Lincoln to Linder, Feb. 20, 1848. *Collected Works*, I, p. 453. Original in Illinois State Historical Library.
28. The name of the defendant nowhere appears in the correspondence between the two.
29. *Robert Todd Lincoln Coll.*, Lib. of Cong.
30. *Collected Works*, IV, pp. 34–5.
31. Since publication of the *Collected Works*, by the Abraham Lincoln Association in 1953, over 200 new Lincoln papers have been located.

CHAPTER XVIII

1. *Monmouth Review*, Oct. 15, 1858; *Collected Works*, III, pp. 244–5.
2. Charter Illinois Central Railroad Co., Act Feb. 10, 1851. *Laws of Illinois*, 2nd Sess., pp. 61–75.
3. *Collected Works*, II, p. 202.
4. *Ibid*., p. 205.
5. 17 Ill. 291.
6. Herndon to Weik, Dec. 5, 1887, *Herndon-Weik Coll.*, Lib. of Cong.

7. *Herndon's Lincoln*, p. 284.
8. Joseph Grensel, "Detroit Memories of Lincoln," *Detroit Free Press*, Feb. 12, 1911.
9. *Ibid.*
10. *Herndon's Lincoln*, p. 284.
11. Original in Chicago Hist. Soc.
12. Original complaint in Chicago Hist. Soc.
13. See William H. Townsend, "Lincoln, the Litigant," *American Bar Journal*, Feb. 1924, p. 86.
14. *Herndon's Lincoln*, p. 284.
15. *Collected Works*, III, p. 331.
16. John W. Starr, Jr., *Lincoln and the Railroads* (New York, 1927), pp. 126–131.

CHAPTER XIX

1. Jacksonville *Constitutionalist*, March 21, 1854.
2. Emerson Hinchcliff, "Lincoln and the 'Reaper Case,'" *Journal* of the Illinois State Hist. Soc., Sep. 1940, p. 361.
3. Lincoln to Watson, Washington, D.C., July 23, 1855, *Collected Works*, II, p. 315.
4. Johnson acted as counsel, in 1865, for Mary Surratt, one of the alleged conspirators in the assassination of Lincoln.
5. Fletcher Pratt, *Stanton:* Lincoln's Secretary of War (New York, 1953), p. 61.
6. W. M. Dickson, "Lincoln at Cincinnati," *Harper's New Monthly Magazine*, June, 1884, p. 62.
7. Harry E. Pratt, *The Personal Finances of Abraham Lincoln*, p. 56.
8. William H. Dowse to Albert J. Beveridge, Oct. 10, 1925. *Beveridge Papers*, Lib. of Cong. (Dowse was a law associate of Harding from 1878 to 1890).
9. Photostat in Illinois State Hist. Lib.
10. *Record*, Sangamon Circuit Court; Angle, *Lincoln Day-by-Day*, 1854–1861, p. 100.
11. Original in Illinois State Hist. Lib.
12. Only two books in the Lincoln field have mentioned the case, which, after numerous continuances, was tried at the April 1857 term of the McLean Circuit Court—Milton H. Shutes, *Lincoln and the Doctors* (New York, 1933) and Sherman D. Wakefield, *How Lincoln Became President* (New York, 1936).
13. From photostat of complaint in Illinois State Hist. Lib.
14. Lulu M. Crothers to Sherman D. Wakefield, Oct. 30, 1935. Harry E. Pratt, "The Famous 'Chicken Bone' Case," *Journal* of the Illinois State Hist. Soc., Summer 1952, p. 166.

15. From Court Record "B", p. 45, *Herndon-Weik Coll.*, Lib. of Cong.
16. *History of Sangamon County*, p. 525.
17. Letter of Thomas Lewis, "Springfield of the Past," *Illinois State Register*, July 10, 1887.
18. *Illinois State Register*, Nov. 24, 1856.
19. *Ibid.*, Nov. 25, 1856.

CHAPTER XX

1. Edwin L. Page, "The *Effie Afton* Case," Fall 1956 *Lincoln Herald*, p. 5.
2. *Chicago Tribune*, April 17, 1857.
3. Frederic B. Crosley, *Courts and Lawyers of Illinois*, I, p. 299.
4. Proceedings of the Republican National Convention, held at Chicago May 16, 17 and 18, 1860, p. 108.
5. Joseph B. Oakleaf, Moline, Ill. to Albert J. Beveridge, Dec. 17, 1924. Beveridge MSS, Lib. of Cong.
6. F. J. Nevins, Valuation Engineer, The Chicago, Rock Island & Pacific Railway Company, to Albert J. Beveridge, July 30, 1925. Beveridge MSS, Lib. of Cong.
7. Unfortunately, the copy of the letter is now "gone beyond recall," inasmuch as the letter copy books pertaining to the period in question were inadvertently destroyed some few years back. William E. Hayes, Executive Assistant, Chicago, Rock Island and Pacific Railroad Company to the writer, Dec. 31, 1957.
8. The supposition is borne out, to some extent, by the following item which appeared in the *Rock Island Weekly Argus* of Sep. 2, 1857: "Hon. A. Lincoln.—This distinguished lawyer who is employed by the bridge company to defend that mammoth nuisance is expected in Davenport in a few days, for the purpose of examining that huge obstruction to the free navigation of the river."
9. Charles Edward Russell, *A-Rafting on the Mississippi* (New York, 1928), pp. 67–72, cited in Elwin L. Page, "The *Effie Afton* Case," p. 10.
10. On Sep. 20 (a Monday) Mrs. Lincoln wrote: "Mr. L. is not at home, this makes the fourth week, he has been in Chicago." Sandburg, *Mary Lincoln*, p. 201, cited in Angle, *Lincoln Day-by-Day* 1854–1861, p. 192.
11. L. O. Leonard, "The Founders and Builders of the Road," *Rock Island Magazine*, Vol. xxi, No. 2, Feb. 1926, p. 6.
12. *Chicago Daily Press*, Sep. 9, 1857.
13. It was not until 1858 that stenography began to figure in the reporting of court trials. In that year Robert R. Hitt, later to become a member of Congress from one of the Illinois districts, commenced taking down the testimony in the more important cases tried in Chicago. John M. Palmer, *The Bench and Bar of Illinois*, I, p. 150.
14. *Chicago Daily Press*, Sep. 25, 1857.

15. F. J. Nevins, Valuation Engineer, The Chicago, Rock Island & Pacific Railway Co. to Albert J. Beveridge, July 30, 1925. Beveridge MSS, Lib. of Cong.

16. Jesse W. Weik, *The Real Lincoln* (Boston, 1922), viii.

17. Richards, *Abraham Lincoln: The Lawyer-Statesman, p.* 72.

CHAPTER XXI

1. The county seat was moved from Metamora to Eureka in 1897.

2. Ernest E. East, "The Melissa Goings Murder Case," *Journal* of the Illinois State Hist. Soc., Spring 1953, p. 79.

3. Testimony of Josephus Goings, son, at coroner's inquest.

4. *Common Law Record B*, p. 313, cited in East, "Melissa Goings Murder Case," *Journal* of the Illinois State Hist. Soc., Spring 1953, fn. 18, p. 82.

5. *Chancery Record Y*, Woodford Circuit Court, pp. 36–43, cited in East, "The Melissa Goings Murder Case."

6. Copy of letter William Ryan, Editor *The Metamora Herald*, to Ernest E. East, Mar. 28, 1941, in Illinois State Hist. Lib.

7. William L. Elwood, of Peoria, for years a member of the Woodford County bar, told the Cassell version at a farewell dinner for Judge George W. Patton of Pontiac in June, 1921. Thereafter, Judge Baker, at Eureka, ordered Elwood's address spread upon the records of the court, East, "The Melissa Goings Murder Case," fn. 20, p. 83.

8. *Herndon's Lincoln*, v.

9. "Young Mr. Lincoln."

10. Original indictment in Illinois State Hist. Lib.

11. From original application in Illinois State Hist. Lib.

12. From account of talk delivered by William H. Weaver to the Optimists' Club, at its regular meeting at the St. Nicholas Hotel, Springfield, on Feb. 15, 1926. *Illinois State Journal*, Feb. 16, 1926.

13. Letter of J. Henry Shaw to Herndon, Aug. 22, 1866. *Herndon-Weik Coll.*, Lib. of Cong.

14. Ewing, who read law and practiced in Bloomington, was a frequent attendant at Lincoln's trials in Bloomington and other county seat towns on the Eighth Circuit.

15. Hill, *Lincoln the Lawyer*, p. 222.

16. Undated statement of Judge Harriott in *Herndon-Weik Coll.*, Lib. of Cong.

17. The large monument at Dr. Stevenson's grave in Petersburg, Ill. was erected by the Grand Army of the Republic, of which he was the founder.

18. See letters, Walker to Herndon, June 3, Aug. 27 and Sep. 17, 1866. *Herndon-Weik Coll.*, Lib. of Cong.

19. From photostats in Illinois State Hist. Lib.

20. J. N. Gridley, "Lincoln's Defense of Duff Armstrong," *Journal* of the Illinois State Hist. Soc., April 1910, pp. 24, 39.
21. *Collected Works*, VI, p. 462. Original of letter in Brown Univ. Lib.
22. Seventh Annual Report of Illinois State Penitentiary, 1863–4, p. 44.
23. *Collected Works*, II, p. 521. Original in Illinois State Historical Library.
24. Lyman Trumbull, Alton, Ill. to Abraham Lincoln, care Hon. Thomas J. Turner, Freeport, Ill., Aug. 24, 1858.
25. J. Howard, Jr., *Atlantic Monthly*, vol. VIII, p. 205, cited in Frank E. Stevens, *Life of Douglas*, fn. 376, p. 671.
26. *Judge's Docket* 1858–1859, Sangamon County, p. 553.
27. Herndon to Weik, Nov. 20, 1885. *Herndon-Weik Coll.*, Lib. of Cong.
28. Hertz, *The Hidden Lincoln*, p. 107.
29. *Ibid.*, p. 108.
30. *Ibid.*, p. 107.
31. This was not the first time Lincoln brought suit against the college faculty. On June 10, 1857 he wrote and filed a declaration in the federal court in an action (*Gilbert* v. *Read, et al.*), seeking $3,000. damages for the plaintiff's expulsion from the college. Angle, *Lincoln Day-by-Day*, 1854–1861, p. 180.
32. Palmer, *Bench and Bar of Illinois*, I, p. 35.
33. Chapter VI, p. 95.
34. Statement of Mary Lincoln to Isaac Arnold, in Arnold, *Abraham Lincoln*, p. 429; Nicolay, *Short Life of Abraham Lincoln*, p. 532; Lamon, *Recollections*, pp. 119–20; Tarbell, *Life of Abraham Lincoln*, II, p. 235.

APPENDIX A

*Lawyers Who Were Associated with Lincoln
on the Eighth Judicial Circuit*

Sangamon County

Edward D. Baker
Albert T. Bledsoe
Mason Brayman
Christopher C. Brown
David B. Campbell
Shelby M. Cullom

Benjamin S. Edwards
John E. Rosette
Schuyler Strong
Jesse B. Thomas
William Thomas

Tazewell County

J. M. Bush
Samuel W. Fuller
Asahel Gridley
Jonathan Haines
William H. Holmes
B. F. James
Edward Jones

William H. Leonard
Amos L. Merriman
W. B. Parker
E. N. Powell
Benjamin S. Prettyman
A. H. Saltonstall

Woodford County

B. C. Brown
William Brown
Charles A. Clark
J. T. Cooper
William H. Davidson
Ira J. Fenn
Asahel Gridley
Henry Grove
William H. Holmes

Amos L. Merriman
Onslow Peters
E. W. Powell
Norman H. Purple
Ezra G. Sanger
Eleazar M. Thorpe
J. H. Wickizer

McLean County

Mason Brayman
Charles Emerson
Asahel Gridley
Harvey Hogg
William H. Holmes
Ward H. Lamon

Clifton H. Moore
William W. Orme
John M. Scott
John T. Stuart
Lawrence Weldon

Logan County

Charles Emerson
Grant Goodrich
Asahel Gridley

Edward Jones
L. P. Lacey
Samuel C. Parks

DeWitt County

Kirby Benedict
Asahel Gridley
Harvey Hogg
Clifton H. Moore
William W. Orme

Leonard Swett
Lawrence Weldon

Piatt County

Charles Emerson
Clifton H. Moore
Joel S. Post

Champaign County

William N. Coler
Oliver L. Davis
Asahel Gridley
William W. Orme

Benjamin R. Sheldon
W. D. Somers
Leonard Swett
Henry C. Whitney

Vermilion County

James C. Allen
Corydon Beckwith
Kirby Benedict
Shelby H. Cullom
Oliver L. Davis
William M. Fletcher

Harvey Hogg
Ward H. Lamon
John H. Murphy
Onslow Peters
John Pearson
Wesley Sloan
Daniel Voorhees

Edgar County

Kirby Benedict
Joseph Blackburn
M. M. Dill
Charles Emerson

Augustus C. French
Usher F. Linder
Josiah McRoberts
James Steele

Shelby County

Orlando B. Ficklin
Samuel W. Moulton
Anthony Thornton

Moultrie County

Charles Emerson
O. B. Ficklin
Usher F. Linder
Anthony Thornton

Macon County

Kirby Benedict
Charles Emerson
Joel S. Post

Anthony Thornton
Eleazar M. Thorpe

Christian County

Benjamin S. Edwards
James M. Mason
William L. May

Hiram Roundtree
Anthony Thornton

APPENDIX B

Roster of Judges of the Illinois Supreme Court
before Whom Lincoln Practiced 1840–1860.

Name	Term of Service
Thomas C. Browne	Oct. 9, 1818 — Jan. 11, 1847
William Wilson	Aug. 17, 1818 — Dec. 4, 1848
Samuel D. Lockwood	Jan. 19, 1825 — Nov. 3, 1848
Theophilus W. Smith	Jan. 19, 1825 — Dec. 26, 1842
Samuel H. Treat	Feb. 15, 1841 — Mar. 23, 1855
Thomas Ford	Feb. 15, 1841 — Aug. 1, 1842
Sidney Breese	Feb. 15, 1841 — Dec. 19, 1842
	Nov. 3, 1857 — June, 1861
Walter B. Scates	Feb. 15, 1841 — Jan. 11, 1847
	June 25, 1853 — Oct. 1, 1857
Stephen A. Douglas	Feb. 15, 1841 — June 28, 1843
John D. Caton	Aug. 9, 1842 — Mar. 6, 1843
	May 2, 1843 — Jan. 9, 1864
James Semple	Jan. 16, 1843 — Aug. 16, 1843
Richard M. Young	Jan. 14, 1843 — Jan. 25, 1847
James Shields	Aug. 16, 1843 — Apr. 2, 1845
Jesse B. Thomas	Aug. 24, 1843 — Aug. 8, 1845
	Jan. 26, 1847 — Dec. 4, 1848
Gustavus P. Koerner	Apr. 2, 1845 — Dec. 4, 1848
Norman H. Purple	Aug. 8, 1845 — Dec. 4, 1848
Lyman Trumbull	Sep. 4, 1845 — July 4, 1853
William Denning	Jan. 18, 1847 — Dec. 4, 1848
Onias C. Skinner	June 4, 1855 — Apr. 19, 1858
Pinckney C. Walker	Feb. 6, 1858 — June, 1875

BIBLIOGRAPHY

I. *Manuscript Collections.*

Albert J. Beveridge *MSS.*, Library of Congress.
Albert J. Beveridge *MSS.*, Illinois State Historical Library.
Sidney Breese *MSS.*, Illinois State Historical Library.
Orville Hickman Browning *MSS.*, Illinois State Historical Library.
John Dean Caton Collection, Library of Congress.
James C. Conkling *MSS.*, Illinois State Historical Library.
David Davis *MSS.*, transcripts in Illinois State Historical Library.
Stephen A. Douglas *MSS.*, Illinois State Historical Library.
Henry Enoch Dummer *MSS.*, Illinois State Historical Library.
Elmer Ephraim Ellsworth *MSS.*, Illinois State Historical Library.
Jesse W. Fell *MSS.*, transcripts made and collated by the Illinois Historical Survey, 1913, University of Illinois, Urbana.
Joseph Gillespie Collection, Chicago Historical Society.
Horace Greeley *MSS.*, New York Public Library.
Anson G. Henry *MSS.*, Illinois State Historical Library.
William H. Herndon-Jesse W. Weik Collection. Microfilm, Illinois State Historical Library.
Robert Todd Lincoln Collection. Microfilm, Columbia University Library.
John A. McClernand *MSS.*, Illinois State Historical Library.
John G. Nicolay-John Hay *MSS.*, Illinois State Historical Library.
William W. Orme *MSS.*, Illinois State Historical Library.
John M. Palmer *MSS.*, Illinois State Historical Library.
George Pasfield Scrapbook, Illinois State Historical Library.
Nathaniel Pope *MSS.*, Illinois State Historical Library.
Stuart-Hay *MSS.*, Illinois State Historical Library. Family papers of Stephen Trigg Logan, John Todd Stuart and Milton Hay.
Leonard Swett *MSS.*, Illinois State Historical Library.
Leonard Swett Scrapbook, Illinois State Historical Library.
Lyman Trumbull *MSS.*, Library of Congress.
James R. B. Van Cleave Papers, Illinois State Historical Library.
Joseph Wallace Scrapbooks, Illinois State Historical Library.

William H. L. Wallace *MSS.*, Illinois State Historical Library.
Jesse William Weik *MSS.*, Illinois State Historical Library.
Richard Yates *MSS.*, Illinois State Historical Library.

II. *Official Publications.*

Journal of the House of Representatives of the Ninth General Assembly
    of the State of Illinois. Vandalia, Illinois.
Journal of the House of Representatives of the Twelfth General As-
    sembly of the State of Illinois. Springfield, Illinois.
Springfield Directory, 1860.
Charter Illinois Central Railroad Company, Act February 10, 1851. Laws
    of Illinois, 2nd Session.
Seventh Annual Report of Illinois State Penitentiary, 1863-4.
Roll of Attorneys of the Illinois Supreme Court.
Proceeding Upon the Occasion of the Presentation of Portraits of Federal
    Jurists to the United States Courts for the Southern District of
    Illinois, at Springfield, on June 2, 1903.
"An Act to Establish a Uniform System of Bankruptcy Throughout the
    United States." U.S. Statutes at Large, 27th Congress.
Records of the County Commissioners Court of Peoria County for the
    Years 1836-1876.

III. *Newspapers.*

The Alton *Telegraph*, Illinois State Historical Library.
The Beardstown *Gazette*, Illinois State Historical Library.
The Bloomington *Pantagraph*, Illinois State Historical Library.
The Brooklyn *Daily Eagle*, New York Public Library.
The Carthage *Journal*, Illinois State Historical Library.
The Chicago *Daily American*, Illinois State Historical Library.
The Chicago *Daily News*, Illinois State Historical Library.
The Chicago *Daily Press*, Illinois State Historical Library.
The Chicago *Journal*, Illinois State Historical Library.
The Chicago *Times*, Illinois State Historical Library.
The Chicago *Tribune*, Illinois State Historical Library.
The Danville *Illinois Citizen*, Illinois State Historical Library.
The Davenport *Democrat and Leader*, Library of Congress.
The Detroit *Free Press*, Library of Congress.
The DeWitt *Courier*, Illinois State Historical Library.
The Jacksonville *Constitutionalist*, Illinois State Historical Library.
The Jacksonville *Morgan Journal*, Illinois State Historical Library.
The Missouri *Republican*, Library of Congress.
The Monmouth *Review*, Illinois State Historical Library.
The New York *Daily News*, New York Public Library.

The New York *Independent*, New York Public Library.
The New York *Tribune*, New York Public Library.
The Peoria *Democratic Press*, Illinois State Historical Library.
The Peoria *Register and North-Western Gazetteer*, Illinois State Historical Library.
The Quincy *Whig*, Illinois State Historical Library.
The Rock Island *Weekly Argus*, Illinois State Historical Library.
The St. Louis *Republican*, Library of Congress.
The Springfield *Illinois State Register*, Illinois State Historical Society.
The Springfield *Republican*, Illinois State Historical Library.
The Springfield *Sangamo Journal* (called also the *Illinois State Journal* and the *Illinois Journal*), Illinois State Historical Library.
The Tremont *Tazewell Telegraph*, Illinois State Historical Library.
The Urbana *Clarion*, Illinois State Historical Library.
The Vandalia *Illinois Advocate* and *State Register*, Illinois State Historical Library.

IV. *Books, Articles and Pamphlets.*

Abraham Lincoln Association, *Bulletin*, Nos. 1–58 (1923–1939). Numbers issued prior to 1929 bear the title Lincoln Centennial Association.
Abraham Lincoln Association, Papers Delivered before the Members. Issued as *Lincoln Centennial Association Papers.*
Angle, Paul McClelland: "Abraham Lincoln: Circuit Lawyer," *Lincoln Centennial Association Papers*, 1928.
———: *A Shelf of Lincoln Books: A Critical, Selective Bibliography of Lincolniana.* New Brunswick, New Jersey. Rutgers University Press in cooperation with the Abraham Lincoln Association, 1946.
———: "Aftermath of the Matson Slave Case," *The Abraham Lincoln Quarterly*, June, 1944.
———: *"Here I Have Lived": A History of Lincoln's Springfield, 1821–1865.* Springfield: The Abraham Lincoln Association, 1935.
———: *Lincoln, 1854–1861: Being the Day-by-Day Activities of Abraham Lincoln From January 1, 1854, to March 4, 1861.* Springfield: The Abraham Lincoln Association, 1933.
———: "Lincoln in the United States Court, 1855–1860: New Light on His Law Practice," Lincoln Centennial Association, *Bulletin*, September 1, 1927.
———: *Marine Bank: The Story of the Oldest Bank in Illinois.* Springfield, 1931.
———, ed.: *New Letters and Papers of Lincoln.* Boston: Houghton Mifflin Company, 1930.
———: *One Hundred Years of Law.* Springfield, Illinois: Brown, Hay and Stephens, 1928.

———— and Earl Schenck Miers, eds.: *The Living Lincoln*. New Brunswick, N.J.: Rutgers University Press, 1955.

————: "Where Lincoln Practiced Law," *Lincoln Centennial Association Papers*, 1927.

Arnold, Isaac N.: *The Life of Abraham Lincoln*. Chicago: Jansen, McClurg & Co., 1885.

Baringer, William E.: *Lincoln's Vandalia, a Pioneer Portrait*. New Brunswick, N.J.: Rutgers University Press, 1949.

Barton, William E.: *The Life of Abraham Lincoln*, 2 vols. Indianapolis: Bobbs-Merrill, 1925.

————: "The Influence of Illinois in the Development of Abraham Lincoln," *Transactions of the Illinois State Historical Society*, 1921.

Basler, Roy P. (Editor), Marion Dolores Pratt and Lloyd A. Dunlap (Assistant Editors): *The Collected Works of Abraham Lincoln*. New Brunswick: Rutgers University Press, 1953.

Baxter, Maurice: *Orville H. Browning, Lincoln's Friend and Critic*. Bloomington, Indiana: Indiana University Publications, 1957.

Bergen, Abraham: "Abraham Lincoln as a Lawyer," *American Bar Association Journal*, Vol. 12, June, 1926.

Beveridge, Albert J.: *Abraham Lincoln, 1809–1858*, 2 vols. Boston: Houghton Mifflin Co., 1928.

Birch, Jonathan M.: "A Law Student's Recollection of Abraham Lincoln," *The Outlook*, Feb. 11, 1911.

Bowers, Claude G.: *Beveridge and the Progressive Era*. Boston: Houghton Mifflin Company, 1932.

Brown, Christopher C.: "Major John T. Stuart," *Transactions of the Illinois State Historical Society*, 1902.

Bryan, Wilhelmus Bogart: *History of The National Capital*, 2 vols. New York: Macmillan Company, 1914, 1916.

Capers, Gerald M.: *Stephen A. Douglas*, Defender of the Union. Boston: Little Brown & Company, 1959.

Chambers, William Nisbet: *Old Bullion Benton*. Boston: Little Brown & Company, 1956.

Charnwood, Godfrey Rathbone Benson: *Abraham Lincoln*. New York: Henry Holt and Company, 1917.

Coleman, Charles H.: *Abraham Lincoln and Coles County, Illinois*. New Brunswick: Scarecrow Press, 1955.

————: "Spelling Bothered Lincoln, Too," *Journal of the Illinois State Historical Society*, Winter, 1956.

———— and Paul H. Spence: "The Charleston Riot, March 28, 1864," *Journal of the Illinois State Historical Society*, March, 1940.

Crossley, Frederic B.: *Courts and Lawyers of Illinois*, 3 vols. Chicago: The American Historical Society, 1916.

Cunningham, J. O.: "Some Facts in the Judicial History of Illinois," *Transactions of the Illinois State Historical Society*, 1902.

Current, Richard N.: *The Lincoln Nobody Knows*. New York: The Mc-Graw-Hill Book Company, 1958.

Daniels, Jonathan: *Prince of Carpetbaggers*. Philadelphia: J. B. Lippincott Company, 1958.

Darrow, Clarence: *The Story of My Life*. New York: Charles Scribner's Sons, 1932.

Dickson, W. M.: "Lincoln at Cincinnati," *Harper's New Monthly Magazine*, June, 1884.

Dictionary of American Biography. Vol. XI, New York: Scribner's Sons, 1933.

Donald, David: "Billy, You're Too Rampant," *The Abraham Lincoln Quarterly*, December, 1947.

————: *Lincoln's Herndon*. New York: Alfred A. Knopf, 1948.

Dupuy, George Alexander: "The Earliest Courts of the Illinois Country," *Transactions of the Illinois State Historical Society*, 1906.

Dyson, Howard F.: "Lincoln in Rushville," *Transactions of the Illinois State Historical Society*, Spring, 1903.

East, Ernest E.: "The Melissa Goings Murder Case," *Journal of the Illinois State Historical Society*, Spring, 1953.

Epler, Judge Cyrus: "History of Morgan County Bar," *Journal of the Illinois State Historical Society*, October 1926–January 1927.

Ficklin, O. B.: "A Pioneer Lawyer," *Tuscola* (Illinois) *Review*, Sep. 7, 1922.

Flint, Margaret A.: *Chronology of Illinois History 1673–1954*. Illinois Blue Book, 1953–1954.

Ford, Thomas: *History of Illinois*. Chicago: S. C. Griggs & Co., 1854.

Fuess, Claude M.: *Rufus Choate*, The Wizard of the Law. New York: Minton, Balch & Company, 1928.

Gaylor, George R.: "The Mormons and Politics in Illinois: 1839–1844," *Journal of the Illinois State Historical Society*, Spring, 1956.

Harris, Gibson W.: "My Recollections of Abraham Lincoln," *Farm and Fireside*, Dec. 1, 1904.

Herndon, William H. and Jesse W. Weik: *Herndon's Lincoln: The True Story of a Great Life*, Angle ed. Cleveland: The World Publishing Company, 1949.

Hertz, Emanuel: *The Hidden Lincoln: From the Letters and Papers of William H. Herndon*. New York: The Viking Press, 1938.

Hill, Frederick Trevor: *Lincoln the Lawyer*. New York: The Century Company, 1906.

Hinchcliff, Emerson: "Lincoln and the 'Reaper Case,'" *Journal of the Illinois State Historical Society*, September, 1940.

History of Champaign County, 2 vols. Chicago: Lewis Publishing Company, 1918.

History of Champaign County, ed. by Joseph O. Cunningham. Chicago: Munsell Publishing Co., 1905.

History of Coles County, Illinois. Chicago: Wm. LeBaron, Jr., & Co., 1879.

History of Christian County, ed. by Henry L. Fowkes, 2 vols. Chicago: Munsell Publishing Co., 1918.

Past and Present of the City of Decatur and Macon County, Illinois. Chicago: The S. J. Clarke Publishing Company, 1903.

History of Logan County, Illinois. Chicago: Donnelley, Lloyd & Co., 1878.

History of McLean County, by Jacob L. Hasbrouck, 2 vols. Indianapolis: Historical Publishing Co., 1924.

History of Menard and Mason Counties, Illinois. Chicago: O. L. Baskin & Co., Historical Publishers, 1870.

History of Peoria County, Illinois. Chicago: Johnson & Company, 1880.

History of Sangamon County, Illinois. . . . Chicago: Inter-State Publishing Company, 1881.

History of Shelby and Moultrie Counties, Illinois. Chicago: Brink, McDonough & Co., 1881.

Past and Present of the City of Springfield and Sangamon County, Illinois, 2 vols., by Joseph Wallace. Chicago: The S. J. Clarke Publishing Co., 1904.

History of Tazewell County. Chicago: Charles C. Chapman & Company, 1879.

History of Vermilion County, by Lottie E. Jones, 2 vols. Chicago, 1911.

Howells, William Dean: *Abraham Lincoln*. Campaign Biography of Abraham Lincoln, Corrected By the Hand of Abraham Lincoln in the Summer of 1860. Republished by the Abraham Lincoln Association, Springfield, Ill., 1938.

Hunt, Eugenia Jones: "My Personal Recollections of Abraham Lincoln and Mary Todd Lincoln," *The Abraham Lincoln Quarterly*, March, 1945.

Kyle, Otto R.: *Abraham Lincoln in Decatur*. New York: Vantage Press, 1957.

Lamon, Ward Hill: *The Life of Abraham Lincoln from his Birth to His Inauguration as President*. Boston: James R. Osgood and Company, 1872.

Leonard, L. D.: "The Founders and Builders of the Road," *Rock Island Magazine*, February, 1926.

Lewis, Lloyd: *Myths after Lincoln*. New York: Harcourt, Brace and Company, 1929.

Light, Ivan Huber: *This Blooming Town*. A Sketch of Bloomington, Illinois. Bloomington, Illinois: Light House Press, 1956.

Lincoln File, Menard County Circuit Court.

Lincoln Herald. Published by the Lincoln Memorial University, Harrogate, Tennessee, 1938-date.

Lincoln Lore. The bulletin of the Lincoln National Life Foundation, Fort Wayne, Indiana, published 1929-date.

Linder, Usher F.: *Reminiscences of the Early Bench and Bar of Illinois*. Chicago: Chicago Legal News Co., 1879.

Lufkin, Richard F.: "Mr. Lincoln's Light From Under a Bushel—1850," *Lincoln Herald*, December, 1950.

Mearns, David C.: *The Lincoln Papers*, 2 vols. Garden City: Doubleday and Company, 1948.

———, Arthur Bestor and Jonathan Daniels: *Three Presidents and Their Books*. Urbana: University of Illinois Press, 1951.

Memorials of the Life and Character of Stephen T. Logan. Springfield, Illinois: H. W. Rokker, 1878.

Monoghan, Jay: *Lincoln Bibliography, 1839–1909*, 2 vols. Collections of the Illinois State Historical Library, Vols. 31 and 32, Springfield, 1943.

Nevins, Allan and Milton Halsey Thomas, eds.: *The Diary of George Templeton Strong*, 4 vols. New York: The Macmillan Company, 1952.

Newell, Mason H.: "The Attorney-Generals of Illinois," *Publication No. 8 of the Illinois State Historical Library*.

Newton, Joseph F.: *Lincoln and Herndon*. Cedar Rapids: Torch Press, 1910.

Nicolay, Helen: *Personal Traits of Abraham Lincoln*. New York: The Century Co., 1912.

Nicolay, John G. and John Hay: *Abraham Lincoln, a History*, 10 vols. New York: The Century Co., 1890.

Oldroyd, Osborn H., ed.: *The Lincoln Memorial: Album-Immortelles. Original Life Pictures, with Autographs, from the Hands and Hearts of Eminent Americans and Europeans. . . .* New York: G. W. Carleton & Co., 1882.

Packard, Roy D.: *The Lincoln of the Thirtieth Congress*. Boston: Christopher Publishing House, 1950.

Page, Edwin L.: "The Effie Afton Case," *Lincoln Herald*, Fall, 1956.

Pease, Theodore Calvin and James Garfield Randall, eds.: *The Diary of Orville Hickman Browning*, 2 vols. Springfield: Illinois State Historical Library, 1925, 1933.

Power, John Carroll: *History of the Early Settlers of Sangamon County, Illinois*. Springfield: Edwin A. Wilson & Co., 1876.

Pratt, Fletcher: *Stanton, Lincoln's Secretary of War*. New York: W. W. Norton & Company, 1953.

Pratt, Harry Edward:

    Abraham Lincoln Chronology 1809–1865. Springfield: Illinois State Historical Library, 1953. 12 pp. Revised ed., 1955.

————: "Administration of Estate of Abraham Lincoln," *Bulletin of the Abraham Lincoln Association*, December, 1936.

————: "Albert Taylor Bledsoe: Critic of Lincoln," *Transactions of the Illinois State Historical Society*, 1934.

————: *Lincoln, 1809–1839: Being the Day-By-Day Activities of Abraham Lincoln from February 12, 1809 to December 31, 1839*. Springfield: The Abraham Lincoln Association, 1941.

————: *Lincoln, 1840–1846: Being the Day-By-Day Activities of Abraham Lincoln from January 1, 1840 to December 31, 1846*. Springfield: The Abraham Lincoln Association, 1939.

————: "David Davis, 1815–1886," *Transactions of the Illinois State Historical Society*, 1930.

————; ed. *Concerning Mr. Lincoln: In Which Abraham Lincoln Is Pictured as He Appeared to Letter Writers of His Time*. Springfield: The Abraham Lincoln Association, 1944.

————: " 'Judge' Abraham Lincoln," *Journal of the Illinois State Historical Society*, Spring, 1955.

————: " 'Lincoln Tries a Suit Well,' " *Journal of the Illinois State Historical Society*, Spring, 1954.

————: *Lincoln's Springfield: A Guide Book & Brief History*. Springfield, Ill.: The Abraham Lincoln Association, 1938.

————: "In Defense of Mr. Justice Browne," *Bulletin of the Abraham Lincoln Association*, June, 1939.

————: "Lincoln and Douglas as Counsel on the Same Side," *American Bar Association Journal*, March, 1940.

————: "The Genesis of Lincoln the Lawyer," *Bulletin of the Abraham Lincoln Association*, September, 1939.

————: "Lincoln Defends Tom Patterson," *Illinois Bar Journal*, October, 1940.

————: "Lincoln's Petitions for Pardon," *Illinois Bar Journal*, February, 1942.

————: "Our Growing Knowledge of Lincoln," *Illinois Bar Journal*, July, 1951.

————: *The Personal Finances of Abraham Lincoln*. Springfield: The Abraham Lincoln Association, 1943.

————: "Lincoln's [Illinois] Supreme Court Cases," *Illinois Bar Journal*, September, 1943.

Randall, James Garfield: *Constitutional Problems under Lincoln* (Revised Edition). Urbana: The University of Illinois Press, 1951.

———: *Lincoln the President.* Springfield to Gettysburg, 2 vols. New York: Dodd, Mead & Company, 1945.

———: *Lincoln the President.* Midstream. New York: Dodd, Mead & Company, 1952.

——— and Richard N. Current: *Lincoln the President.* Last Full Measure. New York: Dodd, Mead & Company, 1955.

Randall, Ruth Painter: *Lincoln's Sons.* Boston: Little Brown and Company, 1955.

———: *Mary Lincoln:* Biography of a Marriage. Boston: Little Brown and Company, 1953.

Rankin, Henry Bascom: *Intimate Character Sketches of Abraham Lincoln.* Philadelphia: J. B. Lippincott Company, 1924.

———: *Personal Recollections of Abraham Lincoln.* New York: The Knickerbocker Press, 1916.

Reep, Thomas P.: *Lincoln at New Salem.* Petersburg, Illinois: Old Salem Lincoln League, 1927.

Rice, Allen Thorndike: *Reminiscences of Abraham Lincoln by Distinguished Men of His Time,* 6th ed. New York: North American Review, 1888.

Richards, John Thomas: *Abraham Lincoln: The Lawyer-Statesman.* Boston: Houghton Mifflin Company, 1916.

Riddle, Donald W.: *Lincoln Runs for Congress.* New Brunswick: Rutgers University Press, 1948.

———: *Congressman Abraham Lincoln.* Urbana: University of Illinois Press, 1957.

Rip Van Winkle, the Autobiography of Joseph Jefferson, rev. ed. New York: Appleton-Century-Crofts, 1950.

Rock Island Railroad. Seventieth Anniversary Brochure, 1922.

Russell, Charles Edward: *A-Rafting on the Mississippi.* New York: The Century Co., 1928.

Sandburg, Carl: *Abraham Lincoln: the Prairie Years,* 2 vols. New York: Harcourt, Brace & Company, 1926.

Shutes, Milton H.: *Lincoln and the Doctors.* New York: The Pioneer Press, 1933.

Sprecher, Robert A.: "Lincoln As A Bar Examiner," *Illinois Bar Journal,* August, 1954.

Starr, John William: *Lincoln and the Railroads, a Biographical Study.* New York: Dodd, Mead & Co., 1927.

Stevens, Frank E.: "Life of Stephen A. Douglas," *Journal of the Illinois State Historical Society,* October 1923–January 1924.

Tarbell, Ida M.: "Lincoln as a Lawyer," *McClure's Magazine,* July, 1896.

———: *The Life of Abraham Lincoln,* 2 vols. New York: McClure, Phillips Co., 1900.

Thomas, Benjamin Platt: *Abraham Lincoln. A Biography.* New York: Alfred A. Knopf, 1952.

————: "A Unique Biography of Lincoln," *Bulletin of the Abraham Lincoln Association,* June, 1934.

————: *Lincoln 1847–1853: Being the Day-by-Day Activities of Abraham Lincoln from January 1, 1847 to December 31, 1853.* Springfield: The Abraham Lincoln Association, 1936.

————: "Lincoln's Earlier Practice in the Federal Courts. 1839–1854," *Bulletin of the Abraham Lincoln Association,* June, 1935.

————: *Lincoln's New Salem,* rev. ed. New York: Alfred A. Knopf, 1954.

————: "Old New Salem," *Bulletin of the Abraham Lincoln Association,* December, 1932.

————: *Portrait for Posterity: Lincoln and His Biographers.* New Brunswick, New Jersey: Rutgers University Press, 1947.

————: "The Eighth Judicial Circuit," *Bulletin of the Abraham Lincoln Association,* September, 1935.

Tilton, Henry Clay: "Lincoln and Lamon: Partners and Friends," *Transactions of the Illinois State Historical Society, 1931.*

Townsend, William H.: "Lincoln the Litigant," *American Bar Journal,* February, 1924.

————: *Abraham Lincoln, Defendant.* Boston: Houghton Mifflin Co., 1923.

Tracy, Gilbert Avery: *Uncollected Letters of Abraham Lincoln.* Boston: Houghton Mifflin Company, 1917.

Wakefield, Eva I., ed.: *The Letters of Robert G. Ingersoll.* New York: Philosophical Library, 1951.

Wakefield, Sherman D.: *How Lincoln Became President.* New York: Wilson-Erickson, Inc., 1936.

Warren, Louis Austin: "Herndon's Contribution to Lincoln Mythology," *Indiana Magazine of History,* Vol. 41, September, 1945.

————: "Sifting the Herndon Sources," Lincoln Fellowship of Southern California, 1948.

Weik, Jesse W.: *The Real Lincoln: A Portrait.* Boston: Houghton Mifflin Co., 1922.

Wetherbee, S. Ambrose: "Lincoln Collection. Illinois State Archives," *Illinois State Libraries,* 1943.

White, Horace: *The Life of Lyman Trumbull.* Boston: Houghton Mifflin Co., 1912.

Whitney, Henry Clay: *Life on the Circuit with Lincoln,* ed. by Paul McClelland Angle. Caldwell, Idaho: The Caxton Printers, Ltd., 1940.

Williams, T. Harry: *Lincoln and His Generals.* New York: Alfred A. Knopf, 1952.

Wilson, Rufus Rockwell: *Uncollected Works of Abraham Lincoln*, 2 vols. Elmira, New York: The Primavera Press, Inc., 1947.

Woldman, Albert A.: *Lawyer Lincoln*. Boston: Houghton Mifflin Company, 1936.

Zane, Charles S.: "Lincoln As I Knew Him," *Sunset Magazine*, October, 1912, reprinted in *Journal of the Illinois State Historical Society*, April, 1921.

BIBLIOGRAPHY

INDEX

Adams, James: 46–8

Allen, Charles: principal prosecution witness in "Almanac Trial," 354; Lincoln confronts, with almanac, 355

"Almanac Trial": Herndon's *Life* devotes but a paragraph to case, 350; defendant lodged in Beardstown jail, awaiting trial, 352; Lincoln exercises great care in selecting jury, 354; Lincoln a psychologist in choosing jurors, 354; Lincoln secures jury of young men, 354; Lincoln's summation in, 357; Lincoln's requests for instructions to the jury in, 357; theory of Lincoln's defense, 357–8; Lincoln secures acquittal in, 357; "spurious almanac" rumor, 358–9

Alsop, Sarah: 217

Alton, Ill.: 30, 361

Alton *Telegraph:* 234

Anderson, George: 330

Anderson, Jane: Lincoln represents, on charge of murder, 330–1

Anderson, Mary and Richard: 46

Anderson, Theodore: 330–1

Angell on Limitations: 155

Angle, Paul M.: quoted, 130, 205; cited, 374 (n. 21), 376 (n. 7), 379 (n. 30), 385 (n. 21), 392 (n. 27), 393 (n. 3)

Armstrong, Hannah: enlists Lincoln's services on behalf of her son "Duff," 353; Lincoln writes, regarding son's release from army, 359

Armstrong, Jack: 351

Armstrong, William ("Duff"): Lincoln's defense of, 350–9; Lincoln orders discharge of, from army, 359

Ashmore, Gideon M.: 131–2; 136; 143

Arnold, Isaac N.: appointed to conduct investigation of Judge Browne, 88; recalls murder trial in Cook County, 120; considers Lincoln "the strongest jury lawyer in the state," 170; compares Lincoln and Douglas as jury lawyers, 190

Atkins, Henry I.: examined by Lincoln, Milton Hay and Benjamin Edwards concerning his qualifications to practice law, 295

Backenstos, Jacob B.: 93

Bailey v. *Cromwell:* 86; 140

Baker, David J.: Lincoln represents, in suit against Faculty of Shurtleff College, 365

[415]

takes no modest view of the extent of his powers as justice of the peace, 14; Lincoln called upon by Mrs. Green to speak at grave, 15

Greene, Henry S.: examined by Lincoln, Browning and Lewis W. Ross concerning his qualifications to practice law, 295

Greenleaf on Evidence: 31

Greenville, Ill.: 225

Gridley, Asahel: 118; 185–6; 194; 196; 200; 328

Hackett, James H.: Lincoln writes, concerning own interest in Shakespeare, 11

Hamlin, Hannibal: 153

Hanks, Dennis: 5; 134; 273

Hanks, John: 146

Hanks, Joseph: 65

Hardin, John J.: 10; 20; 122

Harding, George: 323–4

Harriott, James: presides in "Almanac Trial," 354; 356–7

Harris, Gibson W.: quoted, 112, 123, 189, 198–9, 285–6; cited, 373 (n. 13), 379 (n. 10), 385 (n. 38), 386 (n. 9)

Harrison, Quinn ("Peachy"): Lincoln defends, on charge of murder, 363–4

Hartgen, Jonas D.: Lincoln's defense of, for stealing from the mails, 237–8

Hay, John: on Springfield, 39; characterizes Lincoln as "extremely unmethodical," 43

Hay, Logan: 111; 241

Hay, Milton: serves as law clerk in office of Stuart & Lincoln, 285; forms partnership with Logan, 285; Joseph Fifer on, 285; as-

sociated with Lincoln in defense of "Peachy" Harrison, 285; serves, with Lincoln, as bar examiner, 295

Hayes, President Rutherford B.: 153

Henry, Anson G.: 26; 48

Herndon, Archer G.: 109; 110

Herndon, William H.: on Dennis Hanks, 5; education, 10; on New Salem, 18; on Lincoln's self-confidence, 22; on Lincoln's political career, 26; advertises for law business in *Illinois Journal*, 50; denounces John T. Stuart, 76–7; writes disparagingly of Stephen T. Logan, 94; Lincoln's reasons for offering partnership to, 97–100; and story of Lincoln-Rutledge romance, 99; antagonism toward Mrs. Lincoln, 99; personal use of liquor, 99, 109, 164–5, 321; personality, contrasted with that of Lincoln, 101–2; lack of sense of humor, 102; considers himself a better lawyer than Lincoln, 102; loyalty to the living Lincoln, 102; annoyance with the Lincoln boys, 103; resents Lincoln reading newspapers aloud, 103; no part of a flunkey, 104; active practitioner in Menard County, 104–5; capacity for work, 105; his dislike of the law, 106, 108; as a lawyer, difficult to evaluate, 106–8; intellectual interests, 108; contradictory traits, 108–9; compared by Emanuel Hertz with Boswell, 109; uncomplimentary references to Lincoln, 109; clerks for Logan & Lincoln, 110–

11; becomes Lincoln's partner, 111–2; partnership with Charles Zane, 112; partnership with Alfred Orendorff, 112; lacking in the qualities of a businessman, 113; makes entries in partnership books, 113–4; on Lincoln's "filing system," 114; forever seeking new clients and new cases, 136; and Tonica & St. Petersburg Railroad cases, 136; failure to mention Matson Slave Case, 143; carries on during Lincoln's term in Congress, 151, 164; comments on Lincoln's service in Congress, 153; urges Lincoln to continue the partnership, 163; arrested on drunk and disorderly charge, 164; retains substantial part of practice while Lincoln in Congress, 164; on Lincoln as circuit lawyer, 169; dislike of circuit travel, 198; extent of his work in the Federal Court, 222–3; estimate of Lincoln as a lawyer before the Illinois Supreme Court, 243; share in the winning of Lincoln's cases before the Illinois Supreme Court, 246; research for Dalby case, 270; supervises law students in Lincoln & Herndon office, 287; accompanies Lincoln to polls, 289; Henry B. Rankin charges use of drugs by, 291; on the McLean County tax case, 317; his removal of official probate files, 326; his failure to mention the *Effie Afton* case, 345; Leonard Swett on, 345; John T. Richards on, 345; devotes but a paragraph to the "Almanac

Trial," 350; on the "Peachy" Harrison case, 363–4
Herndon and Weik: literary partnership, 5
Herndon-Weik Collection: 41–2; 108; 245; 268–9; 315; 326
Hertz, Emanuel: 292; 345
Hewett, Josephus: 49; 55
Hickey, James T.: 115
High, George: Lincoln draws pardon petition for, 278–9
Hill, Frederick Trevor: travels over route of the Eighth Circuit, 172–3; interviews Weldon and other Lincoln contemporaries, 173
Hitt, Robert R.: 396 (n. 13)
Hogg, Harvey: 212; 304
Holmes, Justice Oliver Wendell: quoted, 70
"Horological Cradle Case": Lincoln appears in, 259–61
"House Divided" Speech: 360
Howells, William Dean: 16; 23
Hoyne, Thomas: engages Lincoln to form college of homeopathy, 325
Hunt, Eugenia Jones: quoted, 194–5
Hurd v. *The Rock Island Bridge Co.:* See *Effie Afton* case
Hyde, Alfred: 280–1; 391 (n. 11)

Illinois Advocate and State Register: 28
Illinois Central Railroad: Lincoln represents, in resisting tax claim of McLean County, 200, 312–7; Lincoln meets George McClellan in connection with trial of case for, 207; Lincoln tries his first case for, in Urbana, in 1853, 210; Lincoln submits bill